Class, Politics, and Agrarian Policies in Post-liberalisation India

Has there been a shift in agrarian policies in India since liberalisation? What has been the impact of these policies on new class formation and consolidation of existing ones? Did proprietary classes with close relations to the state influence the formulation of these policies? Do class–state relations have to be uniform across nations under globalisation?

Studying post-liberalisation India, this book answers these questions by scrutinising the tenets of agrarian policies of three Indian states – Chhattisgarh, Gujarat, and Karnataka. In doing so, it analyses the political economy of agricultural policy and the class–state relations operating in the country, concluding that class and its relation to the state have come to occupy a defining role in the politics of new India.

This edition has an all-new introduction and a conclusion that consider the farmer movements in 2020–21 and how that impacts agrarian class structure and the role of the state.

Sejuti Das Gupta teaches at James Madison College, Michigan State University. Her research interests are agrarian political economy, public policy, class–caste, state–society and informal economy interactions. She has worked at the Tata Institute of Social Sciences, Mumbai, and in the development sector in India.

Class, Politics, and Agrarian Policies in Post-liberalisation India

Second Edition

Sejuti Das Gupta

CAMBRIDGE
UNIVERSITY PRESS

CAMBRIDGE
UNIVERSITY PRESS

Shaftesbury Road, Cambridge CB2 8EA, United Kingdom

One Liberty Plaza, 20th Floor, New York, NY 10006, USA

477 Williamstown Road, Port Melbourne, VIC 3207, Australia

314–321, 3rd Floor, Plot 3, Splendor Forum, Jasola District Centre, New Delhi – 110025, India

103 Penang Road, #05–06/07, Visioncrest Commercial, Singapore 238467

Cambridge University Press is part of Cambridge University Press & Assessment, a department of the University of Cambridge.

We share the University's mission to contribute to society through the pursuit of education, learning and research at the highest international levels of excellence.

www.cambridge.org
Information on this title: www.cambridge.org/9781009481335

First edition published 2019
Second edition published 2024

A catalogue record for this publication is available from the British Library

ISBN 978-1-009-48133-5 Hardback

To all farmers who toil to feed us
and to Caesar who toiled to convert my naive ideas
into an academic work

Contents

Tables and Figures

Abbreviations

ABD	Accumulation by Dispossession
Amul	Anand Milk Union Limited
APMC	Agricultural Produce Marketing Cooperative
ASSOCHAM	Associated Chambers of Commerce and Industry of India
BALCO	Bharat Aluminium Company Ltd.
BJP	Bharatiya Janata Party
BKS	Bharatiya Kisan Sangh
BKU	Bharatiya Kisan Union
CAG	Comptroller and Auditor General
CBI	Central Bureau of Investigation
CEO	Chief Executive Officer
CII	Confederation of Indian Industry
CPI(M)	Communist Party of India (Marxist)
CPR	Common Property Resource
CSSDCL	Chhattisgarh State Seed and Agriculture Development Corporation Limited
FAS	Foundation for Agrarian Studies
FCI	Food Corporation of India
FDI	Foreign Direct Investment
FERA	Foreign Exchange Regulation Act
FGD	Focus Group Discussion
FICCI	Federation of Indian Chambers of Commerce and Industry
GATT	General Agreement on Tariffs and Trade
GDP	Gross Domestic Product
GGRC	Gujarat Green Revolution Company Limited
GPP	Gujarat Parivartan Party
HDR	*Human Development Report*
HYV	High-yielding Variety
ICAR	Indian Council of Agricultural Research
ICCP	Intensive Customer Contact Programmes
IFFCO	Indian Farmers Fertilizer Cooperative
IMF	International Monetary Fund
IRMA	Institute of Rural Management Anand

IT	Information Technology
JDS	Janata Dal (Secular)
JNU	Jawaharlal Nehru University
JPL	Jindal Power Limited
KHAM	Khsatriya Harijan Adivasi and Muslim
KRRS	Karnataka Rajya Raitha Sangha
LIBRS	Lingayat Brahmin
MGNREGS	Mahatma Gandhi National Rural Employment Guarantee Scheme
MIS	Micro Irrigation Scheme
MLA	Member of the Legislative Assembly
MOU	Memorandum of Understanding
MOVD	Muslim, OBC, Vokkaliga, and Dalit
MSP	Minimum Support Price
NABARD	National Bank for Agriculture and Rural Development
NAP	New Agricultural Policy
NCEUS	National Commission for Enterprises in the Unorganized Sector
NDA	National Democratic Alliance
NDDB	National Dairy Development Board
NHM	National Horticulture Mission
NRI	Non-resident Indian
NRLM	National Rural Livelihood Mission
NSDP	Net State Domestic Product
NSSO	National Sample Survey Office
OBC	Other Backward Classes
PDS	Public Distribution System
PIL	Public Interest Litigation
PPA	Power Purchase Agreement
PRI	Panchayati Raj Institution
PWD	Public Works Department
RFAS	Rural Finance Access Survey
RSS	Rashtriya Swayamsevak Sangh
RTI	Right to Information
SAGY	Swachha Adarsh Gram Yojana
SC	Schedule Caste
SDA	Surat Diamond Association
SEZ	Special Economic Zone
SMF	Small and Marginal Farmers
SSC	State Seed Corporation
SSP	Sardar Sarovar Project
ST	Schedule Tribe
UPA	United Progressive Alliance
VAT	Value Added Tax
WTO	World Trade Organization

Acknowledgements

This book took a decade from conceiving the ideas to bringing them to fruition. The period includes two years at Jawaharlal Nehru University (JNU), four years as a doctoral student at SOAS, University of London, a year at Tata Institute of Social Sciences (TISS), and seven years at Michigan State University (MSU). I thought of a world of people as the I wrote the acknowledgement. The experiences over the past decade have been both liberating and captivating for me.

I learnt a lot at the Centre for Political Studies at JNU, particularly from Professor Gurpreet Mahajan and Professor Gopal Guru, who remained consistently interested in my work. Their encouragement and critique from the early stages of my research meant a lot to me. Professor Asha Sarangi was my M.Phil supervisor and her acceptance of me as a student at the last moment and providing guidance saw me through those years. The one person always keen to help with my work was my doctoral supervisor, Dr Jens Lerche. He was duly critical to bring out sharper arguments, taught me the nuances of arguing and how to use language in an academic way. I cannot thank him enough for reading and re-reading the drafts and spending hours to shape my ideas through debates and discussions. I am also grateful to Dr Subir Sinha and Dr Alessandra Mezzadri, members of my supervisory committee. Teachers are amazing people and here I want to mention Mrs D. Roy, Mrs S. Mazumdar, Mr K. Sengupta, and Mrs Haldar, who taught me at different stages of my school and college lives. They taught me to treasure learning. In 2003, Mrs Mazumdar had taken us on a field trip to Shantiniketan, my first ever field trip. I thank her for opening up the world to us. I thank Professor R. Ramakumar and Professor V. K. Ramachandran for their interaction and engagement during my fieldwork and writing of the book.

I thank the Felix trust and the British Foundation for Women Graduates, without whom this project would have been impossible. Finance is a constraint and is the biggest boon, once secured, in pursuing research. I am grateful to SOAS staff Alicia Sales and Laura Jacob, who always lent a hand in all financial difficulties. The SOAS library was the most important source of books and articles. Two other grants which helped me a lot in the reading year are the SOAS Hardship Fund and the FfWG (Funds for Women Graduates). The British Federation for Women granted me an emergency fund in the fourth year when it was getting harder to manage time and concentrate on work. I am grateful to James Madison College (MSU) for their financial and moral support and the College of Agriculture, MSU, for the summer fellowship to continue my research.

The people who contributed to the fieldwork were Dr Hanumanth Yadav, Professor Hirway, Professor Deshpande, Mr Rajpal Pawar, Mr Shashi, and Ms Savitha Rath. Their academic input and veteran field experience kept me humble and my search for information on track. On several occasions, I asked them naïve questions which were answered patiently, particularly by Bhalchandra, Madhava, Kanan, and other social workers. They made possible accessing such corners of villages which I could have never had reached otherwise.

I must thank Ramya, Asha, Manamee and Kayleigh for taking care of different aspects of my life in East Lansing so sincerely that it allowed me to focus on the manuscript. Aditi Dayal was the main editor who painstakingly read the entire manuscript and gave it the final shape and Divya Singh extended help in dire hours. I am most grateful to the Cambridge team, Anushruti, Anwesha, and Qudsiya, who had their faith in me and worked tirelessly with me. I thank my mentor at MSU, Professor Linda Racioppi, for spending time on the Introduction and Conclusion to help convert them into reader-friendly pieces. Professor Kerr was valuable in boosting my confidence when I needed it most. Over a period of five years, all our conversations and interactions have boosted my faith in humanity. A.R. Vasavi deserves a special mention for being the first to encourage me to propose a second edition. Linda Racioppi for her unwavered support and Amanda Flaim, Melissa Fore, and Rashida Harrison for all our intellectual and emotional conversations. I am truly grateful for your friendships.

Moving to the personal, I am grateful to my family whose dream kept me going. They believed daughters can do all that sons can, if not more, and in India, that is a special place to belong. My Baba (father) believed in me the most while my mother pushed me the hardest. My Mesho (uncle) nurtured my interests carefully and consistently. My sisters, Sohini and Shabori, were and are ambitious and focused. Just by being themselves, they inspire me to work harder. I will be ever grateful to Anna for opening a new world to me by sending me off to SOAS, the place which has made a real difference in shaping the book. My family in London, the Nairs and Naidus who were rock and cushions, deserve a special mention. From them I learnt never to shy away from hard work. Their discipline and commitment inspired me to work harder and their children guarded me from all disappointments on this long journey.

My confidant in this journey was Ishita, a friend and a critic, and she never let me down. She would raise the bar higher and trusted that I could meet it. A mail would be replied in less than an hour, though in fewer words than I would hope for. Her inspiring words were 'jhande gaad ke ana' meaning 'make a difference'. Taneesha, with whom I sailed the seas, made a difference by being around almost always. From sewing a saree to encouraging me to pursue dance and cooking, she lessened the pressure of work. Right till the end, we held hands and faced the trials. I thank Chandrani for being always available for a long chat, by the end of which I would be reassured. Priyanka spent hours making chapters shorter and more readable. Sejuti Basu was an asset when it came to fixing the bibliography; Shabana for helping with the maps, a hard job for me.

Aruna, Francy, and Eliza were the three new friends I made at SOAS, whom I could count on for more than a mere good time. I thank Caesar for debating my ideas and encouraging me to develop nuanced arguments.

My ever smiling, ever loving boys, Trivik and Pranav – it was an incentive to work harder to finish my book in time to be with them. Aadvik joined the gang in 2016 and Aiyira in 2022 to teach me to use my time more prudently. They added to my resolve of finishing the book in a more meaningful way.

I must talk of three people without whom it would be incomplete. Dhibhai for always being there to talk, to cheer me up, to share and to crack jokes in difficult times. Aratrika, my closest friend now for 25 years, who always took my calls and in a sublime way, always sorted out my worries. To end this brief piece, the one person I perhaps cannot thank enough is Kirtimaan Mohan, since he came to life as faith in everything good. He has been part of the journey as a friend, a fellow academic, and family.

I want to thank my colleagues R. Ramakumar, Aparajita Bakshi, Amanda Flaim, Melissa Fore, Linda Racioppi, and Linda Sayed who have all enrichedmy academic journey in the last eight years. A special thanks to Dr A. R. Vasavi, Dr Vakulabharanam Vamsi, Prof. Surupa Gupta, Prof. Aseema Sinha, Dr Jonathan Pattenden, and Dr Kenneth Nielsen for allowing me to present my work and offering their insights and critique.

My deepest gratitude is to my editors, Aniruddha De and Anwesha Rana, who have restored my faith in humanity by working tirelessly on the second edition. And a final thanks to Truman Forbes and Caitlin Santer, my students, who were great research assistants.

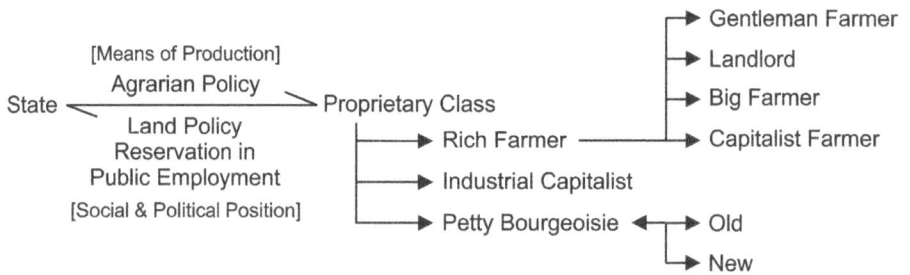

Political settlement after 2004: state–proprietary class relation

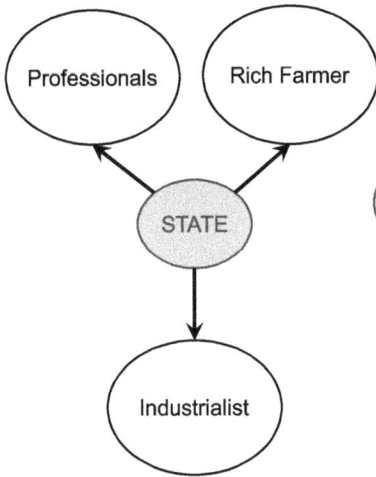

Dominant Classes in 1980s
(Bardhan, 1984)

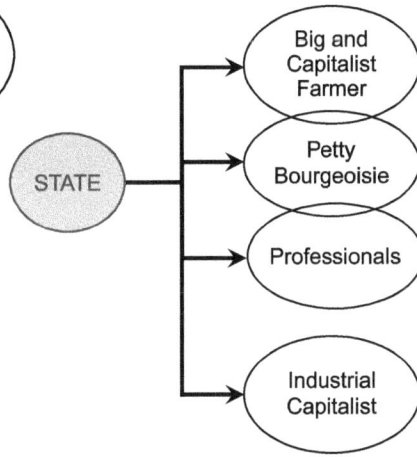

Dominant Classes in New India:
Overlapping Interests and Changing Class Structures

1

❀

Introduction

India has been rapidly changing since globalisation, albeit not uniformly. In 2022, India has been found to be the most unequal country in the world (Chancel et al., 2022). This makes it critical to understand where the inequality came from: is it new or structural or something else? Several characterisations have been attributed to India's transformation since globalisation; some talk about rapid urbanization, fast growth with incoming global investments, the IT boom, and an expanding middle class, while another set of scholars highlight aspects such as the agrarian crises, farmers' suicides, food insecurity, and corruption. The point, however, is to comprehend how each version of this story has a saga of unequal distribution within it, whether in cities or villages. India being the most unequal country in a Marxian term means certain classes are accumulating and others are not even able to reproduce themselves. This makes it even more crucial to look at 'capital', and how it is accumulating, which spreads across the urban and rural. This book offers an in-depth analysis of diversification and various sources of accumulation accessed by the agrarian proprietary class, and a discussion on the other two proprietary classes, the petty bourgeoisie and the capitalist. By disaggregating the sources along fractions of the agrarian proprietary class, it shows how the class adopted new means within agriculture and outside agriculture, to further accumulation during the 2004–2014 policy regime. The policies under scrutiny are agricultural and those related to rural population in general, such as Panchayati Raj institutions (PRIs), land acquisition and affirmative action in employment. The latter may serve caste groups but in addition contribute to consolidating class structure. What these policies demonstrate is the key role played by the state in the globalisation era, thereby maintaining a stable political settlement with the three proprietary classes. The state and the nature of the state are important questions raised in this book, thus 'bringing the state back in', as Skocpol (2010) once argued. This book's third contribution is that it brings an understanding of classes that does not begin from being informed by abstract categories but rather begins with the empirical observations that guide the formulation of the conceptual classes and fractions. Skocpol finds neo-Marxism's conceptualisation of state very abstract, therefore hard to be applied, and hence starting from the empirical to the abstract following a methodology of 'thick description' (Geertz 1973) is an attempt to address that limitation.

In the globalisation era, even though invisible global capital is no doubt powerful, the book argues that the interaction of global phenomena with existing structures is peculiar to the history and materiality of a nation which produce a different trajectory in each context. Therefore, it is relevant to study forward and backward linkages of a state policy to understand the internal peculiarities of social-class dynamics. The book upholds the nature of the state, its policies and their impact on proprietary classes as critical to understanding the politics of class formation.

The scholarly attention in development literature has been divided between those who look at the role of institutions brought by globalisation as the key factor and those who look at the question of agency emerging at the grassroots as the primary factor. This book draws attention to the third question, the structure, and investigates the role of policies in fostering accumulation by proprietary classes, and thereby reflects on the nature of each state. Therefore, it argues that even in the globalisation era, it is critical to study the role of the state, its relation to the propriety classes, and the operating political settlement. In fact, the engagement with regional states demonstrates a peculiar experience owing to its existing structure and owning to the expectations of the regional proprietary classes, and finds that since 2004, states have managed to serve the interest of the fractions of the agrarian proprietary class well. It therefore offers a variation in political settlement of proprietary classes. The book concludes that the state fosters accumulation by a few, builds on the existing structure but also adds a few members into the proprietary class as demonstrated through a foray into agrarian policies between 2004 and 2014 and other key policies affecting rural India. The key themes here are class and fractions, agrarian policies and the nature of the state. The chapter is divided into six sections. It starts with a discussion on the time period and the key questions raised in the book; second, the relevance of an inter-disciplinary frame to study state, policies and agrarian capitalist class; third, a discussion on the matter of the book where the theoretical frame builds on three fields of study, political economy, political sociology and political economy of agrarian studies;

fourth, a discussion on the form which draws methodologically from works in comparative politics as seen in Kohli (1987) and Sinha (2005); fifth, brief overview of the chapters of the book; and finally ends with a reflection on the current political scenario.

Since the publication of the first edition the farmer movement between 2020 and 2021 has triggered a growing attention towards agrarian transformation, agrarian policies and rural movements in India. In fact, after 2020 and the passage of the three farm laws and their repeal thereafter, academics, journalists and activists in India and those who work on India have debated various facets of law and institutions, of political economy and of grassroots mobilisations. The second edition is an attempt to join the conversation with the stalwarts who fought from the grassroots and those who toiled to capture the story of the biggest farmer movement that India has ever seen. A few of the key scholars who have contributed to the meaningful conversation around the issues of larger political economy and agrarian change are R. Ramkumar, Elizabeth Chatterjee and Matthew McCartney, Uday Chandra and Daniel Tagioff, Sudhir Suthar, Shreya Sinha, Ajay Gudavarthy, Surinder Jodhka, Ishita Mehrotra, Aparajita Bakshi, Michael Levien, Alpa Shah and Jens Lerche. The question 'who is a farmer?' has recently received a lot of attention and has been differently argued by Damodaran and Agarwal (2021), Anand, Banerjee and Dasgupta (2021) and Das Gupta, Mehrotra and Bakshi (2022), among others, reflecting on the heterogeneity of rural India and those who engage with agriculture. The reflections in the second edition build on the empirical groundwork of the first edition in which I had conducted field work and added three new interviews of key informants to reflect on the current situation and what lay ahead. That said, the book was among the first to argue that the state and its agrarian policies need to be taken seriously in studying political economy in the globalisation era to understand particularly agrarian India. Policies are framed in response to social forces; specific class and caste alliances influence state actions. Hence looking at the issue of policies through a triangular frame combining social, political, and economic processes becomes imperative. A policy may not have economic gain as its stated purpose and may claim social purpose as its main objective, but a wider consideration of policies could show that those intended for specific caste groups could also lead to class consolidation.

Scholarship on rural India in the post-globalisation era is not a novelty; scholars have highlighted several other themes that reflect on rural India such as corruption, particularly with numerous mining projects and the

2G scam (Bussell, 2012). Mining has also been linked to land acquisition in rural India, both legal and illegal, and the role of the state and changing land relations (Levien, 2017; D'Costa and Chakraborty, 2017). Social movements such as the Plachimada, Niyamgiri and Singur–Nandigram have also revealed the grassroots activism side of rural India (Chandra and Taghioff, 2016; Neilsen and Nilsen, 2016). The rural population moving from non-agrarian to agrarian sectors has put to question the very character of the 'rural', and scholars like Dipankar Gupta and Surinder Jodhka have proposed terms like 'rurban' to capture the transformation (Gupta, 2005; Jodhka, 2008). As stated above, we centre the study around the question of structure. It is to be noted that the major debate around agrarian India has been dominated by two groups: one that talks about a severe agrarian crisis affecting all peasants leading to their pauperisation (McMichael, 2008; U. Patnaik, 2002) and the second about globalisation determining politics across nation states, thus weakening the nation state (Rodrik, 1997; Kennedy, 1993). Both positions assume a kind of homogeneity. The book examines this homogeneity and on the basis of empirical evidence questions such homogeneity. After all, survey reports 83.1 per cent of all land is owned by 20 per cent of rural households in 2015–16 per the National Family Health Survey (Rawal and Bansal, 2022). The Gini coefficient of rural consumers is 0.52, indicating severe inequality (Ramakumar, 2022). The point here is not to oppose the severity of agrarian crisis but to examine if we could nuance the understanding further by looking at the agrarian capitalist class and possible changes within its fractions between 2004 and 2014. Scholars have noted a discontinuity in agricultural budget from 2003/04 (Lerche, 2014; Suthar, 2022). This raises the question of whether the agrarian distress has hurt entire rural India or created avenues of gain for certain classes thereby hurting the rest, and thus this is a story of a few accumulating at the cost of the rest. It is not to deny the magnitude of agrarian distress but rather to highlight that globalisation has not evened out all structures, but in fact built on them and possibly made them deeper. I hypothesize that the state and agrarian policies have contributed to the reinstatement of the agrarian proprietary class (and its fractions) in the political settlement and, more importantly, brought the interest of the three proprietary classes closer than ever before. The three classes are taken from Pranab Bardhan (1984).

The time period the book is situated in is 2004–2014. The National Democratic Alliance (NDA) led by the Bharatiya Janata Party (BJP) lost in 2004 when it launched the India Shining campaign, but in 2014, the Modi wave helped the BJP win the election. A part of the wave was the much-talked-about

'Gujarat model of development' with rapid agricultural and industrial growth which successfully diverted attention from the Godhra carnage. The 2014 victory bears testimony to what the promise of rapid development can deliver in terms of electoral success but, unlike 2004, this time it included rural India's development as well. The book argues that the rural proprietary class pushed the state to include its interests and the state in turn had to reinstate the powerful, agrarian groups in the political settlement since 2004. This was ensured by agrarian policies and non-agrarian policies, such as reservation for Other Backward Classes (OBCs) and Scheduled Castes (SCs) in admissions and government jobs, in the states which allowed the class to accumulate from more than one source. Did this settlement make the state confident that they could pass the farm bills in 2020, since they had the support of the farmers?

To answer the question, the book scrutinises the tenets of agricultural policies and related policies in three states in India – Chhattisgarh, Gujarat and Karnataka. It analyses the effect of agrarian policy on agrarian capitalist classes and the state's consideration towards various fractions of the class in formulating these policies. It addresses four primary concerns in this regard.

First, have agrarian policies since globalisation been continuous and homogeneous across regional states and, if not, is the state an important factor affecting that?

Second, what has been the disaggregated impact of policies, both agrarian and others, on proprietary classes and their fractions? Does it lead to the formation of new class or/and consolidation of existing classes?

Third, what do we know about the nature of the state and its autonomy from proprietary classes? To answer this, the political settlement, the proprietary classes in it, and their relation to the state are relevant. Reference to caste has been made throughout the empirical chapters to keep up the conversation with the existing literature and capture the nuance on the ground. Does the political settlement help us predict what is coming up in the 2024 elections?

Fourth, can agrarian classes be understood by studying only rural processes or do we need to include other productive sectors as well?

Scholars have seriously engaged with issues of peasantry, agrarian transition, rural struggles and agricultural politics since independence. The Green Revolution era had scholars argue that the policy was resulting in a rise of new class in the countryside and subsequently a social movement. Scholars in politics termed them the bullock capitalists (Rudolph and Rudolph 1987). Both societal and political forces were given weightage in the analysis of India during the Green Revolution and its aftermath (Hasan, 1989; Pai, 1993).

Economists may have different names for the emerging class – capitalist farmers or rich peasants – but agreed upon their accumulation under the new technology (Byres, 1981; Patnaik, 1987). Byres found the class to operate as a class for itself. Study of societal forces got a real boost when India witnessed the emergence of an active farmer movement in north India that demanded state subsidy (Brass, 1995; Banaji, 1994; Omvedt, 1988). At the village level, changes were noted with the rich farmers retaining their privileged position through their control on credit institutions and the rural poor facing harder conditions of work due to technology stepping into production (Palmer, 1976; Dhanagare, 1984: 192–93; Bagchi, 1982: 176, cited in Dhanagare, 1987; Jodhka, 1994). Scholars of economics, politics and sociology participated alike in the conversation.

By the late 1980s, a gradual shift was noted across disciplines where each disciplinary group took up a part of the puzzle almost exclusively. Scholars working on Indian politics paid more attention to identity politics and examined mobilisations around cultural identities and their interaction with the state (Christophe Jaffrelot, Yogendra Yadav, Zoya Hasan, Ghanshyam Shah, Gopal Guru, Asha Sarangi and Sudha Pai). They would connect it to the question of the state from a state–society framework. The study of cultural identity garnered further impetus with India's experience of rising communal tensions marked by the demolition of Babri Masjid in 1992 which made the case stronger for why study politics through the lens of identities. Indian citizenry has tended to organise around linguistic, caste and religious identities to demand and navigate the state and that is why studies focused on the same question. These were undoubtedly powerful ways to capture the injustice experienced on the ground (Bailey 2017). These scholars, however, tended to stay away from the class question. The question of state–economy interaction which included state–class relations or the nature of the state was taken up by political economy scholars such as Pranab Bardhan, Ashok Mitra and Atul Kohli, which phased out in the 1990s, and these questions fell into disfavour with both mainstream political economy scholars and political science scholars, as pointed out by Chatterjee and McCartney (2020). During the period, sociologists engaged deeply with the question of caste and community and adopted a frame of Bharat–India, where Bharat was their interest. Jodhka (2014) identifies a tension between the disciplines of economics and sociology which makes each disciplinary group almost exclusively focus on a theme: economists on class and later human development and sociologists on caste community, with exceptions like himself. The question of differentiation within the rural structure, and therefore agrarian classes, was left to scholars of agrarian political economy such as Barbara Harriss-White, V.K. Ramachandran, Vamsi Vakulabharanam, Madhura Swaminathan, Vikas Rawal, Jens Lerche and Ravi Srivastava. For them, reflecting on the formation of rural classes and consolidation is the primary study objective and hence engagement with the state remained secondary.

This book adopts an interdisciplinary frame trying to build upon these disciplines to answer the four questions highlighted earlier. I argue that in the context of growing inequality, economic location forms a critical role in people's lives and their decisions. Growing inequality means it is harder for some classes to reproduce themselves, while other classes have accumulated, probably from multiple sources. Examining the agrarian proprietary class and its means of accumulation would be incomplete without considering the role of the state and its various policies that foster accumulation; for instance, as the state directs its funds to specific caste groups, it may provide an avenue to accumulate for a class, as seen in the case of affirmative action in statutory employment for OBCs in Chhattisgarh. Khan refers to this phenomenon as rent-seeking. Hence I argue the state, policies and their connection to class consolidation and formation due to agrarian policies and rural-related policies need to be explored together to comprehend the entire story. To that extent, caste and class are intertwined. Creating a conversation between caste and class, and even religion and indigenous identity in a few instances, required the book to combine political economy with political sociology. The book attempts to solve the puzzle by applying together aspects from these fields of study and investigating a possibility that a study of agrarian classes may not be located in the rural always. Class, I argue, comes to occupy a defining role in the politics of new India less for organising and mobilising and more for the state to navigate structures. Class is not monolithic and can have fractions and have regional variation across India. Thus, it becomes imperative to conduct this study through fieldwork to capture the changes at the ground level to inform more abstract, conceptual questions. Here the book aligns with the position that what we need is a nuanced and empirically informed picture of agrarian change and the shifting configuration of not only constraints but also opportunities to a few agrarian classes (Harriss-White, 2005, cited in Aga, 2018; Lerche, 2014). Through fieldwork findings, the book questions the populist notion that farmers as a bloc are under threat from an undifferentiated capital.

For the sake of academic rigour, this study focuses exclusively on the fractions of agrarian capitalists and studies their accumulation across the three regional states, then inductively reflects on the changing sources of accumulation of the three proprietary classes that requires a broader engagement with state–society relations, how that affects the interrelation amongst these classes, and finally how it informs the nature of the state in each regional state. Imagine it like a set of concentric circles starting from fieldwork as the core circle, informing the second circle which is fractions of agrarian proprietary classes and their accumulation, informing the third circle as to how this changes the character of the three proprietary classes, informing the fourth circle showing how the interrelation among the proprietary classes undergoes a change, and finally the fifth circle, informing the nature of states. The conversation between the empirical and conceptual parts of the research is critical to answer the research questions. To answer these questions, agriculture and its related policies ought to be studied. First, the agrarian issue is relevant due to its vast reach. The agricultural sector employs 47 per cent of the working population in India (World Bank, 2012), and agrarian issues, such as food prices, affect people widely. Moreover, compared to other policy areas such as social policy, agrarian policy has been under-researched. In recent times, research has tended to focus on social policies such as the Mahatma Gandhi National Rural Employment Guarantee Scheme (MGNREGS),[2] National Rural Livelihood Mission (NRLM), Swachha Adarsh Gram Yojana (SAGY) or the public distribution system (PDS).[3]

Second, since the objective is to comprehend state–class relations and how classes gain means of accumulation, the policies related to one of the three productive sectors – agriculture, industry, and services – were most relevant and, hence, agriculture was chosen. It is commonplace to expect in Marxian political economy that the underlying economic dynamics for policymaking in a productive sector would be more integrally connected to class relations and the means of production/accumulation. This was pivotal to comprehend the differentiation within the agrarian capitalist class taking place on the ground. That said, focusing on an economic policy would not suffice to capture the processes of accumulation and hence other policies were included as these are intertwined in understanding broader agrarian transformation in rural India such as NREGA and the PRI Act. To that extent, social policies have been discussed in the empirical chapters.

This study does not focus on global actors involved in the agricultural sector in India. This is not to disregard their important role. Transnational players such as Monsanto (now known as Bayer), Cargill and DuPont (now known as Corteva), along with organisations like the World Trade Organization

(WTO), International Monetary Fund (IMF) and the World Bank, are exerting tremendous influence on food regimes and, thereby, on national agricultural policies (Bernstein, 2010; McMichael, 1997; Ramakumar, 2022). However, the focus here is on comprehending the ways in which dynamics specific to a country are responding to these global forces and the way classes are working with the state to maximise their extraction and accumulation. A second limitation of the book is the lack of attention to the small and marginal farmers and landless (henceforth referred to as tiller farmers[1]), whose interests have been marginalised despite India's claim to be the largest democracy.

Matter and form

Every research has two elements – matter and form. Matter refers to what it is trying to achieve and form refers to how it will be conducted. We will discuss both matter and form in this section. The objective of the study is to explore the political positions that agrarian proprietary classes take, the extent to which their interests are considered in agricultural policymaking during 2004–2014 by the regional states, and the impact such policies have on their means of accumulation and on the other two proprietary classes. Literature in the past decade has seen renewed emphasis on institutions. Especially regarding China, Brazil and also India, there seems to be more to the story than an imposed uniformity of neoliberal institutions from the outside and the resultant weakening of states (Kobrin, 1997; Chang, 2002). Advocates for a minimalist state argue that discrepancies and high public expenditures are created by the state's social policies, but market forces, left on their own, would regularise these anomalies. Therefore, what we need are 'good' policies and 'good' institutions for market-based development that serve the logic of neoliberalism (Chang, 2002). The aim of this study is to break away from such generalisation and assess the uniqueness of India's political economy and interaction between social structure and political institution, the state.

The theoretical framework used to comprehend empirical findings in this study is borrowed from scholars such as Nicos Poulantzas, Ralph Miliband, Louis Althusser and Bob Jessop. Their theories on the way capitalist classes become an integral part of the state and influence it is helpful in this regard. In stances, such classes may occupy political positions directly. The concept of 'political settlement', formulated by Mushtaq Khan and D. John, is also adopted as a part of the framework to grasp the state and proprietary class relation. Since the categories used by the political settlement scholars differ from those used by Marxists, the work seeks to build a bridge between these categories to create a holistic framework. The category of petty bourgeoisie has been borrowed from both Poulantzas and Khan. Even though these theories are not widely applied to the Indian context, their applicability will be evaluated once the empirical data is analysed.

For political settlement theory, coalition exists among the elites, and the survival of a political system is contingent on maintaining these interests. For scholars belonging to this school of thought, the democratic state is one that is 'neither autonomous nor a social contract, but a bargaining equilibrium or relation among relevant political forces' – the elites engineering such agreement within political institutions – and 'no one stands above the will of the contending parties' (Przeworski, 1991).

Political science literature on India has seen scholars use the 'state–society paradigm', where the state is influenced by social groups but the state is superior to these groups. This is seen in the works of Rudolph and Rudolph (1987) and Francine Frankel (2005).[4] The book keeps that question open, the state may or may not be superior to society if empirical findings so suggest. But it aims to develop a comprehensive picture of society and politics. Therefore, this study takes an interdisciplinary frame, focusing on the role of structures in shaping policies and the way policies affect such structures in turn, where the state may or may not be superior to society. Another interest has been in democracy. India has had stable governments with periodic elections, credited to its democratic system. Surrounded by nation states that have often slipped into military rules and authoritarian governments, India has stood out and attracted much scholarly attention. Regarded as a 'good institution' by the Washington Consensus, democracy has been credited with the resolution of socio-economic anomalies.

This is the vantage point for Varshney (1995) who argues that institutions are the undisputed solution to all social and economic inequality. His work is a critical reference for this study because it is one of those few works that trace agricultural policy decisions over a period of four decades. He sees policies as an outcome of negotiations among the different ministries of the government (Varshney, 1995: 78). Things change decisively in the 1980s as he draws attention to rural voters flooding Delhi to oppose the urban bias in policies. This brings the rural into the political scene as it exerts influence on the institutions. He convincingly argues that this leads to revision in the higher price guarantee of certain crops to tackle the formidable 'rural interest group'. It validates that tension existed between two kinds of interest groups – rural and urban – and that policy had to address the rural demands, thereby rendering a political characteristic to the policy. But he sticks to institution as the primary actor. However, as India becomes a more unequal country, I see a growing need to enquire: what are the social purposes that institutions and policies serve after all? Hence, I step aside from political scientists who explain policies exclusively through a lens of institutions which can take care of socio-economic anomalies, and look at a broader frame of state–class–society interaction.

As stated earlier, this study analyses forward and backward linkages to policy in the sense that interest is taken into account in the event of a policy decision, and how those policies impact existing social structures. Institutions could be serving the interest of existing proprietary classes, and thus furthering inequality, counter to what Varshney argues, which is open to scrutiny. The assumption is policymaking is not an apolitical process; it is enmeshed in politics at more levels than one (Harriss-White, 2002) and even intertwined with social power relations (Byres, 1997).[5] Taking the logic forward, Mitra (1977) argues that 'it is not possible to study the course of economic policy in isolation from the politics of class relations' (p. 5). He explores the forward linkages in the specific case of the Indian Farm Price Policy and finds significant class bias operating. In the 1980s, he found that the terms of trade were improving for agriculture vis-à-vis industry, showing that the rural classes possessed some bargaining power. Such evidence has already shown that policy is political in nature, and it consolidates existing dominant classes or leads to the formation of new classes. This provides the foundational premise of this study, which departs from existing political science literature.

In terms of its 'matter', the study is closest to Pranab Bardhan and Bob Jessop's work. While left-wing activists and political parties have been deeply involved with discussions of class, studies on class–state relations have gone out of fashion since 1990 (Chatterjee and McCartney, 2020; Harriss-White, 2020). Class analysis has either been considered reductionist or abstract, and hence the gap has been filled by an understanding of identity politics as a way to capture the changes in Indian politics. This is a consequence of the limitations of the Marxian frame to take the other identities seriously. By empirically studying class and fractions, the book attempts to capture what Bailey terms 'the on-the-ground experiences' (2017: 876), as cultural identity does, to address the limitation of Marxism which can tend to be monolithic and even an imposition from the top. However, with India globally claiming the first position in inequality, it is safe to deduce that a few classes are gaining;

hence the relevance of the question stands. In fact, reflecting on Bardhan's framework of three 'dominant proprietary classes' (1984, 2002) seems most timely, as pointed out by other scholars (Chatterjee and McCartney, 2020; Harriss-White, 2020). This study, however, differs from Bardhan's work in three ways. First, the unit of analysis in Bardhan's work is India as a whole, while this study is based on the regional state – Chhattisgarh, Gujarat and Karnataka – selected such that they reflect a diversity adequate to comment more broadly on India. This study focuses on agrarian policies, unlike Bardhan, which directly provide pathways for economic gains, and therefore accumulation by the agrarian proprietary class. Third, it considers policies that indirectly create such pathways; by catering to the interests of specific caste groups in rural India, the state consolidates their class position and brings them into the political settlement. Policies such as reservation under PRI has been examined and found to provide rent-seeking opportunities which in turn impacts the class position of elected representatives. Does the same class/fraction gain or are new members recruited into the class? In that sense it is reverse to the work of John Harriss (1999). He explains poverty by looking at socio-economic indicators such as education and health, and links it to the political parties. He also looks for differences among states with special attention on four states. He touches upon class but then swiftly moves on to caste as a more subjective form of differentiation found commonly in rural India. Harriss concludes that policies intended to benefit caste groups end up providing opportunities for a class to accumulate.

Tracing similarities and dissimilarities across states in India in terms of social policy is not new (Kohli, 1990, 2005). Comparative analysis as a method has been adopted by Kohli where he employs cross-state comparisons of specific agricultural policies and their implementation to characterise the kind of regime. For instance, the central question Kohli posed in *The State and Poverty in India* (1987) is whether regime types make a difference in the effort to combat poverty (Gupta, 1989: 790). Regime implies the ruling political party, its ideology, and its capacity to implement policies. Aseema Sinha (2005) probes deeper as she draws a comparative study on three Indian states to answer the central question: 'Which kind of state will provide developmental governance?' (Sinha, 2005: 3). Although she draws attention to regional elites such as the Patidars and Kshatriya castes in Gujarat, who wield pressure on the state, she returns to the state that wields the power to explain economic policy decisions.

This study derives its 'form' of three-state comparison from Kohli and Sinha. By application of inductive method, Kohli concluded that regime types have a determining effect on the efficacy of policy implementation.

The kind of policies he investigated were rural reform policies. Similarly, this book scrutinises agricultural policies adopted after 2004. Agricultural policy in India, in general, has taken a more market-oriented approach. The study assesses how this has played out in three specific states in India. The book differs from Kohli in that instead of comparing policies and regimes per se, it focuses on state–class dynamics. In addition, it endeavours to provide a detailed comparison of agricultural policies – an economic policy – after liberalisation. While Kohli in his 1990 work took a state-above-society position, in his later writings (2004, 2009) he has acknowledged that political institutions have become proximate to economic interest and so the state may not necessarily be above society – a major shift from his earlier position.

India has a federal structure with the union/centre and the regional states. Legislation is divided between these two levels of government with three lists, union, state, and concurrent lists. The subject of agriculture falls in the state list. Thus, the regional state became the unit of research by default. A three-state comparison model has been adopted to present a variation in terms of political settlement among the states, the nature of the state, and class structure. Comparative analysis has, then, been used to draw conclusions about the globalisation era. The main parameters for ascertaining which states to compare included the nature of existing dominant groups, regional disparity within the state, the way political parties have maintained linkages with social groups, and the nature of agricultural policies. The three states selected are unique and not the object of existing studies, and thus their comparison potentially offers some new insights. In terms of economic development, Chhattisgarh, Gujarat and Karnataka are at different stages of development and rely on primary, secondary and tertiary sectors, respectively. During the period of study, these states were under the rule of the BJP, with Karnataka as the only exception because it had a brief interlude of other parties in power. Hence the difference in development and commonality of political party were considered in comparing these states. Chhattisgarh was formed in 2000 and has been ridden with Maoist insurgencies since then. It is, therefore, an under-researched state. Gujarat has been in the limelight due to the high rate of agricultural growth in 2000–10 and its controversial political climate. Addition of a third state is methodologically to deepen the analysis, and Karnataka is chosen as it was ruled by the same political party in 2010 and registered high agricultural growth for the most part of the decade between 2000 and 2010. Its performance in floriculture and horticulture on one hand and high rate of farmer suicides since the late 1990s on the other make it a significant case to explore.

The method employed for the research is inductive. Information was gathered with the help of secondary literature and field-based investigation across 24 districts in three states to make sense of the ground reality. Empirical data gathered and analysed over 14 months were used to answer the large conceptual questions. Inferences have been drawn for each state based on cases from newspapers, existing literature and field interviews across cities and district headquarters. Semi-structured interviews and long interviews as well as focused group discussions were used in the field.

Chapters

Chapter 2 opens with a discussion of works that have theorised on social groups, the state and their interrelation. A few scholars use class as the category, some use class enmeshed with caste, and some use concepts from the pluralist school such as elites, borrowing from the pluralist school. All these schools engage with unequal distribution of power in society. It provides varied notions of different classes from existing literature – big farmers, landlords, small farmers, petty bourgeoisie, capitalist farmers, industrial capitalists, political class, professional class, gentleman farmers and wage labour – which have been reviewed to justify the fraction and class categories on which the study focuses.

Chapter 3 provides a detailed understanding of various aspects of agricultural state policy from the production side. Since agriculture spans huge and diverse processes, there was a need to predetermine which aspects would be concentrated upon. The core sections revolve around credit, seed, fertilisers, water and cropping pattern, and bring in various 'actors' involved in each of the above, such as farmers, traders, moneylenders and input-shop owners. Thinking through these issues helped in ascertaining that the agrarian policies are most relevant to my work, but due consideration has to be given to related policies that impact rural India.

The second half of the book is in keeping with the empiricist Anglo-Saxon tradition. The concepts that have been established as central through the theoretical discussion of class and state have been woven into an inductively oriented assessment of ground findings. Chapters 4, 5 and 6 describe and analyse the field findings that emerged from the states. Each chapter carries a section on drivers of agricultural growth, for example, irrigation, price policy and machinery subsidies. Other aspects are touched upon, including farmers' organisations, land acquisition, and decentralisation, to reflect on class formation and consolidation. It broadly attempts to sketch the dominant classes in each state, their relation to the regional state, possible influence on policy formulation, and what change they have undergone since new agrarian policies came in after the 1990s, and then 2004. A discussion of proprietary classes, especially within rural economy, is followed by their political affiliations since 2004. This affiliation might be an effect of the new opportunities created by the agrarian policy, or certain other policies providing opportunities of class mobility among caste groups. These sections are woven together in the conclusion, proposing causal links to understand the structure, its changes and the nature of the state in the aftermath of liberalisation.

Chapter 7 generalises on the basis of empirical findings and infers that the agrarian capitalist class, and not the rural capitalist class, is part of the political settlement in all three states, though not the dominating interest. The capitalist class has assumed a dominating position, albeit in different equations. The third dominant class is the petty bourgeoisie, with two fractions, new and old. The agrarian class may not necessarily represent a rural interest as they have increasingly taken to non-agrarian sources of accumulation as have the non-agrarian capital which has been invested in agrarian production, especially high value crops. Non-agrarian sources of accumulation facilitated by state policies are trade, input retailing, land brokering, moneylending and even white-collar jobs. Hence, the petty bourgeoisie relates more to big capital than the 'tiller farmers'; in fact, this fraction has become virulent oppressors of tiller farmers trying to maximise surplus from the sale of chemical inputs and land transactions. The agrarian policy highlights input centricity and mechanisation without acknowledging that these are not resource neutral (Byres, 1981); policy benefits thus accrued to the capitalist class and its secondary ally, the agrarian proprietary class. The tiller farmers failing to compete are increasingly squeezed out (Lerche, 2014). The state does not merely deepen the old structure but brings in a few new members, such as elected SC and ST members of PRIs into the fold of accumulation, and OBC members in state bureaucracy thus joining the petty bourgeoisie.

In such a fractured agrarian structure arises the pressing question of who will carry forward the mandate of the farmer in new India. Regional variations are important and need to be considered. For example, recently Punjab and western Uttar Pradesh showed us how the power of solidarity can move even a very popular leadership like the Modi government. This was truly commendable, because the farmer movement held Indian democracy accountable. Further, regional variations of farmer movements also exist within states. For instance, farmers in eastern Uttar Pradesh are not on the same page as their western counterparts. Under these circumstances, it is implausible to assume that all of rural India will unite on farmer issues. Second, farmers are not a homogenous group and are highly differentiated along class lines. In fact, as this book shows, farmers exhibit differentiation within class as well. In fact, with all farmers increasingly reporting non-agrarian sources of income, farmers may not associate with the rural interest as they once did in the 1980s (Varshney, 1995; Brass, 1995; Rudolph and Rudolph, 1987; Mehta and Sinha, 2022). Bharat as we once knew it has transformed significantly, with classes reporting cross-cutting interests and inter-sectoral movements. This has been made possible not just by the market in the globalization era, but also, as the book shows, by the state, which has been a driver in creating these opportunities too. Here the accumulation of the agrarian proprietary class is facilitated by both the state and the market, taking the form of rent and profit respectively.

In the light of the last fact, one factor assumes pivotal importance in the 2024 elections: the variation across regional states in terms of the nature of the state and the kind of political settlement. As we saw, Karnataka and Chhattisgarh have states characterised by clientelist and personal fusion respectively, which means the proprietary classes have a significant dependence on the state for their accumulation, and hence there is a possibility of galvanisation around farmers' interests which want more state support. Even if the farmer is accumulating from market-led sources, he or she will be unlikely to want to lose the opportunity of skewed access to subsidies, rent from PRIs, and so on, which are facilitated by the state. This phenomenon is unlike Gujarat where the state is characterised by relative autonomy, so classes do not lean on the state as much and are more willing to make use of market opportunities. There they may be more supportive of adopting something like the farm laws.

The other key factor in deciding the elections is related to differentiation within the agrarian proprietary class and banks on one fraction in particular, the petty bourgeoisie and its size. The big picture is that rural voters are 64 per cent and urban voters are 36 per cent of the population (World Bank, 2022); post-pandemic, more Indians have moved back to the rural areas and stuck to their land and agriculture. This orientation towards the rural makes one hopeful. However, within the rural population, the top 20 per cent mainly control the land, and they have shifted to align themselves with urban India. If this 12.8 per cent of the Indian population wants to welcome market forces, they will sign up for the BJP. That reduces the rural vote share to almost 51 per cent; if this fraction of agrarian proprietary class votes with the urban voters, the competition's ability to defeat the BJP becomes questionable. But one thing remains unquestioned: the story since 2004, then 2014, and now 2024 shows we cannot understand Indian politics and its shifting political economy without paying heed to agrarian transformation, the nature of the state, and the agrarian proprietary class. Institutions have acted on social structure and created opportunities that allow a few to accumulate, feeding inequality, and therefore an institution should not be studied in itself. The book contributes to the literature in politics, political economy, sociology, development studies and anthropology.

Notes

1. Semi-medium, small, and marginal farmers, even those with semi-medium holdings, who cultivate themselves and directly use their labour in cultivation, work as wage labour, and have no other significant source of income like rent from government schemes, have been referred to as 'tiller farmers' in the book.

2. MGNREGS is an Indian government welfare scheme, legislation for which was passed in 2005. It guarantees work for at least 100 days in a year to one adult member from every rural household. This generally means doing unskilled manual work such as digging tanks, building roads, and other public work. The minimum wage per day is 120 (US$1.80) at 2009 prices.

3. The PDS is another welfare programme of the Indian government under which raw food materials, such as rice, wheat, oil and sugar, are provided to below-poverty-line households at a subsidised price. State governments are responsible for determining the prices of these items and their distribution channels.

4. Both the works mentioned are on the political economy of India, which makes their mention of particular significance.

5. Byres (1997) points out that those social power relations find their way into political arenas, so we can deduce that those who are socially powerful will wield proportionate power over the state apparatus.

❁

2

Policy-making, Class Factor, and Political Settlement
Setting the Theoretical Framework

Political economy offers an insightful way of analysing the influence of proprietary classes[1] on agrarian policy-making and effective class formations in post-liberalisation India. The objective is to identify the key classes dominating the relations of production and their means of production and accumulation, and assess if these means have undergone a change or alteration over the past two decades under the impact of state policy. Once the economic interest of the proprietary classes is ascertained, their relationship with the state is examined. Intervention by classes and representation of their interests in policy-making are usually covert, if such exist, and nearly impossible to study. Instead, their role in policy-making is construed through a study of formal and informal contact, proximity, and relations with political leaders and the bureaucracy.

Identifying the framework

This section discusses two conceptualisations of social group and state relations – the Marxist theory and the 'political settlement' theory – and weaves them into a framework for the study.

The Marxian view on class and state

In the 1970s, two schools surfaced within Marxism with respect to analysis of the capitalist state. Ralph Miliband and Nicol Poulantzas personify the 'instrumentalist' and 'structuralist' positions, respectively. Miliband's position on the state is based on the *Communist Manifesto*, while Poulantzas draws on *Das Capital* and the writings of Gramsci (Barrow, 2000). Both scholars are influenced by Gramsci's analysis of the coercive and ideological apparatus of the state and civil society. Miliband argues that the state is directly controlled by capitalists, rather than by capital. Therefore, the state is reduced to an instrument in their hands. The ruling class of a capitalist society is 'that class which owns and controls the means of production and which is able, by its virtue of the economic power thus conferred upon it, to use the state as its instrument for the domination of society' (Barrow, 2000: 23). He draws on historical instances to understand state functioning.

On the other hand, Poulantzas' understanding of class is more nuanced, wherein he incorporates political and ideological relations in what is otherwise seen as a purely economically determined category. He argues that in the capitalist mode of production, the direct producers are dispossessed from the means of production. Economic power is concentrated in the hands of the owners of the means of production – the capitalists. They are an exploiting class who control the labour process and accumulation of the generated surplus. The process of accumulation is supported by state policies that justify such exploitation in the name of capitalist 'development'. Therefore, the state performs a wider and more complicated role than just carrying out repressive and legitimating functions. It balances diverse class interests to maintain the continuance of the mode of production. The main indicators of an effective state power, therefore, are state policies that propagate both capitalist accumulation and class structure. The dominant classes affect policy-making by their participation in, and sometimes control over, the prevailing political and ideological apparatus (Barrow, 2000: 23).[2]

Overall, Poulantzas' analysis enables a more nuanced investigation of the relationship between 'class', 'state', and 'policies' as it points to the need to enquire into how certain classes directly or indirectly influence state apparatus to act in favour of their class interests, 'lawfully and democratically'. Miliband did this only in part as he spoke of direct capture of political offices. He does not talk about policy-making, which is an integral part of the democratic process and remains mired in class interest.

In the same strain, Byres (1997) argues that state bureaucracy – the policy-making arm of the government – is embedded within social power relations, wherein classes collaborate and compete to form political alliances. These alliances manifest themselves in state planning which, instead of being a rational exercise, reflects power relations between the state and different classes. Similarly, Barbara Harriss-White (2002) argues that policy-making is a political process and enmeshed in politics at several levels, right from deciding budgetary allocation to implementation of policies. Thus, policy-making does not qualify as a technical or a rational process.[3]

What notion of class does the study adopt? It is well known that from a Marxist perspective, classes are constituted by their relation to the 'means of production', and derive their differentia from relations of exploitation, domination, and subordination. Considering this insufficient, Poulantzas held that a class ought to be further classified into fractions and strata, based on differentiations in the economic sphere as well as political and ideological relations (Poulantzas, 1973). He used the term 'power bloc' to refer to different fractions of capitalist and other economically powerful classes, such as the landed aristocracy and elements of the petty bourgeoisie, whose political interests are upheld by the state. Poulantzas highlights that the petty bourgeoisie can be divided into two – old and new. The new petty bourgeoisie emerges as capitalism surges ahead and grows through opportunities created by the market. Whereas the old petty bourgeoisie thrives on state and its resources. The new class is characterised by the help it lends in consolidating the hegemony of the ruling classes, and, in the process, it erodes the labour's capacity to organise. For a complex society, such as India, the idea of fractions within social classes has the potential to explain the societal dynamic better.

Jessop (1983) developed Poulantzas' theory into a detailed analysis of the way the capitalist state interacts with dominant classes in Europe. He argues that, in some instance, the relationship between private capitalist monopolies and the state apparatus is close enough to comprise a 'personal fusion', where monopolists, or their kin, come to occupy seats at the highest echelons of the state. This position of Jessop is aligned to that of Miliband, who characterises the capitalist state along similar lines and highlights 'interlocking of positions'. But for Miliband, this is the only form that capital–state relations take. Jessop is closer to Poulantzas' idea of personal fusion. Other ways are listed here. Political parties can act as instruments of ideological control whose loyalty is captured by monopolies investing in them in different ways, such as election campaigns. Other mechanisms of control include interest associations, lobbies, and contact with politicians, and other individuals who help in influencing policy decisions which are more commonly found under monopoly capitalism. Contact with politicians and public officials take the form of control over means of 'mental production', which operate through control over school curriculum, media, and even religious institutions. The process of mental production received particular attention from Miliband, and remains his seminal contribution.

Two other points raised by Jessop (1983) are of significance for the book. First, as capital consolidates its position, there is a simultaneous and almost complementary process of 'immiseration of proletariat' that takes place. This serves the dual purpose of keeping the supply of labour going, while unemployed labour puts downward pressure on wages. Second, as capitalism advances, a simultaneous process of decentralisation of power to microeconomic and/or local political levels takes place. Decentralisation refines the control of capital over even the smallest areas of surplus production or consumption, and facilitates penetration of state control into all areas of social life (Jessop, 1983: 59).

However, it should be noted that except for Byres and Harriss-White, the scholars discussed here write in the context of the Northern, monopoly capitalist state. Can they prove helpful to understand class–state relationship in the Global South states, where the reality is different? Arguably, it can. The core of Poulantzas' and Jessop's analyses is not specific to a particular aspect of capitalism but outlines the general relationship between capitalism and the capitalist state. The way this relationship plays out in different societies will vary and can only be ascertained once class relations in that society are analysed. To reiterate, while class acts upon the state, the state also plays a significant role in maintaining and shaping classes through its policies. This two-way relation is of utmost interest to the research undertaken in the book.

The 'political settlement' perspective

'Political settlement' as an idea is similar to that of power bloc from Marxism. Mushtaq Khan (2005) explains political settlement as an arrangement between state institutions and the elite, albeit not class. It influences the way in which the state mediates between various group demands, and how it suppresses dissenting groups, thereby perpetuating the interests of the elite. Through this formulation Khan challenges new institutional economics, which view institutions as 'incentive structures' that will propel change (Di John and Putzel, 2009). For Khan, institutions are value laden and not objective entities. They, in fact, operate as a coalition partner to social groups. In developing countries (democracies), social groups and their various fractions are in intense competition, far more than in advanced democracies (Di John and Putzel, 2009). The dependence on state resources and the clientelistic tendency of the state makes the groups more dependent on the institutions.

The 'political settlement' scholars argue for a similar role of the state as Poulantzas did. This was creating cohesion among different groups. However, the two differ in the conception of social groups – the 'political settlement' theorists discuss groups in terms of 'elite', while Marxists use the term 'class'. Elite is a pluralist notion and does not involve an analysis of relations of production, and it, therefore, cannot equate with social classes. However, the two concepts – elite and class – are not disconnected after all. Khan argues that informal arrangements play a key role in facilitating access for the powerful groups to sources of incomes through which they can continue 'political' accumulation, particularly in developing countries (Khan, 2010). For instance, in India, the petty bourgeoisie holds positions of leadership in civil society and exerts political pressure on the state. It uses its influence to guide disbursement of rents by the state in the form of subsidies, tax breaks, and licenses, and tries to obstruct the state from removing unproductive rents. Politics is thus reduced to capturing resources by the powerful, part of which is used to pay the supporters/voters. The elite are, therefore, involved in accumulation through association with state apparatus. Khan finds himself close to Mitra (1977) in making the argument. The twin objectives of such a stable settlement are good governance and protection of property rights, which minimises transaction cost. Good governance and property rights are crucial for the smooth functioning of the economy that any political institution must ensure. Conflict creates a hostile environment for investment, so the need is to mitigate conflict as much as possible.

How will conflict be minimised? Within a polity, stability is best maintained when there is parity between institutions and societal power distribution, otherwise powerful groups will attempt to change any institutional arrangement that challenges or checks their power, argue political settlement scholars. This balance between institutional make-up and the resultant power distribution must be sustainable. The reproduction of particular societies mandate both formal and informal institutions to be in sync to achieve minimum levels of economic performance and political stability (Khan, 2010). In the context of India, such informal arrangements through which powerful groups access the state find mention in the works of scholars such as Harriss-White (2003), Manor (2004), and Jenkins (2000). Such an institutional arrangement secures the power position of a select few, and their benefits make for a stable political settlement (Di John and Putzel, 2009). The elite bargain made in this process secures the state's stability, which enables it to decisively fix taxes or use its monopolised violence. This is akin to Poulantzas' scheme of analysing state–class relations, where he discusses how class assumes a political role and builds coalitions to perpetuate its interests.

Political settlement theory draws our attention to how these settlements have to operate both horizontally and vertically to be effective (Khan, 2010).

In the case of India, this is manifested in arrangements within castes and across classes. How do these settlements stay intact and what prevents them from disintegrating? The answer lies in the 'petty bourgeoisie' which acts as a crucial cementing element that holds together various dominant classes, particularly the bourgeoisie and the landlords, in an effective settlement. It is an intermediate class and does not belong to either, yet benefits from both. Hence, when differences arise between major classes, the petty bourgeoisie somewhat mitigates them.

Di John and Putzel (2009) draw a cross-country comparison to reflect upon the benefits and constraints that a stable coalition can offer. They extend 'political settlement' from a conceptual level to a functional level, where it can interpret the differential performance of states in the developing world. In the case of Guatemala, the scholars observe that a landowner–military alliance obstructs tax reforms. The state finds it hard to impose taxes on the landlords because they occupy a dominant position in the settlement. Whereas in Costa Rica, taxes can be imposed and extracted successfully as landowners are not a part of the ruling alliance of the state. Penetration into the countryside is a mark of any state's resilience. For elites, securing rent allocation remains at the core of any political organisation they enter. Their interest is as much in protecting existing privileges, such as those for the landed groups who have been enjoying tax relief, as in creating new, such as strengthening emerging capitalist groups (Di John and Putzel, 2009). The 'political settlement' perspective has rarely been singularly applied in the Indian context, but its analysis has shown merit in understanding several developing countries. There is a wide acceptance that India has an economic and political elite group, as scholars have acknowledged (Kohli, 2009; Harriss et al., 2012). However, questions such as who they are, where they operate, and what their political interests are remain under-addressed. By adopting political settlement as part of the framework, the book endeavours to answer these questions.

'Elite' is a term that makes it difficult to understand the multiple interests within the elite, such as the landed, industrialists, and political leaders. Hence, the study uses the 'political settlement' framework as the operating arrangement but ascertains the constituent parts by conceptually locating proprietary classes, their means of production, and their link to state apparatus since the 1990s. The question whether such settlement is effective in each of the states is addressed subsequently. The next section discusses the issue of class and why it has been taken as the entry point to understand agrarian policy in India.

Why take 'class' as the lens? Structure over institutions

The aim of this study is to understand how classes have used the political apparatus to protect their ownership of means of production and access to surplus, and how they have benefitted from agrarian policies in the last two decades. This is an important question to investigate, for several reasons.

Since the 1990s, policies of the Indian state have shown a clear inclination towards fostering interests of specific social groups. This has led to what many scholars have identified as crony capitalism, grand corruption, land acquisition, and favouring capitalists. Kohli (2009) observes that the Indian state was rather balanced towards different social groups during the 1980s, and turned markedly pro-business since the 1990s. Harriss, Corbridge, and Jeffrey (2012) acknowledge the encouraging response of the Indian state to the demands of business groups and the elite, which is evident in disproportionate opportunities, such as the initiation of 600 special economic zones (SEZ), made available to them. Some might blame it entirely on globalisation, but it seems the state has assumed a greater role in guiding the market. In fact, it continues to negotiate expectations and demands of other classes to diffuse tension.

Scattered evidence shows that political leaders are dependent on the capitalists to finance their increasingly expensive election campaigns, which has been noted by some scholars. The quote states, 'greater costs of participating in India's competitive politics led a growing number of politicians to finance their campaigns illegally' (Harriss et al., 2012: 15–16; Bussell, 2012). On the other hand, the capitalist classes seek the patronage of the political class for fast business clearances, subsidised institutional credit, infrastructural support, and so on (Bussell, 2012). This symbiotic relationship between political and economic capital is indicative of a pro-business environment. Jayal (1999) has made a similar observation. The increasing cost of contesting elections in India is leading to proximity between propertied classes and political parties. Even though voters have been mobilised along social identities, such as caste, these allegiances are overshadowed by economic interest in demand politics since liberalisation. In the context of the southern state of Tamil Nadu, Harriss-White writes extensively on how local state officials and merchants collude with each other to protect and enhance their interests (Harriss-White, 1996, 2008). Direct capture of political office, such as acquiring a bureaucratic or local government position (*sarpanch* or *mukhia*) by big farmers, is rampant. Jeffrey and Lerche (2000) make similar observations about the northern state of Uttar Pradesh with a detailed account of how economically dominant classes have infiltrated the state's institutions. They note that political brokers and economically powerful farmers exert control on state resources and use state power for their personal gain. Evidence shows deep ties exist between class and state, and thus state policies can hardly be discussed appropriately unless this nexus is analysed.

Pre-liberalisation literature on India suggests that political regimes were built by tapping into the social structure of rural India during the first three decades after Independence (Gould, 1995; Chatterjee, 1997; Weiner 2012). Chatterjee argues that Congress dominance stood on 'incorporating within its own structure of rule the existent dominant groups in the various localities' (Chatterjee, 1997: 299). Although such explanations had been overshadowed, recent references show social groups getting politicised and using parties as platforms to access political power (Yadav, 1999). Bharatiya Janata Party (BJP) rule in Chhattisgarh was recently argued to be thriving by fostering the mercantile capital interest (Berthet and Kumar, 2011). In Gujarat, it is argued, that the shift in land policy was meant to appease the demands of the rising nouveau riche capitalist class (Sud, 2012). Comparable situations where the regime addresses the demands arising from existing dominant social classes to remain in power, rather than altering it, were also reported from Karnataka (Jenkins, 1999). A logical conclusion under such circumstances could be that policy decisions are taken to benefit proprietary classes, and facilitate their reproduction and accumulation, as argued by Poulantzas and Jessop in the context of Western countries. Their suitability in the context of India needs further assessment.

This discussion points to the marked centrality of class in political decision-making, and to the importance of looking at policies through the lens of class in order to conduct a comprehensive assessment of India since liberalisation. Whether this holds true for the three states under scrutiny, and if so, what are its ramifications in the case of agrarian policies, both agrarian and others, will be subsequently examined

State–society discourse in India

This section reviews seminal works in the realm of interaction between social actors and the political system in India. Pranab Bardhan (1984) has written about the interaction between the two, but his emphasis is on class demands and benefits that accrue to three dominant proprietary classes at a pan-India level. A disproportionate part of state resources is allocated to these classes. The rich farmers are 15 per cent of the rural population, and have benefitted from formal credit and support prices; the professional class (bureaucracy at union and state levels) owns social capital, which privileges them to access rent income. The industrial class includes both big and small industries, which have thrived on state support. For Bardhan, state works on class formations and the class exerts pressure on the state. The difference of demand creates a constraint on state resources making it difficult to make decisive policy decisions. Hence, the Indian state is characterised as a 'machine' model of politics. While his work holds much significance, it points at the collective action dilemma created by a heterogenous class coalition but it does not bring out the richness of regional variation.

Writing in the 1980s, the Rudolphs (1987) identified three main actors in India – capital, labour, and the state. They characterise it as a demand polity with groups making demands on the state. Yet it enjoys relative autonomy, and certainly is not subservient to these actors. The state is termed as 'the third actor', which manages the groups and their expectations. Class politics is only a marginal force, as Indian politics is more of an 'involuted pluralism' where interest groups and classes weaken themselves by dividing into fractions. Since the state exerts its authority over them, they characterise India as a command polity. Neerja Gopal Jayal (1999) takes the position that boundaries exist between the state and society, though the two domains are influenced by each other. She observes that Marxists have not written about the Indian polity directly, which shows that this perspective has not found enough leverage in the Indian context.[4] Her larger concern remains with public–private or religion–secular dichotomies, which, according to her, trump economic concerns. Hers is a commendable work on democracy and allied concepts such as justice, freedom, and rights, but not on political economy.

Atul Kohli has worked on state–society relations in India for over three decades. To understand the factors that determine a state's capacity to make strong policy decisions, he compares the performance of three states – West Bengal under the CPI(M), Karnataka under Devraj Urs, and Uttar Pradesh under the Janata Party in the 1970s and 1980s. Each state being bound by the same democratic–capitalist system, ceteris paribus, is faced with similar constraints of resources, institutional frameworks, and pressures from civil society. The primary distinguishing feature between the states is the difference in terms of policy, which can be ascribed to the regional party in power (regime type). His arguments are decisively political, giving primacy to the state and the political party over social groups (Kohli, 1990). After the 1990s, Kohli acknowledges that India's business receives undue support from the state to compete with global capital, a move necessitated by the onset of liberalisation

(Kohli, 2006). During this time, he notes, the capitalist class in India gets divided into two sub-groups: Confederation of Indian Industry (CII), which took a lead in welcoming reforms, and the Associated Chambers of Commerce and Industry of India (ASSOCHAM), which remained protectionist. Despite the academic rigour with which Kohli engages with capital, he overlooks important interest groups such as rural capitalists, who form part of the elite gaining from the reforms.

In his later works, Kohli cites the fragmented multi-class nature of the Indian state as the reason for its limited ability to be a strong state, capable of implementing policies decisively. He reflects on the political determinants of economic performance in India, especially the rates and patterns of industrialisation, raising questions about the design and capacity of India's highly interventionist state (Kohli, 2004: 257). It is critical to understand the nature of state, which the book justly does, but what the author overlooks is the multi-class aspect of the state itself that mandates further breakdown and analysis.

The bureaucracy plays an active role in this shift from a state-above-society approach to a pro-business one in India after liberalisation, both in formulating policies and consenting to changes needed to implement them, an idea that Mooij (2005) and Sinha (2005) discuss in their books. Kohli labels this as a shift from 'socialist India to India incorporated' (Kohli, 2009: 147). He draws a critical distinction between pro-business (state supports existing businesses) and pro-market (state supports new business entrants in the economy), and characterises India as pro-business. That said, he holds that the state is still somewhat autonomous of society as it embraces 'Indian capital as the main ruling ally' (Kohli, 2012: 93). Thus, businesses do not infiltrate the state; instead, the state consciously collaborates with business interests. In this book, this position is put to test in the context of current India. Unlike Bardhan, who argues that rich farmers and the professional class were allies prior to the 1980s, Kohli holds that business is the only gainer, and rentier landlords[5] are losing out in India after liberalisation. Chatterjee (2008) argued that capitalists are hegemonic in this period. This study, therefore, also attempts to understand the composition of the 'ruling elite', which is treated as the political settlement in the book.

State–society relationship analysis in India has been conducted by Aseema Sinha (2005) following the same 'form' as Kohli – a three-state comparison of Gujarat, Tamil Nadu, and West Bengal. Adopting a political economy perspective, she looks at the interaction between regional state institutions and social groups in each state with respect to economic policy decisions. She agrees that electoral competition has significant impact, but she concentrates on institutions and ascribes a central role to the state. However, any analysis of class composition and the extent of its influence on institutions is not the focus of her work. She deals with regional elites and their political choices to explain the failure of India's failed developmental state.

From these discussions, two main positions emerge – the 'state-over-society' approach and the 'state partnering with social actors' approach. These have been widely adopted by scholars who research on India. Both positions are examined in this book and considered in the light of empirical findings from Gujarat, Chhattisgarh, and Karnataka. The third position to be put to test has been discussed in an earlier part of the chapter, outlining how class is seen as integral to political system. The book's approach on class is that definitionally, class is as much a political and ideological relations as economic relations.

Class discourse in India – Different perspectives

This section discusses the theses of scholars who have worked on class as an analytical category in the Indian context. It explains what it means to adopt a political economy framework. The subsequent discussion will refer to several academic and political debates, as well as to operating class relations presented by the mainstream Left parties in India.

John Harriss (1999) emphasises that class formation is a problematic notion. There are 'objective' differences between groups of people in terms of their relations with productive systems. However, the key is to understand how these interact with 'subjective' categories in terms of which people experience and understand their roles which influences the relationship; hence the relationship between 'class in itself' and 'class for itself' needs to be considered. He thus introduces caste as the subjective category. Moreover, not only do social relations exist between different classes, there can be different and often competing interests within the same class such as the old and new petty bourgeoisie or national and comprador bourgeoisie.

The theory of intermediate classes has gained currency in recent years in India, especially through the work of Barbara Harriss-White (2003). She draws on Kalecki and argues that the self-employed and the middle farmers form the intermediate class that dominates the Indian state and its decisions in a major way (Kalecki, 1972). She calls it the intermediate regime. Their differentia is a combination of labour and capital, since their income comes from both labour and risk-taking with capital. Though not rich, they are numerically dominant. They have been the chief beneficiaries of government favours like the licensing policy. This intermediate class tends to dominate the countryside. For Mushtaq

Khan (2005), these are akin to the petty bourgeoisie, which comprises those with college and university education, middle and big peasants, and those indulging in small trade. They often act as agents of political parties, and lead organised and informal politics, cementing dominant classes.

Another class-based analysis is more in line with the classic Marxian thinking. Daniel Thorner, writing in the mid-1950s, put forward a three-fold classification of Indian rural population who drew a living from the land, namely the *malik, kisan,* and *mazdoor.* The *malik*s were landed proprietors who derived their income by employing tenants and labourers. *Kisan*s were those cultivators who 'live[d] primarily by their toil on their own lands', and *mazdoor*s were those who 'gain[ed] their livelihood primarily from working on other people's land'. This is essentially a Marxian notion, given Thorner's emphasis on possession of land, as well as relations of labour hiring and land renting between the proprietary *malik*s and landless *mazdoor*s, with the *kisan*s occupying the middle rank (Thorner, 1956: 9–11 cited in P. Patnaik, 2001).

The class composition in rural India has undergone significant changes since the 1950s. Many of these changes have been affected by land reforms – especially tenancy reforms – and the Green Revolution. The benefits of the Green Revolution initially accrued to farmers from the wheat-growing states of Punjab, western Uttar Pradesh, and Haryana, and gradually spread to other states. The highlight of this change is the emergence of the capitalist farmer class whose nature, composition, and role have been defined differently by scholars.

Byres (1981) argues that a new capitalist farmer class developed in India as capitalist production and peasant differentiation took root in the Green Revolution.[6] The Rudolphs (1987) assign a central role to a somewhat different category of capitalist farmers in agrarian politics of India, who they call 'bullock capitalists'.[7] They are independent agricultural producers and are the products of the abolition of intermediaries. They have been the chief gainers of the Green Revolution, having an average land holding size between 2.5 and 15 acres, which was enough to support their infrastructural requirements. This suffices to engage in capital-intensive agricultural production based on extensive use of machinery and employing labour. According to Bernstein (2010), capitalist farmers are those who exploit labour for profit, invest to expand production and increase productivity, fund new sites for commodity production, and develop new markets for those commodities (p. 33). The fractions do not necessarily emerge from big farmers, but given the need to have surplus – enough to be able to invest capital – big farmers are a part of the class. All capitalist farmers are not big farmers, and all big farmers are not capitalist farmers, despite an obvious overlap between the two.

Utsa Patnaik (1987) empirically identifies classes-in-themselves within the cultivating population in India. Instead of basing the classification solely on landholding and initial resource endowments, she asserts that class position is also influenced by factors such as family size, cropping pattern and intensity of cultivation, and the level of technology employed. An important indicator is the extent to which a household hires external labour, and the extent to which the household members work for others. This indicator and the labour exploitation criteria are used together in Patnaik's method of labour-use index for identifying classes. She identifies five distinct rural classes – big landlords, rich peasants, middle peasants sub-divided into upper and lower peasants, poor peasants, and wage labourers. Big landlords and rich peasants are the net exploiters of labour. The middle and poor peasants are those who work as hired labour and cultivate crops for their own subsistence. However, the upper middle class peasants generate surplus as well as engage in self-cultivation. Wage labourers have no ownership of land and sustain themselves through selling labour alone. The landlord class is reluctant to invest in agricultural modernisation and prefer non-farm sectors since profits in agriculture tend to remain lower than non-agricultural sectors in the event of investing the surplus. They tend to extract rent from leasing out land.[8] In view of the agrarian crisis which hit India in the late 1990s, Patnaik (2006) takes a position that class differentiation within the peasantry is no longer relevant as imperialism is the biggest exploiter crushing all agrarian classes.

The largest Left party in India, the CPI(M), has similar views on the agrarian question. In its agrarian analysis carried out in the year 2000, it held that the ruling class is the big bourgeoisie who are allied to 'landlordism', and this ruling class protects and helps the operation of monopoly capital (CPI[M], 2000: 34 cited in Lerche, 2013), although what 'landlordism' refers to is unclear. It glances over the role of rich peasants, who are also exploiters of labour. Lerche conjectures that 'landlordism' refers to the same class as Patnaik draws attention to in her work. They are capitalist landlords, that is, 'the kind of village-based, relatively small, ex-landlords that Patnaik referred to, who still own sizable amounts of land locally' (Lerche, 2013). The CPI(M) contends that these ex-landlords are now actively investing in agriculture and rapidly adopting capitalist technology in agriculture. To describe the class, a term 'capitalist landlord' has gained currency. Patnaik and the Left party argue that the landlord class goes back to exploitation in the semi-feudal ways of the neoliberal era. The book argues that the changes since liberalisation have not been captured in class formulation and, therefore, the term 'landlord' is misrepresented. Noting a change in mode of production, the agrarian sector being penetrated by market forces, a term like 'rural capitalist' has been proposed by Bernstein (2010) to capture the ground reality. Similar categories are revisited in the following paragraphs.

Several scholars throw light on the intricacies of the rural class, pointing out that there are primarily two segments within the category of those with big holdings, namely the 'landlords' and the 'big farmers'. The term 'landlord' is not used to refer to a feudal category (Vakulabharanam 2010, Kohli 2006, Damodaran 2008). It is a class that has its origin in the feudal mode of production, but has assumed a new character with technological advancement. They are urban-bound and hardly have any stake in the rural sector. They earn from farming, but the surplus is diverted to other sectors. This is a differentiation arising from land reform and tenancy reform. Patnaik characterises the class engaging in labour exploitation and capitalist agriculture as capitalist landlords (U. Patnaik, 1987). However, 'capitalist' and 'landlord' posit a paradox, since an interest in investing in capitalist method is for profit, and thus rent extraction should decline. This is an issue that the book addresses at a theoretical level, in light of new empirical findings.

The big farmers (Assadi 2008, Jeffrey 2002, Rutten 1986, Jodhka, 2014, Reddy and Swaminathan 2014, Lerche 2014) are more rooted in the rural set-up and often directly engage in cultivation, resembling Patnaik's category of rich peasants. Commonly, their holding is more than 10 acres and they engage with cultivation through the employment of wage labour or tenants. Crucially, the surplus thus generated is not necessarily invested in upgrading the technology required for agricultural production, rather diversifying into agri-business and trades.

The categories are unclear and analytically weak. If a class has no direct stake in agriculture and is urban-bound, seeking opportunities in other sectors, then there remains no reason for them to invest in capitalist technologies. Hence, at this point the landlord class should have a minimal relevance to agriculture as a productive sector though they continue to have a political presence.

The categories landlords and big capitalist farmers are used by Ramachandran, Rawal, and Swaminathan (2010). The land is cultivated by either tenants to whom the land is leased out or hired labour who perform agricultural operations. Therefore, cultivation does not involve participation of the owner's family members. Given their monopoly over land, the landlords are economically dominant, but given their high social status and direct or indirect access to political power, they also dominate traditional social and modern political structures. The big capitalist farmers are mostly from upper middle income peasant families and sometimes from rich peasant families. They have acquired more land by inter-generationally investing the surplus, and now employ others to cultivate the land. They commonly derive income from moneylending, salaried employment and trade (Ramachandran, Rawal, and Swaminathan, 2010: 24–25).

In this book, big farmers are those with big holdings, engage in productive agriculture, do not put in their labour but also do not adopt modern technology unlike landlords who live off rent from leasing out landholdings, but do not engage in productive agriculture. Unlike a big farmer, a landlord's role is expected to be minimal in agrarian economy but they wield socio-political power. This book holds that a capitalist farmer is a category distinct from both. The former produces with the aim of accumulating capital (that is, generating profit to reinvest in agriculture or elsewhere) and does so through exploiting other people's labour. Hence, the capitalist farmer does not put his labour in the productive activity. He invests the surplus in improving technology (seeds, fertilisers, and machinery) to increase productivity and hence profit in agriculture. On the other hand, landlords are those who have a rentier-class relation to agriculture, and choose to invest surplus in other sectors. The use of the term 'farmer' rather than 'peasant' is more appropriate in India in the post-liberalisation era where production for self-consumption has reduced; cheap food under the public distribution system has made buying food for consumption predominant among food crop growers, and commercial cropping has registered a sustained increase in acreage. So, the term 'peasants' will not be used.

The concepts discussed above and of importance for the study have been presented in Table 2.1. Since the book lays focus on the capital side of the story, those fractions which constitute the agrarian proprietary class (Badhan refers them as rich farmers) have been listed.

Class and state relations

This section presents a brief discussion on how and why class impacts policy decisions, followed by a class analysis drawn from the works of several scholars. Mitra (1977) theoretically and empirically analyses the relationship between the economy and state. In this unique analysis, he meticulously traces the roots of policy decisions to specific class interests, inferring a kind of class conflict among landlords and the industrial bourgeoisie. He explains how social class power manifests itself: 'the seizure of power is ... to shift the distribution of assets and incomes in society in favour of those groups who support them' (p. 3), which means that there is a mutual advantageous alliance between those in

Table 2.1   Class and its various notions

Scholar	Labour	Mix of labour and capital	Capital	Capital from other sectors
Daniel Thorner	*Mazdoor*	*Kisan*	*Malik*	Gentleman farmers
Utsa Patnaik	Small peasants	Middle and semi-medium peasants	Capitalist landlords and rich peasants	
John Harriss	Small farmers/ lower castes	Middle farmers/middle castes	Rich farmers/ upper castes	
V. K. Ramachandran, Madhura Swaminathan, and Vikas Rawal			Big capitalist farmers and landlords	
H. Bernstein and T. J. Byres			Capitalist farmers	
Rutten 1986, Jodhka 2014			Big farmers	
Kalecki, M. Khan, and Barbara Harriss-White		Intermediary class/the petty bourgeoisie	Agro-commercial capital	

Source: Author.

power and those backing them. Hence, the means of production and accumulation lie at the core of political power. His interest lies more in conflict between classes than on class–state relationship (McCartney, 2010). Such a framework has been rarely put forward in either the discipline of politics or economics, although 'political settlement' theorists make a similar claim when explaining the stability of a democracy. Following Bardhan and Mitra, this book will assess the way the dominant classes influence agricultural policy, and how their class positions are protected and furthered through state policies. Both scholars found that conflict existed between dominant classes – what has become of that conflict shall be examined.

Bardhan (1984) identifies three classes that play the most determining roles in Indian society and uses them as tools to explain the ground reality. These are the industrial capitalist class, the rich farmers, and the public-sector professionals. Taken together, they form the ruling class, but they have severe disagreements among themselves in terms of their specific class interests and, thus, do not form a 'monolithic class enemy'. In fact, they pressurise the state in such diverse directions that the state fails to take decisive economic decisions that can drive growth. This explains why India was in growth doldrums during the 1980s. Rather, the soft state falls behind in economic performance in an attempt to mediate between these powerful groups. The professionals or the third class support the urban industrial class, while the big farmers stand against these two classes. Bardhan points out how a Jat Prime Minister in the 1980s improved the terms of trade towards agriculture by increasing government procurement prices for farmers from ₹100 to ₹240 within one decade, and left the industrial class unhappy. Similar favouratism is implicit in the exclusion of agricultural income from taxation. For Mitra (1977), this indicated the improvement of terms of trade for agriculture. This has only increased the already existing tension between these two classes, pulling the state in opposite directions.

Scholars have classified industrialists as an interest group rather than as a class in action, leaving out their means of production and accumulation from analysis. Stanley Kochanek (1974, 1995) has written about the industrialists' role in Indian politics. Over time, business groups have designed channels for 'interest articulation', like the Chambers of Commerce, trade and industrial associations, and employers' associations. Traders and small-scale businessmen use more informal channels, such as the 'industrial embassy' in Delhi, often employing highly personalised systems of liaison and lobbying. Originally, three chambers were formed in Calcutta, Madras, and Bombay, dominated by regional communities that moved from trade to industry, namely the Marwaris, Chettairs, Gujaratis, and Parsis. For the initial three decades after Independence, there were major caste-, region-, and family-based cleavages within the business community – a situation that gradually changed over the years (Kochanek, 1974: 97). Damodaran (2008) traces the source of capital invested in different Indian states such as Andhra Pradesh and Gujarat, as well as north India, and studies the dynamics within communities such as the Kammas, Khatris, Naidus, Patidars, and Marwaris to list a few. These communities have been instrumental in making such investments possible. The companies investigated fall in the category of ₹1000 million worth companies, belonging to the most reputed business communities. He observes a transfer of surplus from agriculture to industry, but communities differ on how they relate to agriculture after this shift (Rutten, 1995; Damodaran, 2008). Damodaran draws attention to the link between accumulation in the two main sectors of Indian economy – agriculture and industry – and reflects on the role of community in capital accumulation. This is significant, according to Damodaran, as it differentiates Indian capitalism from Western capitalism that thrives on abstract individualism.

However, a new cleavage between foreign and indigenous capital has appeared since the 1980s. The three prominent associations representing the private sector in India, namely the Federation of Indian Chambers of Commerce and Industry (FICCI), the ASSOCHAM, and the CII, show this cleavage (Kochanek, 1995). While the FICCI has the largest membership, it consists of older, more indigenous family-owned businesses. The ASSOCHAM, however, is the oldest but has come to represent both large family-owned indigenous businesses and foreign multinationals, whereas the CII is the newest and the richest apex association. The CII played a pivotal role in pushing the reforms in 1991, and tends to represent new entrants such as electronics, software, and computer technology.

The class nature of these groups is that of Bardhan's industrial capitalist. Classifying further within the class, the FICCI and the ASSOCHAM represent more of the national capital/bourgeoisie, which is protectionist, eager to capture the national market, earn public infrastructure support, and control the surplus. The CII, on the other hand, is pro-foreign capital; it actively lobbied for the reform of the Foreign Exchange Regulation Act (FERA), and was so influential that the Revenue Secretary of the Government of India called the 1993–94 budget the 'Tarun Das Budget', named after the then head of the CII (Kochanek, 1996: 167). Amin (2005) in a similar vein links the 1991 reforms to 'an offensive by obscurantist forces supported by the dominant comprador class and a large proportion of the middle classes' (p. 234) that challenged state legitimacy.

Bardhan's class analysis remains seminal in understanding Indian political economy (McCartney, 2010). Contrary to his predictions, India recovered from the economic doldrums in the 1990s, and experienced a long period of rapid growth. However, his three-class paradigm remains a critical tool to investigate India in the current phase, which the book adopts. It traces the means of accumulation for these classes and the political routes they adopt to influence policies – both of which Bardhan did not engage with. John Harriss'

(1999) work fits perfectly in this gap. He unfurls the class–caste basis of the regimes[9] (political system at both central and state levels) to understand the 'balance of power'. He argues that when taken together, caste and class can bridge the gap between objective and subjective identities and positions, that is, a group's role within the production system (class), and the way a group experiences its identity (caste). For instance, a landlord or a big farmer often earns people's obedience through his upper-caste status, which furthers his interest in extracting surplus.

Harriss classifies agrarian society into three social groups combining class and caste. The most dominant local class of landlords or big farmers comprises the upper castes – Brahmins, Kshatriyas, and Vaishyas. Middle peasants (*kisans*) dominate by way of their control over land and labour, which forms the basis of local political power. They often belong to middle castes such as Jats, Yadavs, and Kumris in Maharashtra. The lower castes, constitutionally termed the Scheduled Castes (SCs), are composed of marginal farmers, sharecroppers, landless labourers, barbers, carpenters, and blacksmiths. Though significant in terms of the proportion of the population, they are weakest in terms of mobilisation and organisation. They enter the political spectrum, if at all, at the bottom. Harriss notes that their role in impacting political institutions is limited, and they are passive recipients of policies. Srivastava (1999) and Paul Brass (1994) differ from Harriss. They collect evidence from north India, which show that dominant classes need not necessarily be the upper castes. Middle farmers had gained substantially (Rudolphs, 1987). Hence, class is a critical tool to understand agrarian structures with/without caste.[10]

On a schematic classification level, caste–class could possibly serve as a starting point, but it analytically falls short. It runs counter to the position that the essential core and driving force of economic bargaining by groups is their class interest, even when this could be intertwined with their caste identity. Hence, Harriss' perspective is not the chosen point of entry for the book. Second, Harriss does not include the intricacies of fractions within a class, like big farmers, capitalist farmers, gentleman farmers, and so on, which have been established as a core component to follow and develop in the study. Third, as Srivastava (1999) holds, class–caste need not always overlap, so to adopt Harriss' categories might be a constraint to the work.

The Green Revolution has contributed to altering positions of some groups in the social hierarchy. For instance, Other Backward Classes (OBCs),[11] from the middle farmers, have made significant economic gains and become surplus-producing farmers. They have come to assume the position of a 'dominant class' in states such as Bihar and Uttar Pradesh (Srivastava, 1999; Lerche, 1999). Political representation of the OBCs is found in regional parties such as the Samajwadi Party (Uttar Pradesh) and the Rashtriya Janata Dal (Bihar), dominated by the Yadavs – a caste group (Stern, 2001). The rise of a new dominant class forms part of an ongoing process, both in relation to economy and the state. The study will seek to investigate the rise of new classes in the three states in question, particularly in the context of new opportunities created by economic reform and the opening of markets in the neoliberal era, and the way their class interests are articulated in the political realm.

The affirmative action policy, commonly known as the 'reservation' policy, has contributed towards class consolidation in India. Given India's deep structural inequality, the Constitution had mandated the implementation of reservation to address historical inequalities. Reservation pertains to educational institutions and government employment, but in the context of the research, a specific kind of reservation will be considered – which was introduced at the local self-government level in the early 1990s. Hence local governments have had leaders from marginalised sections. Reservation policy has often been held responsible for creating a 'creamy layer' – a particular group repeatedly gaining the benefit of a policy – emerging from the OBCs (Chaudhury, 2004; Vaid, 2012). This book contests the position that the policy has mitigated caste inequality. Reservation has, in fact, selectively picked members from the middle/ lower castes, often with prior and better economic means, and absorbed them into the dominant class. Though seemingly random, those with political connections have benefitted disproportionately. The elected members have come to enjoy a share in rent, such as state resources through corruption, and, thus, have been able to generate a surplus. As a result, their interest has been separated from their caste group, and they would tend to associate with the new class and its allies.

Conclusion

To sum it up, the relation between society and the state is the core issue of investigation. Society here is layered into multiple social classes, and the class is further divided into fractions. In keeping with Mitra's argument, this study regards economic policy as a product of interaction between political institutions and class structure. The question of what became of Bardhan's three dominant proprietary classes and their interrelationship will be investigated in the later chapters. Specific attention will be given on the formation and consolidation of agrarian classes and their fractions. However, the other two proprietary classes – professional and industrial capital – will be studied in relation to the state. Literature review will be used to reach a comprehensive understanding and bridge the gaps left by fieldwork.

This approach will be operationalised by utilising Atul Kohli's model of three-state comparison to bring out regional variations. The role of agrarian classes in policy formulation, and the impact of these policies on these classes will be explored. Following the 'political settlement' theorists, attempts will be made to identify which classes form parts of stable coalitions in case of each regional state. Different methods used by classes to influence the state, such as patron–client relations, lobbying, organised farmer representation, and congenial relations with political parties, will be examined.

From the aforementioned discussion on literature, it can be inferred that the rural proprietary classes are constituted of big farmers, capitalist farmers (regionally concentrated in north India), and landlords. They were politically influential in the 1980s, and made economic gains through state subsidies and minimum support price (MSP). It remains to be seen how these classes have coped with neoliberal policies. Have they lost out in the new era or found new means of accumulation and survived? It remains to be seen if all fractions have gained evenly or some have gained more than others. As an offshoot, the question of lack of mobilisation among the numerically large tiller farmers will be addressed.

Other classes under observation are the industrial capitalists such as cotton mill owners, agro-business owners, coal lifting company owners, cement company owners, software and IT company owners, and real estate company owners. For the most part, their functioning as a political ally to the state will be assessed instead of engaging in details of their means of accumulation and self-perpetuation. However, those capitalist classes that are closely linked to agriculture, such as merchant capitalists earning surplus from agriculture-related trade, moneylending, and retail in seeds and fertilisers, will be given due attention. Whether old and new petty bourgeoisie arise from rural classes will also be investigated to comprehend if in the era under scrutiny, new classes are being formed. This will probably require understanding middle farmers and their means of accumulation under the neoliberal regime. Hence, an analysis of dominant classes of each of the three states will be undertaken to understand who formed part of the ruling coalition or political settlement with the coming of liberalisation. This finding will further help in comprehending the political reason behind the formulation of state agricultural policy during the years following liberalisation.

A foray into policies will enable tracing new and old class consolidation. Agrarian, land, and reservation policies for Panchayat Raj Institutions (PRIs) are under scrutiny, because each of them has the potential to influence/ alter class composition in rural society. With the help of categories used in agrarian political economy so far, the fractions and their means of accumulation in agriculture after 2004 will be highlighted to contribute to a nuanced understanding of the agriculture sector. It will pose a question about states that registered agricultural growth, such as the Gujarat model has suggested, and about the agrarian crisis, as Patnaik upholds. Such homogeneous representation of the agrarian sector ought to be questioned to enquire about class differentiation and differentiation within a class. The newly created fractions of the dominant classes could be politically significant as well. They may generate new demands and exert influence on the state to cater to their interests. This study intends to capture two-way state–class processes to seek answers to how the nature of the Indian state has changed in the context of globalisation–liberalisation. Given the three-state comparison, the task is to identify how each state varies in midst of the emerging wider pattern.

Notes

1. Class is a social relation, with capital and labour on its either side. However, this study focuses primarily on analysing classes who own capital.
2. Poulantzas argues that if a class does not have a developed class consciousness and does not struggle in the political realm, then it cannot be deemed as class (Poulantzas, 1973: 77–9).
3. This argument is borrowed from Bernard Schaffer (1984).
4. Marxists such as Byres, Mitra, Harriss-White, Shrivastava, and Lerche, as discussed earlier, are conveniently forgotten.
5. Landlord is characterised as rent seeking, and to that extent, not engaging in productive capitalist agriculture.
6. In his words, 'among rich peasants, clearly, class consolidation has proceeded apace and has been hastened by the availability of the "new technology". They are, more and more, a class of capitalist farmers. Class-for-itself action has been pursued with relentless skill with respect to both subordinate rural classes and to the urban bourgeoisie' (Byres, 1981: 443).
7. The Rudolphs (1987) focus on the emergence of what they see as a modern middle peasantry, thus, discarding the role of the processes of peasant differentiation emphasised by Byres (1981).
8. Patnaik (2006) marks a departure from peasant differentiation to peasant–globalisation dichotomy, affected by the onslaught of agrarian neoliberalism where internal differentiation among peasantry loses significance.

9. In comparative politics, the concept of a political regime refers to the formal and informal structure and nature of political power in a country, including the method of determining office holders and the relations between the office holders and the society at large (Siaroff, 2011).

10. The idea of the dominant class has been used by other scholars, such as Paul Brass (1994), Lerche (1999), Stern (2001), Lieten (1996), Gupta (1998), and Lieten and Srivastava (1999), to understand Indian socio-political and economic life. It is noteworthy that almost all instances are from north India.

11. The Government of India has classified certain castes as socially and economically backward and termed them as the OBCs. The Government of India provides 27 per cent reservation for these castes in the public sector, higher education, and employment. The Mandal Commission had a decisive role to play in gaining these benefits for the OBCs.

✤

3

Privatising the Inputs of Production

A Case of Careful Choice of Beneficiaries and Losers

A discontinuous period for agrarian policies since 1990

The study of class relations in India and their interaction with state policy necessitates an overview of Indian polity in the post-liberalisation era. Liberalisation of India's economic policies started in 1991, aiming to make the economy more market oriented and expand the role of private and foreign investments. That decade was a period of economic, social, and political flux, from which India took about eight years to stabilise. Kohli (2001) points out that between 1947 and 1990, India had five general elections, and five general elections were held during the 1990s alone. Following this, the BJP-led NDA held power for two terms (1998–2004). The period between 1997–98 and 2004–05 registered low agricultural growth at 1.6 per cent per annum, which recovered to 3.5 per cent between 2003–04 and 2010–11 (Dev, 2012). The late 1990s witnessed the lowest agricultural growth since Independence. The period since 1997 has been characterised by agrarian distress culminating in farmer suicides (Patnaik, 2003). Political commentators argue that in view of the agrarian distress across states, the NDA lost support of India's rural voters, which proved to be the NDA's undoing. Against this backdrop, the UPA with the Congress at its helm came to power in the 2004 general election (Birner, Gupta, and Sharma, 2011; Bose, 2006; Mooij, 2005). The rise in agricultural growth right after that makes the problem of who benefitted worth thinking about. The various regional parties that had mushroomed during the 1970s and 1980s came to play a determining role in the formation of governments at the centre, because the national parties were unable to attain a simple majority on their own. Be it the BJP-led NDA or the Congress-led UPA, the coalition had to include regional parties to form governments.

Until 2014, the UPA held power at the centre, while governments changed hands at regional levels. The three states studied here – Chhattisgarh, Gujarat, and Karnataka – have mostly been under the rule of the BJP since 2000. Since its formation in 2000, Chhattisgarh has had a BJP government until 2018.

Karnataka was governed by the Congress until 2004, and has had the BJP in power since then. Meanwhile, politically, Gujarat had a tumultuous time until 2000, with the continuous entry and exit of different leaders and parties who seldom completed a full term. After 2001, the BJP has held power consistently in Gujarat under Narendra Modi's chief ministership until Modi was elected as the Prime Minister of India in 2014.

In spite of the changes in political power and the concomitant differences in party ideology, there has been little disagreement on the overall neoliberal direction of economic reforms (Mooij, 2005). In the 1990s, market forces came to play a greater role in all sectors of the economy, including the agricultural sector, and the control of the state dwindled. In 1995, the Indian government signed the General Agreement on Tariffs and Trade (GATT), thereby committing itself to pursuing liberalisation of trade and privatisation of inputs in agriculture. This government was now under greater obligations to adopt structural changes such as removal of subsidies and reduction of social expenditure as stipulated by the Washington Consensus and to open its borders for import. Even though these policy decisions were taken at the national level, the burden of implementation was paradoxically left to the regional states, since agriculture is a state subject. Different states, therefore, formulated their own policies to bring these changes into effect. These new policies, analysed here through a political economy lens, include land acquisition policy, agricultural credit policy, and agricultural input policy for seeds, fertilisers, and suchlike. Until 2009, the Chhattisgarh and Gujarat state governments addressed these issues under stand-alone initiatives, which were followed by the adoption of an all-encompassing Agrovision in 2010 in both states. Evidence shows that stand-alone initiatives rose around 2004 to push agricultural growth. They aimed at drastically increasing farm output by improving efficiency and increasing chemical inputs and commercial crops. Karnataka adopted two successive agricultural policies in 2006 and 2012 to foster these objectives.

Agricultural policy before and after the 1990s

Agricultural policies in India, without any redistribution commitment, can be divided into three phases – first, the Green Revolution (1967–90), second, the period between 1991 and 2004 characterised by negative reforms, and, third, the period from 2004 onwards marked by positive reforms. Ramakumar (2014) has subdivided the post-1990s phase into two, as shown above, where he demonstrates that agricultural policies in the 1990s show variations between 1994[1] and 2002 and between the years 2003–04 and 2012–13.

Phase I: The Green Revolution Phase (1967–90)

Beginning in the 1960s, the Green Revolution refers to a policy to introduce high-yielding variety (HYV) of seeds to increase productivity in agriculture. The technology was imported from the USA. The distribution of benefits that arose from the Green Revolution has been debated over the years. It is contended that the rich peasantry benefitted much more from the new technology as compared to small and marginal farmers, since the former could afford the use of HYVs of seeds, fertilisers, pesticides, and irrigation technology. As a result, the rich peasantry became more polarised into a capitalist class – a class-for-itself – and exercised increased political influence over policies during the 1970s and 1980s (Bardhan, 1984; Byres, 1998; Rudolph and Rudolph, 1987; Subbarao, 1985). Varshney's (1995) work merits mention because it traces a critical policy change in the 1980s affected by a farmer movement, and how democracy created the space for it to occur; however, he glances over the nuance of what rural interest group means. Despite acknowledging that the rural interest group is not a homogenous category, he incorporates only two categories – rural poor and big landowners – which fall short in understanding agrarian social structure and class differentiation. However, by reflecting on the participation of people, he demonstrates the efficacy of democracy as an institution to scrutinise.

Evidence shows that a big chunk of the subsidies offered during the Green Revolution period was garnered by a small section of farmers, while others did not benefit much. The benefits of the new technology also disproportionately accrued to 'prosperous states' with access to water and irrigation, such as Punjab and western Uttar Pradesh. Within these states, the more affluent sections of farmers gained more than anyone else (Pai, 1993; Rathore and Singh, 2010; Subbarao, 1985). Similarly, crops grown in irrigated areas dominated in terms of cropping pattern and garnered research and development funds (Pal, 2008). Therefore, a kind of class polarisation set in within agrarian structures under the impact of the Green Revolution. It is in this structural context that economic reforms were introduced in agriculture in the 1990s.

The neoliberal policy mandate was unique in its shift from state-driven to market-driven allocation and efficiency. The emphasis on technology in agricultural policy, however, was not new; the Green Revolution had aimed at efficient extraction of natural resources, maximisation of output, and food security since the late 1960s. In that sense, there was continuity in these objectives before and after economic reforms, except with regard to food security. However, there was a greater stress on fast sectoral growth, input centricity, privatisation and crop selectivity with a shift to commercial cropping, and subsequently shift to high-value crops.

Despite GATT, the expected policy change did not take immediate effect. It was as if the reforms were implemented by stealth to avoid public animosity (Jenkins, 1999). Initially, reforms were implemented in the industrial sector,[2] and there was no specific economic reform package for agriculture. The presumption was that freeing agricultural trade would automatically lead to lucrative prices for farmers, resulting in higher investment (Ghosh, 2005). Gulati and Sharma (1995) justified the increasing need for a new policy promoting growth rather than subsidies in the beginning of the 1990s. Subsidies have a specific life, as they are needed in the initial phase of capitalist agricultural development when farmers cannot afford inputs at market-determined prices. Over time, as they avail subsidies, they become capable in terms of resource and knowledge, and are ready to compete with market forces that would allow higher profit. The state provided large-scale institutional support during the Green Revolution in the form of cheap credit, subsidised inputs, and suchlike, to the farmers, which policy-makers in the liberalisation era wanted to divert to research and infrastructure. That said, the positive effect of the subsidies provided by the state was limited to a few agrarian classes, as argued earlier in the section, and they were the ones enabled to compete with the market forces. It was an effort for 'building on the best' (Cleaver, 1973).

Phase II: Post-liberalisation stage one (1997–2004)

This phase was characterised by the state retracting from the agricultural sector. The state assumed a 'negative' role, reducing public investment and institutional support, as well as declining procurement prices. Further, the government withdrew support from banks for providing rural credit and implemented stricter norms for loan recovery, thereby discouraging credit to poorer farmers, withdrawing seed subsidy, and decreasing extension services (Dev, 2012; Ramchandran and Rawal, 2010; Reddy and Mishra, 2009).

In addition, the period witnessed a policy in favour of industry in the form of the SEZ schemes, relaxation in the ceiling law for acquisition of agricultural land in Gujarat and Karnataka, and the government's lack of effort in preventing illegal mining that affected fertile land. These are integrally linked to agriculture because land is the key factor for its production. The changes in political economy because of these changes in policy, as listed in Table 3.1, and their effects have been examined in the book.

Table 3.1 Important measures taken for economic liberalisation in agriculture

Area of liberalisation	*Policy changes and measures of implementation*
I. External trade sector	• In tune with the WTO regime, all Indian product lines are placed in the generalised system of preference (GSP) since 1997. • India is made a part of the WTO intellectual property rights (IPR) regime relating to agricultural products, including plant varieties (seeds) and geographical indications. • In 1998, quantitative restrictions (QRs) for 470 agricultural products are dismantled. In 1999, 1,400 more agricultural products are brought under open general licensing (OGL), and canalisation of external trade in agriculture is almost reversed. • Average tariffs on agricultural imports are reduced from 100 per cent in 1990 to 30 per cent in 1997. • Though India is, in principle, against minimum common access, it is actually already importing 2 per cent of its food requirements. • More liberalised import of seeds is started.
II. Internal market liberalisation	
Seeds	• Since 1991, 100 per cent foreign equity is allowed in the seed industry. The Seed Policy is passed in 2002.
Fertilisers	• Subsidies on fertilisers are gradually reduced since 1991.
Power	• In 1997, power sector reforms are introduced. An increase in per unit cost is introduced to power charges used in agriculture there is resistance from state governments, such as Andhra Pradesh, which have introduced 'free power' to agriculture.
Irrigation	• Water rates are increased in some states. • Participatory water management is sought to be introduced through Water User's Associations (WUAs). • States such as Andhra Pradesh make new large irrigation projects conditional on 'stakeholder' contribution to part of investment, but later the government ignores this condition and increases public investment in irrigation.

Contd.

Area of liberalisation	Policy changes and measures of implementation
Institutional credit	• The Khusro Committee and the Narasimham Committee (1992) undermine the importance of targeted priority sector lending by the commercial banks. Targets for agricultural lending are allowed to be compromised. • A number of bank branches in rural areas are closed. • The objectives of Regional Rural Banks' (RRBs) priority lending to weaker sections in rural areas are diluted since 1997, and RRBs are restructured on commercial considerations.
III. Fiscal reforms	• Fiscal reforms with an emphasis on tax reduction and public expenditure are tuned to reduce fiscal deficit as priority. This has grave implications for public investment in agriculture and rural infrastructure.

Source: Acharya (2004: 677), Chand (2006), Dorin and Jullian (2004: 206), and Vakulabharanam (2005: 975) cited in Reddy and Mishra (2009: 20–21).

Reddy and Mishra (2009) characterise the period from the mid-1990s to 2004 as a phase of reforms that exposed farmers to global price fluctuations and left them to face the vagaries of the market. Harriss-White (2002) argues that during the 1990s, the structure of subsidies changed slowly, be it on credit, agricultural co-operatives, or inputs such as fertiliser, electricity, and irrigation. This is attributed to the farmer lobby's resistance to reforms throughout the first decade of liberalisation. Dubash (2007) agrees with this and notes the continuing influence of an interest group, the farmer lobby, on agricultural policy formulation. Hence, the reforms could only be incremental. Adopting a radical reform approach would have potentially created political tensions, which were best averted at the time when the political situation was already in flux. Overall, when the reforms were adopted, India faced immediate effects in the form of crashing agricultural prices, uncertainty in returns on investment by farmers, and farmers' suicides. A direct consequence of this policy transformation, in conjunction with other long-term structural changes such as land miniaturisation, was the agrarian crisis beginning in 1997, an extreme manifestation of which was the farmers' suicides that took place across India (Patnaik, 2003; Sainath, 2004).

About seven years later, the defeat of the NDA in 2004 taught a forgotten lesson to political leaders – neglect of the agrarian classes' interest can prove to be fatal in Indian politics. This also meant that the new Congress-led government at the centre and the governments at state level had to set a new agricultural reform agenda to accommodate rural voters. This, for the purpose of the book, was the beginning of the second phase of the post-liberalisation agricultural policy. The states under study adopted new policies in and around 2004; was the objective of these new policies to benefit all farmers or benefit certain classes at the cost of the others?

Phase III: Post-liberalisation stage two (2004 onwards)

It is to be noted that in spite of the reform initiatives, farm incomes have continued to enjoy tax exemptions even after 1990. The fertiliser industry gets the third highest subsidy after food and oil, and claims a large chunk of the agricultural budget[3] (Birner, Gupta, and Sharma, 2011; Gulati and Sharma, 1995; Mukundan, 2013). As opposed to the overall policy thrust of reducing subsidies, the fertiliser subsidy registered an increase from ₹43.89 billion in 1990–91 to ₹758.49 billion in 2008–09. As a percentage of the GDP, it is a significant increase: from 0.85 per cent in 1990–91 to 1.52 per cent in 2008–09 (Sharma and Thaker, 2009). What does such an increase in subsidies imply in the face of overall focus on reducing subsidies?

During this phase, agricultural policy was geared to directing public investment towards high-value crops by offering subsidies in sectors such as technology, seeds, and irrigation. This was in line with the philosophy of the Green Revolution that saw technology as an alternative to labour (Singh and Rathore, 2010). Public and private partnerships in agriculture were forged in the new millennium to realise the growth agenda. For instance, Manjit Singh (2012) observes that after 2000, policy-makers specifically stressed on mechanisation and direct-seeded rice to save on labour cost. This has protected employers in Punjab (big and capitalist farmers) from labour problems, but has resulted in the loss of livelihood for tiller farmers who worked as wage labourers. This was evident in the growing involvement of the local Dalit population in non-farm vocations.

At the time these policies were adopted, the UPA assumed power at the centre while the BJP was in power in Chhattisgarh, Gujarat, and Karnataka. What factors led to the adoption of these policies in the three states, and how was their political economy shaped by the political settlement? It is commonly argued that neoliberalism is built on perpetuation of capital where global actors have been studied by academics. But how this agenda manifested itself specifically in the context of these states is being investigated here. Did the regional states have a role to play, or was it subservient to the market and overall economic liberalisation that the country was experiencing? To that extent, is there a variation or does a uniform story unfold across the states? In order to explore these questions, a literature review is undertaken in the next section.

The following sections of the chapter aim to develop a national picture, with special attention to the three field states. Some details are provided in the respective field chapters to ease the process of comparison with field findings. The different sections of this chapter are developed to highlight the details of policy and its effect on access to different inputs – land, credit, seed, fertiliser, and water (as necessitated by agricultural production) – enumerated by the supply-side policy.[4] The attempt is to develop a nuanced understanding of agrarian political economy by identifying the beneficiaries of new policies and its effect on the existing social structures , which is expected to be differentiated across region and class, as indicated by Ramachandran (2011). A simultaneous question posed is: why would the state further the interest of a few classes at the cost of others? Arguably, one explanation could be the political settlement operating in each state, relating it to the classes and fractions that constitute the settlement.

Agriculture and market: Delimiting the study

In today's globalised world, the farmer is neither an isolated nor a self-sufficient entity. Apart from the actual cultivation of crops, a range of activities such as retail; procurement of various inputs like land, credit, seeds, irrigation; global supply chains; trade relations between nations; market prices; and storage constitute agriculture (Bernstein, 2010). The market and transnational forces play a critical role in agriculture today.

Agriculture, like any other sector, is heavily dependent on the market. The multiple ways in which the market penetrates agriculture are through land, credit, and product markets. If the cultivator does not own the land he tills, he has to lease land. The terms of the lease between the landowner and the tenant are defined as much by a supply–demand mechanism as by social networking and caste–class positions. Credit is integral to agriculture as farmers under compulsion to cover the cost of cultivation borrow to buy seeds, fertilisers, pesticides, and farming equipment (tractors, water pumps, harvesting machines, and suchlike) during the cropping season and for consumption during the lean season. After harvest, crops need to be sold; this entails interaction with small and big traders, Agricultural Produce Marketing Cooperative (APMC) actors, and merchants. When it comes to selling, the majority of the farmers are incapable of storage and bringing the crops to urban markets for sale to the customers. The sale is often mediated by traders. However, for cash crops, post-harvesting could also mean dealing with owners of sugar and rice mills.

Agricultural policy is thus the sum of different policies the government promulgates on the inputs of cultivation, and on the post-harvest sale and procurement. Agriculture is a state-list subject in India, but there are aspects such as fertiliser and irrigation policies and public investments that are decided by the central government. Moreover, some issues in agriculture, such as fertiliser, fall under the purview of the industrial sector as well. Therefore, policies concerning these elements affect both the agrarian and non-agrarian classes.

Agricultural policies include both the supply-side and the demand-side of agriculture and its allied sectors, such as fisheries. The supply-side entails pre-harvest activities (for example, production), while the demand-side deals with post-harvest activities (for example, sale and storage). This book concentrates on the supply-side policies while recognising that demand-side policies are equally important. Demand-side issues raised by informants in the field have been incorporated in the sections dealing with empirical findings of the study. The following section discusses the impact of recent agricultural policies on the agrarian social structure.

Who benefits? Impact of the new policy regime

In the previous chapter, we reviewed the 'statist', 'political economy', and 'political settlement' approaches to define the dominant classes and their relationship with the state at multiple levels. In this section, different classes and fractions that have benefitted from the agrarian policies post 1991, and related informal operations, are discussed; particularly, policies related to different inputs of production such as land, credit, and privatisation of chemical inputs.

Dominant classes and their changing equation

The importance of Bardhan's work (1984, revised and enlarged edition in 1998) is undisputed in understanding the political economy of India (McCartney, 2010). Scholars such as Atul Kohli, Barbara Harriss-White, and V. K. Ramchandran have addressed pertinent questions. However, scholars did that by either performing an all-India analysis of policies without adequate attention to class dynamics or by attempting a detailed discussion of any one set of class in particular parts of India rather than a state–class analysis of India. Bardhan identifies the key proprietary classes at the national level, which bargain with the state to meet the interests, they are termed the 'dominant classes' or the 'dominant coalition'. The three dominant classes he identified in India's political economy are the rich farmers, the industrial class, and the professional class. Even though different groups such as labourers and the lower castes have come to the fore pitching their interests, they are not regarded as a dominant class.[5]

The first class from Bardhan's dominant classes, the big/rich farmers form a critical force in pressure politics, 'log-rolling' with other groups (Bardhan, 1984). As a category, rich farmers are not subsumed into the capitalist class or 'subsumed in giant capitalist agro-business enterprises' (McCartney, 2010: 215). Bardhan lists the subsidies and patronage that rich farmers enjoy from the state,[6] especially the regional states, and how they have monopolised cooperative credit and political power.

The beginning of this phase was in the early 1980s with the formation of the Indian Farmers' Association, followed by state-specific movements such as the Bharatiya Kisan Sangh (BKS) in Gujarat, the Bharatiya Kisan Union (BKU) in Uttar Pradesh, the Shetkari Sanghatana in Maharashtra, the Karnataka Rajya Raitha Sangha (KRRS), and the Tamilaga Vyasaseva Vigal Sanghan in Tamil Nadu. Brass (1994) argues that the farmers' movements represented a class of surplus-generating farmers, or those who produce agricultural products for the market. Towards the end of the 1980s, the movement weakened due to cultural and communal fissures. This resulted in the movement splitting into two lobbies. The section headed by Shetkari Sanghatana in Maharashtra came to see liberalisation as a boon, getting its primary support from Gujarat's Khedut Samaj and Punjab's BKU. The other section was led by the KRRS, whose leader, Narayanswami Naidu, saw liberalisation in agriculture as part of the neocolonial project to enslave Indian farmers, and organised protests against the World Trade Organization (WTO).

Scholars such as Brass (1994) and Jeffrey (2002) have argued that the farmers' movement and protests are the techniques adopted by big farmer lobbies for pressuring the state to accommodate their demands. Their protests are more a display of power than actual dissent, because the same class has previously enjoyed state patronage. For instance, farmers who were at the forefront of farmers' protests in Uttar Pradesh, which was noted during the fieldwork conducted in the 1990s, were the same set of farmers who were tapping into government resources through state bureaucracy, particularly police officials (Jeffrey, 2002).

The second proprietary class, the bureaucracy, has been placing distinct demands on the state such as protection and rent, which stand in the way of demands pressed by the industrial capitalist (Bardhan, 1998). Since the 1990s, the industrial capitalists have advocated for wider control of the market with a minimalist state. This runs counter to the interests of the bureaucracy, which

Bardhan characterises as feeding upon state resources. Mooij (2005) addresses the question 'what is the role of the bureaucracy in adopting economic reforms?', while concluding that the bureaucracy is found aligning with the industrial capitalist interests (Das, 2005). Bureaucracy sees opportunities for their next generation in economic reforms and thus shifts its position (Das, 2005).

In the post-liberalisation phase, scholars present evidence contrary to Bardhan, as the bureaucracy acted as the frontrunner in adopting privatisation measures (Corbridge, Harriss, and Jeffrey, 2013; Das, 2005; Jenkins, 1999; Kohli, 2006; Levien, 2012). At a pan-India level, Das (2005) finds that the Indian bureaucracy, namely the Indian Administrative Service, is a chief support lobby for the reforms. He traces this support to the 1980s and argues that the shift of industrial policy to a more competitive model from that of the protectionist (import substitution) model was regarded by the bureaucracy as a new challenging environment to prove themselves. The hope was that reforms would bring in new opportunities such as employment in private sectors and sources of rent collection through export, land deals, and suchlike. These became the primary reasons for the bureaucracy's support for privatisation.

The opportunities, as hoped for, have come alive in the recent decade. Levien (2012) argues that the private sector's agenda of procuring land for new industrial ventures would not be possible without state support. Essentially, the state is 'carrying out the dispossessions'. The bureaucracy, he contends, does not have an interest distinct from the capitalist class. In fact, a 'joint venture' prevails, where the government acts as a business partner with private developers (Levien, 2012: 462). Harriss-White (2008) argues that state regulation enables rents to be reaped, even enforced, by the larger farms. State officials make money – that is, accumulate rent[7] – by using discretionary powers to sell limited public assets and extort money from firms that are not allowed to trade legally. Farmer lobbies are strong enough to influence the state to grant them subsidies but not strong enough to change policies such as land acquisition, in which the state acquires private land for industrialisation/urbanisation from the landowners and compensates them for rehabilitation and resettlement. The reality is far from amicable, and often landowners or farmers have been uprooted from their only source of livelihood without receiving a fair deal or market price for the land. Such accumulation by dispossession (ABD)[8] would be impossible without the policy intervention of the state (Levien, 2012). The scholarship of Levien, Harriss-White, Pattenden, Jeffrey, and Lerche indicates how different dominant classes are gravitating towards one another in the post-liberalisation era, with most of the evidence gathered at the local state level. This merits an enquiry to identify the dominant classes, their sources of accumulation, their political interests, and their connections at the regional state level. These can help understand the nature of coalition of or between such classes, a political settlement.

Apple in multiple baskets: Rural class diversification

The neoliberal era has unleashed new market forces and, arguably, shrunk the role of the state. This has altered class positions and interests through changes in distribution of the means of production. In an agrarian economy, such class differentiation occurred at two levels – class differentiation within agriculture and class differentiation relating to economic activities outside agriculture. There are classes that benefitted from both these aspects. The development of rural class relations is often understood in relation to two phases – the Green Revolution phase from the late 1960s, which was marked by rapid growth in agricultural output, and the period of neoliberal policies from 1991, when agricultural growth stagnated until 2003–04 and had serious implications for poor farmers (Lerche, 2013; Ramchandran, 2011).

Regarding class differentiation within agriculture, Byres' (1981) seminal analysis of the impact of the Green Revolution on class upheld that the new chemical inputs might have been scale-neutral but not resource-neutral. Given the need for high investment, an emerging class of capitalist farmers reaps the benefit of such technology while the rest run the risk of being pushed down further for lack of access and capability. This is a phenomenon that Cleaver (1972) termed as 'building on the best', thus aiming the benefits of the policy towards those already commanding resources and in positions of privilege; it is bound to exclude the majority from the benefits of technology. Some have termed it a 'lumpy technology', in which the use of complementary inputs such as water, seed, and fertiliser is non-divisible (Byres, 1981; Cleaver, 1972; Despande et al., 2004). Hence, access to all inputs was crucial to successfully adopt the technology, making it particularly expensive. This is a common thread between pre- and post-1990s agricultural policy – growth in the sector was carried out through the use of such capital-intensive technology, starting from the Green Revolution, leading to the deepening of structural inequality in the rural economy.

The impact of neoliberal agrarian policies on class differentiation is disputed. Some scholars such as Patnaik (2006) and McMichael (2008) argue that all farmers are losing out with global multinationals penetrating agriculture. Hence, peasantry as a whole is oppressed. On the other hand, studies such as those carried out by the Foundation for Agrarian Studies (FAS) show that class differentiation within agriculture has continued to increase (Ramachandran, Rawal and Swaminathan, 2010). However, in a nuanced analysis, Ramachandran (2011) looks at data on land size, expenditure on inputs, diversification to non-farm avenues, and so on, from the 1990s and concludes that such macroeconomic data can neither be used to identify class differentiation within agriculture nor support the view that class differentiation has ceased to exist. However, the National Sample Survey Office (NSSO) data show that after the 1990s the proportion of population working in agriculture is falling more rapidly than it did before the 1990s, which broadly suggests that farmers are moving out of agriculture. A possible interpretation could be that a class differentiation exists, with a few classes accumulating from non-agricultural sources. Hence, the majority of the agrarian population earning less share of their income from agriculture.

A foray into rural class differentiation cannot focus solely on agriculture, let alone on just cultivation (Harriss-White, 2008; Lerche, 2013; Pattenden, 2005; Rakshit, 2011). Harriss-White (2008) argues that the agro-commercial capital in West Bengal has not been a passive recipient of the impact of political regulation and liberalisation, but is an active shaper of both (Harriss-White, 2008: 13). Since the 1990s, there was a wave of deregulations and decentralisation of controls on import and export, but the commercial elites held on to both power and profit in this new environment by developing newer networks, such that 'the prevalent informal process of rent-seeking[9] was hardly touched' (Harriss-White, 2008: 259). Dixit (2012) points in the same direction in the context of Gujarat, stating that growth in the past decades has led to the concentration of surplus among the numerically few, resulting in a fall in calorific availability to many and adding to existing poverty. Food consumption has stagnated, which is an indication of malnutrition and harder living conditions. Levien (2011) shows that the rural elites gain from land acquisition in Rajasthan. From different regions in India, new sources of accumulation have been noted (Dasgupta, 2013; Harris-White, 2008, Pattenden, 2011; Rakshit, 2011; Sinha, 2017).

Challenging the view that agrarian accumulation is increasing for big and capitalist farmers, Harriss-White (2008) illustrates through case studies in West Bengal that big farmers are accumulating more from non-agrarian sources and, thus, their concern about agriculture has reduced considerably. She raises a definitional question and asks whether it is appropriate to use the term 'big farmer' to describe such a class. In the context of Vinayagapuram,[10]

Harriss-White (2004) elaborates about a family that is primarily accumulating from moneylending. During the last decade, their surplus has assumed such proportions that they employ 'agents' to extract interest and capital from borrowers. In addition, there are pawnbrokers and silk merchants who offer pre-harvest loans (Harriss-White, 2004). The National Commission for Enterprises in the Unorganised Sector (NCEUS) report (2008) notes that 50 per cent of the income for people involved in agriculture is non-agrarian. Dixit (2008) agrees with this and, based on her field findings, confirms that education and non-farm assets also act as sources of income that support non-agricultural interests of the agricultural classes. A common feature that emerges across her sample villages is economic diversification indicating new sources of income (Dixit, 2008). This study has attempted to understand the different sources of income of a rich farmer, and its impact on their differentiated class position, particularly since 2000.

Early signs of diversification of big farmers towards agro-processing, real estate, and trade were observed in the 1980s (Breman, 1993; Nair, 1996). Farmers with a surplus started investing in other sectors such as trade. Damodaran (2008) observes the trend gaining momentum in the 1990s with the big farmers of Andhra Pradesh (Kammas and Reddys) investing in other sectors and in other states, thus becoming a significant actor in the Karnataka economy. In the context of Tamil Nadu, moneylenders have entered the input market by giving loans or even helping in opening shops (Harriss-White, 2004). While the Green Revolution may have increased polarisation in some parts of India, the move towards non-cultivation businesses, commercialisation, and retreat of the state in the neoliberal period has further increased this polarisation. For instance, (re)instated moneylenders now dominate new spheres of the agrarian economy, exploiting the numerous poor farmers (NCEUS, 2008). The market is the obvious source of accumulation but state resources form the unexpected source of accumulation. Gatekeepers were found to accumulate by cornering state resources and non-agrarian sources of income in Karnataka (Pattenden, 2011). Gatekeeping here stands for obstructing the flow of state resources to the marginalised, thereby enabling accumulation by the dominant class. Therefore, within the rural economy, the dominant classes[11] seem to have benefitted substantially from the privatisation policies.

Against this backdrop, it is no surprise that Harriss-White (2008) challenges Kohli (2006), who is of the view that the rentier landlords are at the losing end of liberalisation. She proposes that these classes have been losing interest in rural landed property due to new sources of income outside agriculture, a view seconded by Pattenden (2011). However, the evidence available so far remains regionally specific, and needs to be validated in other regions of the country in order to look for new trends as well as to draw generalisations. Given the hypothesis that the class interests of these dominant rural proprietary classes have undergone a transformation, what interest do they now represent in the realm of politics? Their demands in terms of the inputs of production such as land, credit, and privatisation of inputs, and the way state policies protect their interests, are discussed in the following sections.

Land from the tillers

Land is 'the mother of all issues' that are faced by farmers in India. There is severe inequality in the size of landholdings, and the state has failed to alter these structural inequalities. Generational redistribution has made the holding size even smaller. Small and marginal farmers constituted 84.97 per cent of the landed people in India in 2010–11 (Government of India, 2012). In recent times, literature has focused on land grabbing and displacement of marginalised communities (Fernandes, 2014; Roy, 2009). Walter Fernandes (2014) estimates the number of displaced population, who have lost land and livelihood since India's independence, at 60 million, the majority of whom are tribal people or belonging to the SCs (Corbridge, Harris, and Jeffrey, 2013: 206). This means that the small farmers are situated at the supply end of the resource (land) that has a high demand from different market forces as witnessed over the past two decades. The key question, regarding the political economy of land transfer, is what happens to classes at the demand end and the way it affects agriculture. A tiller for the purpose of the book refers to those who put their labour in cultivation and has agriculture as their main source of income.

The Government of India (GoI) has made legal provisions for land acquisition and transfer, and these have changed over the years. The government acquires land under the Land Acquisition Act of 1894.[12] As per the Act, land can be acquired for the use of the government and its parastatal agencies. But the 1984 amendment to the Act has relaxed this ownership ceiling in such a way that the government can now acquire land for a purpose it deems as serving 'public' need. The Act falls under the 'eminent domain',[13] rendering the issue of acquisition itself as not questionable;[14] only issues of compensation and resettlement are debatable. Governments are, therefore, free to interpret private and non-productive activity catering to the interests of the capitalist class as 'public purpose' (Levien, 2012; Morriss and Pandey, 2007). Any private company wanting to buy land has to liaise with the state, but there is no accountability about what happens to the land after acquisition. Levien

(2012) draws attention to the way land procured under the SEZ provisions is being used for real estate purposes.[15] Cases of acquiring more land than required by private actors have surfaced. The bureaucracy adds to its rent extraction with acquisitions of all sizes of land plots (D'Costa and Chakraborty, 2017; Fernandes, 2014; Levien, 2012). Further, the uncertainties in land titles (such as non-transfer to sons' names on the demise of the father) make compensation for farmers difficult.

After liberalisation, the demand for land for industrial and infrastructural purposes has seen a steady rise. By July 2009, 600 SEZs had been approved across India, concentrated in Maharashtra, Andhra Pradesh, Tamil Nadu, Karnataka, and Gujarat. Though the government has taken a public stance that prime agricultural land[16] cannot be taken over for this purpose, it has continuously done so, leading to protest from various quarters (Fernandes, 1998; D'Costa and Chakraborty, 2017). As Levien interprets the situation, 'the SEZ developer is a state-appointed capitalist landlord who receives windfall returns by commodifying artificially cheap land expropriated from farmers' (2012, 963). The case study on Rajasthan points to a deep nexus between the state and capital, which has been observed in other parts of India as well (D'Costa and Chakraborty, 2017).

Simultaneously, in different parts of India, people have struggled and protested against insufficient compensation for land, use of coercion in acquiring land, and with no assurance of alternative livelihood despite displacement (Chadda, 2012). Most industrial projects are being delayed as a result. In response, the union government drafted the new Land Acquisition, Rehabilitation and Resettlement Bill (LARR Bill) in 2011, passed in 2012, according to which compensation is applicable to cases of direct displacement only.[17] The upper house of the Parliament passed the bill in 2013, causing great anxiety among the industrial capitalist class (*Times of India*, 2013c). The regional states followed this move by amending their respective land acquisition acts.[18] The Act emphasises on better terms of resettlement and compensation, but does not alter the 'eminent domain' treatment to land acquisition.

In Gujarat, Sud (2007) has done extensive work on the political economy of land acquisition and political alignments around the new land policy. According to her, the upper-caste industrial bourgeoisie, dominated by the Patidars,[19] have alliances with the state. This is exemplified by the fact that prominent industrialists have directly assumed political positions. Sud argues that the dominant class controls the state apparatus and illustrates this through land policies in Gujarat after 2000.

Sud's findings are based on the Kheda district of Gujarat, where agricultural and trade surplus have been accumulated over the years and reinvested in trade and industry (Damodaran, 2008). Traces of a class of capitalist farmers are still found here; this class has maintained ownership of land but has moved to urban centres and invested in industry as well as agricultural land (Damodaran, 2008). During the 1960s and 1970s, emerging entrepreneurial groups in the state, began a transition from rural to urban living, as well as from agriculture to agro-industry and other industries, such as plastics, chemicals, dyes, and pharmaceuticals. They continued to base their social identity on their agriculturalist roots and on their landholdings. Gujarat saw a high rate of urbanisation, which grew from 25.7 per cent in the 1960s to 34.5 per cent by 1991. The nouveau riche entrepreneurial groups, different from the Brahmin–Bania–Khoja mercantile groups, came to occupy the urban spaces and were set to take up non-agricultural occupations (Sud, 2007: 621). Despite a shift in their location and occupation, they did not give up their right to land and wanted the legal right to use agricultural land for non-agricultural purposes. Sud argues that this class came to dominate the state machinery, undermining the interests of other groups such as the Bharwads, which transpired in the former being able to affect a land policy change. Bharwada and Mahajan (2006) point out that despite the deficit in *gochur* (grazing) land, the government has been offering land to corporates and justifying its actions in the name of being an 'investment-friendly state'.

The rising dominant mercantile–industrial classes did not see the coalition of the Kshatriya, Harijan, Adivasi, and Muslim (KHAM) as favourable, which was strategically used by the Congress in the 1980s to assume power. The Congress party's support for Dalits and Adivasis, many of whom are marginal farmers and wage labourers, made the dominant classes regard the Congress as antagonistic to the interests of capital. The shift in government from the Congress to the BJP in Gujarat, therefore, is attributed to the dominant class consolidating their support behind the BJP (Sud, 2007).

On the other hand, Karnataka experienced winds of change when H. D. Deve Gowda assumed power in 1994 as the Chief Minister. He relaxed land ceiling, thereby allowing the sale of agricultural land for non-agricultural purposes. He advocated a pro-market position and viewed land ceiling as an obstacle in the functioning of markets and the optimal utilisation of factors of production. This remained his stand even when he became the Prime Minister of India in 1996. Besides this, he declared a revised set of policies known as the New Agricultural Policy (NAP) of Karnataka, which had the potential to adversely affect small and marginal farmers (Assadi, 1995). Although both agrarian and land policies were at a nascent stage then, it is possible to examine the impact of these policies on agrarian classes after they have been in effect for over two decades.

Two decades ago, Assadi (1995) had predicted that the proposed amendments to the Land Reform Act of Karnataka, permitting conversion of agricultural land into non-agricultural, will take the path of corporate landlordism and widen the gap between the rich and the poor. The same amendment overrules the earlier stipulation that only those with an income of less than ₹200,000 are exclusively eligible to buy agricultural land. He argued that such an amendment would lead to 'de-peasantisation', adding to the pool of labourers, with a simultaneous rise of 'gentleman farmers' (Assadi, 1995). Another scholar speculated that these policy changes are to facilitate the free flow of capital. She predicted that not only the urban industrial capitalists stand to gain, but even the big farmers, who took to agro-processing and trade since the 1980s, have an advantage and might gain (Nair, 1996). Fifteen years later, these predictions have become a living reality in a different state, Rajasthan. Levien (2012) notes that the flipside of land grab and the concentration of land by the industrial capitalist has been the creation of a class of labour who have been 'freed'[20] from their means of production. Freedom here is used sarcastically, of course, and the loss is too grave for their individual sustenance because what they lose is not just land but also their livelihood and a part of their self. But how it has played out in Karnataka mandates further inquiry.

In 2011, the Karnataka government announced the integrated agribusiness development policy. Sections 20.3 to 20.5 of the policy encouraged floriculture, horticulture, and animal husbandry. For these purposes, land acquisition would be facilitated by the government (GoK, 2011).[21] The transfer of agricultural land for setting up agribusiness units is also mentioned, which has been the point of focus since the government signed a pact with the World Bank in 2001. Clearly, the state has geared itself towards investing in technology and agribusiness, with little regard for issues of food security and the fall in real income of small farmers, in the face of debt crisis and water crisis, which enhance their vulnerabilty (Banerjee, 2011). The high-value crops have a tacit promise of freeing land, and because it has high productivity, the land required is less than that for traditional crops. Hence, excess land can be diverted to non-agricultural purposes, which is the focus area for the Karnataka government.

As far as Chhattisgarh is concerned, there is not enough secondary literature on either its agrarian and land policy or the political economy around it.

This study aims to bring to the fore these issues based on fieldwork conducted in the state, the findings of which have been discussed in subsequent chapters.

Nationalisation to informalisation of credit

Agricultural credit plays a determining role in what farmers can cultivate, where they buy the inputs and whether they can wait for prices to go up to sell their crops. Indian credit policy entered its third phase[22] in 1991 with the adoption of liberalisation (Ramachandran and Swaminathan, 2001). The distinguishing feature of this phase is a clear shift from redistributive objectives to emphasis on profitability of banks. Among other things, interest rates were deregulated and branch licensing policies – which ensured a minimum number of rural bank branches – were revoked (RBI, 1991, quoted in Swaminathan, 2012).[23]

According to the Rural Finance Access Survey (RFAS) in 2003, 79 per cent of the rural households had no access to credit from a formal source. The situation was worse for poorer households, as bank branches in rural areas appear to primarily serve the needs of richer borrowers – 44 per cent of large farmers have access to credit while 87 per cent of marginal farmers have no access to credit from a formal source (Basu, 2005: 409). A similar picture has been drawn by the NCEUS report (2008), which states that marginal farmers have the poorest access to formal sources of credit, the majority of whom are from the SC and Scheduled Tribe (ST) communities. A limitation of the NCEUS study, however, is that the data it uses ends in 2003 and, hence, is not relevant for commenting on the last ten years.

More recent studies show that the new policy has altered the way in which overall lending was divided among different lending institutions. Cooperative societies have become secondary in providing credit to agriculture, and commercial banks have gained a higher share (Golait, 2007; Singh and Sagar, 2004). This phenomenon may be attributed to the banks taking a market-oriented approach, wherein they have minimised their dealings with tiller farmers and concentrated on big and capitalist farmers or agribusinesses that are more capable of offering collaterals and repayment (Chavan and Ramakumar, 2007; Golait, 2007: 93; NCEUS, 2005; Sen, 2005; Singh and Sagar, 2004; Swaminathan, 2012). This phenomenon is of particular interest to this study because cooperatives fall within the state list and their formation, registration, and functioning are linked to state laws.

Case studies have revealed that the control of cooperative societies lies in the hands of the village elite. Pattenden (2011) gives a vivid account of the intertwining of political and socio-economic powers in the state of Karnataka, which entails both caste and class dynamics. Drawing from his fieldwork, he refers to the dominant class as the gatekeepers,[24] who in other literatures are denoted as political entrepreneurs.[25] Due to the reservation policies that provide access to the (local) government office, a few politically connected low-caste farmers might be able to garner an advantage unlike most lower caste farmers (Rajsekhar, Babu, and Majula, 2011). Some scholars find that these actors actively direct state resources in their favour, creating a skewed distribution of public resources. Others have hinted at a similar concentration of resources by the privileged classes (Harriss-White, 2004, 2008; Singh and Sagar, 2004). Similar observations have been made for the neighbouring state of Andhra Pradesh in field studies conducted after 2004 (Ramachadran et al., 2010). The income thus generated from gatekeeping activities consolidates the proprietary class. The class is a complex combination of older and new members who are being added from lower castes through the process of reservation.

The Ministry of Agriculture, India, has published an authoritative work called the *State of the Indian Farmer: A Millennium Study* (2004) running into 27 volumes, compiling details about Indian agriculture over more than 50 years. The work identified a pattern in the way agricultural lending operated at the national level. It indicated that higher rates of interest were charged by informal sources, and these kinds of loans were the last resort for small farmers. In contrast, big farmers took loans from formal sources, which generally lent loans at lower interest rates than informal sources. The same agricultural credit exploited the small farmers and enabled the big farmers to invest in new high-investment ventures, such as horticulture. For instance, in Warwat Khanderao, one of the sites of investigation, landlords had an average outstanding debt 77 times that of a manual worker household. This was indicative of the landlords using debt to make the transition to high-value crops. The region is known to grow fruits. The variance across caste and class is not only in terms of the amount of loan, but also in terms of the rate of interest charged, shown by case studies to be 36 to 60 per cent (Assadi, 1995; Swaminathan, 2012). The formal institutions favour the big farmers/landlords who prefer them because borrowing from formal sources does not require paying a bribe (transaction cost) to government officials, which makes them unaffordable to small farmers (Basu, 2005; Golait, 2007; RFAS, 2003). Access to credit is the key to better technology, irrigation facility, chemical inputs, and higher yield, which are particularly relevant in the post-2000 period, since agriculture has now become even more driven by private investment, and has simultaneously acquired an input-intensive nature (Reddy and Mishra, 2009).

Bagchi (2005) attempts to understand the political dynamics behind this shift in credit policy. He argues that financial liberalisation since the 1990s has created more sources of credit for the rich, and this is linked to the state having close association with what he terms the 'plutocracy'. Ramachandran (2011) infers that an alliance between the bourgeoisie and landlords is dominating the Indian state. This has pushed small farmers towards informal sources that are often offered by landlords, their relatives, and traders. Adding to this is the long-acknowledged interlocking between farmers taking loans from traders and being tied to selling to that trader at a fixed price. Introduction of forward markets and speculation have further infringed on their right to negotiate prices of their crops (Jan and Harriss-White, 2012). A big part of selling agricultural produce at high market prices is being able to wait for the high-demand season, which requires capital-intensive infrastructure, such as cold storage and warehouses. Traders or big farmers-cum-traders monopolise this infrastructure; hence, small farmers are forced to sell off their produce to these traders at pre-harvest rates (Aga, 2018). Little benefit accrues to them even when prices are high in the market. The high off-season prices benefit traders, whereas farmers get the lowest prices available when supply exceeds demand (Ramchandran, 2005).

Shawn Cole (2009) has contended that there are political lending cycles in India, wherein credit becomes a mechanism to distribute patronage to loyalists, or to buy loyalty by the political leaders. This is evident in the way credit is targeted towards districts in which the majority party has just won or lost an election. Moreover, a separate pattern of targeting is observed for loan write-offs than for lending. Write-offs are highest in the districts in which the winning party enjoyed the most electoral success. All of this requires the skillful assistance of the bureaucracy. Therefore, the nexus of the political class – political leaders and bureaucracy – plays a critical role in such patronage distribution.

The shift in credit policy includes a change in the nature of informal sources before and after the 1990s with the commercialisation of agriculture. Breman (1993) noted that the onset of capitalist agriculture in south Gujarat altered the older arrangements between labourers and employer-farmers.[26] Their relations have become less personal and more business-like, a process he terms as 'depatronisation'. Similar observations have been made in the context of Uttar Pradesh (Lerche, 1999; Mehrotra, 2012). Weakening social ties and a capitalist ethic pervading relations in the agrarian economy, with receding government subsidies for production inputs, have adversely affected wage labourers, as seen in north India in the 1990s (Jodhka, 1995). Srivastava (2012) argues that despite the claims made by the NSSO that there has been a rise in wages of labourers since 2005, the improvement in their life conditions has been marginal. Wage labourers as a class is overlapping with the tiller farmers.

The retreat of the public sector since the 1990s created a vacuum, and micro-credit was introduced as a solution to fill the vacuum (Ramchandran, 2005: xxxi). It has been argued that one reason behind this was to cut the cost of banks, since non-profit organisations (NGOs) were seen as more effective in retrieving loans. Over time, micro-credit has proved to be profit-oriented and has failed to reach target groups effectively. In addition, the interest rates charged have been as high as 20 per cent, thereby failing the purpose of catering to lower-income groups (Chavan, 2011). Taylor (2012) found that, contrary to expectations, micro-credit has pushed farmers further into debt traps. He cites instances where farmers have used new loans to even pay back their old loans.

In terms of region, it has been found that farmers' indebtedness was low in less-developed states and high in agriculturally developed states, such as Karnataka, Maharashtra, and Andhra Pradesh (ESCAP Report; Nagaraj, 2008). This is symptomatic of capitalist agriculture that is input-intensive and highly dependent on credit, where formal credit that is mostly cornered by capitalist farmers. Similarly, other inputs of agriculture have increasingly been procured from market since the economic reforms, hence accessing these has become harder for small and marginal farmers.

Input centricity in policy: Pushing masses of farmers to the periphery

This section deals with chemical inputs in agricultural production, namely seed, pesticide, and fertiliser. The immediate post-liberalisation phase witnessed poor agricultural growth – 2.1 per cent between 1996–97 and 2002–03 – owing to the state's withdrawal of subsidies on irrigation, fertiliser, credit, and suchlike (Mishra and Reddy, 2009; Ramakumar, 2014). It can be aptly classified as negative intervention of the state. The NAP was declared in 2000. It aims at ensuring efficiency and agricultural growth above 4 per cent per annum and advocates the use of chemical inputs to achieve these goals. It has, therefore, been characterised as 'input centric' (Rathore and Singh, 2010). Moreover, the NAP focuses on high-value crops for export, an initiative supported by the National Horticultural Mission. The thrust of these policies is on chemical inputs to increase productivity since land is scarce. A study of the differentiated impact of these policies on different classes and fractions of farmers is mandatory for an understanding of India's agrarian structure.

India's liberalisation-era policies of agriculture can be delineated into two phases.[27] The first phase was marked by the state's withdrawal from public investments in the sector, but in the second phase, the state partnered with private companies by directing subsidies to specific inputs such as hybrid seeds, fertilisers, private research, high-end machinery, and high-value crops. Subsequently, the state governments drafted and adopted their respective agricultural policies in the mid-2000s, sticking to a strategy of subsidising cost of cultivation of certain elite crops and prescribing capital-intensive inputs to push forward agricultural growth. A notable instance of such a shift is observed in the fall in public investments towards surface irrigation (canals), which positively affected many farmers. Instead, state subsidies were observed to have been directed towards private irrigation methods such as ground and drip irrigation, which showed a rise in usage during this phase (Ramakumar, 2014; Reddy and Mishra; 2009). Hence, it cannot be stated that the state has withdrawn from irrigation entirely; rather, it has rearranged its priorities. State governments have proactively invited private players – both Indian companies and giant corporations such as DuPont, Cargill, and Monsanto – into the domain of chemical inputs to foster speedy growth in this sector. In an effort to foster greater privatisation, a seed policy was adopted in 2004. The implications of the policy changes and the impact on different classes are elaborated in the subsequent paragraphs.

Most scholars approach agriculture from a technical or scientific perspective, when assessing the impact of new agricultural inputs. However, it must be noted that these inputs have socio-political ramifications as well. Take, for example, Bt cotton, which is a genetically modified organism (GMO) cotton variety produced by Monsanto. In this case, the adoption of the crop was fast and wide. However, the question that arises is, did all farmers adopt Bt? The answer is no. The well-off farmers with sources of irrigation adopted the new seeds much ahead of others, and, thus, had leverage over the rest in capturing the market (Glover, 2010). As experienced during the Green Revolution, the resource bias caused some farmers to gain much more than others when the new seed policy was introduced. These farmers had access to irrigation, better credit, literacy, and often larger landholdings. As Duvick (2001) points out, introduction of new technology can transform agrarian social structures. He observed this for maize production systems in North America. The advent of hybrid maize resulted in extensive restructuring of agrarian relations, as small family farms were pushed to the wall; only a few farmers succeeded and could use the opportunity (Glover, 2010). In Byres' (1981) words, 'technology does not fall from heaven, and neither does it exist in a social and political vacuum. It is appropriated by specific classes and used to further class interests' (p. 416).

Availability of water and its access are pressing issues in agriculture. Nowadays, with focus on high-value crops and cuts in budget expenditures on dry-land crops, water has assumed a determining role in agricultural production. This section will specifically focus on the status of surface irrigation in India and the privatisation of irrigation.

India has over 20 million irrigation wells and still the number is growing by 0.8 million per year (Shah, 2006). Worldwide, India is the largest user of groundwater for agriculture. The proportion contributed by surface irrigation has had a steady fall, and has been replaced by groundwater irrigation. Simultaneously, there has been a shift from government support for irrigation to privatisation of the sector. Shah (2006) notes that 25 per cent of the farmers in India own irrigation wells, while the remaining, non-owners, depend on the groundwater market. This means that the former 25 per cent of the farmers extract rent by giving their pumps on hire to the rest (NCEUS, 2008). It implies that privatisation of irrigation, as a policy promoted by the Indian government since 2000, has further skewed the distribution of resources among farmers in rural India. Those who can afford to have access to more water, which is required in abundance by commercial crops, have an edge on other classes. In addition, they extract rent from poorer farmers by leasing out pumps, tractors, and other equipment (NCEUS, 2008). Therefore, a combination of all these factors leads to accumulation by big and capitalist farmers.

Rain-fed areas have been neglected in terms of public sector investment right from the Green Revolution era (Singh and Rathore, 2010).[28] India spends 0.5 per cent of the GDP on research, whereas other developing countries spend 1 per cent (Dev, 2012). Negligence of dry land crops in the policies since the late 1990s has been recognised by a review of the research activities of the Indian Council of Agricultural Research (ICAR) system, which focused on the 10th Plan (Dev, 2012). This bias has affected crop diversity, leading to scarcity of food crops for the lower rung of the society, particularly tribal people and tiller farmers. Since 2001, farmers in some states such as Karnataka, Maharashtra, Andhra Pradesh, and Gujarat have tended to adopt monocropping with water-intensive crops such as cotton and sugarcane, as well as by promoting monocropping activities such as horticulture (Alagh, 2004). Adoption of such techniques is partly dictated by market prices and export demand (Shetty, 2004). The government emphasises on the adoption of these practices. Therefore, the rise in cultivation of water-intensive crops in regions where water is a scare resource has deepened the class divisions in agrarian structures.

A brief description of access to water and irrigation and how that is connected to cultivation of certain crops which excludes most has been provided in this chapter. It results in a bias that has negatively affected the majority of farmers, because commercial cropping and high-value crops thrive on abundance of water and, thus, irrigation. A more comprehensive discussion on water for each state has been included in the respective chapters. What follows in the next section is a detailed discussion on the other chemical inputs in agriculture.

Seed: From autonomy to slavery

In traditional India, the farmer was the owner of the seed which was a chief source of her/his autonomy and food security. Things started changing from 1967. The GoI initiated a National Seed Project with the World Bank's financial assistance and expert guidance. As a part of this effort, seed processing plants were set up in 17 states with the mandate of producing certified seeds.[29] In the 1980s, the seed sector was opened to private players, as embodied in the New Policy on Seed Development in 1988. This allowed the import of certain seeds for a limited period by Indian companies in either technical or financial collaboration with foreign companies. The objective was to make the best of seed inputs available to Indian farmers to increase productivity and income.

The National Seeds Policy of 2002 recognised the central role of private players in securing national food requirements, especially in areas of seed production and export promotion. The policy encouraged private research and development by advancing intellectual property protection. The Hooda Committee Report (2010) emphasised a move from HYV to hybrid seed technology for the sake of higher productivity. It stated that because the hybrid seed technology is more expensive, the government should incentivise the private sector to carry out such research. It changed the fundamental relation of farmers with seed, who until then would store seed from one year to be reused in the next year. The farmers had a degree of autonomy from the market. With seeds becoming the private property of companies, farmers' autonomy is converted to slavery. They can no longer use their seeds but have to buy them from the market (Shiva, 2007; for more details see seedfreedom.info). In the same vein, the expressed aim of the 2004 Seed Bill was to 'provide for regulating the quality of seeds for sale, import and export and to facilitate production and supply of seeds of quality and for matters connected therewith or incidental thereto' (Saggi, 2006: 6). It seeks to hold sellers legally accountable for quality by making registration of all seeds mandatory. This Bill has been criticised for neglecting community rights, overlooking risks associated with GM crops by allowing them to be sold in India, and not dealing with issues relating to seed pricing and intellectual property rights (IPR) (Shiva, 2007).

Kloppenburg (2010) has described this conversion of common property into private commodity as 'accumulation by dispossession'.[30] He argued such legislation furthered the neoliberal agenda of pushing forward the private sector and reducing the government's role in seed production and distribution. It was regarded by Shiva (2007) as an onslaught of multinational companies (MNCs) on India's indigenous resource, such as Cargill and Monsanto. The policy requires the farmers to adopt the technology the MNCs make available, as opposed to what might be the most suitable, given the region-specific peculiarities. Experts have raised the concern that there is a need for growing seeds based on specific requirements and the suitability of the ecosystem, such as that of rain-fed and arid areas, something that has largely been overlooked in current policies (Singh and Rathore, 2010). Pulses, coarse grains, and mass crops have been excluded from private technological innovation, which has resulted in poor yield, forcing farmers to opt out from growing these crops (Singh and Rathore, 2010). This has added to the trend of monocropping.

The Indian seed market was estimated to be worth ₹20 billion by the turn of the century and would touch ₹60 billion in another 7–10 years as per predictions by Monsanto (Shiva and Crompton, 1998). In 2012, the domestic seed industry stood at ₹70 billion ($1.14 billion) and exceeded the predicted figure with a production of 40 million quintals of various kinds of seeds (*The Economic Times*, 2012b). In 2012, the Secretary of the ASSOCHAM commented that the growth of the seed industry in India is driven by scarce land resource and government subsidies towards the sector (*The Economic Times*, 2012b).

The seed market has witnessed a wave of privatisation. With a 67 per cent market share, cereals dominated the certified seed market in 2008–09 and pulses came in second with 20 per cent share. During the same period, maize, oilseeds, vegetables, and, most importantly, cotton dominated the hybrid seed market (Ramakumar, 2014). The seed replacement for paddy and wheat stood at 30 per cent and at 50 per cent for maize and other high-value crops in 2010 (Ramakumar, 2014). Verma (n.d.) has estimated the share of the private sector to be 80 per cent in the turnover in seed. The seed distributed by the government is also bought from private companies.

Since 2002, Bt has registered a dramatic rise covering 90 per cent of the cotton area. The demand for hybrid seeds soared up to 220 per cent over the last decade (Paroda, 2012). It is safe to infer that the seed market is being appropriated by the private sector. By 2008, the market for hybrid seeds was dominated by the private sector – 100 per cent for cotton, sunflower, and vegetables, 98 per cent for maize, 90 per cent for paddy, and 82 per cent for millets (Schenkelaars, Vriend, and Kalaitzandonakes, 2011, cited in Ramakumar, 2014). Over 300 companies are part of the seed industry and part of a formal organisation, which is the National Seed Association of India.

Within the public sector, the State Seed Corporations (SSCs) have gained precedence over the National Seed Corporation in regulating seed breeding and distribution. The SSCs buy seeds from private companies for crops, such as oilseeds and sunflower, and circulate them among farmers. The state's bureaucracy, its political leaders, and its whole machinery in general play an important role in realising and implementing such policies. For example, in Gujarat, the government provided tacit support to Navbharat to produce and sell Bt cotton seeds despite the patent of Monsanto, going against the verdict from the central government (Herring, 2005). The seeds were, thus, made available to farmers at one-third the price of the patented seeds. However, state governments such as Andhra Pradesh and Karnataka advocated for dominance of foreign companies in the seed market. This approach is evident in Karnataka offering its fields to private MNCs for experimentation with private seed varieties. The state agricultural policy documents mention agro-business and the transformation of agriculture into industry as the way forward for the agrarian sector. Productivity is crucial in the face of rising population and falling land availability. However, how the productivity rise is to be achieved is a political economy question. The Asian-Pacific Seed Association meet, held in Bangalore in 2000, marked the beginning of a new era of propagating hybrid seeds. The concessions given to agribusiness companies by the state government were tabled and signed here, symbolising the state's allegiance to private companies (Assayag, 2005: 74). Some of the prominent Indian agribusiness companies are Nuziveedu Seeds Limited, Ajeet Seeds, Century Seeds, and Eagle Seeds, and among MNCs, DuPont, Syngenta, and Monsanto came to dominate the market.

The success of new seeds is associated with the availability of corresponding extension and support services. However, since the economic reforms, the state has steadily withdrawn extension services to reduce public expenditure. With poor access to information, the majority of farmers face a crisis with regard to adopting the new seeds (Dev, 2012; NCEUS, 2008). On the other hand, the big and capitalist farmers have access to education, as well as contacts with companies and/or bureaucracy, aiding adoption of new inputs more effectively (Assayag, 2005). Meanwhile, the small farmers are dependent on retail shop owners, dealers, and traders to learn about using the new seeds (Rao and Suri, 2006). With this inequality between different classes of farmers steadily increasing, agricultural universities and state agriculture departments had a role to fill the information vacuum faced by lower classes, which has not always been met. Instances of institutional bias for elite crops and against orphan crops have been registered. Poor sharing of holistic information about adopting GM seeds and scarcity of extension services have been listed as factors causing confusion in GM seed adoption (Kulkarni, 2004). State universities and Kisan Vikas Kendras[31] have not been forthcoming in offering corrective measures or providing extension services (Patnaik, 2003; Ramachandran et al., 2010; Reddy and Mishra, 2009). Since 2000, greater emphasis on private inputs has meant further roll back of extension services. In the absence of any authority to advise farmers on new crop technologies, local retailers and dealers have come to occupy a prominent position as knowledge providers (Rao and Suri, 2006; Aga, 2018).

By encouraging public–private partnerships, the seed policies of 2002 and 2004 have pushed cultivation costs higher, which is a probable cause for land dispossession (Janaiah, 2002; Raghavan, 2008; Shiva and Crompton, 1998). Seeds are priced at a premium in order to maximise profits, but this makes them unaffordable to tiller farmers (Janaiah, 2002; Mishra, 2008). Tiller farmer means those farmers who work on their land, and definitely includes the small and marginal farmers and even semi-medium farmers. The high price excludes these farmers from adopting new technology, which makes their produce non-competitive. Hence, it is unlikely that they will ever generate enough surplus to shift to commercial crops. A vicious cycle continues. More technology is available for cultivating commercial crops than traditional food crops; therefore, once commercial crops are adopted for farming, the rise in productivity is faster.[32] The resource crunch, as in lack of capital, has made survival of small and marginal farmers harder in the given context. Scholars have drawn attention to these issues (Shiva, 2000, 2006, 2007; Das Gupta, 2013).

The Green Revolution has been linked with the emergence of a class of 'capitalist farmers'. Termed as progressive farmers, or bullock capitalists, they have been identified in different parts of India. Therefore, when transnational and national companies are entering the input sector, structural inequality already exists. This context plays a crucial role in how the liberalisation–privatisation package unfolds in rural India. With the coming of private capital in the agricultural sector, and the government support that accompanied it, transnational and national corporations emerged as the biggest gainers (Ramakumar, 2014). However, the corporations do not sell to the farmers directly, but have to go through local networks to maximise the sale. Since the late 1990s, shops selling chemical inputs (seeds, fertilisers, and pesticides) have been established. Proliferation of newer brands have been noted who also gained market share in suburban and rural areas. Murugkar et al. (2006) offer an explanation of how these traders have created a niche for themselves. Seed companies dealing in big brands offer a 15 per cent margin on seed price whereas companies dealing in lesser-known seeds offer 35 to 50 per cent of the seed price as the dealers' margin to provide an incentive for selling their products. In the case of less popular brands, the social capital of the dealer is crucial for the products to gain prominence in the markets. On the other hand, the networks of small and middle farmers play a role when it comes to securing credit to meet the high cost of proprietary seeds. Here, the social ties and personal connections of these farmers with the seed dealer act as collateral for availing credit. Once the farmer is indebted to a dealer in a credit relation, his choice of seeds is heavily influenced by the dealer. This dependency is exploited by both transnational and indigenous seed companies, which try to acquire local knowledge and build informal networks to expand their customer base and gain market share. This is not to suggest that everyone uses proprietary seeds. Illegal Bt has also been a source of higher margins and accumulation for seed dealers and producers. The proceeds are shared with local government officials who have the authority to enforce seed laws (Deshpande, 2002; Murugkar et al., 2006; Nagaraj, 2008). The price of hybrid seeds is significantly higher than public seeds, which are readily pushed for sale by both government officials and the local dealers (Pray and Ramaswami, 2001). Studies dealing with social networks and the way they affect seed dealers' operations are scarce, but one finding emerges: even the biggest company makes use of local rural networks to penetrate the market. The issue has been addressed in a later section of the chapter.

The rural network works on credit in a big way. Harriss-White (2004) has argued that the producer–product market interlocking is a source of dominance of one class over others, as she finds in the case of paddy crop in Tamil Nadu. Similar observations have been made in Punjab (Gill, 2004). The seed trader uses credit to tie the producer/farmer to pre-harvest conditions of paybacks

(Aga, 2018). Spurious seeds add to the agony, as they often result in failed crops. Since dealers get higher margins of profit – up to three to four times more – for unbranded seeds, they encourage farmers to use them. Government certified seeds can also be spurious. For farmers, the use of inferior inputs, in the face of reduced government-certified inputs, has resulted in poor or failed harvest while adding to the cost incurred on pesticides, as found in Andhra Pradesh (Ghosh, 2005; Rao and Suri, 2006). A spiral seems to have unfolded, leading to the requirement of higher investment in order to sustain agricultural production, which is oppressing the resource-poor farmers, often owning small holdings.

Shiva and Crompton (1998) highlight other aggressive means employed by private companies to capture the market and convince farmers to shift from open-pollinated seeds to hybrid seeds. The methods listed include intensive advertising, campaigns in local languages, and farmer-to-farmer advocacy by industry representatives. The state provides financial assistance to some of these initiatives in the name of providing greater variety and better quality of seeds to the farmers. For instance, Cargill, a privately held multinational based in the USA, spreads the word about their seeds in the rural areas by identifying ten farms where their seeds are used with increased yield. Then they organise visits to these fields, and owner-farmers of these farms speak about their experience with the seeds to 300 farmers invited to the event. On these occasions, experiments are conducted to demonstrate the expected high-quality output. Cargill also organises Intensive Customer Contact Programmes (ICCPs), where the company holds long and detailed informal sessions with farmer groups. To cite another example of corporate marketing strategy, ITC Zeneca, an agro-business company headquartered in India, provides farmers with free seeds for planting. During the time of harvest, up to 500 neighbouring farmers are invited to a 'Farm Day', where farmers narrate their experiences of using seeds provided by Zeneca, and the technical staff of the attending company back their claims. In this seemingly harmless way, private companies have been replacing public extension services and using innovative strategies to increase their market share.

To sum it up, the government's New Seed Policy is not resource neutral, and has been benefitting to those who have other inputs of production – irrigation, credit and, in some instances, education – at their command. This is reminiscent of Byres' analysis of the way technology introduced during the Green Revolution in the 1970s benefitted the capitalist farmer class. Further, it appears that small and middle farmers necessarily have to incur debt to procure the investment capital critical for new technology (inputs) for crops.

Commercial crop is prescribed as a way out of poverty but in fact is pushing them into poverty. Ironically, these methods perpetuate their dependent and subservient position and even force many farmers to commit suicide (Frankel, 2005). Farmers are increasingly polarised into two classes – one is composed of those who are finding new accumulation opportunities like retail seed shops, and the other (numerically the majority) who are forced to borrow from informal sources to cope with rising costs of cultivation in order to deal with input-centric technology, leading to their further marginalisation.

Fertiliser and pesticides

Success of the National Seed Policy is heavily dependent on the use of fertilisers and pesticides. Again, taking Bt cotton as an example, its increasing adoption has by default entailed the use of pest-prone seeds and, hence, added to pesticide consumption among the farmers as their last resort. This has led to the spread of proprietary hybrid seeds (Herring, 2008). Data from the Cost of Cultivation Surveys over the years have shown that the expenses incurred by farmers on insecticides have increased steeply over the years. The all-state average expense per hectare on insecticides was less than a rupee in the 1970s and over ₹25 in the 1980s. It shot up by 365 per cent in the 1990s and by as much as 1,115 per cent in the first half of the decade following 2000 (Bhaumik, 2008; Raghavan, 2008). Shetty (2004) argues that pesticides now form nearly 30 per cent of the cost of cultivation in the southern states. In the case of wheat, fertiliser was second in operational cost of cultivation, but it was replaced by the cost of machine power after 2000 (Sen and Bhatia, 2004). The high rate of mechanisation of agriculture has increased the cultivators' expenses, but this has happened particularly in some regions and selectively for certain crops.

The cost of cultivation increased due to the rising costs of fertilisers and pesticides, and private players came to dominate the production of these inputs (Ramakumar, 2014). Even before the NSP 2002, incremental use of fertilisers along with high-yield seeds had contributed greatly to the success of the Green Revolution. In the reform period, the government has offered subsidies to encourage farmers to use fertilisers though it is still expensive. Scholars have held that a large portion of the fertiliser subsidy benefits the industries or manufacturers and the large farmers (Birner, Gupta and Sharma, 2011; Ghosh, 2005).[33] Until 2004, the subsidy to fertiliser decreased following SAP prescriptions from international organisations such as WTO, but the subsidy increased exponentially by 530 per cent during 2004 to 2009, with about 90 per cent of the increase being due to the rise in the international prices of fertilisers and chemical inputs. Pesticides have been deregulated and put under the monopoly of a few firms that can dictate terms and prices (Ramakumar, 2014). These subsidised inputs reach the farmers through government agencies such as the cooperative societies (GoI). The access to subsidies is a question to be assessed on the basis of field research.

With the widespread argument against subsidy for the past two decades, and austerity becoming the order of the day, it would be commonplace to expect that the fertiliser subsidy should decrease after liberalisation. Scholars find the opposite to be the fact. A summary note states that 'the cost of India's agricultural input subsidies as a share of agriculture output almost doubled from 6 per cent in 2003–04 to 11.6 per cent in 2009–10', with the main two components being fertiliser and electricity (Grossman and Carlson, 2011). Another study finds that fertiliser subsidy fell between 1997–98 and 2002–03, and then rose steadily after 2004 (Paul, Sharma, and Thaker, 2010). It has increased by 17 times between 1990–91 and 2008–09. It poses a question about the politics within India, as well as the power exerted by agrarian proprietary classes since 2004 on the government, which could have affected such a change in budgetary allocation, against the global forces' prescription. Chemical industries have certainly gained in pushing their agenda.

Fertiliser consumption is not always proportional to landholding size. In fact, small farms have been applying fertiliser and pesticides at higher intensity to maximise yield, with some regional variation (Sen and Bhatia, 2004: 220). In Rajasthan, the size of farm and the use of fertiliser and bullock labour are inversely related, whereas in Punjab, seeds, fertilisers, micro-nutrients, and machine labour are more intensively used in big holdings than small and medium ones (Sen and Bhatia, 2004). Others have found no variation among farm sizes in the application of fertilisers (Paul, Sharma and Thaker, 2010). Alagh (1988, 2004) found that the usage of pesticides is as high among small farmers as among those with larger holdings. The technology has been effective and well accepted by different classes of farmers. However, there exists some regional variation. In the 1990s, five states – Punjab, Andhra Pradesh, Maharashtra, Madhya Pradesh, and Uttar Pradesh – consumed 60 per cent of fertilisers, which has changed post-2000, with Gujarat and Karnataka catching up, and the share of the former falling to 55 per cent (Paul, Sharma and Thaker, 2010).

The access of big and capitalist farmers to cooperatives among other state institutions has already been affirmed above. Cooperatives are the source of subsidised fertilisers and micro-nutrients. This means that those who cannot access these formal institutions have to buy the inputs from private dealers

(Nagaraj, 2008). It transpires that the proprietary classes have benefitted from the increase in subsidy that the state has sanctioned on fertilisers since the early 2000s. The small farmers are left to buy fertiliser at high prices, thereby incurring debt. Nagaraj (2008) argues that traders selling inputs are of a predatory nature who charge exorbitant amounts from farmers, thus pushing the cost of cultivation higher and putting farmers' livelihood in jeopardy. He does not provide the details of the evidence, but the study borrows from a geographically wide sample. Jeffrey and Lerche (2001) and Gupta (1998) have presented evidence that the village elite and the local state[34] share a close association in which public resources are channelised through the former to the rural beneficiaries. The authors argue that a disproportionate share of this fund is used for the elite's material and political reproduction, making the state a source of accumulation. The rural elite act as intermediaries between the village members and the local state officials, wherein they charge rents and/or political leverage for settling the transaction (Jeffrey and Lerche, 2001; Gupta, 1998). The elite, for the sake of the study, include big and capitalist farmers and, on rare occasions, middle farmers with political ties. The possibility of the rise of new fractions around the distribution of state resources and electoral politics in the last decade cannot be overlooked. However, it is probable that the rural elite continues to procure fertilisers and seeds from government institutions at subsidised rates. Given that there has been a rise in fertiliser subsidy, a question arises about who the beneficiaries are, and whose interest is crucial to the political settlement which the state is trying to protect, as evident from higher spending on fertiliser subsidy since 2003. This shall be pursued in the empirical chapters.

Input privatisation has had differential impact on different classes of farmers. Lack of education and disappearing public extension services have created a disadvantage for small farmers who are left at the mercy of unscrupulous moneylenders and traders to buy these inputs (Dev, 2012). As argued earlier, many of these actors are big capitalist farmers who have access to more knowledge and, thus, use the inputs in judicious quantity and ensure better quality. Extension service is also following a highly top-down trend and does not allow participation of farmers (Dev, 2012). The NSS farmers' survey (2003) has shown that awareness about bio-fertilisers, minimum support prices (MSPs), and WTO is associated with education levels, which are privileges of the big farmers and those with urban connections, while tiller farmers suffer owing to poor education. Market imperfections alongside privatisation of inputs eat into the income of the small and marginal farmers. As NCEUS (2008) found, 'consumption expenditure of marginal and small farmers exceeds their estimated income by a substantial margin and presumably the deficits have to be plugged by borrowing or other means' (p. 12). They borrow not only to cultivate crops but even after sale of crops to cover consumption expenses.

In this situation, common sense would dictate farmer interest groups and would highlight the pressing issue in agriculture and the steep rise in the cost of production due to chemical inputs; yet what surprisingly dominates the conversations in agrarian circles of the big and capitalist farmers is how the cost of labour has become unbearable over the past decade. This feeling is shared among those classes of farmers who do not cultivate themselves. However, a cost-of-cultivation survey reveals that average wages as a ratio of operational costs have not increased at the same rate as its other components over the past two decades. Yet the input that has been fast replaced is labour, as seen in the survey conducted by the author; wages paid to hired labour as a proportion of operational costs have stagnated through the same period (Raghavan, 2008). Though this study focuses on wheat, the trend is worth exploring. Does emphasis on technological innovations gear towards replacing wage labourers, and thus pushing the latter to non-farm sector given the fall in employability within agriculture? Political representation of farmer interest is a perplexing aspect of agricultural transformation, which merits further research.

Changing cropping pattern: Why and where

The previous section outlined how different classes of farmers have varied access to inputs of agriculture, and resources are heavily skewed in favour of big and capitalist farmers. Against this background of structural inequality, agrarian policy emphasised a change in cropping pattern. Along with producing for the market, modernisation of agriculture has meant adopting more marketable crops.

Crops are commonly classified into cash and food crops (Fafchamps, 1992). Food crops are those that the farmer produces for self-consumption, and include crops such as paddy, wheat, and pulses. Cash crops are produced for sale and to be exchanged in the market. With increasing commercialisation of agriculture, cash crops such as cotton, sugarcane, groundnut, silk, areca nut, and flowers have seen a rise in acreage. It is possible for a crop to be cultivated for subsistence as well as commerce. For instance, paddy and wheat are cash crops in Punjab, where they are produced mostly for sale, while they are grown as food crops in Chhattisgarh.

In the 1990s, field and horticultural crops together occupied 43 per cent of the research and development budget, livestock and natural resource management research covered 18 per cent and 15 per cent respectively, forestry and fisheries accounted for 8 per cent each, while non-commodity research such as agricultural engineering received 7 per cent (Pal, 2008). This can be understood as preparation for focusing on high-value[35] crops (Pal, 2008; Singh and Sagar, 2004; Swaminathan, 2007; Vyas, 1994). As the years progressed, in 2000 under the National Horticulture Mission (NHM), subsidies were offered to farmers who wanted to set up orchards and nurseries. The state governments took similar initiatives to encourage cultivation of high-value crops. Privatisation of seeds has made the availability of seeds for high-value crops greater, and higher price for exportable crops – evident in high demand for cotton, flowers, and maize, among others, from urban India and export markets – has made investment in these crops more lucrative. Therefore, land has been increasingly reallocated from food to commercials crops. In most states, there has been a shift from growing traditional crops (cereals) to horticulture crops, sericulture, and animal husbandry (Deshpande et al., 2004; Chakravarti and Kundu, 2009). In the Tenth and Eleventh Five Year Plans (2002–2012), stepping up of export and diversification of agriculture towards export-oriented crops were emphasised, and large investments were allocated for developing high-technology agriculture. Crops such as maize, sunflower, silk, rubber, pepper, cotton, sugarcane, and silk have been in demand due to their export market. It has been argued that floriculture and horticulture are in an especially favourable position in the new policy regime, given their capacity to earn foreign currency (Chakravarti and Kundu, 2009; Gowda, 2009).

There has been a shift in the policy agenda of the state, as evident from the thrust towards commercial cultivation. The primary concern of the state vis-à-vis agriculture was to ensure food security until the 1980s. Post-liberalisation, agriculture has been dealt as a profit-making enterprise. The 1990s were marked by gradual withdrawing of procurement by the states[36] and reduction of subsidy on inputs, and the resultant exposure of cultivators to the market (Alagh, 2004: 39; Reddy and Mishra, 2009). The minimisation of the state's role in certain aspects of agriculture has been construed as a negative effort on the part of the state. However, since 2002, the state has proactively made positive efforts, such as introduction of high-value crops, to make agriculture profitable. For instance, Gowda (2009) finds that high-technology floriculture has registered high growth since 2004, and ascribes a part of this success to favourable government policies. A fundamental shift in cropping pattern of Indian agriculture has been implemented willfully by the state. India has entered a new phase in the new millennium, where efforts are strongly directed towards technology, chemical inputs, meant for specific crops that have high commercial value.

Adoption of commercial crops is further encouraged by the fact that there is low financial security in cultivating traditional crops. Despite the Food Corporation of India (FCI) regularly raising the ceiling of agricultural prices, its quantity of purchase of cereals has fallen sharply with the opening of the sector to international trade. This has seriously reduced the security of those producing more traditional crops which, when sold to traders, have low profit margins, if at all. This has resulted in farmers taking up cultivation of market-viable crops to cope with low profit margins of food crops. However, these farmers have landed in a trap of spiralling high cost of inputs owing to the lumpy[37] nature of the technology, thereby finding it harder to sustain themselves. In fact, adopting high-value crops is more suitable for large farmers as access to land, credit, and other inputs of agriculture is heavily skewed in their favour. The burden of interest makes sustenance harder for small farmers, because adoption of high-end technology almost always requires credit (Minot and Roy, 2006). This possibly explains Alagh's (2004) prediction in early 2000 that small farmers would continue with cereals (coarse and non-coarse) and would only devote a part of their holdings to commercial crops. Today, non-food crops have steadily gained in acreage but adopted by small farmers only in part of their holdings. Commercial crops such as oilseeds, on the other hand, have been adopted by big and medium-holding farmers who have moved out of cereal farming (Alagh, 2004).

India's policy to encourage commercial cultivation has encouraged numerous private enterprises – both national and multinational – to flood Indian markets with inputs for horticulture, floriculture, poultry, animal husbandry, and meat processing, as these are important products for export. Internationally reputed agribusiness corporations including Cargill Seeds, Pioneer Overseas, Monsanto, and Kentucky Fried Chicken started to spread branches across Indian states individually or in joint ventures with Indian enterprises (Panini, 1999). In the new policy climate, these private ventures are looking to spread technology for high-value crops.

As previously mentioned, crop diversification and high-value crops came into focus due to the NAPs adopted by state governments after 2004. These crops require investment and technology costing as much as ₹100,000 per acre as per Cost of Cultivation data.[38] Post-2002, state governments have directed subsidy towards buying machinery such as drip irrigation instruments, inputs for greenhouse technology, and so on, to assist those who can share the cost of these capital-intensive machinery for high-value crops. Those farmers who are reeling under the mounting debt and rising cost of chemical inputs cannot afford the exorbitant cost of machinery, and the technology is not suitable for small landholdings. To reap the benefit of high-value crops, small farmers have shown preference towards joining contract farming for big agribusiness, where the latter decide what is to be produced, provide inputs, and take the crops post harvest. The decision-making and autonomy that farmers once enjoyed are seriously curbed under such circumstances (Ali and Harriss-White, 2012; Panini, 1999). Therefore, crop diversification as an agricultural strategy has the potential to widen the gap between capital-rich farmers and the rest.

The policy found support from the government in terms of monetary allocations. Analysis of crop diversification strategies in Chhattisgarh, Gujarat, and Karnataka has been undertaken in the respective empirical chapters to understand the shifting cropping pattern post-1990s, changes that have occurred post-2003, state policies regarding cropping pattern, and who the adopters are of these new crops.

Big farmer and emerging gentleman farmers: Converging interests

Urbanisation has created a consistent demand for land, and the rural economy has failed to generate enough employment opportunity for the majority of farmers to retain their landholdings. Use of land, therefore, has unidirectionally moved from agricultural to non-agricultural purposes due to push-and-pull factors (Alagh, 2004). Within agriculture, floriculture has dominated land use due to its export potential. Floriculture has entered its third phase since the early 2000s, and the government support has been directed towards it. In 2005, subsidies for machinery, irrigation, and other inputs were granted under the National Horticulture Mission to encourage high-technology nurseries (Gowda, 2009).[39] While the income from floriculture is more than any other crop (wheat and sugarcane), the input cost is proportionately higher, leaving most farmers incapable of cultivating flowers. Further, scholars note that large farmers adopt high-value cultivation more than what small farmers adopt, and are able to sustain it for a longer duration. Education and knowledge are the other factors that exclude the majority of farmers (Minot and Roy, 2006; Reddy and Mishra 2009). In Uttar Pradesh, similar findings are reported when farmers growing cut-flowers were surveyed (Sen and Raju, 2006). Sud (2008) writes how this is similar to the open offer made by Modi to the corporates and big farmers to come and take up *gochur* land and convert it to orchards or other profit-making agricultural enterprises. While Gujarat has been keen on involving urban players, Indian corporate giants hitherto engaged in the industrial sector have displayed ardent interest in agriculture, particularly in floriculture. This trend was noted even earlier, as is evident from Karnataka (Panini, 1999). The narrowing gap between India and Bharat is evident from these cases. The phenomenon has already been noted by other scholars, such as Dipankar Gupta (2015) and Jodhka (2008). Chakravarti and Kundu (2009) point out that the crop diversification policy – land and credit are the most significant focus of the policy – can reap desired results only when complemented by extensive infrastructural facilities, as well as financial and technological support, particularly for micro-labour-intensive enterprises (p. 74). In the absence of these, the benefits will remain limited to big and capitalist farmers. High-technology floriculture and horticulture are beyond the capacity of the small farmers and, by inference, they are not the target of the subsidies offered by the state.

A few key questions emerge from this discussion. How has the crop-diversification policy affected land use, and who has it benefitted? Has the capitalists' takeover of agricultural land brought them in conflict with the rich farmer class or has a new alliance been forged for common interest?

Decentralisation or accumulation at lower state level?

The policy of decentralisation has had implications for processes of agrarian accumulation and class relations in India. A constitutional change that occurred around the same time as liberalisation was the amendments to the PRIs[40] in 1992–93. In 1992, the PRI was given constitutional status, and reservation for the SC and ST was introduced in the PRIs. Even before that, PRI had occupied a central position in rural politics in India and many had pinned their hope on these to bring about social transformation. John Wood (1987) finds that despite the signs of decreasing untouchability in Gujarat, a parallel trend of recruiting SC members into the middle class by electing them into PRI was observed in the pre-liberalisation era. Therefore, the question he posed is whether in the guise of empowerment of a caste, reservation has actually created class loyalists from the deprived castes. Manor (2004) has indicated that in many ways the local self-government acts as a facilitator of the state's penetration at lower levels of the federal structure and generates consent among disadvantaged groups. The state is found playing a decisive role in class formation. What this does not answer is whether the link is only top-to-bottom or the other way as well. Patnaik (2001) provides some direction in this dilemma at a conceptual level. He argues that decentralisation in India has taken place in the broader context of the class nature of the state. It is, thus, most likely that PRIs work as a 'mechanism for doling out [state] fund[s]' (p. 58), signifying that access to the institution is a limited access to resources for the dominant classes. As argued by Poulantzas (1973), access to state resources leads to accumulation by the old petty bourgeoisie. Following Jessop's (1983) prediction, decentralisation could be the key in helping private capital penetrate Indian villages, but its impact still needs to be explored. This has been addressed through empirical evidence in this book.

In the early 1990s, Rajiv Gandhi had declared Pradesh Congress elections, realising the need to penetrate the countryside and build a wider party base. Soon after, it was called off. The Congress party has thrived on party loyalists at the grass-roots level by co-opting social structures into the party hierarchy (Chatterjee, 1998). What followed was the formation of the PRI under 73rd and 74th amendments. The succession of these events might be coincidental, but it can be suggestive of the PRIs helping to fulfil the party's objective to recruit loyalists at the rural level through patronage distribution. Jalal's (1996) analysis of the local elections in Pakistan during Zia's regime[41] unfolds the hidden agenda of the government to build a base at the village level to support his regime from the lower rungs of society. Therefore, the roles of the state and district bureaucracy, the *zilla parishad* and *panchayat* heads, are crucial for resource allocation and interest mobilisation in each state. By virtue of holding dominant positions at the district level, local government functionaries have the capacity to be the voice of rural people. However, whether this power is transforming the entire rural life or transforming only these elected members' class position by bringing them into the circuit of capital is a question pursued in the fieldwork. In today's globalised India with the classed nature of state, Patnaik (2001) predicts these institutions would operate as lower level comprador agencies, aiding the penetration of foreign capital into rural parts, but simultaneously the rural dominant class would be accumulating themselves by accessing new opportunities created by the entry of foreign capital.

Evidence from a study conducted in three villages in Andhra Pradesh shows a tendency of big farmers and landlords to cordon off political posts and resources (Ramachandran, Rawal, and Swaminathan, 2010). For instance, fieldwork during the study revealed that a landowning family owns about 280 acres of land, and members of the same family exert tremendous control over the village *panchayat*. One of the family members is a professional politician and has held a cabinet rank in Hyderabad; another family member functioned at the *mandal* (second tier) level, while another was a part of the state bureaucracy (p. 26). The significance of those with the ownership of the means of production coming to hold positions in self-government institutions suggests the concentration of political and economic interest at the local state level. Institutions meant for decentralisation of power are found to be perpetuating concentration of power.

The Constitution envisions PRIs as units of local self-government that strengthen India's federal system, but the political and economic ramifications of these institutions have been quite different. PRIs have emerged as instruments of patronage distribution and an easy access to the class ladder, as Jeffrey (2002) enumerates in the case of Uttar Pradesh. The authors cited by Jeffrey have done considerable work on struggles between different rural classes and establishes how the classes owning capital successfully co-opt local government bodies (*panchayats*). This is significant, because such co-option leads to a new round of accumulation, since the local bodies are responsible for the disbursement of development funds in rural India and thus provide access to state resource, such as contracts, employment, and grants. (Gupta, 1998; Lieten, 1996; Lieten and Srivastava, 1999 cited in Jeffrey, 2001). *Panchayat* leaders have found new sources of income through the MGNREGS, which has been heavily ridden with corruption since its implementation (Bhatia and Dreze, 2006; Vanaik and Siddharth, 2008). Khan (2004) terms this as the 'patron-client network' existing in the Indian state, which has intensified under a corrupt regime. Corruption and patronage have a close relationship, and the Indian political system is sustained through it, as Manor (2004) points out in his discussion on political fixers. Dominant classes in rural areas thrive and grow by influencing and permeating state institutions at different levels (Jeffrey, 2000). Still others have characterised the Indian state as an embedded particularistic state (Herring, 1999). The state police aid when the dominant class of moneylenders have to illegally appropriate land from poor borrowers who are in debt. Thus, the dominant class accumulates in the process of dispossessing the resource-poor (Jeffrey, 2000). All these instances can be interpreted as various people using their political power – local district officials, the police, and the *panchayat* secretary – consolidating their class position through access to state resources.

Based on the fieldwork in Karnataka, Pattenden (2011) concludes that 'fiscal decentralisation has thickened state–society interactions at the village level, and triggered a substantial increase in the levels of appropriation of public resources by the village gatekeepers' (p. 192). It is indicative of how *panchayat* institutions are becoming yet another source of income for the powerful classes, which helps in accumulation by capitalist farmers and big farmers. There is also the issue of leaders from deprived castes and tribes who join the dominant classes because of caste reservation in public employment and local institutions. Thus, the people for whom the advantages of state apparatus have previously been a distant dream potentially become part of a creamy layer and enjoy strong patron-client relations with the state bosses (Herring, 1999; Vaid, 2012; Weiner, 2001).[42]

Accumulation of capital happens in various ways and simultaneously in the agrarian economy. Credit and land are two factors of production that the dominant classes control and mediate for their class advantage, as argued earlier. In this context, the incentives that their political connections to the state bring have been affirmed. The growing demand for land in post-liberalisation India has arguably opened new opportunities for the same classes that have connections with the political bosses. The agrarian capitalist class is often instrumental in buying land from the small and marginal farmers or selling their own land (partly), where they get to negotiate on the terms of transaction to be carried out with urban stakeholders. This is yet another source of accumulation, wherein they receive perks for settling the land deed (Levien, 2011). A similar role has been ascribed to them by Manor (2004), who found that 'political fixers' have an important role of being the negotiator between rural masses and political leaders. This is a form of winning patronage for the former, while taking a part of the pie home for the middleman. Palaniswamy and Krishnan (2012) note the evidence of elite capture of state resources through the PRIs. Land acquisition of the common property resources (CPR) requires approval of the *panch*s,[43] thus excluding villagers from the decision-making process. For this consent, the *panch* receives a cut from the broker or contractor. The political elite have gained access to the resources that have risen through new governmental schemes and programmes, such as the MGNREGS (Rajshekhar, Babu and Manjula, 2011). This has, therefore, transformed the class character of elected members of the PRIs from farmers into allies of capital.

This section has outlined numerous cases, mainly situated in Karnataka, Gujarat, Uttar Pradesh, and Tamil Nadu, where political connection is ensuring enhanced sources of accumulation. Thus, political connection is instrumental in consolidating the proprietary class position at the district level. Fieldwork will address if such practices were prevailing in the states under scrutiny during the liberalisation phase, when the state's role was supposedly going to retreat.

Conclusion

In the decade following 2000, Indian agriculture has become more chemical input-centric, high-value-crop oriented, irrigated, and mechanised. The land reform policies of the government in the 1950s and 1960s were broadly unsuccessful owing to the lack of political will, followed by the Green Revolution that deepened class inequalities, widening both regional and interpersonal disparities (Alagh, 2004: 48; Byres, 1981). On this unequal social structure, policy makers decided to build the edifice of privatisation, which has likely perpetuated inequalities even further. Given that the state is a socially embedded category facing multiple social pressures and, at the same time, making policies which heavily impact the lives of the people, an analysis of state agricultural policies (as listed in subsequent chapters) has the potential to reveal the nature of the state. This is a question pursued in depth across the chapters.

The political factors that necessitated a policy shift, after liberalisation and again after 2004, is a crucial question pursued in the study. A comparison has been drawn with agricultural policies prior to the 1990s. Building on the main argument presented in Chapter 2, the relevance to study the specificities within a state rather than ascribing all causality to global forces has been presented. Regional political settlement will be investigated to explain the new policy regime. Existing studies that address the effect of these policies are limited to Andhra Pradesh, Punjab, Uttar Pradesh, Karnataka, and Tamil Nadu. Therefore, when it comes to the three states studied here, the effects of privatisation of inputs, new cropping pattern, and rapid land acquisition by capitalists will be emphasised. An understanding of classes and fractions that have benefitted from adoption of chemical inputs, new sources of accumulation such as land transactions, and informal moneylending already exists in the literature, but not necessarily based in Chhattisgarh, Gujarat, and Karnataka. With the help of empirical data, an understanding of state–class relations in these states will be developed.

This chapter discussed various inputs of agricultural production, namely land, credit and chemical inputs, and identified its beneficiaries. The post-liberalisation era, particularly after 2002, has seen significant policy changes in these domains. To realise the objective of high productivity, the agricultural sector has increasingly accommodated the private sector that has brought in expensive, high-value, and low-volume inputs. This also altered the class relations in the rural economy, which will be explored in the subsequent chapters.

A selective literature review enumerates three scholars, Pattenden (2011), Levien (2011), and Sud (2007), who shed light on the associated themes of land acquisition and decentralisation in Rajasthan, Gujarat, and Karnataka, and draw overlapping inferences. They place the 'state' at the centre of their analyses and find a particular class accumulating through access to the state resources. In Karnataka, the relation among these classes is found to be closely intertwined with the relation between each class and the state, making the state very much a contributor to accumulation and self-perpetuation (Pattenden, 2011). In Gujarat, the economically powerful classes use political leverage to further their interests. Sud (2007) finds an unholy marriage between the political class and the economically dominant class. In Rajasthan, the state is at the core of land acquisitions, and is characterised as a 'land-broker' (Levien, 2011). Such studies have proven helpful in providing a direction to the path of enquiry followed for this book and in situating the empirical findings in a wider context.

With the thrust of commercialisation and privatisation in Indian agriculture, new classes and actors emerged. That the trader, the retail shop owner, and the moneylender overlap with the proprietary classes of the big and capitalist farmers was indicated in several cases. It can be argued that agricultural policy has opened new avenues for the proprietary classes to diversify into chemical input retailing, moneylending, and earning rent from hiring out pumps and tractors at an unprecedented magnitude.

The cases presented point to two trends. First, the close proximity between big farmers and the political leaders and state officials persists even when the state was propagating anti-farmer policies, particularly after 2004. The rural proprietary class' access to political institutions continued after liberalisation, as several such instances suggested from the literature based on case studies and surveys undertaken in different regions of India. Second, the big farmers are directly or indirectly instrumental in fostering accumulation by the capitalists, as seen in the few studies on land deals. This is evident in how land grab is a process facilitated by big and middle farmers. Likewise, big farmers along with traders sell corporate brand seeds. Hence, these two classes develop seemingly overlapping interests.

The point of investigation is whether these interrelations among different class interests – even overlap between classes – are exclusive to the cases discussed in the literature, or if there is a pattern across India. Such a finding can potentially illustrate if a class linkage has emerged or is emerging between rural proprietary classes and capitalists, and whether the bureaucracy plays a role in that relation. To make sense of the relationship, the vantage point remains the classic work by Pranab Bardhan (1984, 1998), in which he drew up the three-proprietary class model involving these very classes.

Methods and methodology

The fieldwork carried out in the states of Chhattisgarh, Gujarat, and Karnataka was structured in such a way that adequate empirical data could be gathered to address the issues raised here. Respondents included a variety of stakeholders in the agrarian sector, including political leaders, journalists, social activists, big farmers, middle farmers, tiller farmers, and academicians. Even though respondents among farmers were selected on the basis of their class position, caste data was also collected to assess if patterns emerge within each state and between the three states. The methodology adopted was inductive and, during fieldwork, the method was in-depth/long interviews. A number of districts were covered in each of the states to capture regional variation in how agrarian structures are organised and the way political settlement operates within a state. A qualitative study approach was adopted to conduct fieldwork, because it was logistically not possible to cover the relevant social groups through statistically significant samples. The aim was to reach an understanding of the existing major qualitative tendencies by gathering views and information from a variety of stakeholders.

I consider case studies as the most effective way to unearth qualitative trends from across a wide geographical area and with varied stakeholders. Therefore, information is gathered and presented in this study in the form of case studies. Case studies are mainly of two types – synchronic and diachronic (Gerring, 2004). In a synchronic case study, a particular case is studied over a period, while in a diachronic case study, several cases are studied in a particular period. This study is diachronic, because it compares three states from post-1990 to 2014. During this time, as noted in this chapter, Indian agricultural policy underwent a fundamental change, and it moved from focusing on food security to treating agriculture as a profit-driven enterprise. The change in agricultural policy has been analysed with a political economy approach, wherein the concern is with the interaction of political and economic forces within the Indian society, the way power and wealth are distributed between different groups, and the way their relationships are created and sustained.

Many uncertainties lurked during the fieldwork for this study. Individuals are unpredictable entities, and there were also limitations in the kind of respondents chosen. For instance, in Karnataka, owing to the language barrier, the respondents I could access were mostly academicians and activists, and fewer farmers and traders, who conversed mostly in Kannada. I depended on the former to understand the ground reality and verified the trends by visiting districts later. In Gujarat, some respondents were not keen on talking about politics and focused only on the technical aspects of policy. However, a logical and coherent work strategy was adopted and attempts were made to cover all relevant stakeholders across the three states. Chhattisgarh was the easiest in terms of finding contacts and respondents and Gujarat the hardest, with many contacts declining to give interviews. For the sake of objectivity, an attempt has been made to clearly mention any prejudices I may carry in interviews, to include different types of stakeholders as respondents for the sake of appropriate representation of ground reality, and to cross-check information with key informants (Mehrotra, 2012).

Case studies were augmented with triangulation, a method that entails agreement from at least three stakeholders on a point to consider it a valid evidence (Guion, Diehl, and McDonald, 2011). Triangulation is a method used by qualitative researchers to check and establish 'validity' in their studies by analysing a research question from multiple perspectives. Data triangulation involves 'using different sources of information in order to increase the validity of a study', most often from different stakeholders. To regard a finding as valid, and reflecting ground reality, the number of respondents in agreement has to be at least three. The authors provide an example when they are assessing the impact of a social programme, where the different stakeholders constitute participants, other researchers, programme staff, and other community members (Guion et al., 2011). This is what I followed in this study, by focusing on few cases and gathering multiple views on them from different stakeholders.

Operationalising objective: Choosing sites and interviewees

The fieldwork for this study was conducted at three levels – state, district, and village. Out of these, maximum attention was focused on understanding the power dynamics at the state level by studying the functioning of political parties and exploring their relations with the farmer lobby. There were several challenges during the course of the fieldwork. First, some stakeholders were more difficult to approach than others. Bureaucrats proved difficult to access and their views repetitive; therefore, their direct views have been included sparsely in this study. However, this challenge was resolved through persistent contact and communication with most other stakeholders, such as traders, businesspersons, political party workers, and journalists. They proved to be much more accessible and willing to share information. Second, not all state governments had the reputation of being forthcoming in sharing information. For instance, Gujarat is one state where the government has been known for its tight control on information. Therefore, building a vertical linkage from class to state was a challenge. To circumvent this, a pilot survey was conducted in each state, based on advice from academics and activists from both Delhi and the respective state. I met academics in each state to make a list of districts to be visited and ascertain the location of the big farmer lobby. The pilot survey would take a week to 10 days before embarking on the phase of interviews. Third, there were security issues. In particular, Chhattisgarh has been going through periods of severe unrest owing to tribal displacement and the rise of Naxalism,[44] and the state is reputed for its oppression of civil society activists. One example is the case of Dr Binayak Sen, who was imprisoned[45] on charges of sedition for his contact with Maoists. Even before I reached India to start the fieldwork, I had to be cautious at every stage of acquiring information, and even meeting people became a constraint. Unfortunately, the security risks were multiplied since I am a woman. I had male family members accompany me in the initial phase of my work in Chhattisgarh, and where I did not, I faced adversity in the field.

Fieldwork was conducted first in Chhattisgarh, then Gujarat, and finally in Karnataka. At the state level, stakeholders were approached depending on contacts and availability, with a focus on tiller farmers, big farmers, traders, industrialists, *panchayat* leaders, senior officials in various ministries of each state, political party cadres, farmer leaders, state-level party leaders, senior journalists, and academicians working on these issues.

Data was collected by combining a number of methods, such as case study, participant observation, long interviews (semi-structured), and focus group discussions (FGDs). Semi-structured checklist interviews were conducted at the state and district levels, and a checklist was used for these to ensure all relevant points had been addressed. FGD proved to be more time efficient with small farmers. As pointed out by Roche (1999), it provided an opportunity to observe peoples' interactions with each other, how their views and opinions developed and formed in conversations with one another, allowed group verification of information, and the debating and dialoguing involved in these FGDs helped generate new insights. Data was collected from seven districts in Chhattisgarh, eight in Gujarat, and nine in Karnataka to account for regional variations within the states. The number of interviews conducted were 47 each in Chhattisgarh and Gujarat and 40 in Karnataka. Since the evidence on political leaders was found inconclusive, evidence from newspapers, books, and reports by the Association for Democratic Reforms (ADR) published on the candidates' financial and criminal backgrounds during every assembly election have been incorporated to substantiate the qualitative trends with quantitative data.

The chapter has appraised the agrarian policy since 1990 and its effect on access to different inputs – land, credit seed, fertiliser, and water (as necessitated by agricultural production) – on the supply side.[46] Different aspects of the agrarian policy have arguably opened new opportunities for the agrarian proprietary classes. Evidence showed privatisation of inputs has opened trade opportunities and informal credit lending, while high-value crops have created a fraction, the capitalist farmers reaping profit from agriculture. Seed and credit policies have paved a path to greater inequality within classes of farmers in particular. Class differentiation persists in an agrarian economy, as fractions within rich farmers are not equally placed. By delineating their means of accumulation, fractions and classes have been identified. The lumpy nature of technology has made sustenance harder for capital-poor farmers. The state has been playing an active role in forging these policies, which have fostered opportunity for some classes and oppression for others. Another policy that has helped accumulation through the political channel is reservation at the local state level. Arguably, one explanation for such policies could be the political settlement operating in each state, which has aided rent-seeking by members of deprived castes, who in turn aid accumulation by proprietary classes.

Notes

1. This is the year when the WTO agreement was signed.
2. The private sector was de-licensed and MRTP (Monopolistic and Restrictive Trade Practice) restrictions were removed. To promote growth, the government granted tax concessions to business and formulated regulations against strike; there were some efforts to discipline entrenched labour (Kohli, 2009: 156–57).
3. This includes those industries that supply feed stocks to the fertiliser industry (for example, Oil and Natural Gas Corporation and Indian Oil Corporation).
4. The need to cover three states and the distance travelled to meet the interviewees operated as constraints on the time spent with each interviewee. For many interviews, the first 15–20 minutes in a two-hour-long session would be spent talking about what I generally do, in order to build rapport. As a result, I was left with an hour to ask questions. This made it essential to ask focused and pointed questions. Therefore, I limited the questions to the production side and the inputs of production.
5. Yogendra Yadav (1999) terms it the 'second wave of democratisation', as the marginalised sections use democratic institutions to be included in the political system.

6. State means different things to scholars; for Levien (2011), it is the regional state, but for Bardhan, it is the national state.

7. Barbara Harriss-White defines rent as 'when a specified area is demarcated for sale of products [such as APMC], then it brings buyers and sellers together which leads to competitive pricing. In the case of evasion of competition, this becomes a source of rent seeking' (2008: 260).

8. The concept has been written extensively by David Harvey (2009), where he characterises the new imperialism – the one the world is experiencing since the 1970s – by over-accumulation. What underlies the process of ABD? It is an adaptation of the Marxist notion of primitive accumulation.

9. 'Rent seeking in air' is an expression for an income enjoyed by a class by the sheer ownership of resources such as land and capital in the form of machinery, without indulging in the productive process that generates a profit. Mushtaq Khan (2004), however, uses the term 'rent' to refer to the income generated from corruption and co-option of public resources.

10. A village in Tamil Nadu where Harriss-White has conducted field surveys for decades.

11. In Chapter 2, we outlined the classifications of rural propertied classes by Ramchandran et al. (2010) and Lerche. To recapitulate, the distinct sense in which the two classes, namely landlords and big farmers, are referred to in the thesis is that the former is an urban-bound rentier class whereas the latter is generating surplus from agriculture and involved in other means such as trade, input sale, moneylending, and government jobs, and maintaining closer links to rural life. Neither class involves itself in self-cultivation. The third fraction mentioned is that of the capitalist farmers who have taken up technology-intensive agriculture and generate huge profit from agriculture itself, thus engaging in capitalist agriculture.

12. This was the case in 2011 when fieldwork was conducted. Right after that the new land acquisition policy was introduced in 2012.

13. The power to take public property for public use.

14. The only exception is Jammu and Kashmir.

15. It is mandatory to use only 50 per cent of the land acquired under the SEZ Act for industrial purposes. The rest can be used as the private companies deem fit.

16. Prime land is defined as land with irrigation or land that gives two crops or more per year.

17. Walter Fernandes (2014) highlights how those dependent on land for livelihood but not direct owners of land are adversely affected by such land acquisitions.

18. This policy is not discussed in the study, because it came into force after my fieldwork, towards the end of my doctoral study.

19. It is a caste that has historically been middle peasantry. Post-Independence, this class has shown tremendous upward mobility, invested in different agro-industrial sectors, and accumulated land, becoming the most important caste among the big farmers.

20. It has the same double meaning as Marx used: free to become a wage labourer, and deprived from other means to make a living.

21. For further details, see http://www.investkarnataka.co.in/assets/downloads/integrated agribusinessdevelopmentpolicy.pdf (accessed on 18 July 2018).

22. The first phase began in 1969 with nationalisation of 14 commercial banks with the objective of enhanced rural liquidity. The second phase began in the 1980s with emphasis on directed credit under the Integrated Rural Development Programme (Ramachandran and Swaminathan, 2001).

23. Under the Narasimham Committee's recommendations.

24. 'Gatekeepers act as intermediaries between villagers and state officials, merchants, etc. in interactions which may benefit one or both parties. Such interactions – securing votes, distributing government resources, accessing a police officer, etc. – are often informal and involve a fee for the gatekeeper' (Pattenden, 2005: 15).

25. James Manor (2004) uses the term in the context of Karnataka.

26. It implies those farmers who do not cultivate themselves, mainly big and middle farmers.

27. To note, a significant difference exists between the Green Revolution period and the economic reform period; at a fundamental level, the post-reform period is driven by the private sector, whereas the Green Revolution period was under the direct control of the public sector.

28. Only 30 per cent of Indian agricultural land is irrigated. Rest of the crops are grown under rain-fed conditions and termed rain-fed agriculture. It refers to the areas with very low or no irrigation. Dry land crops are those cops that are grown in these areas.

29. Certified seeds are those seeds that meet the standards laid down by the Government of India. The certificate works as a quality assurance. It is up to three generations of seed from the foundation seed that is considered a certified seed. The production and distribution of quality/certified seeds is primarily the responsibility of the state governments.

30. Accumulation by dispossession is a concept propounded by David Harvey (2009).

31. Extension service offices.

32. In the Indian context, Bt cotton and wheat dominate the literature on seeds. This limits a comprehensive political economy analysis of seed production and distribution.

33. For more details on yearly subsidy on fertilisers, see http://data.gov.in/dataset/details-year-wise-subsidy-fertiliser-products (accessed on 27 May 2014).

34. The state is seen operating in layers. The national politics is ascribed the highest layer, then the regional state and then district, which is often referred to as the local state.

35. High-value crops generally refer to non-staple agricultural crops such as vegetables, fruits, flowers, ornamentals, condiments, and spices.

36. The effects of procurement are regionally concentrated in four states, Punjab, Haryana, Uttar Pradesh, and Chhattisgarh.

37. Lerche argues in essence that modern technology to give high yield requires seed and fertiliser to be adopted with water and pesticides. He thus terms the technology a 'lumpy technology'.

38. The data are collected and published by the Directorate of Economics and Statistics, Department of Agriculture.

39. For details, see www.nhm.nic.in/Horticulture/RevisedNorms.pdf (accessed on 19 April 2014).
40. PRI is a three-tier local self-government institution operating at district, sub-district (*zilla*), and village levels.
41. Zia was the fourth President of independent Pakistan. He was an army general who assumed power and ruled between 1978 and 1988.
42. For more details, see Chapter 2.
43. Elected head of the *panchayat* institutions.
44. 'Naxal' is a generic term used in India to refer to extreme left guerrilla groups who are under the influence of the Communist Party of India-Maoist. The movement originated form a West Bengal village, named Naxalbari.
45. Indra Sinha, 'A Plea for Binayak Sen,' *The Guardian*, 14 April 2011.
46. 1991–1997 was the period when the economic reforms were being initiated and implemented. So, it took that long to see the effects of policy shift.

❖

4

Chhattisgarh

New State, New Opportunities for Old Class Domination

Overview

This chapter addresses three primary concerns. First, what kind of political settlement is operating in the newly formed state of Chhattisgarh. Second, what has been the impact of (class) interest on the state apparatus with respect to agricultural policies. Third, in the era of liberalisation, has the market's free play caused a retreat of the state from the sector of agriculture? Additionally, with regard to the consequences of prevailing agricultural policies, if the existing three proprietary classes have transformed themselves, remained unaffected, or have been replaced by new classes since the formation of the state. Land acquisition policy and the political economy around it have been addressed as well. Simultaneously, the implications of these policies on the different fractions of rich farmers and their means of accumulation alongside the other two dominant proprietary classes – industrial capitalist and petty bourgeoisie – have been developed.

Chhattisgarh was created under the Madhya Pradesh Reorganisation Act, 2000. Its creation was more a decision of the national political parties than having been driven by the struggle for regional autonomy under the Chhattisgarh *Mukti Morcha* (Berthet and Kumar, 2011; Tillin, 2013). The popular story is that the high proportion of tribal (*adivasi*) population, who had a claim to a separate state, was the basis for the formation of the state. The new state would make things favourable for the tribal population, who would then be able to assert themselves more in the new political entity; this would turn development in their favour. However, arguably, this was not the only reason for the new state formation. The concentration of natural resources fostered the need to make the region into a political entity, so as to facilitate smoother economic access to the resources (Berthet and Kumar, 2011). The state has registered high incidence of food insecurity and low human development. What really has happened since to the political economy unfolds in the following sections.

Geographically, Chhattisgarh is divided into hills in the north and south and plains in the centre. The total population of the state is 26 million (approx.) as per the 2011 census. Scheduled Tribes, who form one-third of the population, inhabit the hills. The Scheduled Castes (11.61 per cent) and other communities, including the Other Backward Classes, form the remaining 55 per cent of the population and live in the central plains. The arterial Howrah–Mumbai railway line passes through Bilaspur (headquarters of South East Central Railway) dividing the state roughly into the northern and southern regions, with the more developed parts of the state located in the immediate north and around this famous line. The southern districts are underdeveloped, and have witnessed severe Naxal disturbances and faced state oppression in the last decade. Naxals are also active in certain areas of the neighbouring states of Andhra Pradesh, Jharkhand, and Orissa. The state apparatus has limited access to these parts, and even food supply and government schools are few. With little physical link and no political link to the state, Abujmarh, a hilly region spread across three districts, operates like a 'liberalised zone', hence functionally not under the state though within the boundaries of the state (Guha, 2010). Lately, the government has tried to reclaim this area through military intervention under Operation Green Hunt.[1]

Between 2000 and 2010, Chhattisgarh's economy grew at 10 per cent annually, and the state has consistently maintained its position in the top five fastest growing states in India. It was third among the Indian states in 2007–08 in receiving investments and slipped to the fourth position in 2011–12 in attracting FDI with a fall in total (domestic and foreign) investment in the financial year (*Indian Express*, 2008; *Times of India*, 2012a).[2] Backward states such as Orissa and Chhattisgarh have emerged as real competitors to the old big players, such as Gujarat.

Sectoral distribution: Economy shifting to the service sector

According to the available secondary data on income and livelihoods, the per capita net state domestic product (NSDP) in Chhattisgarh stood at ₹12,476 in 2001–02. The per capita NSDP has increased at an average rate of about 2 per cent per annum at constant (1993–94) prices since then and by 2009–10 it was 11 per cent. As shown in Table 4.1, the share of agriculture in the state's NSDP has fallen by 20 per cent between 2001 and 2010. During the same time, the tertiary sector's contribution to the NSDP has more than doubled. The shift in population from primary to other sectors has decreased marginally, by 1 per cent over the period.

Table 4.1 Sectoral shift as percentage of NSDP

	2001–02	*2009–10*
Agriculture	38	18.65
Industry	38.5	31.74
Services	24	49.61

Agriculture is the predominant occupation in Chhattisgarh with 80 per cent of the population engaged in the sector. The central plains of Chhattisgarh are referred to as the 'rice bowl' of India. Paddy is the staple crop, and crops such as coarse grains, maize, wheat, pulses, oilseeds, and groundnut are cultivated. The region has abundant capacity for cultivation of fruits, vegetables, and other varieties of high-value crops. Nevertheless, on the composite index of food insecurity mentioned in the report of the state of food insecurity in rural India, states such as Jharkhand and Chhattisgarh appear in the 'very high' level (Vijayshankar, 2005). Minor forest produce such as lac, tendu leaves (tobacco), bamboo, honey, sal, and seed contribute to the state's economy. The government claims to pay special attention to boost the use of irrigation facilities, but even after a decade of assuming power, the area under irrigation was low at 33.1 per cent against the national coverage of 46 per cent (Government of Chhattisgarh, or GoC, 2012). Since irrigation is available to very few villages, most farmers can undertake only single cropping, which prevails across the state (Bhakar et al., 2007). Taking a disaggregated view, the plains have 43 per cent of cultivable land under irrigation, while a mere 5 per cent in the southern districts and 11 per cent in the northern districts are under irrigation. Women play a significant role in agricultural production. Traditional methods of removing husks are common and often performed by women. Women also take a lead in gathering forest produce used in households and sold in nearby weekly markets.

When it comes to cropping pattern, food crops continue to dominate the cropping area in the Chhattisgarh region, occupying 77 per cent of the net sown area (GoI, 2012); kodo-kutki (millet), primarily grown in the Bastar region, and maize are next in line. These are consumed by the local population. Soybean and sunflower cover about 100,000 hectares. The kharif crops grown here are paddy, urad, arhar, jowar, and maize. The rabi crops include til, alsi, moong, mustard, and gram. The kharif crop (summer crop) forms the main source of income. Collection and sale of forest produce and other forest-related work supplement the meagre agricultural incomes for STs.[3] Crafts form another source of income. Capitalist agriculture is at the stage of inception.

A few difficulties faced by the agricultural sector include a consistent fall in water table, poor employment opportunities to the extent that an estimated 87 per cent of the labour force does not find employment all year round, price fluctuation, partial procurement of paddy, and shift in cropping pattern erasing traditional crops such as millets. Debt afflicts those who want to adopt commercial crops, and informal sources charge exorbitant rates of interest, which makes the adoption harder.

The political landscape

Following a brief discussion on economy, this section paints a sketch of politics since 2000. Raman Singh of the BJP had served a full term as the Chief Minister of the state and was in power for a second term at the time this field study was conducted in 2011–12. The BJP claimed that their electoral victory was a reflection of people voting for better infrastructure – power, water, and roads. The election campaign drew on socio-cultural appeals, but the main plank used by the party was the 'anti-conversion' issue (against Christian missionaries), around which it consolidated the tribal majority. It used schools to inculcate the politics of Hindutva among the tribal population by including Hindu scriptures and practices as a part of the curriculum (Chattopadhyay, 2015).

Engineer (2003) attributed the BJP's success to two electoral strategies. First, it adopted a more secular and development-based agenda after its leaders failed to evoke Hindu sentiments in the parliamentary elections. 'Good governance', based on the agenda of international organisations such as the United Nations and World Bank, worked well as an electoral promise. Provision of good roads, PDS, and water became some of the key issues around which the BJP rallied its agenda. Second, it appealed to Hindu sentiments to consolidate the community's votes. In doing so, the BJP received strong support from the Rashtriya Swayamsevak Sangh (RSS),[4] which mobilised support among three sections – tribals, dalits, and the OBCs – and even formed a committed cadre base in remote Naxalite-controlled areas of Bastar (Jaffrelot, 1996: 3207). The RSS leaders have claimed that their work in *vanwasi ashrams*[5] in tribal areas has earned dividends. The RSS has been concentrating on tribal areas and working on generating pride in their 'Hindu' identity, despite the fact that the tribals are not Hindus (Basu, 2015).[6] The BJP came to power in Chhattisgarh for a third term in 2013 and continues to dominate the political scene. They rode on the success of an effective PDS mechanism, *anganwadi*,[7] and elections at the *panchayat* level in rural areas, and speedy urbanisation, mining, development in Raipur and Korba, and adopting an overall market-oriented approach in the urban areas. A similarity between Chhattisgarh and the other BJP home state, Gujarat, becomes relevant here. During the post-Godhra[8] carnage, tribals and dalits were used on a large scale to massacre Muslims. As reported, people in the tribal areas of Baroda and Panchmahal districts were massacred. This led to these social groups joining the BJP support base. The Congress has not employed any such organised intervention among the tribal communities and had taken these tribal votes for granted. In Chhattisgarh, which used to be a traditional Congress stronghold, the party lost heavily and the BJP was the main beneficiary of tribal votes. A similar trend can be seen in Jharkhand state, another primarily tribal constituency. Cultural questions provide an important background to the study, though are not pursued as central to it, since it seeks to answer questions of political economy.

Key findings from fieldwork

Owing to the state being new, research and available literature focusing on Chhattisgarh was limited. Further, left insurgency movements such as Naxalism/Maoism had rendered the region difficult to investigate.

The fieldwork for this study was largely based in Raipur, the state capital of Chhattisgarh. Out of a total of 47 interviews and 3 FGDs conducted in the state, 30 were undertaken in Raipur. Others were done in 8 nearby districts, namely Jagdalpur in the south and Durg, Bemetara, Bilaspur, Dhamtari, Korba, and Janjgir-Champa in the central plains that have a concentration of big and middle farmers, as highlighted in Figure 4.1.

The total number of interviewees in Chhattisgarh was 47, out of whom 19 were farmers (primarily big), 10 were academics working with state institutions, 7 were social activists or development professionals, 4 were journalists, 5 were state officials and politicians from various political parties, and 2 were private fertiliser company employees, as shown in Figure 4.2. A farmer could well be a state official or a social activist or a petty bourgeoisie, because these are not water-tight categories. Hence, the farmer might be counted in two categories. Therefore, the sum of the subgroups might exceed the total. Three FGDs were held – first in Bilaspur with female small farmers (August, 2011), the second in Durg with youngsters (18–20 years) studying in a District Institute of Education and Training, who were all from rural backgrounds (September, 2011), and the third in Raipur with big farmers belonging to OBC fighting for better compensation in lieu of their land taken over for the Naya Raipur project (September, 2011).

Figure 4.1 Chhattisgarh – districts visited and regional divisions

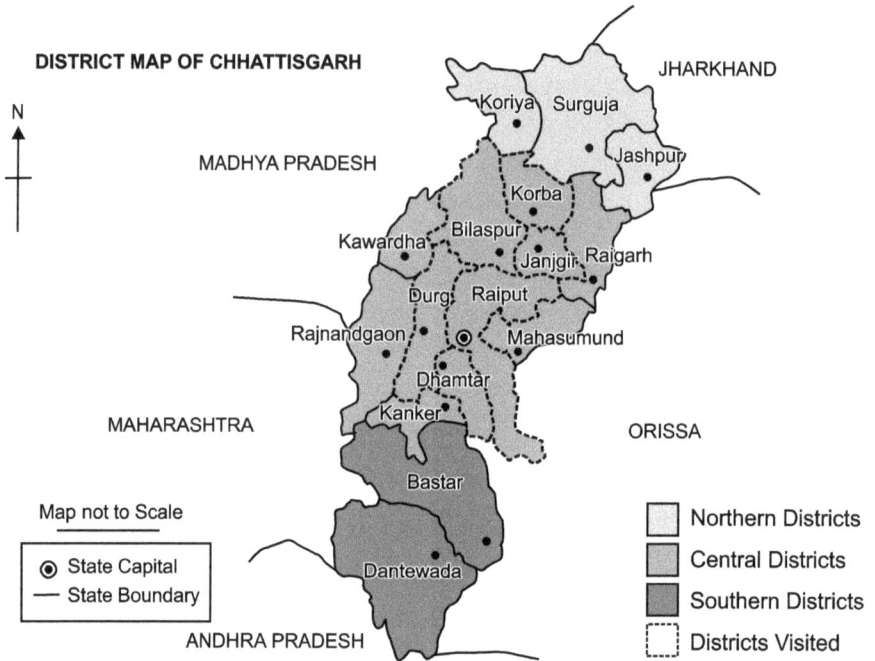

Source: Maps of India.

Figure 4.2 Occupational breakup of interview respondents

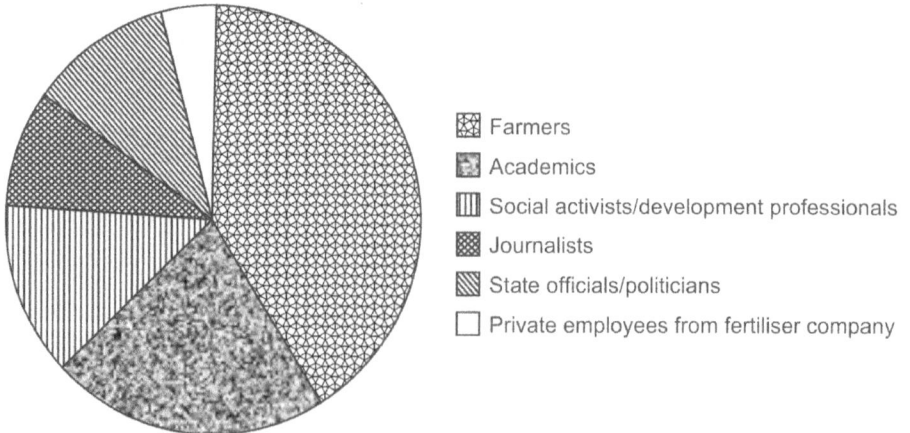

- Farmers
- Academics
- Social activists/development professionals
- Journalists
- State officials/politicians
- Private employees from fertiliser company

Balance of power and lobby politics

This section discusses the political settlement or dominant class constellation of the state, alongside their means of accumulation and their relations with different political actors. Several respondents stated that among sectors, agriculture has been neglected, and primary industries – those that extract raw materials from nature, such as oil extraction and mining – have been offered favourable conditions to grow. This is explicit in government policies and by the support for primary and big industries such as cement and steel, as triangulated in interviews. For example, Jhanjgir-Champa is the most irrigated district with 77 per cent of its agricultural land under irrigation, and traditionally an SC-majority area with large landholdings. The Rajnandgaon area of the district has Khurji settlers from Maharashtra, and they own more than 20 acres of landholding on an average. In 2001, the government filed an affidavit that the Hasdeo dam located in the district should not provide water for *rabi* (winter) crops, because water from the dam would be used for industrialisation. With public irrigation water diverted to industry, in this instance, the only farmers who can survive are those who can resort to private means of irrigation. The subsidy provided for drip and sprinkler irrigation had been increased until 2014 to encourage private irrigation. Since 2011, the district has also seen 54 power plants approved on agricultural land, most of which were being used for double cropping. The respondents saw these developments as a clear case of neglect of farmers and agriculture (Mishra, Bilapur, 2011; Singh, 2011).

At the same time, agriculture has received 10 per cent of state plan allocation since 2005, which is the highest among the three states under scrutiny.[9] The displacement of farmers, skewed water access, and seasonal unemployment need to be understood in the light of the high budgetary share allocated to agriculture. The political settlement operating in the state has a huge bearing on the way the state's resources are distributed. The class that controls the economy is the trader class (Berthet and Kumar, 2011). As observed during fieldwork, this class has been fast transforming into an industrial capitalist class since the formation of the new state. The new state has brought in opportunities in mining and industry. Land acquisition for corporate projects has been made easier, and laws such as environmental clearance, land ceiling, or stipulation disallowing purchase of land in Schedule V areas have been flouted (a lawyer in Bilaspur interviewed in 2011 and an activist in Korba, also interviewed in 2011). The surplus generated by merchants tapping into these new opportunities has been steadily invested in industries. The class is chiefly constituted of Agarwals, Gujaratis, and Sindhis, with some Bihari Brahmins, who dominates trade, agribusiness, real estate, cement, and mining (Berthet and Kumar, 2011).[10]

Within the dominant class, the Agarwal community deserves special mention. They form the core of the capitalist class – mercantile and industrial. 'The Agarwals are the kings here', stated Jha (interview in September 2011). In the 1950s, they came to Madhya Pradesh to trade in kosa silk which was produced in the region and had a huge market all over the country. Internally, a rigid and orthodox community, they steadily bought land and soon gained control of the market in spices, rice, precious forest products, such as saffron (*kesar*), and nuts. They have come to exert tremendous control on the natural resources of the state, and lately have extended their control to mining by investing in primary industries such as aluminium making from bauxite and coal mining.[11] Apart from the Agarwals, Sindhis are another important business community. They settled in this region after the Partition, and originally lived in refugee camps located in Indore and Nagpur, from where they moved to erstwhile Madhya Pradesh. What sets them apart from Agarwals is that despite economic influence, they have been relatively distant from the state apparatus.

A large amount of investment has been poured into this state owing to its natural resources. Along with regional and national players such as the Agarwals and Sindhis, international players such as Vedanta and Lafarge Cement are investing in this region. Industrial capitalists were found investing in political elections because they need political allies to run an efficient and profitable business. Investments ought to be protected by a friendly policy regime for the sake of rapid industrialisation. Access to land, labour, and water are a few such elements that have been channelled towards industry by the state. Instances of capitalists entering political parties to fight elections were noted, while their close ties with the BJP as a whole were evident. Their partners in the state ensure that business at the ground level functions smoothly, and both players reap huge profits from these projects. An ADR report from 2013 has noted that between 2008 and 2013, the percentage of legislative assembly election candidates from the BJP and the Congress who are *crorepatis* (that is, have assets worth more than ₹ 10 million), has increased from 22 to 71 and 49 to 77, respectively. The average assets per member of legislative assembly (MLA) in the 2013 legislative assembly election for BJP candidates was ₹21.9 million, which for the Congress Party was ₹174.9 million. The average asset for independent MLAs was ₹74.7 million (*Times of India*, 2013b). By implication, more rich people are getting into political parties and elected positions. It remains to be seen who they are in terms of class position.

The traditional business community has managed to entrench itself into positions of political power that can influence the content of policy. This came across clearly in an interaction with Sriram Wagela in Raipur – a Gujarati businessman who settled in Chhattisgarh 50 years ago, but continues to own businesses in Gujarat. He owns a quarry and is an elected representative. Chewing *paan* (betel leaf), he expressed disbelief in and disregard for the people of Chhattisgarh. 'They drink a lot and at sundown, become a source of nuisance,' were his words. Wagela's interests lie with the capitalist class, but his political portfolio demands him to look after marginalised sections of the rural society. These are conflicting interests – the motive to secure profit even through extractive means perhaps dominates other responsibilities. He also has the ability to influence policies to realise such profit motives, as did many high-profile ministers who were often capitalists themselves and entered politics after the formation of Chhattisgarh state. A journalist, Nitin Sahu argued, 'They have shares in all upcoming power plant projects and would do anything to see these projects sail smoothly. So, when they are the decision makers of agricultural policies, the policies are bound to be against tiller farmers, as it is in their class interest to make land acquisition easy' (interview in Bilaspur, October 2011). The adjudicator and beneficiary – meaning those who make and enforce policy/laws and those who are meant to benefit from a policy – should ideally be two different set of actors in a modern democracy for the sake of justice. But in this case there was an overlap between the two, turning policies into a biased tool. Through the Marxian paradigm, the phase of capitalism where the capitalists can give up direct control of the state was not where Chhattisgarh is situated (Poulantzas 1973). In fact it is under the tight grip of the capitalists, who partake in every decision of the political apparatus. Thus, the state seemingly does not enjoy relative autonomy.

There are five important political lobbies in the state, as an academic Professor Reddy listed, namely rice-miller lobby, sponge-iron lobby, big-farmers lobby, mining-cement lobby, and liquor lobby. The list is not to suggest distinct interests because significant overlap of interests exists among these lobbies; capitalists often have investments and interests in multiple sectors. What follows is a discussion on what are the different lobbies operating, and what kind of state support they seek to accumulate, which determine their political demands.

The rice millers are traders from mostly Marwari, Sindhi, Sikh, and Gujarati communities. They require paddy at cheap prices to run a profitable business, and the government facilitates this by procuring paddy from the *mandis*.[12] Government procurement is only done over three months a year and is limited to *kharif* crop; therefore, for the *rabi* (winter) crop, the farmers have no choice but to sell to the middlemen or traders at exploitative rates. Apart from this, the government offers a heavy subsidy for setting up godowns (warehouses). Respondents indicated that up to 80 per cent of the subsidy for these projects has been cornered by rice millers who now own private godowns.[13] Raipur,

Dhamtari, Durg, Bilaspur, and Mahasamund districts together account for more than 50 per cent of the rice mills' daily milling capacity (Chhattisgarh Government), and 60 per cent – 896 in number – of all mills are located in these districts. These are taken on rent by the FCI[14] and other government agencies to store rice. The policy to subsidise warehouse symbolises state funds being directed to creating a stronger capitalist class, who can then take the agenda of profiteering forward instead of building a stronger public sector. Since the government does not own these godowns and instead subsidises them, it makes it easy for the traders to own them. The small and marginal farmers, who cannot afford storage on their own, are forced to sell their produce right after harvest at the price quoted by traders, often low prices. Speculating in crops is in the hands of the middlemen with urban connections who belong to petty bourgeoisie and rarely, rich farmers. Why can they speculate? Their standing power to wait until the season changes and prices rise makes it possible. While big and capitalist farmers have made economic gain from speculative practices, they have one more channel of gain: they are of significance to the political parties. The government needs the support of the rich farmers because of their control on rural votes and ability to garner support at the grassroots level, given their socio-economic power. This is particularly true given the fact that in many parts of Chhattisgarh, traditional loyalties and allegiance to erstwhile landlords such as the Judeos and Singhdeos (Jashpur and Raigarh) are still prevalent. Similarly, Thakur or Chandrakar enjoy similar social status in other districts such as Raipur, Dhamtari, and Janjgir-Champa. These classes, therefore, formed the dominant lobbies till the end of 1990s, throwing up eminent politicians like Shyama Charan Shukla (Congress party). They have lost the dominant position to other lobbies such as cement, real estate, and mining, though they continue to maintain deep ties with the state.

Dominant class members who have assumed political office were found using their position for furthering their source of accumulation. Recently, they maintain their legitimacy with the masses by distributing patronage. This was found in the case of a political leader, who comes from a predominantly tribal district that is also a hub of industrial growth within the state. He was regarded as a symbol of the common man – a tribal and political worker when he fought elections. Today, he owns a rice mill and has recently started a 500 mega-watt power plant. Politics has acted as his source of accumulation which is a common path among farmers using their identities to seek political leverage. He maintains a huge rest house in Raipur, where food is prepared for 100 to 200 people each day. Whoever from his constituency visits Raipur is welcome to eat and stay there free of cost. As a villager narrated the story, he noted that this helps them a lot when they have to go to Raipur for any work, as it is expensive for them to rent a room or eat in the capital city (interview in Korba, September, 2011).

However, Jivan Haran, the Left Party President, said in his interview that the rice mill lobby has recently lost a part of its authority vis-à-vis other lobbies. This is caused by a kind of monopolisation by the Raipur millers who are exercising greater control on the rice trade owing to their modern machinery and capacity to produce more. The smaller millers are now forced to sell their produce to Raipur millers. The government has refused to allot single wagons in goods trains to the small millers, so they cannot transport their produce to other states. This has brought down their capacity to negotiate for higher prices or sell their products in the deficient states. Only those millers who can send a truck or train wagon full of rice can now trade. The respondent suggested that this monopoly has made these mill owners effectively partners to the government, instead of a lobby. Dinesh Deewan (interviewee from Raipur, July 2011), a petrol pump owner and a politically well-connected capitalist, confirmed the trend in the state.

Two other lobbies operating in the state are liquor and mining. The capitalists from across these lobbies have reaped benefits from the new state, thus transforming from trade to industrial capital. Interestingly, despite operating as lobbies, the interest represented by each of these lobbies is not exclusive. Evidence showed that the rice mill owners or their kin are fast investing in mining and power plants. A mining company owner was reported to have stakes in real estate. Cement factory owners had stakes in other sectors. Hence, the class is accumulating from multiple sub-sectors, such as real estate, mining, quarry, rice mills, and cement.

One common interest pervades different lobbies or fractions of capitalists – keeping wages low by maintaining a pool of underemployed labour. Agriculture continues to work as a bargain sector, providing labour for industrial sector, as it did prior to liberalisation (Chakravarty, 1987). This is why the transfer of tiller farmers into the secondary sector as unskilled and semi-skilled industrial workforce has been crucial to ensure rapid economic growth. Displacement and dispossession of farmers in Chhattisgarh has been an important focus for scholars working on the state (Shah, 2010). Tiller farmers have been selling their land to industries in different pockets, given the unfeasibility of small-scale agriculture and coercion. As a senior technocrat and agriculturist stated, to remain in agriculture, 'the best position is that of the labourer; he does not have to worry about resources and profit. He just takes his day-to-day payment that has steadily increased in the last 4 years' (Raipur, September 2011). However, it cannot be concluded that all tiller farmers are willing to make this shift. It was evident from tribal farmers that they have not taken to the market ethics entirely and are still unwilling to part with their land. Interviews with tribal small farmers did not reflect a similar disdain for agriculture despite all the problems they were facing. On the contrary, they displayed eagerness to hold on to their land for cultural and emotional reasons (interview in Raigarh, 2012).

Migration has been on the rise in the state, particularly so from Champa district, owing to a very rapid rate of industrialisation. Richard Parry (2003) has presented evidence of migration in his study to another region in Chhattisgarh. However, migration from tribal districts is more seasonal than permanent. To quote a businessman, 'for attending every festival in the village, adivasis run back and overstay' (interviewee from Raipur, August 2011). Given their attachment to their native land, the tribal population make an erratic work force that is interested mainly in seasonal employment in the city, saving some money to spend in the village, and then moving back to the city to earn more. A mill owner mentioned in his interview that irregularity of labour is one of the key reasons why the mills have adopted machine-based processes.

In other interviews, dominating lobbies that had recurrent mention were rice millers, mining, and sponge iron. The media personnel reiterated that these lobbies do not represent distinct political interests. The owners of rice mills and other sectors are the same or their kin. The brother of a power plant owner heads the current (2011) Rice Millers' Association in the state, which operates as an organised lobby on the government. While interviewing a *Doordarshan* reporter, it was found that the rice millers return only 25 to 30 per cent of the paddy given to them for processing by the state granary, whereas on an average 65 to 67 per cent ought to be returned. The government does not question this, as in many cases, the rice mill owner is close to politicians.[15] The presence of such influential leaders who carry their class interest into the party probably explains the government's soft treatment of industries and support for other pressing issues, such as land grabbing. Thus, being in politics was observed to be gainful either directly or indirectly. The financial gain of elected leaders reflects in the following figure. In 2008, 22 MLAs who owned average assets of ₹12.7 million had assets of ₹31.6 million on average when re-elected in 2013. Hence, the average asset growth is of 147 per cent (ADR, 2013).

Tight networks among proprietary classes

This section brings out the interconnection between different proprietary classes, operating at different levels of state administration. Owing to extensive mining activities, Korba district has witnessed agricultural land being diverted for other purposes; more land is in the process of acquisition, and several landholdings have fallen barren or have reported poor fertility owing to pollution and inappropriate disbursal of industrial waste (interview of an activist in Korba, July 2011; PRIA, 2010). Given that the primary skill of these local inhabitants is agriculture, losing their land has translated into a loss of livelihood, forcing them to work as wage labourers (interviews in October 2011 and September 2011). An instance of a private company extracting more coal than permitted by the state government was found out through a Right to Information (RTI) Act application filed by a local environmental activist.[16] Ironically, the government that sets the permissible limit of coal extraction per year has given an award to the company for its highest extraction, which is above the stipulated limit. The political connection of the company is such that illegal exploitation of natural resources and violation of environmental regulation are overlooked by state bureaucracy.

The nexus between petty bourgeoisie and capitalist class, on one hand, and between capitalists and political leaders, on the other, form the basis of undue accumulation by few and results in exclusion of competitors. With such relationships permeating every level of administration, economy does not foster competition the way a free market would be expected to operate. In fact, a kind of personal fusion was noted between the capitalist class and the state. One of the key contacts during the field study, Kamleshwar Jha, is a small businessman. To get each contract, he has to bribe state- and central-level ministers, who recommend the particular company that should be given the contract. Jha had bought three houses in government housing schemes, which he showed me; one house is in the lower-income colony and another in the middle-income colony.[17]

The petty bourgeoisie act as an ally for the capitalist. If need be, these petty bourgeoisie would go against the interests of their community. Caste and kin are weakened as economic interest takes precedence. Their motive is self-accumulation and often securing a permanent job in the companies. For this, they offer inroads into village land and put interests of members of other classes at stake.[18] Such an instance had surfaced in a small village where the kin member used the trust of his tribal group members to get signatures on land deals and sold off land to a private company for a good monetary reward for himself. This was also evident in a scam in Chhattisgarh in June 2011, when a minister's son was reported as acting as a *dalaal* (land broker) for Videocon, an electronic company (*Times of India*, 2011). Being a tribal, he transferred tribal lands to his name and then sold it to Videocon. Even though it surfaced as a notorious case, this is a commonplace process of land acquisition in the state. In fact, Bilaspur and Korba have hundreds of such agents (interviews of Pramanik from Bilaspur, 2011, Shukla from Raipur, 2011, and Dixit from Korba, September 2011). They have moved from rural to urban areas, and have started a shop or small business in the town. However, they work as *dalaal* providing information on good quality land to big companies, acquiring land as small plots from farmers, and selling them to big corporates. They often have connections and kin in such villages, whose land they buy. On need basis, they even negotiate prices on behalf of the companies. There are also cases where the *sarpanch* (headman) acts as a *dalaal*, because he has political connections with the higher authorities and wants to make the most of the opportunities the market has brought in.

Environmental activists in the districts of Bilaspur, Raigarh, and Korba reported that industries and mining have resulted in drying up of the natural streams and lowering of the level of the water table, creating acute water problems in the villages. Parashar (2010) in his study finds similar environmental hazards caused by methane mining. The health of soil has deteriorated in the villages around the mining area in Raigarh and Korba, owing to presence of fly ash in the area and little effort from the private companies to adhere to environmental regulations. The disposal system of coal ash is also ineffective, and thus it has been steadily contaminating the bodies of water. Through water bodies, toxic contents have entered into the crop cycle, and the same water supply is used by cattle and households.[19] Therefore, mining is adversely affecting the day-to-day lives of the local inhabitants, particularly in Champa, Korba, and Raigarh districts. Environmental concerns are very high among civil society organisations that are addressing it through writing in newspapers, advocacy, and filing RTI applications (Purohit, 2013; Sharma, 2011). Similar observations were made by a woman lawyer who has been filing public litigation on behalf of the local people and against private companies with twin purposes – to get compensation for affected people and challenge the private companies for violation of environmental regulations. This has contributed to a crisis in agriculture, forcing tiller farmers to out-migrate from villages in search of employment elsewhere (interviews of activists from Bilaspur, Raigarh, and Korba, August 2011).

Industries promised employment to villagers at the time of acquiring their land for industry, but rarely was this promise met. Most of the displaced villagers work as daily wage earners, and none of them have been employed on the regular pay roll of the company. The officials claim that they are unskilled and lazy, so employing them would be a burden on industries. There are no industrial training institutes, so transition for the huge mass of small farmers and agricultural labour to skilled labour force capable of employment in the secondary sector seemed rather difficult. Most labour used in mining sites are from the other states, especially Bihar and Jharkhand. Another observation was that with numerous farmers[20] losing land, which is significant given that the tribal lands fall under statutory non-alienable Schedule V[21] areas, a new pool of labour is being created that cannot be absorbed in skilled and formal employment. It is resulting in casualisation of labour, as the labourers cannot continue with self cultivation any longer, either due to loss or poor productivity of land due to release of chemical waste in water bodies. The respondents argued that tiller farmers are facing increased hardship due to these factors (three interviews, 2011: tribal farmer from Korba, non-tribal farmer, and senior official from Bilaspur). Displacement and dispossession were observed across the districts; outright displacement exists, and so do numerous tiller farmers' struggles under deteriorating land and water conditions.

Classes within farmers and their caste identity

One of the objectives of this study is to understand the different classes of farmers that operate and their political interests. Theoretically, and in line with classic agrarian class analyses on India, it was suggested that this was best done by basing it on empirical observations and focusing on five main classes.

Landlord: Rentier and urban-bound

It is well known that no systematic abolition of *zamindari* (landlordism) or proper land reform was undertaken by the Madhya Pradesh government. Field interviews reconfirmed that the ceilings were never adhered to seriously. One example of this is the Rajgond landlords, who continue to own major landholdings. The Rajgonds ruled over tribal villages in Bastar and Jabbalpur in the pre-Independence era. It is their dominance that gave this region the name 'Gondwana' (Varma, 1995). They originated from Rajasthan and settled in erstwhile Madhya Pradesh, parts of which later became Chhattisgarh. In post-Independence India, they sent their younger generations to colleges in New Delhi and even to foreign universities to study, for example the Kanker royal family sent their children to Delhi University.[22] They have come to occupy positions within urban professional classes, including the bureaucracy. The landlords (feudal lords of princely states) have entered politics, diversified to business and, as said, also continue to own big landholdings. However, agriculture is certainly no longer the main source of their accumulation; neither does it define their class position.

In this region, the pre-Independence landlords were referred to as Gotias and consisted of members from Thakur, Kumri, and a few Satnami (SCs) communities. Farmers with large holdings from within these castes have shown upward mobility and engaged in urban migration since Independence, and flourished particularly, in the past two decades. Thakur is one such caste that has traditionally owned large landholdings. It is said locally that they migrated to this region over the past 100 years from Madhya Pradesh and Rajasthan. They now commonly use surnames such as Singhdeo and Judeo. Originally Rajputs, they continue to command a lot of respect from the tribal population. The Thakurs have entered the realm of politics, as in the case of Dilip Singh Judeo in Raigarh. His huge landholdings stretch from Raigarh to Jashpur, two adjacent districts. His son was a MP from Congress party, while Dilip Singh was in the BJP. They enjoy significant political power cutting across party lines. 'The father and son are the kings of these districts', as a social worker from district Raigarh stated. Government jobs and benefits of government schemes are said to come through them; hence, there is prevalence of strong patron–client relation. The local state operates on strong traditional hierarchies, where the Judeos are addressed as 'raja' (king), and at the same time Dilip Singh has held ministerial position in the union level of Indian Government. They have forged ties into politics, business, and education, but they have not transformed into capitalist farmers. Agriculture is not the primary source of their accumulation, neither do they consistently invest in the sector.

What became of the traditional big and middle farmer?

The class of middle and big farmers have an overlap with castes such as Chandrakar, Sahu, or Kumri, who are a part of the OBCs. With the formation of a new state, these farmers migrated to urban centres for white-collar jobs or trade. Over the last 15 years, they have been able to tap into the opportunities that industrialisation has brought into the state. They have come to constitute the petty bourgeoisie, but have continued to retain their landholding and in some instances even acquire more land. They have also diversified into government services by making use of caste reservation, and related opportunities (Tillin, 2013). However, they are not decisive in terms of political power.[23]

In Dhamtari, Bilaspur, and Korba districts, the landholdings of big and middle farmers from OBCs were of better quality and located closer to the highway or main road. This gave them better access to markets and towns. Over the past three decades, the fractions of rural proprietary class (rich farmers), big farmers, landlords and even middle farmers, primarily from the plains have tended to acquire higher education and move to urban areas by procuring jobs in the service sector. The transition has been aided by the state as seen in Karnataka in the 1980s. They have found more support under the ruling party, BJP, who by using OBC-based politics carefully and by providing reservation in state bureaucracyhave gained the loyalty of these classes (Berthet and Kumar, 2011).

In words of a respondent, well-off Indian farmers prefer investing outside the sector of agriculture. Purav Mishra, a farmer, scholar, and political leader, stated that agriculture has become non-viable, leading to agricultural surplus flowing out of the sector. Few are interested in investing to consolidate their landholdings. This has been caused by government policies, which have led to falling returns from agriculture, for example, offering poor prices for crops, such as paddy. Hence, farmers have opted to move their next generation to urban professions, primarily into the service sector. 'The first thing a big farmer would do is buy a house in Bilaspur.'[24] He accepted that he himself was not an exception (interviewee from Bilaspur, October 2011). A similar case of surplus flowing out of agriculture was observed in the Dhamtari district. Anand Chandrakar narrated that his family had moved to a town with four sons, about 20 years ago. The sons gained education and now work in urban centres. Two of them are in government service, and one is in the police. The family owns 30 acres of land and falls in the big farmer category. The eldest son has continued to live in the village and supervise the farm with the help of wage labourers, but is not keen to continue.

Similarly, several local interviewees mentioned that big farmers in Bilaspur and Dhamtari districts have moved to cities and leased out their land. Barring those employed in the services of Coal India Limited and Indian Railways, the rest of the urban population comprises rural middle and big farmers, as well as traders, as explained by a journalist (interview in Madhvi, Bilaspur, October, 2011). They tend to retain their landholdings and visit their villages periodically to collect rent. Owners and cultivators are entitled to equal shares of the crop. The cost of cultivation including seed, fertiliser, and labour is paid by the tenant. In some cases, the now city-based landowners also employ agricultural labourers. It could be inferred from the interviews that the middle farmers have managed to keep their landholding because of non-agricultural income from other sources, such as government employment. Agriculture may no longer be their primary source of income, but land is an asset that they still value. They are urban, but rent extraction links them to agriculture. This is also regarded as a source of power that is enjoyed by their caste groups.

The case studies indicate two conclusions – first, the big farmers and a few of the middle farmers, mostly from the OBCs and a few SCs, have taken on the class character of a petty bourgeoisie. They have access to political institutions either as part of bureaucracy or through the political parties. Second, compared to investment in other sectors, agriculture has lost its glory because of poor financial returns. Farmers with big holdings in Bilaspur and Dhamtari districts reflect a landlord class behaviour in relation to agriculture, as they are not investing in capital-intensive technology and are averse to commercial crops. Rent from agriculture is an important source of accumulation, but it is used to gain skills in order to settle in urban areas, where they seek white-collar and government jobs and, less frequently, enter trade. This is in contrast to the big farmers' behaviour in Raipur, Bemetara, and Durg since east and west Chhattisgarh display two different trends.

Emerging gentleman farmers

A class of urban investors has emerged, who buy farms of 100–200 acres, but have no interest or stakes in agriculture. Their interest in land is due to the fast-escalating appreciation of real estate in Chhattisgarh. Legally, they can be classified as farmers since they draw a part of their income from agriculture which helps evade taxes. Given the scale and technology involved in corporate agriculture, it is seen as a growth driver, and the state actively encourages such investors to put their capital in land. Monsanto, Reliance, Pepsi, and numerous corporates are investing in land for contract farming but reserving more land for non-agricultural purpose. The entry of new participants is leading to unequal competition in which real farmers, 80 per cent of whom are small and marginal, are finding it almost impossible to compete.

Tax exemption emerges as the biggest concession for the farmers. It is particularly conciliatory for big farmers who have moved on to capitalist farming and are eligible for paying taxes, or landlords whose primary source of income is no longer agriculture. The state's reluctance to impose any tax despite all the talks about fiscal discipline is a clear indication of these fractions of rich farmers being a part of the political settlement operating within the state. In fact, it would be fair to conclude that this is a sign of a weak state which does not challenge the status quo or alter the political settlement, and is deeply influenced by the dominant classes.

To summarise, big farmers survive by resorting to other means of accumulation such as input retailing, moneylending, tractor renting, and urban professions, while the middle farmers primarily sustain themselves by gainful employment in the public sector. However, it is the capitalist farmers who are the main gainers of the state's policies on agriculture. Big farmers thrive by extracting surplus from small and semi-medium farmers who face severe food insecurity (World Food Programme, 2008). The STs constitute 50 per cent of the poor people despite constituting only 33 per cent of the population, thus indicating the steep deprivation faced by the STs (World Food Programme, 2008). Based on police records, the Chhattisgarh *Kisan Sabha* has reported that the state has had nearly 9,000 farmer suicides over the past three years. Nagaraj (2008) ascribes a critical character to the agrarian crisis in the state, where small farmers are faced with poverty and dispossession with market forces penetrating the sector. A kind of polarisation has set in with the agrarian class structures not just persisting but deepening the gap between classes.

Key issues in agricultural policy

Chhattisgarh has been hailed as a farmer-friendly state. The highlights of the state's agricultural policy since 2006 have been in regard to its intensive agriculture, modernisation of inputs and technology, adoption of cash cropping such as horticulture, and rice procurement from farmers at MSP.

The state's Agrovision 2011–12 lays down that seed, fertiliser, pesticide, irrigation, transport to market, and credit are key to furthering growth in the sector and, therefore, they must be the focus of the state agricultural policy. Among the three schemes put forth by the government in the 2008 elections, 'payment of a bonus of ₹270 on procurement of every quintal of rice' was included. 'Chhattisgarh is a power-surplus state, so providing free supply to farmers' and 'giving concessions to farmers to dig tube well' have also been on the agenda of the government. It would be pertinent to mention that except the first one, the other two were started by the Congress government and continued by the BJP. No bonus has been distributed in the three years of the BJP rule, as reported in 2011. Moreover, the government has continuously supported the transfer of public water resources from agriculture to industry, leaving private source of irrigation as the only alternative available to farmers.

The government-run societies at the village level are entrusted with the responsibility of supplying seed and fertiliser to farmers at a subsidised rate. These are supposed to reach the villages in the month of April every year. The farmers place their demand village-wise and, on the basis of that, inputs are allocated. The only condition is that to avail loan one cannot be a defaulter in credit repayment. The borrower farmers[25] are given seeds and fertilisers first. These two conditions, being a borrower and a non-defaulter, make the big and few middle farmers the only ones eligible for government supply. As reflected in interviews with tiller farmers across five districts, supplies often reach the cooperative societies late, by which time the crop is ready to be harvested. As a result, these farmers are left at the mercy of the traders to save their crops. Their only option then is to take loans from the seed and pesticide dealers who thereby become claimants to their produce. Why do farmers buy these inputs from private dealers when the government offers them at a subsidised rate? The reason is that the state is often faced with shortage of fertilisers.

Fertiliser is procured by the central government. Fertilisers are mainly imported, and a few are manufactured in India, which are then distributed among the states for sale to farmers. Urea and potash, the two most commonly used fertilisers, are not produced in Chhattisgarh, and the state government has to depend on the centre for their allocation to farmers. Their demand exceeds the allocation. The state government claims that the shortage in fertiliser supply is caused by the central government, which has repeatedly disapproved the state's demand. The state government has no decisive role to play. Two points need to be noted in this regard. First, the disbursal of inputs is the responsibility of the state government that it has been failing to meet; second, the non-availability from government sources means having to buy the commodities from traders. Tiller farmers are often cheated by these traders, and the latter sell inputs in excess than required by using fear tactics. As discussed earlier, government procurement from the paddy farmers is limited to three months. For the remaining nine months of the year, farmers are dependent on private buyers who buy at less than the MSP. This acts as a disincentive for growing rice in the *kharif* season.

In the case of pesticides, the government's involvement is lesser than with regard to fertilisers, and the government does not give any subsidy. The distribution of pesticides is privatised, and both national and international players are doing well in capturing the market. Companies like DuPont have opened a new centre in Raipur after establishing their presence in Punjab, Maharashtra, and Gujarat. They chose wisely as the company had its highest sale in Chhattisgarh in the financial year 2010–11, reflecting an expanding market for agricultural inputs. Another company, Union Carbide, has increased its presence in the state over the last decade. They exert control on the lab-to-land extension work, and work closely with university and government departments. The cream of fresh graduates from agricultural universities are absorbed by these MNCs, and these well-paid professionals work hard to maximise sales of the company (interviews of Mishra, November 2011, and an MNC employee from Raipur, 2011). This shows how the professional class is siding with capitalist interests.

The state government continues to patronise the small farmers by making false promises to them. In the 2013 elections, Raman Singh promised ₹300 to each farmer if he won the elections and free power supply in the form of five horse-power pumps. In the 2008 elections, the promise was ₹270 per quintal of rice. However, once the election was over and the BJP was back in power, the government made the use of pumps chargeable. The pump set was distributed for free, but its usage was chargeable beyond 6,000 units, a limit that covers approximately 45 days of usage. Beyond this limit, farmers have to pay ₹2,000 per month for electricity usage (interviews of a technocrat and a local government member from Dhamtari, August 2011). Furthermore, the government has gradually receded from investing in surface irrigation, leaving water supply for agriculture in private hands, which has resulted in water supply being limited to those who can afford the capital investment. As Byres (1981) would argue, this is not a resource-neutral policy.

The government officials' interviews were most often repetitive and procedural. As an official Mr Kumar said, 'From this chair, I can say no more' to any question asked. They provide a rehearsed official version of the processes. But one thing that stood out is the understanding of a 'kisan/farmer'; Mr Kumar repeatedly mentioned that *kisan*s now face a lot of problems in hiring labour. They ascribed the new negotiating power of labour to NREGS, which has given them other opportunities to earn money. This is adversely affecting farming in this state. In effect, only those who employ *mazdoor*s or wage labour in his vocabulary are 'farmers' (*kisan*s), and he was concerned with the limitations this class is facing in cultivation. Another official I spoke to viewed rural social structure as a dualistic one, which is classified into farmers and agricultural labour. Anyone who tills his own land and works as agricultural labour does not qualify as farmer in his categorisation. Therefore, any policy envisioned by officials who operate with the notion of farmers as those owning land and employing labour is bound to be in favour of big farmers and capitalist farmers, thereby glancing over the requirements of tiller farmers/wage labourers.

The skewed nature of resource allocation gets further emphasised in the way agricultural extension services remain limited to the big and capitalist farmers alone. The focus of the government is on growth and diversification in agricultural production, and they incentivise those who can help the government achieve these goals. Quoting a respondent from Raipur, 'For agricultural growth to be made possible, efforts have been directed to farmers who can afford such a change. Small holdings of two–five acres cannot boost agricultural growth' (interviewee from Raipur in September 2011). Tiller farmers have poor credit-taking capacity and hardly ever have the resources to do high-value cropping, thereby categorising them as risk-averse.

Government officials blame the MGNREGS for the rise in wages – up to twice of the rate only a couple of years ago – and for all the difficulties faced by 'farmers'. Under the MGNREGS, ₹125 per day, with 100 days of work, has been assured to those on the roll. As a result, wage labourers demand ₹80 to ₹100 per day for agricultural work. Big farmers find it difficult to sustain agriculture, because returns in agriculture have not gone up proportionately, and higher wages eat into their profit margin. No mention is made of chemical inputs that have triggered similar rise in cost of cultivation. They envision that the solution lies in adopting appropriate technology that can salvage the farmers, although that would further heighten the cost. The overt faith in technology and disdain for labour was seen among many technocrats, indicating the course in which agricultural policies shall be directed.

Monopolisation of land and natural resources

Land is central to tribal lives and livelihood, and its centrality – the need to protect tribal land rights – was believed to be the reason behind the formation of Chhattisgarh. Land is also central to the capitalist class' interest. Since its inception, the state has seen an overt emphasis on rapid industrialisation such as mining and cement, which have caused displacement of agrarian population, particularly the tribals people and posed a threat to their livelihood. During the interviews, a veteran from the Congress party pointed out that industries in Chhattisgarh were of primary nature, with little effort to develop secondary or downstream industry. The capitalist class is simply interested in exploiting natural resources and extracting surplus. The employment potential of these industries is limited. He added,

Mineral lobby or coal mafias are outsiders and their approach to the state's minerals and state's people is of pure exploitation, the same one as the British colonialist. Industrialisation in the state should wait till the tribals can be beneficiaries. They can participate as equals, not as coolies and unskilled labourers. I made this point but none would listen to me in the government. So the way mining and industrialisation is taking place is helping accumulation and reproduction for the existing industrial capitalists, with further marginalisation of the agrarian labour force who are losing land without proper alternate employment. They are having to migrate to urban centres to work as construction workers or unskilled labourers. Even in these, they are facing stiff competition from labourers from other states. Women have historically been used by the trader class as sex objects (lived as second woman or prostitutes) and men as coolies and casual labour. Neither do they have permanent jobs nor a share in the industrial development taking place in the state.

An academic described a similar scenario. Mining in the state has been directed towards export rather than being used in manufacturing industries within the country. Hence, natural resource extraction has not contributed to a more self-sufficient economy or higher employment opportunities. Those who originally accumulated through trade (such as Marwari and Agarwal) went on to invest in industries since the formation of an independent state. Extraction have been rampant but achievements in terms of value addition are limited and not as conventional capitalism would expect. He condemned the policy of Chhattisgarh government for allowing export of minerals and ores to China, Japan, and Korea rather than starting manufacturing industries (interviewee from Raipur, 2011). It appears that the state made policies to benefit the emerging indigenous industrial capitalist class but thought inadequately about employment generation. This scenario is similar to what Sud (2007) identified in Gujarat's new land acquisition policy, where class demands are being catered to by the state through its policies.

The capitalist and petty bourgeoisie have had support from the state in more ways than one. The legal procedures laid down to protect tribal land rights prior to starting off a project have been flouted regularly. Despite going against state laws, the government has failed to take action against such private companies. For example, there has been a series of protests against Jindal Power Limited (JPL) by the local population who were affected by loss of land. These protests were led by an environmental activist in Raigarh. The allegation was that the public hearing procedures were not followed, and even their clearance for four million tonne per annum of coal was cancelled in 2012 (*The Hindu*, 2012).

But the same company has managed to sell power at a rate that they decide and to clients of their choice. It was reported that 'the coal-fired power project in Chhattisgarh's Raigarh district is the first ever project in India to operate on a 'merchant power' basis'. This means that unlike other projects bound by tariffs fixed through long-term power purchase agreements (PPAs) with state governments, the state has given JPL freedom to sell power at rates fixed on the spot to any buyer (Sharma, 2012). Preferential treatment can also be noted in the allocation of coal mines. Jindal has been allocated the highest number of captive mines in the last decade. This has helped them in procuring coal at cheap rates, thus pushing up their profit margin (Sharma, 2012). This is in violation of the government regulation, which stresses on allocating mines on the basis of competition and protecting natural resources by ensuring that environmental standards are followed. The state is the adjudicator, but in Chhattisgarh it seems to flout both laws and stipulations to suit the private companies and ensure fast economic growth. This is narrowing the gap between the adjudicator and beneficiary, with government officers coming closer to those running private companies and subsequently sacrificing pubic interest (triangulated interviews with a lawyer in Bilaspur, an activist in Korba, and a journalist in Raipur, 2011).

Several interviewees argued that the forest produce market is monopolised by capitalist classes. Even before the state was formed, they had been buying and procuring land in remote areas, and now have access to forest produce and dictate market sales. In the process of acquiring land for corporate projects, political cadre, *gunda* (ruffians), and often *panchayat* elected members or, more rarely, middle farmers who have urban connections, operate as agents of big capitalists. It can be argued that a petty bourgeois class has arisen, which is engaged in assisting natural resource monopolisation by the proprietary classes. It is not to suggest membership of the class is numerous, rather that the members share overlapping characteristics of being educated, urban-bound, and politically connected.

Convoluted processes have been used to procure land from tribal people for mining. Land brokers, *dalaal*s,[26] have often been used by private companies to convince local people to sell their land for lesser prices. They are influenced individually (as some instance shows), instead of allowing land price to be decided collectively. The middle men for land transactions hail from both farmers' and traders' families, and have entered the land *dalaali* market. Traditionally, exploiters of farmers, however not all traders, invested their profits in industries. So, they have joined hands with the industrial classes to facilitate land buying. This is because the profit margin has risen steadily, up to 60 to 100 times over the past one decade. Land has emerged as the most lucrative commodity in the state, whose benefits are reaped by the capitalist and its allies who are part of the political settlement operating in the state.

On interviewing a senior bureaucrat,[27] it was confirmed that the bureaucracy has been sabotaging the entire process of 'public hearing' that is supposed to be held before any new mining or industrial project. This went to the extent that if it so happened that in a public hearing the villagers refused to give up their land, minutes of its proceedings were not recorded. Soon, another public hearing was called, keeping the villagers uninformed about it, and in this meeting the project was passed (interviewee from Korba, 2011). Devyani Srivastava (2008) has compiled a number of instances where land acquisition laws have been inappropriately used to force industrialisation and mining on the local people. Legal provisions are bent to suit interest of capitalists, which was evident in the way land given to Tata in Jagdalpur, Bastar, where the land was classified as fallow was later claimed back by the tribal farmers, since it was their most productive land. Tribal rights were grossly violated in this case, since the Constitution makes land belonging to tribal people inalienable from them.

A common observation during the fieldwork in Chhattisgarh was the way institutions and legal processes are bent, especially the environment impact statement (EIS), to suit dominant proprietary class interest. In a FGD, several local villagers highlighted how despite six *gram panchayat*s (village council)[45] of Raigarh district that passed a resolution refusing to give land for a project, DB Power still acquired the land in question. Kohli (2009) writes, 'anyone who has seen the fate of public hearings over the last 15 years … it would just mean adding on to the endless list of hearings which mock at the face of affected and concerned citizens, and find their routine way to the desks of the decision makers.'

The political leader and state officials were also found to accumulate directly through such land transactions. An elected member of the municipality, as reported by two local respondents, takes *theka* (contract) for Bharat Aluminium Company Ltd. (BALCO) and so does an elected politician and his relatives. So, when it came to BALCO constructing a wall that obstructed the public access to the main road and cutting off the villagers' shortcut to the town, there was little action that the state took. It resulted in the villagers having to walk 4 kilometres extra to come to the town, which is difficult on a daily basis. BALCO has a weekly market in the village, and villagers are forced to buy their household goods at the market at arbitrary prices. The state has remained silent to protect their (kin, relatives of political leaders, and bureaucracy) private stakes. A close relation helps the political leader use BALCO as a source of accumulation, which can explain the poor adjudication of laws and side-lining of public welfare over private profit motives. Again, the overlapping function of adjudicator and beneficiary almost defeats the purpose of legal institutions.

The biggest gainers are no doubt the capitalist class, both mercantile and industrial. Even though neoliberal policies have created beneficiaries within agrarian society, it has been at the cost of the majority.

State coercion to silence protestors

The state has been playing a crucial role in creating a congenial environment for investments by suppressing protests and democratic voices emerging from the tiller farmers and the landless. It has resorted to coercion time and again in the name of safety and public welfare, which has been legitimised by pointing at the Maoists. On enquiring about the reasons as to why there were limited public protests despite such discrimination, Mansi Gaur, a *zilla panchayat* representative, informed that 'when it comes to organising public protests, the government is strict and repressive. In Dhamtari, in an event of a protest by the middle farmers, the state apparatus crushed it mercilessly'. The protest upheld farmers' rights, demanding higher MSP, more subsidy, and access to credit. About 40 people were put behind bars, out of which many were not even present in the protest (interview of Shashi from Dhamtari, October 2011). The violence was so severe that few of the farmers have still not physically recovered from the injuries, including the respondent himself.[28] The legal prosecutions continue, and they are still fighting them. Going to court consumes their time and energy. This has left the farmers who were part of the protest fearful of any further action against the government. The respondent pointed out that the farmers have been unwilling to mobilise themselves since. Farmer protest has received little response as seen in Rajnandgaon. The attitude of the government was instrumental in suppressing the political opposition, the respondent felt.

What works more effectively, a social activist named Dixit in Korba argued, was the patronising schemes from the government, which divide the farmers and curb any possibility of forming a unified movement. Conciliatory schemes such as irrigation subsidy are important to farmers, given the erratic rainfall and low irrigation coverage in the state. In the hope of receiving subsidy for installing new pumps, farmers maintain good relations with the state officials and are reluctant to be part of protests. Further, after the formation of Chhattisgarh, reservation for STs was made compulsory for government employment and the PRI. In 2011, the ST reservation for government job was increased to 32 per cent and that for the SC remained at 12 per cent. For the political parties, it had aided the process of recruiting members at the grassroots level, thereby dividing the dissatisfied masses and stalling the process of any kind of class action. Hence, the unity among the class of tiller farmers who often are also wage labourers, who could potentially transform into a class-for-itself, is broken down by the effort to gain political opportunities or state patronage. Few among them who become petty bourgeoisie lure others with chances of self-preservation. This trend was confirmed by respondents in Dhamtari and Raipur.

Over time, the protest movements that have survived are either sponsored by NGOs or are meant to negotiate for higher land prices or better settlement packages and not for any long-term change, as observed in the Land Bachao Andolan (Save the Land movement) in Raipur (interview of Vijendra from Raipur, 2011). Such instances have been observed in other districts, where protests are organised on the issue of land acquisition, and once the intermediaries offer higher prices for land, the protest is withdrawn. Such movements are not for sustenance of agriculture or to save land, or even food security, but are rather to negotiate for better compensation alone.[29]

An instance was reported when a woman dared to report against a state official. During an MLA visit to her village, she informed him that the local bureaucrat did not listen to their complaints, and their payment under the MGNREGS had been irregular. The bureaucrat threatened to alienate the village from all further government schemes. The following day, the whole village along with the woman was summoned to the bureaucrat's house to apologise and the former had to meet the MLA to convey the information was wrong. With prevailing patron–client relations and dependence of local bureaucracy, it is very difficult to create and sustain a movement (interview of Bala from Bilaspur, October 2011). A veteran politician observed that social movement has lost its steam; 'it should be like the flame of a lamp, steady but at present it is sporadic, like a sudden flicker', and only those who have enough to eat can organise themselves and protest. Those who have dearth of food cannot participate in it (interview of an activist, December 2011).

The close tie between the politician/bureaucrat and capitalist, and the attitude of political leaders as the patrons on whom common people are dependent, is further marginalising the poor (tribal, SC, wage labour, and tiller farmers) and shrinking the democratic space of protest. The state has commanded authority using coercion and consent to retain its dominance.

Credit disbursal for the resource-rich

It has already been asserted that formal credit has seen a skewed distribution in the 2000s with proliferation of private moneylenders (NCEUS, 2008; Ramachandran, 2011). The state government has introduced loans at 3 per cent interest to the farmers. It was used by the BJP to project itself as pro-farmer and pro-agriculture. These, however, are two distinct things. In an annual celebration of a reputed NGO, credit availability was reiterated proclaiming the government's concern for farmers' needs. However, the chief of the same organisation working with farmers stated in an interview that NABARD figures show that one million farmers can access formal loans and this is approximately 30 per cent of total farmers, given the total number is 3.4 million. This fits well with 30 per cent of the state that is constituted of big and middle farmers, leaving out small and marginal farmers who constitute almost 80 per cent of the population and have little access to formal sources. The data shows that 40 per cent of the total number of farmers in Chhattisgarh are in debt. The average debt burden in Chhattisgarh is ₹4,122. Sixty per cent of those in debt are small farmers. Informal sources still account for over 40 per cent of the total debt incurred by the farmers. This high incidence of debt is more to do with non-productive expenditure, such as marriage, education, and travel (UNDP, 2005). This was the case when use of HYV seeds was not high, but since its use has risen during the 2000s across the state, adding production-related expenditure such as chemicals and irrigation as factors to incur debt.

Several factors collated from various respondents show why small farmers in Chhattisgarh rely more on informal than formal credit sources, a trend observed among this class across India. First, the technical details and legal documents required to avail a loan is possible only for the big farmers. The banking system, like all bureaucratic procedures, are particularly unfriendly to the tiller farmers. They also require a map of their land from the *patwari* (village accountant) who has to be bribed for the same. Second, the payments are so steep for getting a loan, that it is faster and easier to take a loan from informal sources at usurious rates. Third, big capitalist farmers have diversified into vegetables and soybean cultivation, and thus have a profit margin enabling them to repay loans, which is an important criterion to be eligible for formal credit. In contrast, most tiller farmers continue with traditional farming of paddy, which has a low profit margin. Many interviews revealed, small farmers could barely cover the cost of production, so they would often default in repayment, thus rendering formal avenues for credit unviable (interviewee in Bilaspur, August 2011 and activist, Dhamtari, 2011).

When big and tiller farmers from the same district were interviewed, they narrated two contradictory experiences. For the former the government system had improved in the last five years, and they had access to all the facilities, including subsidised seed. Loan is given by cooperatives and, if they are not a defaulter, it is easy to reapply for loans (NSSO, 2005). As has been well documented at the national level, a divide has come to prevail in Chhattisgarh over the decade between 2010 and 2020. Tiller farmers are increasingly being pushed towards informal sources, while big and capitalist farmers are being protected by assured access to formal credit. This is crucial for the state to register a high growth in agriculture, which leads them to be favourable towards big and capitalist farmers, thus ignoring resource-poor farmers who cannot drive agricultural growth. The state is purportedly considering the sector more seriously, but that does not mean that the state is equally friendly to all farmers.

New Agricultural Policy brings opportunities for rural proprietary classes

This section focuses on change in cropping pattern and privatisation of inputs and its differential impact on different classes of farmers. Chhattisgarh is one of the few states that has allocated more than 10 per cent of state plan resources and also has access to centrally sponsored schemes in the agriculture and allied sectors to increase production and productivity. During 2005–06, the agricultural sector received ₹2,247.5 million (6.49 per cent), which grew to ₹3,168.0 million (6.20 per cent) during 2006–07 and ₹8,762.4 million (13.66 per cent) during 2007–08 out of the state plan. In 2008–09, the agricultural sector was allocated ₹12,259.2 million (12.08 per cent) out of ₹1,01,463.7 million state plan. In the first two years of the Eleventh Five Year Plan period, the state government spent ₹21,021.6 million for the agriculture and allied sectors. It can be concluded that the state has been investing to transform agriculture into a high-growth sector as the Agrovision 2010 document and agricultural policy (2012) envisioned. The state Agrovision document (2010) mentions that big farmers, constituting 30 per cent of farmers, will be the drivers of growth. The first phase of reforms is focused on those farmers who are capable of investing in commercial crops. In this light, the question of distribution among different classes of farmers can be usefully analysed.

Building on the experience of respondents, the following sections explain how benefits from public investment have accrued to different rural classes, particularly focusing on three aspects, namely shift in cropping pattern, chemical inputs, and irrigation. The pattern that emerges conforms to that documented by NCEUS (2008), Ramachandran et al. (2010), and Barbara Harriss-White (2004, 2008).

Policy-induced change in cropping pattern: Soybean, Jatropha, and horticulture

The promotion of multi-cropping has been emphasised in Chhattisgarh's policy documents as the main tool to achieve agricultural growth. In 2011, the government was planning mechanisation including a Green Revolution, better irrigation facilities, and enhanced market access to optimise productivity. The cropping intensity of Chhattisgarh in 2011–12 was 134 per cent, while Punjab's was at 183 per cent. This has been seen as a major lacuna in the sector. To change this, 'phasal chakra parivartan' (crop cycle change) was adopted; this has been instrumental in introducing commercial crops.

Within commercial crops, focus has been on high-value crops such as maize, soybean, and horticultural crops such as capsicum. Apart from these, *til* (sesame), groundnut, *ramtil*, and *urad* have also shown an increase in acreage between 2006–07 and 2009–10, while crops such as kodo-kutki, millet, and rice have lost their acreage (CoG).[30] The government actively discouraged farmers from growing paddy by using the slogan 'paddy brings poverty' (Menon, 2014). It was a way to publicise the potential of fruit (mango, banana, guava, and apricot) and vegetable cultivation, as is evident from government websites. Though horticulture occupies only 13.41 per cent of the net cultivated area invested, the total income generated from the sector accounts for over 33.83 per cent of the total income derived from the combined agriculture sector (CoG). It was triangulated that the districts situated west of Raipur were more developed in commercial cropping than the districts east of the state capital, such as Dhamtari and Bilaspur. Interestingly, these western districts have a higher incidence of capitalist farmers and are geographically closer to Mumbai and Nagpur, and probably benefit from the resulting market linkages.

During interviews with officials in various departments in Chhattishgarh it was highlighted that large-scale farming, mechanisation, and commercial crops are key to disrupt poor agricultural growth and income cycle. It has taken farmers over a decade to adopt commercial cultivation such as that of soybean. The officials pointed out that, during this time, farmers were taken to view – through government initiatives – to see successful farms. The hope was that by demonstration effect more farmers would be convinced to adopt new technologies and opt for cash crops. The state has not only made seeds and technology available but has also facilitated easy availability of loans for the farmers. The farmers who benefitted from these schemes have become capable of buying more land in the past decade and, as of today, have landholdings of more than 50 acres an average. On meeting one such farmer (recommended by the state officials) who owned nearly 100 acres holding, it was ascertained that he was a capitalist farmer and invested in pesticide retailing as well. Therefore, the state has focused on big and middle farmers to adopt soybean cultivation given the high capital investment required.[31] The bureaucrat who recommended meeting this particular farmer did not share a similar relation with the tiller farmers, because the latter were incapable of capital investment and contributing to agricultural growth. They therefore fall out of the schemes taken up by the state. The farmer also informed that the fellow farmers in his village were very satisfied with the services received from the state. On more than one occasion, the local farmers got together to stop the transfer of the bureaucrat who served in the same district for 15 years and had thereby developed a close tie with the capitalist farmers (interviewee in Raipur, September, 2011).

Commercial agriculture, horticulture, and technology have been successfully adopted by the capitalist farmers in Durg, who have taken to mechanised methods of production; usually these farmers belong to the OBC and upper castes. The others who grow horticultural crops are capitalist farmers (more than 20 acres), who are already armed with the tools and modern technology and live within gated farmhouses (Jha, 2009). The latter have come from Haryana, a Green Revolution state. They were already equipped with capital-intensive methods and have settled in Chhattisgarh, where they use these methods in agriculture. They have bought land by coercing the local Dalit[32] community, thereby reducing the latter to wage labourers working their own fields (Jha, 2009).[33] According to the local media, this could be because the state was planning to undertake a 'Green Revolution', that these capitalist farmers were looking to use as an opportunity. While the contention that they are here to utilise these lands could not be confirmed, it was evident that the state has taken no proactive steps to stop such land acquisition.

The state is all set to modernise agriculture. Following the Green Revolution prescriptions set by other states, the objectives will be achieved by higher mechanisation and change in cropping pattern. Under mechanisation schemes, agricultural implements have been exempted from value added tax (VAT),[34] and an additional subsidy of 25 per cent has been granted on such implements. Financial assistance up to ₹50,000 per pump for energisation has been provided, along with an additional 30 per cent subsidy for SC and ST farmers and 10 per cent for other farmers under the micro irrigation scheme (*Business Standard*, 2014). However, mechanisation as per Byres' analysis is more economical in large landholdings. Consequently, it is not resource-neutral because adoption of such mechanisations can be easily achieved by availing of subsidies; however, despite subsidy, only those who can bear the remaining part of the cost can use the subsidy fruitfully. A direct evidence for the argument was reported by a respondent in Champa. He was from a big farmer family but owns a tractor shop. He stated that though the government gives subsidy to small farmers for buying tractors, these farmers cannot pay the remaining amount. Therefore, they forge documents, and a big farmer buys a tractor in the name of a small farmer. Often this small farmer is either a tenant or wage labour in a big farmer's farm.

As the government prescribed, the sale of machinery has gone up significantly under the new policy regime. Government report shows that the number of power tillers have increased twenty times between 2006–07 and 2009–10 and other power-driven implements have tripled in the same period under various departmental schemes (CoG). But who is selling the equipment? Evidence of diversification to input and machinery trade was observed among farmers. In the agriculturally advanced districts, the big capitalist farmers had diversified to these trades, while the districts dominated by traditional cropping had the presence of traders from non-agrarian background, who own such machinery shops. The entire highway to Durg was dotted with numerous tractor and other agricultural machinery shops. Dhamtari also has a similar pattern, with a number of chemical input shops, but the shops belong to traders from other states and urban Chhattisgarh. In Champa and Durg districts, some big farmers and capitalist farmers were found owning seed and pesticide shops. The diversification has picked up pace since 2000 with agrarian surplus being diversified.

Farmers in Durg have diversified to horticultural crops such as tomato and have gained from good market linkage and even supply to Mumbai and Kolkata; this linkage has been facilitated by introduction of soybean cultivation in this region since the 1980s, which was the first cash crop of the state. By 2011, the big and middle farmers were capable of buying machinery on their own. A big farmer from Durg claimed, 'In 2010 the bank branch in his district has a deposit of ₹330 million, which was ₹80 million only ten years earlier. What is more significant is this money belongs to the farmers, each of whom on this date has a savings of ₹10 million. This has been made possible by shifting to soybean cultivation from rice' (interview of a farmer, Durg, September 2011). These are big and middle farmers who are best categorised as capitalist farmers in the present context. They have been receiving support from the state agricultural department since the 1980s and have generated enough surplus to adopt horticultural crops on their own. He added that 'we can now buy tractors with down payment and our children proudly associate with agriculture'. Clearly, they have generated surplus through agriculture, which is being invested in other avenues; however, their interest in agriculture persists. A representative of a global NGO informed that tiller farmers have averted the change to cash crops due to the high-risk potential. The change has been slow at their end. The agrarian policy stated upfront that 30 per cent of farmers will drive the sectoral growth, and it is likely that the class of capitalist farmers were being referred to. This reflects that the state did not pay much heed to to the rest of the farmers in terms of their economic role since they cannot drive the much-needed economic growth.

Despite the emphasis on cash crops, the government has not neglected paddy farmers. In 2013, the election manifesto said that the government would buy all the paddy produced in the state. In 2014, Chhattisgarh received the prestigious National Krishi Karman Award for the second time after 2010 for the highest paddy production. The state government has been negotiating with the central government for ₹3 billion subsidies for paddy farmers. However, the real attitude can be understood only by comprehending what the government invests in paddy cultivation and paddy farmers. The research done by universities in developing new varieties from indigenous seeds has been slow, while there have been rumours of samples of indigenous seeds sold illegally to Monsanto for developing private seeds; whereas six colleges have been started for conducting research on horticulture. As discussed in earlier sections, the government has supported the sale of private seeds in the market, thus preservation of indigenous varieties has been compromised. Private seeds are more expensive, even if high-yielding, and can only be afforded by rich farmers, something that has adversely affected most farmers.

Small and landless farmers have been harmed further by the prevalence of state support to contract farming. Contract farming refers to agricultural production carried out in accordance with an agreement between the buyers and farmers, wherein the conditions for production and marketing of agricultural product(s) are agreed upon. Interviews held in Jashpur and Champa highlighted the way in which the government has been leasing out land to contractors from Bihar and Uttar Pradesh for a period of three to four months in a year; this land was traditionally used for potato and watermelon cultivation by local farmers. These contractors bear the cost of farming inputs and hire labour to do the cultivation. They are capable of making high investments, own tractors and other machinery, and have good market linkages. All these factors together translate to a higher rate of agricultural growth.

Another factor behind small farmers incurring debt and finding it hard to repay is the pricing of food grains by the central government, as pointed out by respondents. In 2011, the cost of production per quintal was reported to be ₹2,000, while the MSP declared by the government was a mere ₹1,100, as informed by respondents. Further, procurement by the government was limited to *kharif* crop that stretches over a period of three months per year only (interviews with an activist in Korba, a state official in Raipur, and a farmer in Bilaspur). This policy-induced change has resulted in farmers trying to grow other crops that require several chemical inputs to be purchased from the market. This directly reduces the autonomy/sovereignty of the farmers. The other effect of moving out of paddy cultivation is that it leaves tiller farmers food insecure in different parts of the state.

The state is reluctant to support resource-poor farmers, but is more than willing to extend support to contractors, as well as big and capitalist farmers. They are keen to promote horticulture, because it generates revenue and, in this case, the government displays preference towards those who can undertake capitalist agriculture (Menon, 2014). While productivity is an important concern, the lack of focus on indigenous varieties and the sole effort at creating space for corporate products, both directly and through spurious means, is hurting the marginalised classes. The alignment of the state (political leaders and bureaucracy) and the professional class to the capitalist class that owns the new machinery and technology is apparent. There are few exceptions, where organisations are trying to develop alternatives to protect indigenous seed varieties. I interviewed one such NGO owner. However, even in doing so, they have to adhere to the framework laid out by the state. In the instance I encountered, the scientist had to maintain good relations with the state leadership despite being fully cognizant of its anti-farmer policies.

While the policies are focused on shift in cropping pattern and input centricity, their success is contingent upon access to hybrid seeds, fertilisers, and irrigation, and these resources do not accrue equally to all farmers. In fact, class plays a determining role in terms of access to these inputs, which decides which class of farmers can avail these opportunities.

Seed, pesticide and fertiliser, and lumpy technology

With a budget of ₹105.2 million to promote the production and distribution of quality seeds, seed supplied by the state government has grown in 400,000 hectares of cultivable land, which is 10 per cent of the total demand. For the remaining requirement, farmers depend either on their own seeds or buy from private companies (interview with a technocrat in Raipur; UNDP, 2005). A manager at a private seed company, when interviewed, described how seed companies look at Chhattisgarh as a huge market with potentials to be tapped into. He is a highly paid professional, and part of the new petty bourgeoisie benefitting from market opportunities. They sell their highly priced inputs through retail shops in small towns and suburbs by employing local people as agents. During the fieldwork, many such privately run shops were seen, particularly in the districts of Dhamtari, Durg, Raipur, and Champa, where commercial cropping has been adopted more than the others, but with one chief difference. In Durg and Champa, the big capitalist farmers were the owners of these shops, while in Raipur and Dhamtari, these were owned by traders belonging to Marwari or Gujarati communities.

A Left Party veteran pointed out that the need for chemical fertilisers has given rise to a class of *sahukars* or traders. They give loans to farmers to buy chemical inputs and machinery. Defaulting in repayment of these loans results in tiller farmers losing their land. The influence of these traders in the lives of farmers is rather deep owing to the interlocking of markets. So, when paddy is ready to be harvested, and it is time for it to be taken to the rice mills for processing, the traders buy the rice from the mills directly, which is how they settle the famers' loans and interest amount. An interlocking of markets for different agricultural inputs is noted.

Multinational companies have gained control of the fertiliser and pesticide market in the state by successfully penetrating the rural districts during the last decade. In discussion with a senior manager of a private pesticide company, it was stated that corporate entities employ various means to get farmers to buy their products. They employ agents in all the districts to convince the suppliers and farmers that their product would ensure a safe and big yield. The agents and shopkeepers resort to the fear tactic that less chemical fertilisers would lead to crop failure and poor yield to coerce farmers into buying more fertilisers. The informal credit system and existing social networks play a role in achieving this objective. The middle and small farmers are usually unable to buy fertilisers and pesticides with cash payment. Hence, a part of the strategy of private traders is to sell the products during cultivation on credit and collect the cash after harvest. In order to retrieve their payments, they use a network of village kin, who go visiting village to village, collecting money after harvest. This picture is similar to the situation from Murugkar et al. (2006), which has been discussed in Chapter 2.

In the face of high prices of agricultural inputs and poor availability of information and support on how to use them optimally, tribal farmers have mostly remained loyal to indigenous seeds for food crops such as paddy and millets. However, fertiliser and pesticides that are used are now increasingly bought from the market. Farmers across districts have complained in many instances that hybrid seeds cause pest attacks right from sowing to cutting. Consequently, the farmer incurs a high cost of pesticides without effective results (NCEUS, 2008; Menon, 2014; interview of Mishra from Bilaspur, October 2011). In 2011, 90,000 litres of banned insecticides were discovered by the Department of Agriculture from godowns in the state (Agronews, 2011).

In terms of access to these inputs, big and capitalist farmers repeatedly reported easy access to cooperative societies, while the rest found supply through the same cooperatives to be delayed and undependable. Laxman Prasad, a small farmer from Raipur, added that the 'BJP government was very corrupt and anti-people. They do not understand our needs. Seeds and fertiliser from government sources are of inferior quality, and farmers are at the mercy of private sellers'. Farmers in Korba and Bilaspur had a similar experience. The fact that capitalist farmers in two FGDs in Raipur and Bemetara suggested that the BJP has ensured easy supply of inputs through cooperatives indicated the prevailing bias by the state towards big farmers and against the tiller farmers.

The input-centricity policy under the Raman Singh government was regarded as the key factor contributing to increases in the cost of cultivation, leading to debt liability (interview of a technocrat in Raipur, September 2011 and Mishra, December 2011). Chemical fertilisers have heightened the cost of inputs manifold, and so the has cost of pesticides that are hugely expensive and are administered in large quantities (Arjjumend, 2001). Given the lumpy nature of technology, inputs have to be applied together for a good yield. Most respondents in Village Reports[35] demand that traditional methods of cultivation should be promoted, as modern methods are expensive. However, the state is surging towards modern technology. The results of the 59th Round of NSS provide evidence of the worsening situation of farming households due to indebtedness (NSSO, 2005). The cycle of floods and droughts makes livelihood extremely vulnerable. Farmers, with preponderance of small farmers, resort to moneylenders in times of crisis. In the early 2000s, the incidence of poverty was high, owing to the absence of alternative employment opportunities (UNDP, 2005: 202). Chhattisgarh has the highest poverty rate in India. Poverty in Chhattisgarh in 2005 was 51 per cent, which by 2011–12 fell to 40 per cent.[36] For the same period, the all-India figures were 38 and 22 per cent, respectively.

The state has lagged behind the all-India average with regard to the rate of poverty reduction (World Bank, 2011–12). The state policy of using private chemical inputs has, therefore, contributed to the worsening situation of tiller farmers, forcing them to opt instead for contract farming.

The state strategies discussed in this section have worked in favour of both big and capitalist farmers and private companies. The former have cornered subsidised fertilisers from cooperative societies, which has been facilitated through their BKS membership. The membership gives them higher political bargaining power. A respondent noted, 'A typical agrarian cooperative society has either a Suryavanshi [Thakur], Chandravanshi [Yadav], or Kurmi [Sahu, Chandrakar] as its head, who allocates the resources within their kin. This prevents the tiller farmers from getting any benefits. Often a Maheshwari is also involved in these transactions but from outside' (interview of Deependar from Raipur, August 2011 and a journalist from Raipur, 2011). All these castes basically include big, a few middle, and capitalist farmers leveraging their political connections.

Big and capitalist farmers have a hold on seeds from government sources as well. Since the separation of the state from Madhya Pradesh, seeds for cultivation have been developed by the Chhattisgarh State Seed and Agricultural Development Corporation Limited (CSSADCL). The mother seed goes to an agricultural university for testing, and a foundation seed is produced from it. Produced annually, the seeds are then sent to the Seed Board. Around 27,000 varieties of seed come to the Board annually to be reproduced before circulation among the farmers. The CSSADCL owns only 500 hectares, but it needs 3,000 hectares for seed germination, and, therefore, land from 7,000 registered farmers is leased for reproduction of seeds. Once again, well-connected farmers with big landholdings or those with political connections are the natural choice of the government. In the final stage, seeds are sent to the State Seed Certification Agency to ensure genetic identity, purity, quality, and health of the seeds. Interviewees reported that government-sourced seeds that are better in quality are given to big farmers who are politically connected.

It can be inferred that access to government sources of subsidised inputs have been limited to big farmers and capitalist farmers, concentrated in the plains. Policy has presented them with new opportunities to diversify into input shops, earn from renting out tractors and other machinery, bought at low prices owing to the subsidies on machinery offered by the government. A fraction of the class has moved to high value crops and adopted technology and transformed into capitalist farmer. Some big farmers remain in the eastern districts, thus not moving to capitalist agriculture. In addition, contact with

BKS has been an advantage for capitalist farmers in the western districts in accessing cooperative societies. Hence, it can be tentatively inferred that high budgetary allocation towards the sector has made little difference for tiller farmers, who are left at the mercy of private companies, petty bourgeois traders, and retailers to procure inputs.

Water, but not for everyone

Chhattisgarh is naturally rich in water resources, with 9 rivers – Mahanadi, Sheonath, Indravati, Arpa, Hasdeo, Kelo, Son, Rehar, and Kanhar – flowing across the state. Despite that, merely 29 per cent of the agricultural land in the state is irrigated, and there has been negligible effort to start minor irrigation projects (GOC, 2012), even though nearly 80 per cent of the state's population is dependent on agriculture. Therefore, cycles of floods and droughts leave the farmers vulnerable and add to their debt dependence. During a group discussion, a respondent stated that 'the erratic rain pattern and lack of irrigation management has left one village flooded and an adjacent one dry within the same district' (Korba 2011). The extent of irrigation in northern and southern districts is particularly poor, 11 per cent and 4 per cent, respectively. In recent policies, focus has been laid on irrigation but, if discerned, the focus has actually been on subsidising private irrigation. Quoting from a government website, [37]

> Assistance of ₹750 thousand is provided to the entrepreneur as credit linked back ended subsidy on a package of machines worth ₹1.5 million for Sub-Plan Area and ₹1 million for a package of machines worth ₹2.5 million in other areas. Under Shakambhri scheme, started in the year 2005–06, 75 per cent subsidy is given on diesel/electric/kerosene/open well submersible pump sets (up to 5HP) and 50 per cent on dug well to the small and marginal farmers. [38]

The government has initiated a new scheme called the 'Indira Gaon Ganga Yojana' to provide assured water supply to every village by pumping up the available ground water and augmenting traditional water resources.

Except for the 50 per cent subsidy on dug wells as mentioned, and may be the Indira Gaon Ganga Yojana, the benefits of other schemes accrue to the big farmers and capitalist farmers, who can bear the high cost of pumps. Subsidy for installing tube wells, a landmark initiative of the present government, has been cornered by the big farmers with political contacts in district bureaucracy (interviews of FR Mishra, 2011, and Sahu, a driver, 2011). Like Shah (2007) has described in the case of Gujarat, small farmers in Chhattisgarh have had to resort to informal credit and take pumps on rent to irrigate their lands. The

Human Development Report (*HDR*) of 2005 points to the dearth of alternative employment opportunities for small farmers as one of the main reasons for the high incidence of poverty in the area (UNDP, 2005: 202).

To add to the plight of tiller farmers, water has been continuously diverted to industry. In Champa, the diversion of water to power plants has forced farmers to opt for irrigating their lands with pumps instead of natural sources. The process of getting pumps installed is complicated by the need to secure permission from the Sub-Divisional Magistrate.[39] Further, difficulties in securing adequate documents for completing governmental formalities, as well as the presence of corrupt officials, make the process inaccessible for tiller farmers. A local activist filed an RTI to find out about the quantity of water annually supplied to farmers, but no data could be given by the government.

The income from cultivation has fallen for the poorer farmers, and the desperation and helplessness they undergo has increased. Sugarcane growers have suffered because the government has filed a caveat in the High Court in 2015 and banned the farmers from making *gud* (jaggery) at home and selling it. This has been done to ensure a steady supply of sugarcane to the Kawardha sugar mill, because the mill had not been receiving enough raw material. Another sugar mill has been opened at Sarguja, which will hike up the demand for raw sugarcane. Sugarcane cultivation and selling does not offer a high margin of profit. Farmers earn about ₹2,100 per 10 quintals of sugarcane, and spend ₹500 on transporting the crop to the buyer, thereby resulting in low profit margins. In states such as Uttar Pradesh, farmers get around ₹3,000 for the same quantity of sugarcane, as a farmer noted (interviews of a farmer in Kawardha, 2011, and an activist in Raipur, 2011). The helplessness of tiller farmers is exemplified in the sad reality of a rising number of suicides in Champa district between 2001 and 2006. The rate of suicide is lower among paddy farmers, because cultivation of paddy incurs lower debt.

Overall, the overwhelming importance the state has accorded to the adoption of labour-saving technology inherently perpetuates undervaluing labour in both agricultural and industrial sectors, which has acted as a push factor for tiller farmers to join the non-agricultural labour pool.

Mechanism of pacification: Public distribution system and RSS intervention

The PDS in Chhattisgarh has paid rich dividends to the government. Under the PDS, rice is distributed at the rate of ₹1 a kilogram to below-poverty-line (BPL) households, and ₹2 a kilogram to above-poverty-line (APL) households. Making rice available for cheap prices and thereby saving people from starvation in a poor state has resulted in the people developing a sense of gratitude towards the government. This is particularly important, because the price a paddy farmer gets for his produce is lower than the cost of production, as triangulated in fieldwork, and inflation has added to their suffering. Despite such deprivation, it has not resulted in bitterness towards the government. Instead, food security has earned public loyalty for the government. Social workers and academics, however, have a different assessment of PDS. They contend that PDS has destroyed the capacity of the people to judge the oppression they are being subjected to and the way their land is being bought over by external agents. This has prevented the people from organising themselves for protest against the government (interview of a journalist in Raipur, 2011).

A politician regarded PDS as instrumental in the local population's reluctance to work. PDS was acting against the tribal farmers, pushing them into social malpractices and economic poverty. The rice that they get from PDS is often sold in the black market, and they use this money to buy *desi daru* or country liquor called *mohua* (interviewee from Raipur, 2012). He contended that 'drinking *mohua* has left the masses too drowsy to raise their voices, or even realise how they are being robbed off' (interview of Dixit from Korba, 2011). He pointed out that the production and sale of *mohua* has been legalised under the BJP government, which he feels has added to the further deterioration of awareness of the masses. Even though the government keeps promising to close liquor shops and puts up huge posters with Gandhi in Raipur city appealing people to give up drinking, respondents reported that actually the number of shops has gone up in the last few years.

Developmental efforts to change the lives of the tribal population decisively have been few. However, persistent means have been employed to politically bring them within the fold of the BJP. Jashpur has 11,000 RSS full-time workers, who are entrusted with the responsibility to convert the tribal population to Hinduism, and turn them into BJP supporters. Dilip Singh Judeo, a BJP MP, organised huge festivals for reconversion in order to polarise the local population[40] (Saxena and Rai, 2009). The effect of these efforts has been the creation of a mass support base for the party at the grassroots. By organising periodic conversion programmes, the Hindutva card acted as an ideological plank to bring voters together. Movements to organise masses along class lines have been systematically weakened in the process. Other means have been employed to capture support in the rural parts of Chhattisgarh, as discussed in the next section.

Different ways of choosing allies in the countryside

Given the large forest cover in Chhattisgarh, the tribal population living in remote parts of the state have had little connection with farmers in other parts of the state. The region of Madhya Pradesh that came to become a separate state, Chhattisgarh, was one of the most neglected areas in the state before a separate state was carved out. The last decade in Chhattisgarh has, thus, seen various attempts by the state to penetrate the countryside. This has involved selecting groups as allies of the state, to achieve a stable political settlement. Two bodies have served the objective in rural Chhattisgarh – the farmer organisations and the local government institutions.

Role of the Bharatiya Kisan Sangh and its ties to big farmers

The areas where BKS has influence lie mainly in the plains of Chhattisgarh, specifically in Raipur, Bilaspur, and Durg. Its members were part of the Land Bachao Andolan (Save the Land Movement) that was active in Raipur in 2011. The movement waged a battle to protect the land of 27 villages around Raipur which was being acquired under the Naya Raipur project.[41] It has a membership of over 6,000 farmers with landholding size varying from 2 to 100 acres. Members of the Sangh were interviewed during the fieldwork, and all were noted to be big farmers, owning more than 10 acres each, while the Sangh's President owned 25 acres. They belonged to OBC – either Sahu or Chandrakar – communities. They are distinct from the industrial class and are not capitalist farmers. None of them own rice mills or have any connection with mining, though over the past decade, they have diversified by opening small retail shops, trading in agricultural inputs, and taking up *thekedari* (construction contracts) and government jobs. These are opportunities thrown up by the market and the growing importance of Raipur city (FGD in Raipur, September 2011).

The movement listed their demands as higher land price and jobs in the new factories, universities, and hospitals coming up on their land. One of their demands was that jobs requiring Class IV or V qualification be reserved for their people. For instance, the security guard employed in the Central Law University, Raipur, was from their village and had lost his job; their demand was that he be reinstated. Another demand was free medical treatment in the Vedanta hospital coming up on their land. They added that the land was given for free to this hospital because, on paper, it was an NGO. However, their perception was that Vedanta worked only for profit. Therefore they were unhappy with land allocation to Vedanta for free. Further, education for the next generation was one of their main concerns. A few of their sons were studying engineering, while others were pursuing computer courses. They repeatedly argued that this would help their children move out of the village life. Their demands were region specific, and they were expecting small favours from the state, mainly operating along lines of patronage. They confirmed that private *dalaal*s made four times as much as a farmer made in a land deal. They wanted to sell land directly to industries. It can be inferred that industries or land loss was not seen as a problem; rather they were seeking better prices for land and opportunities.

If one can consider the BKS as a movement, and for the sake of argument let us assume it is one, two unique characteristics of the movement were identified – organisation and political contact. The BKS operations are absent in districts other than Raipur, especially the tribal majority districts with concentration of small holdings. This is probably because the aim of this organisation is to mobilise the big and middle farmers who are better informed and educated than farmers in most other parts of the state. These farmers are also mobilised and, thus, operate as a definite vote bank. Their OBC caste affiliation also makes them an ally to the state, which has made serious attempts to entertain their demands. In Durg, big capitalist farmers show political connection with the BKS and are also well educated. Their strength was exhibited when they organised a successful resistance to stop industries from coming into their district, Bemetara. Bemetara was newly demarcated as a district from Durg, hence they were essentially the same farmers. They cashed in on the opportunity presented by new and high-value crops such as *karela* (bitter gourd), *chana* (chick peas), and tomato (interview of Deependar from Raipur, October 2011). There is a coexistence of soybean cultivation and horticulture in these districts. Champa presents a reverse case of Durg, where despite land sale being high, organised farmer resistance has not emerged. Possible factors could be a lack of connection to the BKS and a majority of farmers in Champa still being engaged in paddy cultivation. Given the low profit margin in paddy, if at all, farmers have been caught up in the struggle for survival with a low level of politicisation.

A close relationship between capitalist agriculture and political organisation among big farmers can be speculated, which has also received state support. The big farmers and capitalist farmers are important for the state, which envisions large-scale, highly productive mechanised agriculture as the only way forward. Hence, the demands of these farmers are treated more seriously. It indicates that these specific fractions form a part of the political settlement; however, their position is weaker than that of an industrial capitalist, the other class which forms part of the settlement.

Panchayati Raj Institutions

A key contribution of the BJP government has been the running of *anganwadi*s under Panchayat Raj Institutions. The Panchayati Raj system[42] covers around 20,000 villages in the state and has a total of 136,393 representatives. Altogether, close to 150,000 people in rural Chhattisgarh are involved in the strengthening of self-government and the democratic process (UNDP, 2005: 159). *Anganwadi*s have been effective in addressing the issue of food and nutrition for children below the age of seven years and providing them with preliminary education. Several respondents acknowledged that *panchayat*s have effectively created an elite within the village, who enjoy access to the upper echelons of the government. Its chief role has been to implement the central government schemes, rather than making the grassroots a part of governance processes.

In one village I met the *upsarpanch*,[43] who is involved in the recovery of bank loans.[44] He informed that the only huller (rice dehusker) in the nearby area, where paddy from adjacent villages is also processed, is owned by a big farmer with 20 acres of landholding. This particular farmer held the position of *sarpanch* for eight years between 2003 and 2011. He maintains close contact with urban traders and lives in the nearby town, is the owner of the only tractor in the area, and charges a high rent for it. In this case, the *panchayat* head was not only a big farmer, but was also into agro-processing. Additionally, he was a capitalist farmer who was able to adopt machinery, unlike the rest. This points to the concentration of economic and political power at the village level, thus leading to class consolidation.

With the 73rd and 74th Amendments to the Indian Constitution and the resultant wave of decentralisation and introduction of a three-tier system at the village level, a lot of hope was pinned on upholding the demands of the rural population. However, success in this regard has been limited in most parts of India. This is the case in Chhattisgarh as well. As reflected in several interviews during the fieldwork, *panchayat*s have rarely empowered village communities, nor have they created channels for representing demands from below to the top in the three-tier system. They operate as implementing agencies of the state and central governments. The administrative officers seem more occupied with implementation of the central government policies and do not know much about land acquisition or mining projects. They are generally disconnected from the ground reality of the villages around them. A legal loophole that makes the *panchayat*s heavily dependent on the bureaucracy is associated with rules such as convening meetings. *Panchayat*s are powerless to the extent that they cannot even convene a meeting of the *gram sabha*[45] without prior permission of the Collector. The procedure states that if one-third of a village community demands a village meeting, then it must be convened. However, it is noticed in several cases that even if such applications are made, the Collector/CEO rejects the application on the ground that 'meeting on such issues can disrupt the peace' (interview of an activist in Korba 2011). In implementing the state policies, the *sarpanch* must be careful in maintaining loyalty to higher authorities. It creates subservience of politically elected members to the state functionaries. Respondents mentioned that corruption is rampant in the functioning of PRIs. In any new project, the Collector, the block officer, the *zilla parishad* head, the *sarpanch*, and the *sachiv*[46] have fixed cut rates, as laid out by informal rules of the nexus. The elected representatives act as allies of the ruling class – both political and capitalist. In the process, they get alienated from people of their caste and tribe and the state maintains a stronghold.

The consensus among interviewees was that winning a *panchayat* election requires an investment of ₹1 million on an average (ADR, 2012 and 2013). Two elected PRI members admitted having spent such money in their past elections. A local activist said, 'Farmers in many instances cannot afford such money, so they seek help from local rich people – *dalaal*s, local contractors, or political fixers – and so once one assumes power, his allegiance lies with the patrons rather than his fellow villagers' (interviewee from Korba, August 2011). If it is their own money, post-victory, they indulge in corrupt practices to earn the money back. Money assumes a central role in deciding a candidate's chances, and being in office involves recovering the money spent and eventually accumulating further (interview of Gaur from Dhamtari, 2011). It was also reported that the *dalaal*s work for legislative assembly members and bureaucrats, but the latter also have family members occupying positions at local institutions. These members receive rent for being part of the local institutions and accumulate through state resources, thus transforming into the old petty bourgeoisie.

An MLA's kin, for instance, is presiding over a *panchayat* in Chhattisgarh plains. On visiting the *zilla panchayat* office, we were informed by her secretary that she was largely absent from the office and did not take much interest in the *zilla parishad*'s functioning. In case anyone wanted a meeting with her or had a complaint to lodge, they would have to go to her home or talk to her husband, a political leader. Clearly, at least in this case, institutions of decentralisation seem to be mere arms of state control and women reservation has contributed to deepening social structures of hierarchy rather than challenging them.

On the eve of elections, the President of the *zilla panchayat* organises huge parties where villagers are invited to enjoy 'murga and daru' (chicken and alcohol). She also goes to women's self-help groups (SHGs) to find out what is needed and supplies the same. During the last election, she supplied *dari* (mats) to several such SHGs and earned their support. This is a case of personalisation of power, since, most often, the representative expects to be visited at her residence for official or unofficial work. This case elicits how patron–client relations operate and keeps any organised protest from small farmers at abeyance (interviews of Dixit from Korba, September 2011, and Mohanram from Korba, September 2011). A fascinating fact emerged in the field.

Although an ST candidate, she and her husband have Brahmins among their political cadres, who act as the link between the party and the village. In Banshankari, a village adjacent to South Eastern Coalfields Limited mines, the village's Brahmin family has a lot of reverence among the local population, which includes both SCs and STs. A member of the family is a member of the BJP and works very closely with politicians. The Brahmin cadre uses his traditional status and social respect to earn allegiance from the local population. Pursuing his studies in law, he is also seen as someone better educated and informed than the rest, which adds to the confidence people have in him. His father continues to be the *purohit* (temple priest). Otherwise a middle farmer, they have done better than other families because of their access to education and political connections. Here, the case exemplifies belonging to the political circle being more crucial than adhering to caste hierarchy.

In another instance, a woman *panch* (member) whom I interviewed informed that she hardly participated in the functioning of the *panchayat*, because she did not get to know the date and time of these meetings. She had restrictions on stepping out of the house, imposed by her male relatives, so participating in public life was a remote possibility. On asking why she did not attend meetings, her reply was that she had no information. The case shows that formal political institutions can impact socio-economic structures, where information acts as a tool to exclude these new entrants into the public realm (interview of Sunita from Korba, September 2011).

Democratic consciousness is important to realise the potential of decentralisation, which is grossly lacking among the uneducated farmers. So even if they get elected, it is only titular. A case was narrated where the *upsarpanch* and the secretary controlled the decisions taken without listening to the *sarpanch*, an ST candidate. If the latter is absent, the SDM[47] reserves the power to cancel his post or ask him to leave on account of irregularity. In cases of corruption accusations, the *sarpanch*, who is the main signatory to any document, is penalised, and, given their illiteracy, often do not understand the language used in the documents. They always live in fear of getting framed on illegal charges and have to depend on the secretary (interview of Rao from Bilaspur, 2011). Once again, state bureaucracy exerts tremendous control on decisions made by the elected candidates. Instances have been reported where contractors have pumped money into local institution elections to ensure their candidate's victory. This essentially paves the way to buying the candidate's agreement for any new projects or land acquisitions that the contractor might propose (interviews of the CPM President, July 2011, and a PRI member from Dhamtari, August 2011). The contractors are part of the new petty bourgeoisie who have accumulated through rapid industrialisation and seldom from the capitalist class.

All the findings suggest that PRIs have not brought about democratic empowerment at the grassroots. Instead, a class of beneficiaries has been created who feed on state resources and consolidate their class position. Even though they are farmers, they have become part of the old petty bourgeoisie. The state, as it emerged, is fully aware of this and is happy to have loyalists at the grassroots who will endorse the state's positions on land acquisition and other initiatives, when needed. Political position has also acted as a means of rent extraction from other farmers, when the elected leader is the sole owner of machinery such as huller or tractor, thus adding to accumulation by big capitalist farmers. A few middle farmers have accumulated through political leverage. Caste, where relevant, is used to win people's support for electoral purposes. Where caste is not relevant, other doles (patronage) serve the purpose. Patron–client relations are rampant in the functioning of PRIs. A furtherance of the old petty bourgeoisie through reservation has been identified, where a few members from the SC and ST gain access to state resources and, thus, accumulate, while they participate in exploiting numerous tiller farmers from their social group.

Conclusion

Political settlement consists of a coalition between the industrial capitalists, big farmers and capitalist farmers, and petty bourgeoisie (includes professionals). The state and class relations in Chhattisgarh can be aptly characterised as 'personal fusion', a term used by Bob Jessop (1983) to define almost overlapping relations between the state and the capitalist class, as discussed in Chapter 1. The state is not at a mature stage and, to that extent, does not enjoy autonomy from the capitalist class.

Within the political settlement the industrial capitalist undoubtedly dominates, which consists of interests such as mining, cement, and real estate, and is pervaded by one common agenda, that is, extraction of natural resources such as forest, land, and water. As discussed earlier in the chapter, to call it a 'lobby' would be a misnomer, as the representatives of the industrial class are an integral part of the state – both bureaucracy and politician – and hence do not operate outside the state apparatus. To quote a veteran journalist, 'They are not lobbies, but are the government itself.' The capitalist class discovers new opportunities to perpetuate its accumulation. For instance, the rice mill lobby, despite losing its central position to other lobbies over the last decade, has managed to preserve itself by tapping into the godown subsidy. During the decade following 2000 the rice mill lobby has shrunk, because fewer but bigger mills are now operating in the domain, fostering a kind of monopoly.

The second member of the political settlement is the big and capitalist farmer. The call for input centricity in agriculture and support for cash/high-value crops reflect the concern of the state for this class, which is a distant second to the capitalist class in terms of clout. Unlike Gujarat, agrarian surplus does not contribute to the industrial capital in Chhattisgarh. The investment for industries comes from external capitalists such as Vedanta and Jindal and, within the state, the surplus is generated by merchant capital. The state guards the interests of the big and capitalist farmer class by providing new opportunities, higher income through cash crops, supporting them in receiving loans from formal sources, and providing subsidy for private irrigation. Alongside, new avenues of diversification are also ensured in the state's agricultural policy, such as retailing in various agricultural inputs from seeds to machinery and moneylending to tiller farmers.

The western districts of Chhattisgarh have diversified more effectively and moved ahead in capitalist agriculture than the eastern districts, which are mostly paddy-producing districts. In the eastern districts, a significant presence of traders such as Marwaris was noted who control the seed-pesticide-tractor business as opposed to western districts, where the big capitalist farmers have diversified into these trades. The western districts show the presence of capitalist farmers from Haryana, who are involved in cultivating horticultural crops in a technology-intensive manner. With cash crops gaining ground, the role of traders has assumed a critical position as they provide godowns and storage facilities.

State-level politics is undermined by politics at local levels of administration. In gaining control on natural resources and land, the class dominating the district-, block-, and village-level politics plays a pivotal role. This class typically includes members of the bureaucracy such as the District Collector and the elected members of PRI. The PRI members have accumulated through rent collection in the past decade, with more state resources diverted to rural accounts under schemes such as the MGNREGS. The bureaucracy[48] has had direct economic benefits as observed in Korba, where a bureaucrat's kin is the local contractor for a corporate. There are also indirect benefits such as being in the good books of the ministers by serving their interests and earning extra through corruption. Looking at the functioning of the state, Jung (2011) sums it up appropriately, 'Local government officials and petty contractors seeped in corruption and insensitive to local cultural traditions have presided over the interior hinterlands and deprived these areas of even basic infrastructure like roads, drinking water, schools, small irrigation facilities, or markets where local products can sell at a profit.' State-level leaders do not have to visit a village; in fact, they operate through fine networking with big farmers and the petty bourgeoisie (interviews of a technocrat, 2011, and a political leader, 2011). The professional class also benefitted through urban opportunities such as being employed by seed-pesticide companies or mining companies. DuPont, among others, has employed well-educated professionals at high salaries, thereby minimising their dependence on the public sector for any kind of employment. It makes them a part of the political settlement, providing support to the interest of the dominant classes in the settlement.

A complementary role is being played by the PDS in the state by keeping an ideological control on the masses. The respondents suggested that it has been effective in muting voices of protest so far. Across interviews, it emerged that PDS and reservation are the two policies that have effectively appeased the public. The PDS system in the state runs smoothly, and people perceive it positively. The control of rations remains in the hands of the village *sarpanch*, the *panchayat* head, but most people do receive provisions under the PDS. Fear prevails when it comes to mobilising against the state, though there are small pockets of fearless activists. Protests and movements have been directed to earning favours such as higher compensation in the Land Bachao Andolan. People's struggles are mercilessly crushed by the state, as seen in Dhamtari. Distribution of state favours such as PRI seats and share in public funds such as the MGNREGS effectively dissipate people's united struggle by creating patron–client relations.

As the Chhattisgarh government focuses on two aspects – good governance and good infrastructure – the state's role becomes that 'of an enabler and facilitator of creative energies of its people' (Berthet and Kumar, 2011: 105). It moves away from a redistributive role, and does not rank social justice as a high priority. Economic growth is the ultimate objective and, for the agricultural sector, tiller farmers cannot be its drivers. Hence, the state subsidies and schemes are directed at big and capitalist farmers. The emphasis on technology-driven solutions for replacing labour as a factor of agricultural production is a direct indication of the state's disdain for tiller farmers and wage labourers. The line of argument adopted by bureaucrats is, 'We should favour consolidation of holdings and increase mechanisation to facilitate large scale agriculture' (interview in Raipur, September 2011), a crucial part of which is releasing land to ensure a continuous supply of land for proprietary classes to procure and further the process of accumulation. This is a case of ABD, realised through the state's policy on agriculture. The state emerges as an actor steering facilitation of the capitalist class' demand for land (Levien, 2011).

Another significant class comprising the political settlement in Chhattisgarh is the petty bourgeoisie. Poulantzas (1973) has argued that the petty bourgeoisie can be divided into two – old and new. The new petty bourgeoisie emerges as capitalism progresses and grows through opportunities created by the market, while the old petty bourgeoisie thrives on the state and its resources. Drawing from this argument, it can be inferred that the big farmers and landlords are part of the political settlement, but other sectors do not depend on agricultural surplus as a source of capital, which explains why big farmers actually draw their power more for political reasons than economic. Their presence in bureaucracy and access to state funds through the MGNREGS and cooperative societies are ascribing the character of the old petty bourgeoisie on some of them. At the same time, a new petty bourgeoisie has been emerging from opportunities created by the neoliberal policies by the market. Big farmers are accumulating through land contracting, land deals, retail shops of agricultural products, moneylending; the professional class working for multinationals are gaining by investing into high-value agriculture. The merchant capital is dominant, investing in primary industries, but, in this transformation, the kind of capitalism unfolding in the state has to be characterised as predatory. Surplus extraction emerges as the dominant objective with little regard for any kind of skilled employment and long-term vision. Bureaucracy is found enjoying political authority and gaining from rent due to corruption. Its interest has made it a closer ally to the capitalist class than it was in the 1980s, as Bardhan (1984) had argued. The nexus has left the marginalised more vulnerable which possibly explains why Chhattisgarh is so low on the food security index and continues to have incidents of violent conflict with Maoists.

Within agriculture, the trends are twofold. Farmers in the plains such as Raipur and Durg districts are trying to consolidate their landholdings and increase acreage, while those in other districts such as Kawardha are selling land to real estate and industry due to the unviability of agriculture. A veteran farmer-cum-politician commented, 'A common farmer is twice oppressed, once when they sell their produce for low prices given the urgency to pay back debts, and once again, when they buy food items from market at inflated prices,' because PDS does not cover the entire food demand of the family (interview of Mishra, October 2011).

The capitalist class and the old petty bourgeoisie (state officials and leaders) ensure sources of accumulation for the rural proprietary class, the third member of the political settlement. Fieldwork showed that the 'middleman' is taking advantage of rampant land acquisition; the big farmer and capitalist farmer have thrived by getting loans from formal sources and seeds and fertilisers from cooperatives. The traders selling new inputs are economic gainers. Several of these apparently diverse stakeholders who have gained since the new state was formed actually belong to either the big or capitalist farmer class or petty bourgeoisie. These classes have a political entity, tied to the ruling classes based in district headquarters or even the state capital. The two sets of actors work to secure mutual gain. The rural proprietary classes further their interest in land acquisition and access to forest resources, duly supported by the capitalist class and the state.

Small-holding cultivation has been steadily becoming unviable, and a key argument of the study is that this change is induced by the state's agricultural policy since 2000, which emphasises on input-centricity and high-value crops. Farmer interest has ruptured along class lines, and big and middle farmers are pinning their energy on negotiation for better prices such as in the case of the Land Bachao Andolan in Raipur (Save the Land movement). Such instances have been observed in other districts where protest is organised on the issue of land acquisition, and once *dalaals* offer higher prices for land, the protest is withdrawn. The divorce between small and big farmers' interest has weakened the overall interest of rural Chhattisgarh.

If things are not bad enough, agrarian small holders are facing competition from gentleman farmers. They are the new players in agriculture, who are gradually gaining an upper hand in the sector. They are essentially bringing investment into agriculture from other sectors. It is driven by the logic that land is the most lucrative investment, and horticulture and agribusiness are profit-making enterprises. With state support, it is even more profitable. Reliance Industries has entered the soybean market already.[49] They are procuring from sources in the districts of Champa and Bilaspur. They have taken up huge tracts of land to conduct contract farming. Monsanto, Reliance, Pepsi, and numerous corporates are investing in land and using a part of it, at best, for agriculture. The state is supportive of them in the hope of fast growth in the sector. However, sectoral support for agriculture cannot be equated with support for all farmers, as scholars, media, and politicians commonly argue. The agrarian proprietary class has made its way into the political settlement, albeit less significant than the industrial capitalist and the petty bourgeoisie.

Notes

1. A programme was taken up by the Indian government in 2009 to cleanse the Maoist groups from the affected states. Paramilitary forces were used, and the state governments also provided their forces.
2. The amount was ₹17,671 crores (6.2 per cent share) in 2007–08 as compared to ₹2,365 crores earlier, as part of MP.
3. They are statutorily permitted some access to forests.
4. It is the right wing, voluntary, Hindu nationalist group maintaining close contact with the BJP.
5. Forest-dwelling religious centres run by the party.
6. Tribals historically are worshippers of nature and are thus not followers of Hinduism.
7. It literally means courtyard shelter. The government of India started a programme in 1975 to provide food and medical facilities to village children to combat hunger and malnutrition.
8. Godhra refers to the communal violence that occurred in central Gujarat in 2002 and evidence finds that it had support from the state officials and was thus a part of the BJP agenda (Oommen, 2008).
9. More than the other two states being studied.
10. There are many families such as the Deewans who have lived here since pre-Independence, while many have come in over the past two decades. I met them in Raipur; they are into diamond business and also have several petrol pumps and own land all over the state. They have contact with ministers and rice millers.
11. Their relationship with the tribal population was of pure extraction – the natural resources of tribals, their land, and even tribal women were exploited by the Agarwals.
12. Local market often located in suburbs or small towns where wholesalers and farmers sell their produce.
13. Government of India has launched the 'Grameen Bhandaran Yojana' with effect from 1 April 2001. It is generally 33.3 per cent of the total cost.
14. The FCI is in charge of management of food security issues, so it has been procuring crops and distributing then under the PDS since 1964.
15. I met a junior bureaucrat who shared the same experience. Instead of abiding by the rules, they are expected to obey the politicians to remain in office.
16. The papers filed for RTI were shared with me.
17. Unfortunately, it is difficult for a researcher to break into social circles of businessmen and get details of how they secure their deals. Though I could not directly triangulate

the information, I deemed it fit to include it in the book given how rarely such information appear in print. I verified these findings with a politician whom I knew personally to understand how deals in the mining sector were forged.

18. These categories of farmers are often uneducated and unaware of paperwork.
19. See Savita Rath India Unheard at https://www.youtube.com/watch?v=lfzuhACUjGY, accessed on July 2018.
20. The primary objective of their production is self-consumption, and given their poor connection with suburban centres, they are quite removed from the market.
21. Schedule V under the Indian Constitution is meant to protect land rights of the tribal/indigenous population whose identity and rights are linked to their land. It covers nine states in India.
22. For more details, refer to Bhatia and Banerjee (1988) Varma (1995).
23. However, the Chandrakars, who were big farmers and were located closer to Raipur, are said to have managed to build political connections. There are a few ministers and bureaucrats from this caste group who are members of the BKS, the RSS farmer wing. This membership is not common in other districts. Like all political parties in India, the BJP through the RSS has organised different interest groups. This is to provide a specialised support group; one of them is BKS. There is a detailed discussion on BKS later in the chapter.
24. Bilaspur represents a big city.
25. The farmers who have already borrowed money from the cooperative society.
26. Intermediaries who set up land deals.
27. It took me three visits to actually meet the officer concerned.
28. I met one farmer who was present in the protest.
29. An exception was noted in Raigarh district, in a movement named Coal Satyagarha.
30. The government websites often do not have a year of publication.
31. Big and middle farmers are 24 per cent of the farmers in total and own 66 per cent of the cultivable land.
32. Death of a local Satnami Dalit was reported, who was presumed murdered for resisting the procurement.
33. When I visited these farms, I could see little of what was happening inside. High gates and dense fencing kept it away from the public.
34. Value added tax (VAT), an indirect tax collected by the government on all sales, has been waived on agricultural implements to foster faster mechanisation. This is a kind of subsidy.
35. These are district reports prepared by the United Nations Development Programme (2005) on the basis of survey covering 15 per cent of the local population.
36. See World Bank (2016).
37. Department of Agriculture, Government of Chhattisgarh, available at http://agridept.cg.gov.in/agriculture/Agri_Engg_Activities.htm, accessed May 2016.
38. For more details, visit http://agridept.cg.gov.in/agriculture/enginee.htm.
39. District-level administrative officer.

40. Hindutva groups opine that tribal people are Hindus, though the latter's religious beliefs and practices are very different from mainstream Hinduism.

41. The city of Raipur, the state capital, is being extended to accommodate the demand for urbanisation which is termed as the New Raipur project. It will incur an investment of ₹400 billion and will have an area of 36,000 hectares to accommodate 540,000 people, planned.

42. There are 9,139 *gram panchayat*s, 146 *janpad panchayat*s (at the block level), and 16 *zilla panchayat*s in the state (*Human Development Report*, 2005).

43. Second highest post in the village level body of local self-government.

44. He grows vegetables from the seeds distributed by the state government. When I asked him if he would want to live in the city, he replied, 'Even if I am out till 10 p.m. I come back home. The village is my home.'

45. Lowest level of the three-tier system of PRI.

46. The government officer who works as secretary to the *gram panchayat*.

47. He is a member of the bureaucracy heading the *tehsil* office.

48. On field, I encountered a few bureaucrats who were honest and hard working. My apologies to those very few individuals who uphold the law. In characterising the general tendency, it is hard to do justice to those exceptions.

49. They offer farmers ₹12, while the market rate is ₹10.

❖

5

Gujarat

Strong State-directed Capitalism across Sectors

This chapter addresses three primary concerns. First, whether political settlement in Gujarat has undergone a change since liberalisation. Second, the impact of 'class' interest on state apparatus with respect to agricultural policies and, because of such policies, if the existing proprietary classes have transformed themselves, remained unaffected, or have been replaced by new classes. Third, given that the state has been welcoming market forces, particularly under Chief Minister Modi, whether the market's free play has curbed the state's role in agriculture. These questions have been addressed by assessing various aspects of Gujarat's agrarian policy after 2000, in addition to land acquisition policies. Simultaneously, an analysis of what these policies entail for different classes of farmers is developed alongside the other two proprietary classes – the capitalist and the petty bourgeoisie. This analysis is, thus, undertaken from two angles – classes' influence on the state and the state's role in forming, altering, and consolidating classes. It is based on field research in Gujarat, conducted between October 2011 and January 2012.

The first section of the chapter offers a brief history of the state and outlines the changes in its economy in the past two decades. This is followed by sections presenting the fieldwork findings, in combination with a review of secondary literature. These sections first elaborate the main tenets of agricultural policy and the key factors behind the agricultural success of Gujarat, and then evaluate through a politico-economic lens, differential impact across classes and their fractions that have contributed to the agrarian success in Gujarat, particularly after 2000.

Brief overview

Geographical divisions

The present state of Gujarat historically constituted of two parts: Saurashtra and mainland Gujarat. During the colonial period, Saurashtra was a feudatory[1] state and was constituted of 112 principalities, while the mainland was under the British rule. Baroda was an exception; it was situated in Gujarat but was ruled by an enlightened royalty reputed for its benevolence towards its subjects, contributing to the pursuit of education and arts among its population (Bakhle, 2005). Baroda merged with Gujarat in 1949. In 1960, the regional state of Bombay was divided into two states, Maharashtra and Gujarat. Thus, Gujarat gained independent statehood. Traces of caste dominance and landlord dominance can be observed in agrarian relations till date in Saurashtra, where landlords command social and political respect among lower caste tenants and labourers. Meanwhile, mainland Gujarat has progressed speedily with respect to the industrial growth along the so-called golden corridor (Mahadevia, 2005), which falls between Mumbai and Ahmedabad. It is the fourth most urbanised state of India, with 42 per cent of its population living in urban areas (Census of India, 2011).

The state can be divided into the following four regions, agro-climatically as well as economically: central Gujarat plains known as the canal districts (where the golden corridor runs through), north Gujarat, Saurashtra and Kachchh, and the eastern tribal belt (Shah et al., 2009). Table 5.1 lays out an agricultural profile of these four regions and the districts they include.

Table 5.1 Economic and social profile of the four regions in Gujarat

Tribal areas	Dahod, Panchmahal, and Dangs	Low level of economic enterprise; rainfed farming; semi-arid to humid climate
North Gujarat	Gandhinagar, Ahmedabad, Patan, Mehsana, Banaskantha, and Sabarkantha	Enterprising farmers; groundwater is the main source of irrigation; dairy cooperatives
Canal districts (south and central Gujarat)	Anand, Kheda, Vadodara, Bharuch, Surat, Narmada, Navsari, and Valsad	Humid and water-abundant part of Gujarat; canal irrigation systems, through farmer initiative; enterprising farmers; strong dairy cooperatives.
Saurashtra and Kachchh	Amreli, Bhavnagar, Junagadh, Jamnagar, Porbandar, Rajkot, and Surendranagar	Arid to semi-arid climate; groundwater the main source of irrigation; agriculture dependent mostly on monsoon; poor dairy cooperatives.

Source: Shah et al. (2009: 49).

Note: The fourth region, the Eastern belt, is not relevant to the study.

These divisions are not demarcated along rigid lines. For instance, the state agricultural department further divides Saurashtra into north, south, and Kachchh. Moreover, the northern region does not include Gandhinagar and Ahmedabad in numerous classifications. However, Shah's classification holds significance because it helps in understanding where the powerful lobbies operate from and, hence, explaining which districts hold key positions for this study. For instance, Table 5.1 indicates that agriculture in Saurashtra and Kachchh has not had as large scale an adoption of capitalist methods as in central and south Gujarat. As literature suggests central and southern districts have had exemplary performance in capitalist agriculture, access to canal irrigation, agrarian surplus invested in agro-industry, and industry that has fed back into agriculture and brought about land consolidation, as well as organised and effective cooperatives – these areas were the areas of focus for the investigation.

The fieldwork was based mostly in Ahmedabad, the largest city in the state, about 25 kilometres away from Gandhinagar, the state capital. Most of the interviews were conducted in Ahmedabad, and some farmers, activists, politicians, and academicians were interviewed in the districts of Anand, Kheda, Mehsana, Rajkot, Surat, Baroda, and Banaskantha. Figure 5.1 shows the golden corridor around which all the districts visited are located, except Rajkot. The corridor gives these districts a strategic advantage.

Figure 5.1 Map of Gujarat showing districts visited and the golden corridor

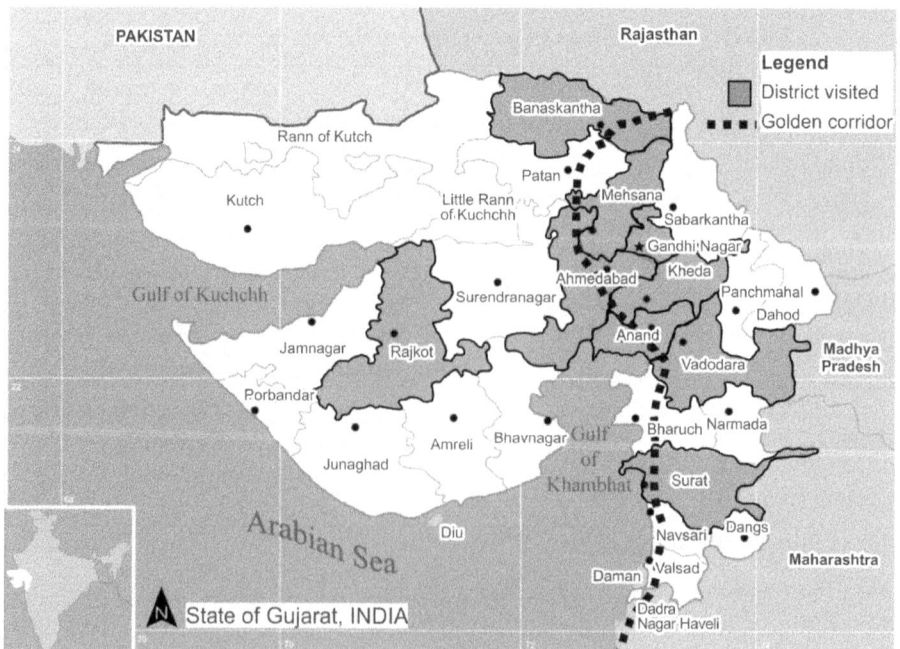

Source: Maps of India.
Note: Map not to scale and does not represent authentic international boundaries.

State-driven economic growth

One characteristic that differentiates Gujarat from Chhattisgarh and Karnataka is that the source of economic investment here has been capital originating within the state, rather than foreign capital or capital emanating from other states (Rutten and Patel, 2002), although the state has been partially successful in attracting foreign investment after liberalisation (Awasthi, 2000; Parekh, 2012). In fact, a significant part of the capitalist class of India – merchant and industrial – originates from Gujarat (Damodaran, 2008; Mahadevia, 2005). This fact is particularly significant since, after liberalisation, there has been a rise in competition between states to attract foreign capital, which is triggered by withdrawal of central funds in the form of grants-in-aid (GoI, 1997). Gujarat has performed particularly well in this regard.

Gujarat has followed the all-India economic development trajectory but has outperformed the rest of India across sectors, as reflected in Table 5.2. It has experienced consistent high growth in the manufacturing and service sectors throughout the last several decades. The agricultural sector fared worse than in other states until 2000, but has bounced back stronger than the all-India average, with high growth rates until recently.

Table 5.2 Sectoral growth rates (compound annual rate of growth) in Gujarat (1980–81 prices) (in %)

Sectors	1960–61 to 1970–71	1970–71 to 1979–80	1980–81 to 1989–90	1990–91 to 1999–2000	2005–06 to 2012–13	All India growth figures, 2005–06 to 2012–13
Primary	2.91	4.15	−0.44	1.95		
Agriculture	2.27	4.22	−0.59	−0.18	5.36	3.88
Secondary	3.62	5.64	6.51	7.25	9.58	7.68
Tertiary	3.51	5.86	7.10	7.39	11.45	9.36
Overall SDP[2]	3.32	4.95	5.02	5.53		
Per capita income	-	-	3.14	3.94		

Source: Hirway and Mahadevia (2003) and Planning Commission (data from 2000–01 to 2009–10).

Gujarat is now among the most urbanised states in India, but the growth of the urban economic sectors has not led to a simultaneous and proportionate movement of population from agriculture to industry and services. The NSSO reports show that the share of employment of the primary sector in the total employment has increased from 49.9 per cent in 2004–05 to 54.4 per cent in 2008–09 (Hirway and Shah, 2011). The last decade's growth, instead of improving the living conditions of those in the primary sector, has widened the gap among the classes (Hirway, 2000; Hirway and Shah, 2012). Arguably, this is a continuation of what Breman (1989) had identified in the late 1980s as a fearsome widening gap between the urban and the rural. He portrays how tiller farmers and wage labourers have to struggle to sustain themselves. This gap has also translated into a regional bias, where agricultural growth for the first five decades after Independence was concentrated along the golden corridor of the state (marked in the map). Both the northern and eastern districts have lagged in terms of development, education, and industrialisation (Mahadevia, 2005; UNDP, 2012). The state has remained negligent towards Kachchh and Saurashtra[3] in the west as well as the eastern districts that are dominated by tribal populations. Both these regions are dry areas. After 2000, Saurashtra has received some attention in the form of industrial investment and developmental concern. However, scholars note that small farmers and agricultural labourers lie at the bottommost level of society, facing poor living conditions and food insecurity (Breman, 2007; Dand and Chakravarty, 2006).

Gujarat's success in making fruitful use of liberalising policies can be accredited to the state bureaucracy, a feature distinct from the usual lackadaisical picture of Indian bureaucracy. Since the 1960s, it has been channelling investments into the state. Sinha (2005) terms it the classic role of 'guiding the market'. Gujarat's capital has received assistance from the institutional machinery through the years. The state bureaucracy's skills were sharpened during the licensing period and put to good use after 1990. The 'monitoring cell' in the regional industries and mines department was used to screen every investment proposal. This constant check from the cell explains why the state has a high ratio of investment to proposed projects, which is one of the highest across India. Sinha (2005) sharply puts it as that 'the bureaucracy has developed a killer instinct when it comes to wooing the investors' (Sinha, 2005: 155). This wing of the government in Gujarat, unlike other states, has been collecting detailed information on investors willing to invest in the state. Gujarat has successfully propagated the 'industrialisation and globalisation' slogan that has come to dominate the public psyche, serving as the means to build 'Gujarati' self-esteem. Along with this, it has also provided support to industries through infrastructural facilities, input supplies, and by abolishing turnover tax (Dholakia, 2000). The state has retained a positive role in a market-led development model.

The favourable position of the state bureaucracy can be seen in the huge revenue expenditure that the state incurs in paying them (UNDP, 2004). A large part of the government budget goes towards payment of interest, wages, and salaries, in addition to subsidies and transfers. Sharma (1999) found that while these items accounted for around 48 per cent of the state's revenue expenditure in 1980–81, by 1997–98 their share had increased to nearly 65 per cent. In addition, the argument that IAS officers managed to convert a rule-based system into a relationship-based one, with the help of the political masters, possibly holds true (Das, 2005). Latest figures show that Gujarat is leading when it comes to grand corruption (Bussell, 2012). It has become a part of everyday transactions, with local inspectors paying frequent visits to small-scale industries to make extra money (Dholakia, 2000). Rent accumulated by the bureaucracy means they directly gain from the economic growth of the state transforming them into old petty bourgeoisie. The success of the market is, thus, routed through the proactive functioning of the state, an argument made for the neighbouring state of Rajasthan, which can well be applicable also to Gujarat (Levien, 2011).

A glance at the sectoral growth of Gujarat from 1960 to 1990 reveals a shift from a balanced growth among three sectors to an overt emphasis on secondary and tertiary sectors, affecting the composition of the state domestic product (SDP) (Dixit, 2008; Table 4.2). Several scholars argue that until the 1970s, there were close linkages between the agricultural and manufacturing sectors. This is evident from the southern districts of Gujarat (Rutten, 2003; Damodaran, 2008). In the transition of surplus, Damodaran (2008) finds cooperatives making a strong contribution. The rise of agribusiness owes much to the agrarian surplus, which sets it apart from Andhra Pradesh, where the surplus has been directly invested in the tertiary sector, skipping investment in the secondary sector (Damodaran, 2008).

In the neoliberal era, states in India have had to compete against one another to attract private investments. Increasing export and generating revenue have become a core goal of the state governments. States have invested in SEZs, as per the central government regulations of March 2000.[4] Gujarat has offered special incentives and facilities, such as land, at unbelievably low prices to developers of SEZs; the other industrial units working within it prefer land at a cheaper rate, tax exemptions, and relaxed labour laws (Levien, 2012). These efforts have facilitated high rates of growth in both the secondary and tertiary sectors.

Along with this growth in the secondary and tertiary sectors, the state has witnessed over 10 per cent growth rate in the agricultural sector between 2005 and 2012. What does this indicate about farmers' relations with political leaders and parties? Have they been able to reach a political bargain despite the overall atmosphere in favour of rapid industrialisation? These questions make it crucial to understand the ways in which class–state relations function within the state. One mode of operationalising these relations is lobbying. The subsequent sections critically examine lobby politics in Gujarat by drawing upon existing literature as well as by substantiating them with evidence from fieldwork.

The general election held in 2014 brought the then Gujarat Chief Minister, Narendra Modi, to national politics as the new Indian Prime Minister. Before this, a few voices from media, academia, and the development sector have often referred to the state's success as the 'Gujarat development model', implying a type of neoliberal development that prioritises industrial development and capitalist agricultural development over and above social development of the majority of the population (Jaffrelot, 2015). Intellectually, there are parallels between this and the classic two-sector 'Lewis model' that dominated development thinking in India from Independence onwards. This model stressed on industrialisation and capitalist development of agriculture. It was expected that this would lead to a gradual shift of the population from agriculture to industrial employment, thereby contributing to better living conditions for them. However, Gujarat has a marginally above-India average proportion of the population working in industry and a slightly below-average proportion of the population working in agriculture. Compared to the all-India average, Gulati and Shah (2011a and 2011b) argue forcefully that this does not amount to a Lewisian development trajectory because there was a significant *reverse* employment that developed between 2004–05 and 2008–09 when the primary sector employment increased by 5 percentage points. Gujarat is a high per-capita income state, but the fruits of development are not benefitting the majority to any significant extent (Hirway, 2000, 2012). Food insecurity is high (Global Hunger Index, 2011), human development is low, and regional disparity has continued (Hirway and Shah, 2011b). In line with this, the fieldwork shows that the focus of the state is strongly on economic growth exclusively and, at best, the economic and social well-being of the population is expected to follow at a later stage.

Key findings from fieldwork

For Gujarat, the total number of respondents was 47, out of whom 18 were farmers, and the others were 1 senior bank official, 2 capitalists, 3 political party members and state officials, 8 social activists and development sector professionals, and 9 academicians-cum-researchers. Here again, petty bourgeoisie is an overlapping category with big and middle farmers and, hence, not spelt out separately. The academicians could be classified into two sections – a few who were working closely with the state and the rest who were critical of state policies. One old gentleman acted as a key informant. He accompanied me in the initial phase of fieldwork and would share old newspaper cuttings to acquaint me with the background of agriculture in Gujarat. When I was unable to grasp certain issues, he would explain various local practices for better understanding. Across the state, two FGDs were held, one in Mehsana with big and a few middle farmers and the other in Anand (Petlad) with organic farmers, who owned more than 10 acres each.

The aim of the fieldwork was to identify the propertied classes owning capital and land in Gujarat, and explore the way they act within the political realm. Do they convey their interests through lobbies and, if yes, how has this changed in the post-liberalisation phase? This question is addressed by identifying the lobbies that operated during the 1980s and 1990s. The post-2001 Modi regime in the state is described mainly through data collected during fieldwork, and it is relied upon to establish whether capitalists are able to earn state favours and support towards private investment. This is followed by a discussion of issues specific to agrarian policy – credit, land, and chemical inputs – using a political economy lens. In the final section, relations between new and old institutions and propertied classes are examined to throw light on how proprietary classes influence the institutions, both theoretically and in the formulation of schemes and policies.

Political lobbying in Gujarat: Before and after liberalisation

The domestic bourgeoisie in Gujarat is constituted of different communities including the Shah, Thakkar, and Vohra (Muslim) groups (three interviews: bureaucrat, activist, and academician in Ahmedabad, November 2012). These were the first communities to invest in the secondary sector, and are now mostly based in Mumbai, Surat, and other metropolitan cities. The Patels became financially influential later, but since then their importance has been rising steadily. Unlike the Patel community, the Shah, Thakkar, and Vohra communities moved out of agriculture once they invested in the secondary sector, and are, therefore, dissociated from farmers' interests (Chandavarkar, 1994; Shah, 2002; Damodaran, 2008). The industrial capitalists, comprising

Banias, Jains, Parsis, Khojas, and Brahmins, have had a historical advantage in the industry. The presence of a few capitalists in agribusiness can be traced back to as early as the 1960s. For example, industrial houses such as Mafatlal invested in both oil-processing and cotton mills. The Patel community was a late entrant in agribusiness, and their initial investment was in agro-industries, such as cotton, rice, and oil mills, and dairy processing, but their strength was in the formation of cooperatives (Rutten, 2003). Relevant literature and field interviews establish the investment for setting up workshops and factories is generated from agricultural surplus (Breman, 1989).

In the context of Gujarat, the Patel community holds particular significance, given its continued ownership of agricultural land and investing its surplus back into the agrarian sector. They are an important caste group constituting the capitalist class. Even though several of the mill owners and diamond merchants in the state are Patels, these capitalists are a numerical minority within the community itself. The Patels work mostly as *karigars* (diamond cutters and polishers), and face hardship, violence, and poor living conditions (Engelshoven, 1999). Therefore, class, and not only caste, becomes more appropriate in explaining the phenomenon. Often both owners and workers belong to the same caste, but stand at two ends of the production relation.

The interest of capitalists is surplus accumulation and a common modus operandi to seek state support has been forming political lobbies. Until the 1990s, the lobby that dominated Gujarat politics was linked to agro-processing. To start with, the *teli mafia* (vegetable oil goons), who hailed from Saurashtra and were landed (but not cultivators), controlled the oil mills (Mahadevia, 2005). With the advent of Bt cotton, cotton production increased manifold, and the groundnut crop that formed the raw material for the oil mills slowly lost its pivotal position to cotton. Instead of groundnut, cotton seeds came to be predominantly used for extraction of oil now. With groundnut losing its monopoly and relaxation of restriction on oil import, the *teli mafia* faced severe challenges. However, this did not result in the loss of influence of the industrial class on the state; rather only a small part of this class was impacted. The industrial class maintains its hold on the state's economy by diversifying capital to new industrial sectors. Similarly, rich farmers from Kheda, Bharuch, Surat, and cash-crop producing regions of Mehsana are considered an important political force in the state (Mahadevia, 2005). The dominance of a crop might vary from decade to decade, but the power remains with the same class of capitalist farmers (Breman, 2007; Rutten, 2003).

The second important lobby was that of rice mills owners, but with rice mills closing down in great numbers since the end of the 1980s, the lobby has lost relevance. The lobby mainly comprised of capitalist farmers. Loss of relevance was caused by the fast adoption of commercial crops (interview of a political leader from Ahmedabad, December 2012). This lobby mandates no further discussion. The third important lobby was part of the industrial capitalists with control on multiple sub-sectors from chemical, pharmacy, to real estate.

The diamond industry is another lobby of significance. Scholars have inferred horizontal unity among its members based on a common caste identity along with regional roots in Saurashtra. They were originally middle farmers, and have migrated to Surat since the 1960s. The early migrants gradually accumulated enough to open workshops and factories, while those who came later did not own adequate surplus and, hence, were forced to work as *karigars* (craftsmen) (Engelshoven, 1999). The owners and traders are organised under the Surat Diamond Association.[5]

While scholars have pointed out that the state has been furthering the interests of the urban classes by treating the secondary and tertiary sectors as vehicles of growth, this book argues that the big farmer class has not been left out of the list of beneficiaries. Urban and rural is not an effective way to categorise beneficiaries since the fieldwork was replete with instances where an urban businessman held land in rural areas and a farmer had an urban shop or trade.[6] Gulati (1988) and Archana Dholakia (2002) show that the Gujarat government has offered huge subsidies to the farmers; these subsidies are significantly more when compared to other states.[7] The subsidy has not been uniformly distributed; for instance, groundnut production was highly subsidised over other crops in the early 1990s (Dholakia, 2002). Cotton, in fact, was thoroughly exposed to international market price fluctuations in the 1990s.[8] This support in the form of subsidies did not translate into immediate high growth rates in the agricultural sector at that time but paved the way for significant changes in agriculture in the following decade.

New millennium: State and class enter a new relationship

During the decade preceding Modi's ascent to power in 2001, the political climate of the state had been largely unstable. Modi's regime was marked by decisive governance and promotion of high economic growth, often related to Modi's successful wooing of investors by means of organising events such as the Vibrant Gujarat Global Investors' Summit. Evidence suggests that during this period, the capitalist class built stronger linkages to political parties, especially in the form of different lobbies funding major political parties and contributing to election funds (Mahadevia, 2005; *The Navhind Times*, 2012).

The high growth rates, 10 per cent in the secondary sector and the service sector, experienced in the state after 2000 can be ascribed to the state's careful manoeuvring of policies. Sud (2007) argues that land acquisition has been possible because of a convergence between political and economic powers in Gujarat that resulted in concentrating resources to nurture capitalists. Several respondents during fieldwork – activists, academics, and political leaders – located in different districts also pointed to the existence of such a nexus between the state and big corporate houses. An extensive study on electoral candidates of the Gujarat 2012 assembly elections found that 372 (22 per cent) out of a total of 1,660 candidates were 'multimillionaires',[9] which was only 1 per cent more than the 2007 Gujarat assembly elections (120 out of the 563 candidates analysed) (ADR, 2012). Out of the 182 newly elected MLAs in 2012, 74 per cent were *crorepatis*. In fact, 75 per cent of the BJP MLAs, 70 per cent of the Congress MLAs, and 100 per cent of the Nationalist Congress Party (NCP) and Janata Dal (United) (JDU) MLAs were *crorepatis* (ADR, 2012). It is evident that the political leadership is composed overtly of those already holding wealth as capital or land. The industrial class also directly assumes position of authority within the state apparatus. For instance, the former chair of the Gujarat Chamber of Commerce and Industry became the Chief Minister of Gujarat for a brief period. He changed his party affiliation thrice, between 1990 and 2002, being a member of the Rashtriya Janata Dal, the Congress, and the BJP (Sud, 2007). Party ideology, hence, becomes secondary to class interest.

The state government in Gujarat has been proactive in acquiring land in the new millennium for private companies and signing memoranda of understanding (MOUs) to facilitate land procurement, thereby reflecting its industry friendliness. As a result of this industry-friendly nature, Gujarat has emerged as a favourite destination for corporates such as Maruti and Tata. The bureaucracy plays a conducive role in these transactions. 'It is commonplace to accept that the government belongs to Reliance and Adani,' remarked an activist interviewed during fieldwork.[10] At the same time, weak labour laws and easy availability of labour have facilitated capital accumulation in the state. Further, it was found that the high growth rate has been at the cost of small enterprises. Hirway (2012) makes similar observations about labour rights violations. According to an Accenture study, the incidence of crony capitalism in Gujarat is high, tying together large domestic industry and the state in a common interest. The argument is substantiated by Bussell (2012), who characterises Gujarat to be on the top in relation to grand corruption. During field work, a respondent indicated that such a nexus is a factor constraining the entry of international oil companies and MNCs into the state (interview of Wagela from Ahmedabad, 2012). The state has been a ripe ground to breed a few domestic capitalists.

Another reason for the high growth witnessed in Gujarat is the support of the bureaucracy to industrialisation efforts. In part this is linked to the high rents that accrue to the bureaucracy because of processes involved in industrialisation, such as licensing and contracting which boosts a class of old petty bourgeoisie. Gujarat registered the highest grand corruption among states in India, establishing inappropriate inter-linkages between the bureaucracy and the capitalist class while experiencing low petty corruption. The latter affects citizens in day-to-day activities (Bussell, 2012). Further, the government, led by Modi, has focused on ideation to bring about economic growth. The Chief Minister was reported to inculcate his vision into the bureaucrats by interacting with them, particularly by organising workshops such as the Chintan Shibir, a three-day exercise in which he, his cabinet, and officers interacted to exchange ideas and understand the agenda of the state (Mahurkar, 2011). It gave the state coherence in both operation and vision which is rare to find.

During interviews with an academic, a CII member, a veteran political leader, and a political cadre in Ahmedabad, the respondents explained how growth has been achieved by giving undue advantage to corporate and big business houses. The political cadre stated that the total subsidy to the corporates was ₹200,000 million between 2007 and 2011. For example, out of this amount, Essar, a leading corporate house, was a major offender, and the government has been reluctant in recovering this money. Reliance bought land in Bhavnagar with the purpose of establishing an industry in 2010–11. Only a part of the land has been devoted to industry, and the remaining land is allocated to growing mangoes. Legally, they are now growers and exporters of mangoes, and thus qualify for tax exemption[11] on agricultural income. In addition, the company has been demanding more land from the government for staff quarters. The High Court has dismissed this, and has asked them to use the mango plantation land instead (interview of a political cadre from Ahmedabad, 2011). Arguably, all figures might be coloured by political difference and could not be verified, but academics indicated a similar biased treatment on the part of the state towards the industrial class.

In 2013, the Comptroller and Auditor General (CAG) found similar problems with the Gujarat government (*The Hindu*, 3 April 2013). It found undue benefits amounting to ₹520 million being handed out for the benefit of the Reliance Group. In another instance, the Gujarat Urja Vikas Nigam Ltd.

failed to recover a penalty of ₹1,600 million from Adani Power. Essar was found defaulting on sales tax payment of ₹61,690 million by the High Court (*The Economic Times*, 2012a). Similar observations have been made by other scholars (Hirway and Shah, 2012). The capitalists, big or small, have extracted surplus from the respective sectors and invested heavily in real estate all over the state. The state has ensured that land is made easily available to the industrial capitalists. The crystallisation of the new capitalist class has been pinned as the support base for the state pursuing such proactive industry-friendly policies. Sud (2007) argues that the class was disenchanted with the Congress and its pro-poor, lower caste, and pro-agriculture policies. They needed a decisive, pro-industry political voice, which they found in the BJP.

Gujarat has experienced an incoming of important political forces since 2000, and this has led to a shift in dominant political lobbies. Two respondents, an activist working on labour issues for over three decades and a senior member of a left party, stated in their interviews that since the late 1990s the grip of the indigenous economic capital on the political apparatus has tightened; however, the dominance has shifted from the earlier powerful lobbies such as diamond and textile to real estate (interviewees from Surat, April 2012 and from Ahmedabad, December 2011). The interests of the industrial capitalist class are represented by different organisations, such as the Southern Gujarat Chamber of Commerce and Industries (SGCCI). Southern Gujarat has cornered the lion's share of capital within the state for the past five decades until 2000, and has garnered 93 per cent of the state resources (Mahadevia, 2005). They maintain close contact with the Gujarat government to earn these favours. They also represent the interests of chemical, pharmaceutical, and IT companies. Another organisation representing industrial capitalist interests is the Federation of Gujarat Weavers' Association (FOGWA), which is a union of power loom owners. Many of the looms are unregistered and exist on paper in the name of different owners, all of whom belong to one family. This helps in evading labour laws applicable to big power looms (interview of Mehta from Ahmedabad, November 2012). Power looms are concentrated regionally along the golden corridor, and each loom has a leader who comes together to form a federation. A well-known spokesperson of the industrial lobby reiterated that under the present regime, big corporates enjoy a direct link with the state administration, are privy to information, and enjoy faster processing of their paperwork. The small firms are left to negotiate through organisations such as the FOGWA. The vision of the state is 'big is beautiful'.

The state extends protection to its allies by granting subsidies of different kinds. According to a Left party leader, the big power looms are given huge subsidies for buying new machinery once every five years. To avail the subsidy, they often sell old machinery at low prices. Some mills have converted to small-scale operations with 20–30 people to avoid adhering to labour laws and follow fewer rules in an informal economy. This helps generate higher surplus. Textile firms such as Mafatlal and Vimal have taken to outsourcing their work to these small looms, while they use their brand labels and organise the packaging of products. Interviews with social activists revealed another development has taken place in the textile industry after liberalisation. Put in Marxian terminology, small firms are being engulfed by big capitalists. A trend of monopolisation can be observed, where economic power is getting concentrated in the hands of the few who are surviving by producing non-cotton textiles such as rayon and polyester. The owners of small textile firms have gone on to invest in the stock market and real estate, moving away from manufacturing. A part of the labour force has gone out of formal employment and have found the conditions of the informal sector hard to adjust with. As a result, several hundred units have closed since liberalisation, as shown by an academic study by the Centre for Social Studies, Surat (n.d.).

The Modi government weakened the implementation of labour laws in the state in order to create a congenial climate for all industries, as was triangulated across three interviews. While the state was actively supporting big capitalists, its passivity about recruitment of labour officers helped further the interests of the same class. This smoothened the casualisation of labour, making Modi a favourite among business houses. The entire machinery for protection of labour was largely suspended, and labour laws had little meaning. In all of this, women workers were among the most marginalised (Hirway and Shah, 2011). In 2011, there were 75 per cent vacant seats in the labour department; even posts such as the Assistant Commissioner of Labour, the highest post in each district, was left vacant. In Saurashtra, among seven districts, only one Assistant Commissioner post was filled. A similar situation has persisted since. Two respondents, an academician and a trade union leader, argued that this systematic weakening has made issues such as minimum wage, timely payment of wages, and grievance redressal relating to labour laws redundant. 'Where will people register their complaints in absence of an operational department?' On the other hand, because of this informalisation of labour, industries have increasingly been using contract labour from other states such as UP, Bihar, MP, and Rajasthan. The liability of the employer with regard to contract labour is significantly less than in the case of regular employment of workers, thereby leaving workers even more vulnerable. The institutional vacuum has allowed class oppression to persist and thrive (interviewees from Ahmedabad, October 2011). There was a dearth of official data on wages available in the state and, as an activist stated, 'Modi, in his attempt to befriend industries, has crushed the rights of labourers.' The same attitude is reflected in the indiscriminate transfer of agricultural land to industries under the present government. Both the national parties, the BJP and the Congress, have labour unions registered to the political party, but both have attracted limited numbers of members. The closer alignment to capitalist interest since the late 1990s in contrast to party strategy during the 1970s and 1980s, when parties sought labour support, has dissuaded labourers from taking membership in unions.

In the aftermath of the liberalisation policy, across the field districts, the continuing hegemonic dominance of the mercantile–financial–industrial class was noted, even in 2000, but in a distinctly new guise. What the class seeks and stands for is different. The Patidar community, along with old business communities such as Parsis and Khojas, has been at the forefront of this class. The state government has welcomed and depended heavily on investments from non-resident Indians (NRIs). In Bardoli, roads and community centres have been reconstructed with NRI investments. However, it is not a benign capital investment to reap profits from, but has a communal overtone as well. An instance can be traced to the Godhra riots in 2002,[12] when various NGOs and trusts received funds from foreign investors to propagate hate sentiments against the religious minority in Gujarat (Oommen, 2008). The inflow of foreign capital has continued after 2002. The most desired areas of investment are banks and shares (financial capital), as well as real estate (farmland, residential plots, and apartments). Other than this, NRIs have invested in family businesses, as a broker pointed out in Kheda (2011). This forms the spine of Gujarat's economy, and makes it less dependent on foreign capital from MNCs and corporate enterprises (Rutten and Patel, 2002; Hirway, 2012).

In the decade following 2000, large-scale agriculture has become an increasingly profitable enterprise. The relation has been maintained between agriculture and industry as seen during earlier decades, where surplus from agriculture feeds into the other sector as capital. The phase has, however, reduced dependence on tillers and wage labour, who are fast being replaced by technology, unlike the case of Chhattisgarh. The emerging entrepreneurial groups who transitioned from agriculture to agro-industry and then to the industrial sector (such as plastics, chemicals, dye, and pharmaceutical) simultaneously moved from rural to urban living yet hold interest in the agrarian sector. This is evident from the rapid urbanisation in Gujarat, exemplified in the rise from 25.7 per cent of its population living in cities in the 1960s to 43 per cent by 2011 (Census, 2011).

Game of gold: Politics requires more than connection and character

Contesting elections in India is an expensive affair. This is particularly true in the state where numerous indigenous capitalists hail from. Alliance with the rich is almost a necessity to access capital to cover the cost for contesting elections. An ADR report (2002) has shown that expenditure per electoral candidate can run into millions of rupees.[13] Political leaders either are mostly economically powerful by virtue of belonging to propertied class, and, therefore, enter politics to promote their class interests, or acquire power with the help of the capitalist class and big capitalist farmers and serve the latter's interests once they assume office. A close exchange with capitalists was evident since most of Modi's visits to different parts of India during elections and abroad were directly funded by the corporates, and he travels in their private jets (*DNA*, 2012).

Industrialists have emerged as favoured candidates of both national parties, the Congress and the BJP. Candidates, especially in south Gujarat, are industrialists who hail from the textile, real estate, and diamond industries. The Congress spokesperson candidly argued that this is because they understand the interest of the industrialists better. Literature suggests that the industrial class invested ₹10,000 million in the 2007 elections in the state (*IBN Live*, 2007; Krishnakumar, 2007). Respondents across districts, including a senior member of the industrial lobby in Ahmedabad, maintained that the industrial capitalist class had close links with the Modi government.

As Jessop (1983) had predicted, the state and capitalists have come to interchange their positions, and forged a 'personal fusion' that results in the state actively helping in capital accumulation. For instance, a sugar factory owner in Surat heads the cooperative bank and, therefore, has access to finance; in addition, he also heads a dairy cooperative and owns large landholdings. He can easily be classified as a capitalist. He contested the state assembly elections and exerts significant political power. When election funding and politicians both come from a particular class, where does the state support go once the elections are won? This is, of course, a rhetorical question. In Gujarat, democratic practice and political ethics have weakened. The number of politicians with a criminal background has increased considerably (CSS report[14]). With the market and the state coming uncomfortably close over the decade since 2001, the adjudicator and beneficiary interests have become the same, sidelining democratic institutional arrangements.

Investment has been attracted to the state by playing the 'development' card as well. The government has actively promoted development in the state by facilitating land transfers and water from agriculture to industry. A few interview respondents indicated that Narmada water under the Sardar Sarovar Project (SSP) has been diverted to industry at the cost of agriculture. Such industry-friendly policies have made Modi immensely popular among urban professionals (new petty bourgeoisie) and the capitalist class alike. Traders and industrial capitalists have been the BJP's traditional support base, but the urban professional class has aligned itself to the party by identifying with precisely this 'development model'. It has been established that the industrial capitalist class is the most dominant part of the political settlement, with a few instances of 'personal fusion'.

Agricultural policy for big capitalist farmers

This section outlines the key elements of Gujarat's agricultural policy since 2000. It draws on an article by Gulati and Shah (2009) which states that policies are substantiated by the Gujarat government's websites. This article has dominated all discourses on the Gujarat agrarian economy since its publication and offers a holistic understanding of the agrarian situation. The article offers a classification of agro-climatic and economic factors, which holds particular significance for a political economy perspective. The classification has been adopted in the chapter over other classifications. This is followed by a discussion of the possible implications these policies have for different classes of farmers. The overall argument is that the government has drawn a sharp distinction between resource-rich farmers, or 'capable' farmers, as a senior government officer termed them, and the rest of the farmers. The government has taken a classic developmentalist policy approach that is favourable to industry and large-scale farming. A pivotal problem of such a vision is the implicit neglect of the small and marginal farmers and wage labourers, who form 88 per cent[15] of the state's agricultural population. They are resource poor and lack access to formal credit and irrigation, which are imperative when it comes to surviving in the investment-heavy and input-centric agricultural world that the state envisions. The government is keen on pushing chemical inputs and hybrid seeds procured from MNCs to achieve higher growth rates. Proprietary class interest is inherent in the kind of agenda the state has set up for the sector, which will perpetuate inequality given that the beginning already had structural inequality.

It was often stated by respondents, scholars, and activists alike that there is no comprehensive agricultural policy, and that several aspects relating to Gujarat's agriculture policies are contradictory. Several standalone policies have been pursued since Modi assumed power, which need to be seen as an integrated system.

A 'Gujarat Agrovision 2010' document exists, which mainly sets certain goals rather than providing a planned path. The central goal and emphasis of all policy and interventionist schemes is achieving economic growth in agriculture. It has been openly admitted that the state will facilitate a linkage between farmers and international markets under the WTO regime (Gujarat Agrovision, 2010: 305). This situation is not one of policy vacuum or chaos. Rather, the state has conceived a coherent vision that is driving the agrarian sector.

A detailed analysis of the state agrarian policies indicates a class bias, which will surface as a foray into specific policies undertaken. In the following section, several aspects of the policy have been discussed to unravel a political economy understanding of each.

Access to power

During 2003–06, the Gujarat government introduced the Jyotirgram Yojana (JGY) to provide 24 × 7, three-phase power supply to the rural areas of the state. To achieve this, an effective rationing of farm power supply was undertaken (Shah, 2006). This led the government to invest ₹11,700 million in separating agricultural feeders from non-agricultural/domestic feeders throughout Gujarat (Shah and Verma, 2008).[16] Scholars have found that increased access to electricity has made a difference in cultivation, but only for those who can bear the cost of an electric pump for irrigation. Resource-poor farmers have to bear the additional cost of hiring pumps to irrigate their fields (Kumar et al., 2004; NCEUS, 2008), a finding that was corroborated in field interviews.

Intense water shortage and poor public irrigation in the region have resulted in tremendous emphasis on agricultural mechanisation. As it stands, private underground irrigation covers 78 per cent of the total irrigation, only an insignificant 18 per cent of which is covered by canals (Mehta, 2012). The Gujarat Electricity Industry (Reorganisation and Regulation) Act, 2003, was implemented with an aim to 'improve efficiency in management and delivery of services to consumers'.[17] There was no social agenda attached to the policy; thus it has ensured better supply of electricity not to the tillers but mainly to the capitalist farmers who can bear investments in adverse water table conditions (Joshi and Acharya, 2005). Coupled with the fact that technological innovation has reduced labour use, in the present era, tiller farmers are losing control of resources, land, and water. Middle farmers have coped by diversifying into trade and business.

Infrastructural support

Gujarat has invested heavily in infrastructure development, particularly for building roads. This has acted as a catalyst in improving rural road connectivity. For instance, transfer of milk now takes place twice daily from villages to cities. Given the direct impact of better road connectivity to foster the dairy business, many dairy unions and other private investors have contributed to the construction of roads (Breman, 1989). The National Dairy Development Board gave a large loan to the Gujarat government to construct or resurface rural roads. Today, Gujarat has 37.77 kilometre of roads per 100,000 of population, and the road length per square feet is 0.01, which for Karnataka is 0.02 (Pradhan Mantri Gram Sadak Yojana). Road coverage is approximately 98.7 per cent in the state. At 146 kilometre per 100,000 of population, Gujarat's road density is higher than the all-India average of 126 kilometres per 100,000 of population. Rural Gujarat is very well connected in relation with other frontrunners such as Kerala, Haryana, and Punjab (Pradhan Mantri Gram Sadak Yojana). The government claims that while Gujarat invested ₹34,840 million on roads during 1960–2001, it has invested ₹47,830 million between 2001 and 2007 (Gulati and Shah, 2009). It is, therefore, evident that the government's focus on building robust road connectivity has increased manifold in recent times. The impact of better road connectivity on tiller farmers and the income they generate remains an open question.

Access to market

Gujarat was among the first states to amend the APMC Act in 1963, calling it the Gujarat Agricultural Produce Market Act to enable farmers to directly sell their produce to wholesalers, exporters, industries, and large trading companies without having to operate through *arhatia*s or commission agents. APMC is limited to a few crops. It also allowed large players to establish spot exchanges. The amendment also helped to create conditions conducive for the spread of contract farming. Sourcing from farmers directly has transpired in big corporates, impacting which crops are grown, and thus affecting cropping patterns. The government has been welcoming large corporates to establish retail chains and source their requirements directly from farmers. Corporates prefer sourcing from capitalist farmers for bulk purchase, but in the process influence farmers' autonomy – how to grow and what to grow. Market access bequeaths more inequality as it builds on existing structural inequality. The access to market also is consistently reducing autonomy of the farmers.

Higher subsidy for commercial crops

The Gujarat government has pursued aggressive policies to promote diversification to high-value crops, especially fruit, vegetables, spices, and condiments. For example, it began offering farmers direct capital subsidy of ₹250,000 to set up green houses, besides 25 per cent rebate in electricity duty. These measures have produced some positive outcomes. Between 2000–01 and 2005–06, Gujarat's horticulture production increased by 108 per cent (Government of Gujarat, 2009a). 'It was under active government consideration to lease out wastelands so as to cultivate it using modern technology for horticulture and biofuel trees to the big corporate houses and individual resourceful farmers' (Bharwada and Mahajan, 2006). Individual resourceful farmers are the capitalist farmers who are capable of putting in the kind of capital that high-value crops require. High-value crops are water intensive, and require chemical inputs that are more expensive; in addition, high-value floriculture requires greenhouse technology; hence, to be able to grow these crops, capital is the necessary prerequisite.

Efficient disbursal of institutional credit

Gujarat farmers have moved in terms of fertiliser usage from a 13:7.5:1 nitrogen–phosphorous–potassium composition to a 6.5:3.5:1 composition, thereby reducing cost, optimising production, and improving net income. The farm credit system too has been revitalised. Agricultural loan disbursements in Gujarat have clocked 22 to 25 per cent annual growth rate mainly due to supportive government policies. In the four years between 2003 and 2007, for example, agricultural loan disbursals in Gujarat doubled from ₹47,350 million in 2003–04 to 1,04,680 million in 2006–07. Even though subsidy seems like a welcome step to support agriculture as a sector, it shows two things: first, a strong state intervention and, second, the market's need for the state in order to thrive.

Minimum support price and its impact on cotton production

The Government of India announces the MSP for certain crops at the beginning of the sowing season to insure farmers against any sharp fall in the prices of agricultural produce during bumper production years. The MSP has provided strong incentive to farmers to increase production (Shah et al., 2009). For farmers in Gujarat, high MSP for cotton has been particularly beneficial, as the Cotton Corporation of India has sizeable procurement operations in the state. Along with this, export demand for cotton has been strong. In recent years, Gujarat has come to dominate India's cotton export and is a major cotton supplier to China (Hamer, 2012).

However, Bhaumik (2008) highlights that Gujarat farmers have poor awareness of price policy and procurement agencies. Only 26.7 per cent of the farmers are aware of the MSP, while only 14.3 per cent know the whereabouts of the procurement agencies (p. 148). Thus, Bt cotton has increasingly been sold at market prices, because it has a high export demand; therefore, farmers prefer selling to traders rather than state agencies. Further, the food grains that are primarily produced by tiller farmers, namely jowar, bajra, and maize, do not feature in the central government's procurement priority. The MSP is fixed to encourage farmers to make capital investment in their farm and motivate them to adopt higher crop-production technology to improve productivity and revenue from land. So, these food crops are disincentivised. As already discussed, only capitalist farmers are capable of making such capital investment without incurring debts and, therefore, such pricing policy's benefits get limited to a certain class of farmers.

Irrigation systems

Water is a premise on which the Green Revolution and its success rest. Making water available to farmers has been a claim to fame for the Modi government. The Sardar Sarovar Dam, which had staunch government backing despite the long years of protest in the 1990s to stop the dam construction under the Narmada Bachao Andolan,[18] has been key in providing canal irrigation in the southern districts. However, canal irrigation accounts for only 18 per cent of the total irrigation in the state, while 4 per cent is done by tanks and other sources. In the northern districts, 90 per cent of the irrigation is covered by private borewells and tubewells alone, while the state average is 78 per cent for private borewells and tubewells (Mehta, 2012). The overuse of groundwater has been ascribed to the introduction of high-yielding seeds and incentive-oriented pricing policy (Mehta, 2012). The public irrigation system is regionally biased towards the southern districts, which have fertile soil and have had a strong farmer lobby. Gujarat has raised the dam height under the Sardar Sarovar Project to 121.5 metres, and there is enough water in the dam to irrigate 1.8 million hectares, as planned. However, the water is catering to Ahmedabad and the southern districts exclusively. The eastern and northern districts as well as Saurashtra have not gained any access to canal water, despite many political promises in 2013.

The Gujarat Green Revolution Company Limited (GGRC) was established in 2005 to implement the micro irrigation scheme (MIS) of the Government of Gujarat and the Government of India in a uniform subsidy pattern of 50 per cent of the total MIS cost or ₹60,000 per hectare, whichever is less. It will subsidise new means of irrigation such as drip and sprinkler and, thus, bolster agricultural productivity while retaining the efficiency of water usage. The scheme provides water to the root zone of the plants – a technological measure to address the environmental hazard caused by conventional irrigation though it is highly capital intensive. Under the scheme, bank loans are directed towards the beneficiary farmer as per need; insurance coverage is provided for the irrigation system for a period of five years; agronomical services are rendered to the farmer for two crops; and the irrigation system is maintained by the MIS suppliers. By 2014, 6,40,853 farmers had adopted MIS, and subsidy of ₹2,866.43 crore had been disbursed.

The policy measures discussed here have been pursued by the state government during the decade following 2000, and their resource-intensive nature implies that they clearly favour the big and capitalist farmers. These are reinforced in the 'Gujarat Agrovision 2010' document. In the new millennium, the government's emphasis has been on high-yielding seeds and input-centric agriculture that relies heavily on chemical pesticides, high-value crops (horticulture–floriculture), private irrigation, and a differentiated credit policy that favours the resourceful. Modi stressed that the state would facilitate linkages between farmers and international markets under the WTO regime (Bhaumik, 2008: 305). As seen with Chhattisgarh, the state aims at increasing productivity by using technological solutions and completely abandoning the distributive aspects of agrarian policy. Given that each of these measures is capital intensive, it is expected to have differentiated impact across different classes of farmers. Tiller farmers who primarily bring labour to the production process cannot easily reap benefits of such developments. In the words of Shah (2005), 'nature's agency makes cotton cultivation a risky and uncertain enterprise to the extent that the nature of work needed to compensate could potentially be afforded by those mighty enough, historically, socially and materially'. Breman (2007) likewise argues that such growth has excluded the huge majority of small farmers from its benefits. He contends that the indifference of local authorities and 'downright sabotage' by village elites are two critical factors in preventing upward progression of landless farmers in south Gujarat. He argues that the landowning castes are conscious that empowering the lower castes, who are located at the bottom of the economy, would corrode their power base. On the other hand, local authorities are indifferent to the interests of landless farmers because they do not matter to the kind of economic development model the state has envisioned. They have no valuable influence to exert. It seems fair to conclude that the state is intentionally designing policies not for the tillers as seen in earlier decades but for the capitalist farmers.

During the fieldwork, interviewing a technocrat helped in understanding the big picture of agricultural policies (interviewee from Ahmedabad, November 2011). He argued that agriculture is not a viable occupation given the small size of landholdings. Further, small farmers are moving out of agriculture and are selling land for their 'lifestyle aspirations'. Therefore, the need of the hour is 'to craft a policy to allow people to move out of agriculture'. Questions around the 'viability of agriculture' arose repeatedly. This indicated that the state is instrumental in carrying out systematic conversion of small farmers into landless labourers who, ideally, would find work outside agriculture. Moreover, the state allows concentration of landholdings in the hands of few, resulting in large landholdings that are useful for technology-driven commercial agriculture. The attitude of an advisor to the government, taking the productivity argument and reiterating government success by repeatedly quoting growth figures, dismissive of any question on inequality or rising cost of cultivation, is indicative of the development agenda pursued by the state. The core principle of the agrarian policy of Gujarat under Modi had been to 'maximise production of high-value/commercial crops to drive rapid growth in the agricultural sector'. In the process, subsidies have been directed to specific crops, private irrigation, and capital-intensive machinery and other agricultural inputs. The high growth rate in Gujarat is, therefore, not because of the market alone, but the policies resulting from the proactive role of the state in guarding the interests of capitalist farmers who are part of the political settlement. In ensuring growth, the state has supported the entry of corporates in the agriculture-related market and created opportunities for the agrarian proprietary class to diversify into non-cultivation activities such as moneylending and the seed–fertiliser–pesticide trade.

The essence of the agricultural policy thus identified gets support from Sud's (2007) writing, where she mentions the *Viswa Samvad Kendrait,* a pro-industry publication of the Hindu right wing, that argues that corporatisation of agriculture is the only way to make it commercially viable. As expected, it has no mention of all those classes of farmers who till the land but cannot afford capital-intensive machinery such as irrigation pump or tractors. In an interview with a senior bureaucrat, it was found that that the government is all for those who can make use of opportunities – 'they ask and we give'. Migrant labourers are causing a lot of problems for the farmers of the state due to their irregularity and demand for high wages. Hence, mechanisation is seen as a solution to this precise problem as it lowers the demand for labourers in agriculture. Those migrating from other states are forced to go back because of lack of work. Once again those who hire labour are those who qualify as farmers for the bureaucracy, similar to the other states. Social and economic redistribution went unmentioned in this interview again. To quote him, 'We are not pro-poor, we are pro-rural economy growth.' A sectoral focus should not be deduced as a 'farmer-friendly' policy. He admitted that only big farmers can adopt any new technology first, be it tractor or pumps, but, to him, this has a 'demonstration effect' that helps in spreading the use of such technology to other farmers. He claimed to know of at least 500 farmers who earn more than ₹10,000,000, and he narrated many stories of how horticulture and floriculture have increased farmer income by leaps and bounds. Of course, flowers and vegetables have been taking commercial agriculture to a new stage, but the political economy around it needs probing. The biggest factor in cultivating high-value crops is capital, which is only possible for the rich capitalist farmers or gentleman farmers.

Class and caste in Gujarat's agrarian society

Based on secondary literature and fieldwork findings, this section details the different classes and castes operating in Gujarat's agrarian economy, their regional location, crop preference, and methods of cultivation.

Landholding consolidation and emerging fractions within rich farmers

To understand recent changes in agriculture, Table 5.3 shows the pattern of change in landholding size between 2005–06 and 2010–11. The steep rise in land area under large holdings over a period of five years indicates a consolidation of big holdings, unlike in the case of Chhattisgarh and, as we will see subsequently, Karnataka. This indicates that for a certain class of farmers, agriculture has proved to be a profitable enterprise. Another possible interpretation is that large-scale farmers are adept in capitalist agriculture and have received support from the state in the form of subsidies that have made agriculture profitable. This might be a result of the leverage they gained with the state in the decade following 2000.

The effect of the state government's policy initiatives to encourage capitalist agriculture has been varied across different classes of farmers. These farmers are differentiated by their class positions based not only on landholding size but also their access to credit, technology, irrigation, and surplus from trade and agribusiness. The following sections discuss the different fractions within farmers with large holdings, relating to their means of production and their location in political and economic arenas.

Table 5.3 Landholding distribution in Gujarat

Categories of farmers as per holding	2005–06		2010–11		Variation (in %)	
	Number of landholdings (in thousand ha)	*Area of landholdings (in thousand ha)*	*Number of landholdings (in thousand ha)*	*Area of landholdings (in thousand ha)*	*Number of landholdings (in thousand ha)*	*Area of landholdings (in thousand ha)*
Marginal	1,585	792	1,748	857	10.28	8.13
Small	1,345	1,959	1,380	2,004	2.57	2.28
Semi-medium	1,081	3,004	1,042	2,886	−3.53	−3.95
Medium	582	3,380	496	2,835	−14.75	−16.13
Large	68	1,133	72	1,397	5.49	23.3
Total	4,661	10,269	4,738	9,979	1.66	−2.83

Source: Agricultural Census, 2010–11. Department of Agriculture and Cooperation, Ministry of Agriculture, Government of India.

Landlords faded out

Landlords are those with traditional big landholdings and drawing rent. The Kshatriyas and the Darbaris were the original big landlords, but their social dominance has diminished significantly. The Kshatriyas lost their land to their tenants, the Patidars. Absentee landlordism paved the path for the efficacy of tenancy reforms in Saurashtra. Under tenancy reform, land ceiling was introduced; 16 acres of arable land was the permissible largest land holding size. As a result of tenancy reforms and the extravagant habits of the Kshatriyas, they lost their property, leading to downward mobility of the caste. Excess land had to be transferred to the tenant farmers. During acquisition of land, the state paid huge sums to landlords for land that was forfeited (interview of Shah, 2011). The Kshatriyas invested this cash in industries and earned profits on it. Their rising purchasing power fuelled the demand for industrial commodities. Thus, despite losing their erstwhile position in the agrarian economy, economically they remained among the proprietary classes. They retained political significance as well. In the 2012 Sadbhavana fast undertaken by Modi, members of the former princely family of Dahod were seen on three occasions with former state minister and former Devgadh Baria MLA, Urvashidevi Maharaul. The presence of the erstwhile royalties in politics reflects their hold on the local population as continuance of traditional loyalties in contemporary politics, a probable factor enabling them to gather votes in certain parts (Sharma, 2012).

The landlords in Mehsana district owned a huge share of the desert, and those in Banaskantha had a prevalence of jewellery makers and stock brokers. They have gradually divorced themselves from agrarian income as the main source of accumulation. Across interviews, it was confirmed that they do not occupy the central stage of politics or economy. Their relevance has been restricted to their respective districts. The landlord class has not invested in capitalist agriculture, neither have they consolidated their landholdings. The surplus has been moved to other sectors. With rapid industrialisation and urbanisation, they no longer form an important part of the agrarian structures, nor play a decisive role in related policies. Information on landlords was limited, as fieldwork did not engage with the category.

Big means capitalist

An anonymous article published in the *Economic and Political Weekly*'s October 1966 edition brilliantly analysed district-level dominant classes and castes in Gujarat. It provides a useful starting point to understand the roots of big and capitalist farmers in the state. It contends that Sabarkantha, Mehsana, and Banaskantha districts in the north, Baroda and Kheda in the south, and Saurashtra had a significant presence of big farmers. These farmers were engaged in agriculture as well as trade. Being commercial crop producers, agro-processing and agro-business came to them as an 'automatic appendage of cultivation'. Cooperatives surfaced in many districts as an important institution of agribusiness. 'Cooperatives were the launch pad for the Patidars who in the past two decades have steadily moved to other industries, leaving the cooperative space for other castes' (Damodaran, 2008). This movement of agrarian surplus to the industrial sector was channelled through cooperatives in Gujarat unlike Chhattisgarh.

Kheda was an area dominated by the Patidars. Several members from the Patidar caste group moved to Africa in the early nineteenth century because of the Great Famine that made agriculture a high-risk enterprise and propelled the community to start trading. The 'better off' within the Gujarati business community were the first to migrate, with Charotar Patidars leading the pack. The other factor for migration was generational land division, resulting in progressively smaller landholdings. Migration reached its peak with the Great Depression of 1929–39, which had a severe impact on the Indian economy. Famine and plague in their native villages, contrasted with upcoming white-collar job opportunities in colonial Africa, pushed and pulled Patidars (Rutten and Patel, 2002). Subsequently, many of them migrated to the United Kingdom in the 1950s. The accumulation of capital that the community undertook gained them socio-economic power (Rutten and Patel, 2002). The next phase of accumulation came with tenancy reform, when they gained land titles. During the Green Revolution period, fast adoption of technology and commercial crops generated agricultural surplus. Along with trade surplus, this was reinvested in trade and industry.

The Patidars, however, did not divorce themselves from land, unlike other communities (Banias, Jains, Parsis, Khojas, and Brahmins) who invested in non-agricultural sectors. In the Patidars, therefore, were traces of the beginning of a capitalist-farmer class, who paid attention to consolidating big landholdings, and buying technologically advanced farming equipment (Rutten, 1986; Sud, 2011). Along with investing in agriculture, Patidars simultaneously moved to urban centres and invested in industry (*EPW*, 1966; Rutten, 1989 and 2003; Damodaran, 2008). The big Patidar farmers from southern Gujarat had bought huge tracts of land in other districts such as Sabarkantha. They reproduced their dominance in the agrarian economy across districts. Likewise, Panchmahal district had similar linkages with the districts of Baroda, Anand, and Kheda. As early as the 1960s and 1970s, a political alliance operated in Kheda between the Kshatriya big landlord and the Patidars, both supporting the Swatantra Party, and showing early signs of a class alliance being forged across castes (Shah, 2002).

In Mehsana, big farmers and traders often overlapped, and wielded political power in the 1960s (*EPW*, 1966). Prakash (2005) observes that when dug wells started drying up in Sangpura village in Mehsana district in the 1960s, rich farmers adopted deep tubewells. The technology was underpinned by a class bias – the rich got richer, but small farmers faced twofold suffering because agricultural productivity fell and they incurred rent for hiring pumps from big farmers, adding to the cost of production (Prakash, 2005). With improved irrigation facilities, agricultural surplus grew steadily. In Saurashtra district, groundnut cultivation generated enough surplus to allow big farmers to invest in other sectors, leading to oil processing units starting in various parts of Saurashtra (*EPW*, 1966). It should be noted that during the same time, Saurashtra registered the highest number of absentee landowners. It can be inferred that those who were farmers on documents had little to do with agriculture, which explains why the region failed to turn completely towards capitalist agriculture.

So far, we have found a continuous exchange between two sectors – agriculture on one hand, and trade and agro-processing industry on the other. In recent decades, capital from other sectors – industrial and foreign – has penetrated the entire economy, including large-scale agriculture, and has altered class equations.

It is interesting to note that out of the randomly selected big farmers during fieldwork, there were none who had not taken to capitalist methods and cash crops. The sample size was limited, but respondents from different districts (Kheda, Mehsana, Banaskantha, Baroda, and Anand) as well as development professionals working with farmers were in agreement with this finding. This is different from Chhattisgarh, where not all big farmers were capitalist – there were those who continued with paddy and old farming methods, and there were big and middle farmers who adopted capitalist methods and engaged in commercial crops. What led big farmers in Gujarat to adopt capitalist agricultural practices? This can best be understood through case studies from the fieldwork.

In Mehsana district, I held an FGD with the Wagela community; the group comprised one big farmer and six middle and small farmers.[19] The village had Dalit *bastis*[20] that consisted of small farmers or wage labours who were working on the respondents' land. Haribhai took me to his field, which was a sprawling tomato plantation. He has four sons, and they have invested in other businesses in nearby cities. The grandchildren have also migrated with their parents, and only the eldest grandson lives in the village and supervises the cultivation. On being asked why the eldest grandson had stayed in the village, Haribhai promptly replied, 'He too has a shop of water purifier in Khudi. He goes every week to supervise the sale and check the accounts. But he chooses to live in the village and take care of his grandparents.' He showed me around the village and the ghetto where the lower caste people lived. He informed that they work in the field, but are not allowed to interact with upper castes. The farmer earns surplus from multiple sources, a part of which has been utilised to consolidate landholding. They earn from urban business, but pull back surplus to consolidate agrarian holding. This is the general trend that agricultural classes have followed in Gujarat. During the fieldwork, a reputed academic and activist had explained, in Gujarat, 'agricultural surplus is invested in service sector by big and even middle farmers. However, what is unique to the state is that a part of income generated from the service sector is also invested back into agriculture for buying land and expanding property'. Rutten (2003) had made a similar observation earlier. As a result, land tends to get concentrated in the hands of capitalist farmers, as reflected by landownership statistics between 2005–06 and 2010–11 and given in Table 4.3. The small and marginal farmers tend to become wage labourers because of loss of land ownership.

Ganapatbhai Somabhai from Khudi, Mehsana, was the contact person who organised the FGD.[21] The village he resides in is located closer to the city than where the FGD was held. He informed that most well-off farmers have opened stores in the nearby city market. They also have shops in Mehsana and even in Ahmedabad, commonly textile shops selling clothes and running material. Some farmers have opened agro-input shops in the last decade.

Gurubhai is a big farmer from Saurashtra. He owns 35 acres in a village 25 kilometres from Rajkot city. He narrated the story of rapid industrialisation and urbanisation in his district. On the way to his village, I observed huge five-star hotels being built, and the entire stretch of road had various ongoing constructions. He informed that in these villages, land was being acquired for constructing resorts and houses. The farmers have lost their livelihood in Iswariya village and now only own residential/homestead plots. There were 257 farmers a decade ago, of whom only 20 remain in the village. Some of them have opened mobile phone stores in the city, while some have opened *paan* and *bidi* (betel leaf and cigarette) shops. Some farmers who owned bigger landholdings sold their land in a staggered manner to have income over a longer period of time. Admittedly, a large part of their income was spent on consumption such as buying motorcycles and house repair. Several cases were reported where individuals were living off the money from the sale of their land without entering into any productive employment or business, thereby disrupting their work life. As I entered his village, I saw a few two-storeyed houses with iron gates and glass windows similar to those in the city. When I enquired about the owners of these houses, he told me that both families were into the iron business and lived in the village. The houses were big and did not resemble a common farmer's house. He started off with 'hum sabhi kisan hain' (we all are farmers), but during the course of the interview, he revealed that most big farmers do not cultivate their land and hire wage labourers to do so. A few families live here, but all of them have businesses outside the village, and their land has been leased out to small farmers. These families are the owners of the huge two-storey houses. He added,

... in my community [Patels], tilling land is not regarded as a prestigious profession. It is difficult to get sons married off if they are farmers [meaning cultivators]. We hire labourers, who come seasonally from Madhya Pradesh, Godhra, Vadodara, and Rajasthan. This has been prevalent over past one decade and they come with their families. The wife and sons also work in fields, especially children who are useful in plucking cotton seeds. Some of them have small holdings in their own villages and learn techniques from us over 3-4 years. We have the most advanced techniques. Some of them stop coming back and lease land in own villages and cultivate with these new techniques. We go to *mandi*s [local market] to sell our produce, and there the *dalaal*s [middlemen] fix prices. Even in election of *pramukh* [head] of APMC, there is politics and parties push their candidates. Though 50 to 60 per cent of price goes to *dalaal*, we still prefer selling to them. If we try to sell in cities, people offer us low prices. Urban people can differentiate between farmers and *dalaal*s, and always pay us less. (Interviewee from Rajkot, May 2011)

In Charotar district, I interviewed a farmer who has been awarded by the state government for adopting organic methods in agriculture. This area is known for tobacco plantations, a commercial crop, and is a forerunner in the formation of dairy cooperatives. His uncle is a *khedut* (farmer), who owns the local rice mill that is used by almost every farmer in the region – it is a case of diversification of a big farmer into agro-industry. He mentioned that people continued to return to villages because life in the village was as good as in the city, complete with modern amenities such as television and air conditioners, and had the added benefit of the quiet and greenery of a village. He explained that villages took longer to progress because families were not keen to send their children abroad to study; however, this mindset was gradually changing, bringing more remittance to villages and adding to their prosperity. This picture of rural life was starkly different from the broken down *jhuggis*[22] I saw in the same village – the *jhuggis* are where the migrant labourers whom I met in trains live. The quality of life of big farmers in Gujarat is certainly better than that of this class in Chhattisgarh and Karnataka.

A senior academic who has conducted fieldwork in Anand district argued that the big farmers have invested in tobacco-curing plants, linking this class to another agro-industry. In case of Surendranagar, small farmers started working as labourers in the tobacco-curing plant, but recruitment remained limited to those within the community until recently (Hitesh, 2011). A caste-based community is held together by trust, and opportunities are thus limited to members of the group. Kin relations have played a similar role in diamond polishing, as recognised in literature. To that extent, caste held a significant role in agrarian class relations.

Although the respondents were limited to big farmers, south Gujarat presented itself as a severely segregated society. Class oppression is rampant; big farmers exploit the landless farmers and many of them belong to lower castes. Speaking to small vendors on trains or while visiting nurseries on the highway outside Surat gave some insights into capital–labour separation. Despite migrating out of the country, the NRI community continues to own land or even buy new land. They appoint agents, often a family member who acts as a manager, to supervise the cultivation of land by wage labourers. Managers make labourers work under harsh conditions. This is a clear case of absentee landownership, albeit of a new kind. This allows the landowners to retain hold on land, the most-valued asset. While adoption of new technological practices has been seen across farms, some farms are headed by capitalist farmers and others by absentee big farmers (Breman, 2007). The investment in trade and agribusiness continues in the present era. Some new sources of accumulation have been added, such as input shops and hiring out of machinery. Thus, the capitalist farmers are the beneficiaries of neoliberal policies and are the oppressors of tiller farmers, earning profit by selling inputs and earning rent by hiring out machinery that make labour redundant. These regions remain in focus in the next section due to the rise in acreage of land under high-value crops grown by a new fraction.

Gentleman farmers in driver's seat

A wave of adoption of technology-intensive agriculture has been ongoing in the state. There has been a steady shift from food grains to cash crops (Dixit, 2008). Given the high profit margins, floriculture and horticulture have steadily been adopted by capitalist farmers. However, more peculiarly, urban professionals are entering the production of these crops. Such evidence surfaced in south Gujarat areas such as Bardoli and Navsari. In interviews, evidence showed that the farmers (on paper) are NRIs who have bought land in south and central Gujarat over the last decade. Though land law bars outsiders – those residing outside the village – from buying land, outsiders' land acquisition processes seem to have gone through smoothly. These new farmers invest surplus from other sectors into agriculture, and the sale of their products is geared towards metropolitan and export markets. They are not dependent on debt from informal sources and are not affected by agrarian crises. The state is attentive to their needs and provides them subsidy on agricultural inputs and facilitates market connections for them. A typical example of a gentleman farmer[23] is the following:

> Bhakta has planted about 60,000 Gerbera plants and 56,000 carnations as well as several other flowers in his farm set-up. He has incurred a cost of ₹13 million in setting up this project in 2005 and is expecting a turnover of ₹35–45 lakh (0.1 million) this year. (*The Economic Times*, 2007)

Even capitalist classes from other parts of India are investing in agriculture. For instance, a journalist informed that Mumbai-based businessmen are investing heavily in horticulture and floriculture firms through contract farming in Surat and Bharuch. 'Both capital and land are theirs, so profit accrues to them. Despite the labour contributed by local tiller farmers and landless labourers, the latter has little benefit from the new cropping pattern. It is possibly true that there are smaller farmers who are also adopting these crops, but they are too small to make a difference in such a big export market or get a decent share in the pie.' Under the new policy regime, the sector has assumed an organised character, facilitated by access to latest technologies, global markets, irrigation, and inputs made available by foreign companies. The investor is called a 'farmer' who hires managers to run the production. Naukri.com, a popular recruitment website in India, advertises for hiring managers for floricultural firms in Gujarat. The manager hires the labourers who work for wages. These firms include private companies such as KF Bioplants and Pepsi. The dominance of capitalist and gentleman farmers has meant more competition for tiller farmers, driving the tillers to a point where self-cultivation seems impossible. Even bigger players such as Champion Agro Fresh, a private company, have entered the agricultural rural market. Their promise is to provide end-to-end solutions to farmers, from fertilisers to technology, and teach them how to farm fruits. Companies such as these have developed farms of over 1,000 acres near Rajkot, for instance, where they grow these high-value crops. This model of applying the demonstration effect to attract other farmers to these seemingly successful techniques has become increasingly popular. Their clientele consists of middle farmers with 4–8 acres of land. The owner was originally a farmer, but invested the surplus in the Magnetic Electric Company until 2009, and then switched to the agro-input sector.

Table 5.4 shows that the area of land used for cultivation of fruits in Gujarat has risen ten times over the last three decades, while that for vegetables has grown about eight times in the same period. It constituted a mere 1 per cent of the total area under cultivation in 1982–83, which has grown to 10 per cent of total area under cultivation in 2010. This has certainly pushed agricultural growth upwards, but fieldwork suggests that the players behind it are in fact the petty bourgeoisie, capitalist farmers, and even capitalists who are aggressively investing in this sector. These are distinct classes attracted to the sector for its high export potential. The state has contributed to making these crops lucrative through appropriate subsidies.

Table 5.4 Area under cultivation and production of flowers, vegetables, and spices in Gujarat

Year	Fruits		Vegetables		Spices	
	Area under cultivation (in thousand ha)	Production (in thousand tons)	Area under cultivation (in thousand ha)	Production (in thousand tons)	Area under cultivation (in thousand ha)	Production (in thousand tons)
1982–83	73	1,666	84	1,467	110	287
1992–93	110	2,127	104	1,637	116	171
1998–99	177	2,388	190	2,534	179	314
2000–01	0	3,150	0	2,950	0	345
2003–04	0	3,351	0	4,580	0	377
2004–05	0	4,019	0	4,867	0	420
2006–07*	253	4,467	253	4,076	318	501
2010[24]	706	15,536	645	11,472	0	

Source: Kashyap (2006).

To summarise, the state has taken a focused and direct approach to further the interests of capitalist farmers and welcomed other classes to invest in agriculture. As a result, small farmers who own 88 per cent of the total number of landholdings in the state (GoG, 2010–11)[25] are facing severe competition. Census (2011) data point out that landlessness has increased among small farmers as has the number of agricultural labourers, rising from 4 million to 5.4 million in the decade following 2000. This is a combined effect of shift in land policy, poor income from low-value crops such as pulses and wheat, and high cost of inputs and technology that has reduced the profit margins in agriculture. Among different social groups, the worst affected are the ST farmers (Chakravarty, 2006). A farmer in Ahmedabad put this aptly, 'Jab phasal khedut ke ghar hota hain uska koi bhao nahin hota, jaise hi who vepari ke paas ata hain, uska kimat dugna ho jata hain' (when the crop is at farmers' home, then its prices are low, and once it reaches the trader, the price doubles). The farmer cannot wait for a high-demand season given his inability to hoard, because the cold storages are owned by traders and merchants who charge high rents for leasing them. Cases like this signify that those who have other means of income or have access and capacity to play on the basis of the terms laid by the market have gained from the Green Revolution and have transformed into capitalist farmers. They can employ high-end technology or, even better, bring in capital from other sectors into agriculture. They are the winners of the New Agricultural Policy in Gujarat.

Shift in cropping pattern: Annihilating tiller-farmer crops for exportable crops

As evident from the discussion so far, the state government in Gujarat has focused on increasing agricultural productivity by using technological solutions, rather than looking at distributive aspects of the agrarian structure (Hirway, 2000; Sinha, 2012). The new agricultural policies of the government have resulted in a change in cropping pattern across the state, as is apparent from Table 5.5.

There has been a shift from mass crops such as dryland cereals and pulses to high-value crops, particularly cotton, spices, sugarcane, flowers, and vegetables (categorised as 'other crops'), between 1980–89 and 2009–10 (Gulati et al., 2009; Mehta, 2012). The adoption of Bt cotton has been layered and fragmented, and access to irrigation, credit, larger holding, and higher income from livestock can be identified as common characteristics of Bt cotton adopters, as opposed to the rest (Morse et al., 2007; Glover, 2010). Commercialisation has deepened, as crops that have greater market-orientation have consolidated their share (Mehta, 2012). This is in line with the general focus on capitalist agriculture in the state. It has become an acceptable practice in the state, so much so that only a few among those interviewed saw a problem with the state's approach to agriculture. The change in cropping pattern shows that the crops grown traditionally by tiller farmers have lost out under the new policy regime.

Capsicum, sugarcane, tomato, and flowers were some of the crops that different respondents regarded as promising, marketable, and thus worth investing in. Given that most of the farmers interviewed owned landholdings between 10 and 50 acres and were capable of investing in new technological means of production, such preference was not a surprise. It has already been discussed that urban professionals and capitalists are also investing in these crops. Big capitalist farmers' sons were found doing courses in biotechnology to equip themselves in adopting high-value crops. The changes in cropping pattern is another indication of the changes in the agrarian class structure, with surplus accruing to the proprietary classes and polarisation setting in between capitalist and tiller farmers.

Table 5.5 Changes in cropping pattern in Gujarat: 1982–83 to 2009–10

Crop	1982–83	1987–88	1992–93	1997–98	2003–04	2009–10
Rice	5.44	5.78	6.12	6.67	5.99	6.18
Jowar	10.19	10.65	6.18	3.98	1.71	1.32
Bajra	13.8	14.82	13.32	11.8	9.56	6.5
Wheat	5.64	4.26	5.42	5.83	5.2	9.17
Maize	2.82	3.48	3.51	3.8	4.36	3.55
All cereals	40.27	40.64	35.52	32.76	27.27	26.77
Gram	0.96	0.71	0.84	0.98	0.78	1.48
Arhar	2.86	3.97	3.97	3.54	2.92	2.26
All pulses	7.87	8.43	8.66	8.11	7.04	6.79
Food grains	48.14	49.07	44.18	40.86	34.31	34.11
Groundnut	19.79	17.78	17.62	16.57	17.89	15.8
Sesame	1.22	1.29	2.39	2.53	3.39	2.16
Castor	1.79	2.12	3.14	3.79	3.02	3.43
All oilseeds	19.79	17.78	17.62	16.57	17.89	15.8
Sugarcane	1.02	1.27	1.62	2.13	1.84	1.76
Cotton	14.06	12.42	10.65	14	15.42	20.48
Tobacco	1.1	1.29	1.29	1.22	0.86	0.45
Spices	1.22	1	1.82	1.58	2.18	4.41
Other crops	9.81	11.32	13.77	14.22	18.5	15
GCA ('000 ha)	10883	9484	10750	11088	10948	11787

Source: Season and Crop Reports, Department of Agriculture, GoG (various years).

Political links to the farmer – exclusive to one kind

Gujarat farmers have been fervent adopters of privatisation in agriculture. Gujarat was at the forefront of the farmers' movement in the 1980s. Contrary to the common perception that farmers' movements are cross-class social movements, studies have found that these represent the interests of big farmers

(Brass, 1994). In fact, the BKS, an RSS-affiliated farmer organisation, welcomed the privatisation of inputs and mechanisation with open arms. The organisation has a Hindu cultural overtone and has been close to the BJP.

A common position is that farmer organisations dissipated after the 1980s (Omvedt, 2005).[26] Field case studies indicated otherwise. A farmer in Petlad, who was a member of the BKS, had a good network among farmers across the state. He was happy to provide contacts of farmers in other parts of Gujarat, such as Rajkot and Sabarkantha. He was well-versed in new technologies and had benefitted from government extension services. In fact, he received an award from Modi for experimenting with organic techniques and refrained from commenting on the government (interviewee from Anand, October 2011). The contacts he provided were eventually interviewed, and they confirmed having ties with the BKS, except in the district of Rajkot and Saurashtra. Traces of the farmer organisation operating were identified, but more as an exclusive lobby for capitalist farmers in central Gujarat to whom the state is providing extension services, new technology, and assistance.

During fieldwork, a BKS leader was observed seeking to organise and represent the cotton growers of two northern districts, Banaskantha and Sabarkantha. The *pradesh adhyaksh* (state head) belonged to the Sabarkantha district, which was facing severe water shortage. All the demands he listed were related to cotton farming, such as crash in global prices, which affected the local price at which farmers had to sell their produce and the cost of HYV seeds. The RSS has been emphasising on similar demands, particularly on allowing pump sets in these districts and free electricity to salvage the poor-irrigation situation.[27] He made an emotional speech about how farmers have been adversely affected by liberalisation. However, the core demands he reiterated were fundamentally to make use of the opportunities the market was bringing in and he expected state support for precisely this purpose. He pointed out that water shortage in this region had affected agriculture negatively, especially the Narmada SSP Dam's canals reaching up to the southern districts of the state, but the branching of canals for the northern districts had been suspended. An activist argued that water was being reserved for industrial purposes in the southern districts, thus explaining the suspension of canals to the north; the case is similar to that of Jhanjgir-Champa district in Chhattisgarh, where the industrial sector seemed to command influence over the state's allocation of resources.

The almost exclusive hold of cotton growers on the BKS became clear from several respondents and through interviews with non-cotton growers in Mehsana and Kheda, which are located in the central plains, where the same was confirmed.

It was confirmed that the BKS was not as active in their districts that predominantly grew tobacco, sugarcane, and so on, which were not the crop lobby the BKS was working with. Regional concerns overpower farmer organisations, such that it is a select few whose interests are represented through the BKS. Similar to the situation in Chhattisgarh, where the BKS is more active in the western districts where commercial cropping has taken roots and is largely absent in the eastern paddy-producing districts. The collective voice of the real tillers remains unrepresented through the BKS, and their gains, if any, are accidental.

Two months after the interview, the power of the BKS became evident while I was still on field. In March 2012, they held a huge protest in Gandhinagar, and right after that the BJP announced that the use of pump sets in the northern districts was permitted. However, only those farmers who could use drip or sprinkle irrigation could put in pump sets in the 'dark zone'.[28] Both methods of irrigation need high capital investment and are economical only in big landholdings. Hence, this is one more policy measure to benefit capitalist farmers alone (*Times of India*, 2012a). The expansion of new technologies in irrigation has contributed to the high growth in the sector, but only for some classes. The rent charged by pump owners, who are inevitably capitalist farmers, exploits the tiller farmers, further adding to their cost of cultivation.

Location matters. Proximity to the capital city and the significance of the golden corridor in Gujarat's economy are factors that determine which farmers are heard by the state more seriously. Like in Surat, the sugarcane farmers also displayed significant organisation and access to resources through cooperatives. A farmer from Rajkot district clarified that both the BKS of the BJP and the Khedut Samaj of the Congress have marginal presence in Rajkot, and there is hardly any difference between them in terms of their agenda. He added, 'They work very closely with the government and represent the interest of few farmers who live closer to the state capital.' It was quite apparent that visibility through *khedut* (farmer) organisations was reserved for specific regions, crops, and class of farmers.

A common finding that emerged from the interviews was that between 2000 and 2010, a large number of farmers shifted to cotton cultivation, particularly in the northern and central districts. This was caused by the import of oil seeds at cheap rates that made oil seed cultivation less lucrative (Despande, 2008). As an academic suggested, 'Figures show that 30 per cent of farmers are devoted to cotton and 20 per cent of farmers in the state are big and middle farmers.' He suggested that these 20 per cent have taken to cultivating cotton along with vegetables and tobacco (interviewee from Ahmedabad, 2011). Cotton cultivation requires high capital investment, because the crop demands large quantities of water and, therefore, mandatory use of pump sets for irrigation. Good rainfall in Gujarat in the years 2005–12 was a congenial factor for cotton cultivation which also brought in other farmers into cotton. However, this is not to suggest that no small farmer grows cotton, but within the crop lobby they only added numerical strength; when it comes to the distribution of benefits, they are the last to receive state support. The main demands of the lobby were lower price of inputs, irrigation subsidy, and globally competitive output prices to be secured for their crops. These are issues faced by the capitalist farmers who are involved in commercial cropping (interview of a farmer cum activist from Baroda, April 2011). They manage to mobilise widely on these demands, as is evident from the December 2011 protest in Gandhinagar when thousands of farmers assembled to demand water subsidy and better prices. That said, tiller farmers have lost out their political bargaining power within Gujarat. Class lines have fractured the farmer movement into capitalist farmers and tiller farmers.

With cotton becoming the dominant crop, the cotton lobby has become a much sought-after group by all political combinations. A senior Congress leader expressed eagerness to capture them as a vote bank, and was confident that in the 2012 elections the lobby would be decisive in Gujarat politics. A similar strategy was expressed by another political leader. The cotton producers are numerous, and those who have moved to commercial agriculture are organised and have a collective interest that is easy to address. The growing significance of capturing a crop lobby indicates that caste is losing its relevance in mobilising voters (interview of Parekh from Baroda, April 2012 and Jyotibhai from Ahmedabad, December 2011).

Another respondent (interviewee Gandhi from Ahmedabad, 2011) pointed out that within the Patel caste there is a rising divide. Until the 1990s, the family members who went abroad would always come back to their family for all religious festivals and would put a part of their income into the village property to consolidate landholdings. However, a disjunction is increasingly developing between urban and rural interests, and he predicted that this will change the face of Gujarat politics and society. The same issue recurred in a veteran political leader's response, who was the last prominent spokesperson of small and middle farmers' rights. While it was suggested that the ties to rural life are getting weaker as generations pass, with the younger people reluctant to return to village life, many regarded it as a prudent idea to invest in land and agrarian production. The binary between rural and urban no longer holds true with the exchange and movement between the two sectors at an all time high. Some felt that villages offered life at par with cities, while others pointed out that investment from other sectors is flowing towards the agrarian sector, and NRIs continue to buy land in parts of rural Gujarat. Hence, several respondents held that the exchange between the rural and the urban has increased many times over the past decade, which is a change from Breman's (1989) position. The emergence of the rurban space has not meant detachment from the state. In fact, it has been accompanied with the state maintaining a stronghold among the capitalist farmers, who act as an organised support base. Rural–urban difference may have blurred, but class difference is still stark, and the BJP operates through the BKS to use the class cleavage to its advantage.

Input centricity: Financial and chemical

The total cropped area in Gujarat is 12.8 million hectares, which accounts for 65 per cent of the total area of the state (GoG, 2009–10). In 2005–06, out of the total state budget of ₹1,10,000 million, allocation for the agricultural sector was ₹5,893.8 million (5.36 per cent). By the Eleventh Five Year Plan period (2007–12), it rose to ₹88,798 million, accounting for 6.9 per cent of the total state plan budget (GoG, 2012). In the same period, Karnataka's expense on the sector was 6.8 per cent of total state plan budget (GoK, 2012). The government aimed to contribute 8.9 per cent of the Twelfth Five Year Plan outlay to agriculture; however, subsequently, the Planning Commission itself was dissolved. As per annual plans, of the total budget, the share allocated to agriculture and allied sector was 9 per cent in 2012–13, which rose to 13 per cent in 2013–14. Another 14.2 per cent of the state plan is set aside for irrigation under the Eleventh Plan. In the annual plan of 2012–13, it rose to 18.1 per cent. The rise in percentage share of agricultural outlay illustrates that the neoliberal prescription of withdrawing support from agriculture and subsidies does not hold true. However, a foray into which heads within the sector have attracted main investment will help develop a nuanced understanding.

Credit policy: All about targets and higher yield

It has often been argued that agricultural credit is guided by market ethics in the post-liberalisation era. Chapter 3 discusses the issue at length, although literature specific to Gujarat was found to be quite limited. In an interview with a senior official of the Reserve Bank of India (RBI), it was explained that banks in general prefer lending money to those farmers who can show land deeds or some asset to ensure returns. This excludes resource-poor small farmers from availing services from formal credit sources. They also are often in need of immediate disbursal of cash, and the banks cannot cater to this need. For the banks, these tiller farmers are not big clients and are treated as 'secondary citizens'. Bank officers often ask them to come back another day, which is difficult given the distance and the cost of transport. This helps the informal economy of credit to thrive. Market ethics should mean free play but structural inequalities translate into the formal lending institutions treating a certain class of farmers as desirable customers and the rest, who do not bring in enough business, as undesirable.

Data from across India show that large landowners have disproportionate access to bank credit (National Commission for Enterprises in the Unorganised Sector, 2008: 14). In Gujarat, a respondent pointed out that tiller farmers are facing stiff competition, as corporates are entering the credit market. Since the 1990s, the banks have preferred giving loans to big and capitalist farmers and even corporates 'to fulfil the quota for which companies like Pepsi Co. are given farmer credit to meet the target'. This ensures timely repayment of loans. Small farmers often spend loans on family functions and repairing houses, which are consumption expenditure (interviewee from Baroda, December 2011). Unequal competition puts the majority of tiller farmers at a disadvantage when it comes to this crucial input in agriculture

As elsewhere in India, trading and moneylending were found to be tied together. A big farmer from Ahmedabad stated that

> *khedut* has to take loan for multiple reasons, and often from more than one source. Be it fertiliser, seed, pesticide, at every stage of cultivation they take loans. This makes it mandatory to sell their produce immediately after harvest to avoid interest from piling up. They have dearth of storage capacity, and access to good infrastructure like cold storage facilities. They are, thus, forced to sell their produce to the moneylender who is often also a local trader. Debt further reduces *khedut's* negotiation powers, since they are bound by pacts to sell their produce to the trader-cum-lender. Each time the *khedut* goes to the APMC, the police man, the gatekeeper, and even the vehicle driver [*choti hati*] would demand the khedut's produce for free. This is a way of paying tax. Then the *dalaal* comes and takes 4–5 gourds for his family. In social hierarchy, small farmers are the lowest and have to oblige everyone to sell his products. The trader takes 75 per cent of the profit, while the *khedut* gets 25 per cent only.

A bleak picture emerged in other interviews. An academic (interview of Kiran Desai, Surat, 2012) shared his fieldwork findings from Surat district, and confirmed that 'pre-contracts' operate in agriculture. Pre-contracts imply that traders fix the selling price of a particular crop with farmers much before the harvest when farmers buy inputs on credit. Hence, if it was decided that the farmer would sell wheat to the trader at the rate of ₹500 per quintal and the market price rises to a higher level like ₹800 per quintal after harvest, the farmer would still be required to sell his produce at the prefixed rate of ₹500. Interlocking between factor and output markets persists in agriculture, as the trader is often the moneylender (interview of a scholar from Anand, 2011; Rutten, 2003). Hence, the opening of the market and competitive global prices have not translated into new opportunities for small farmers who are tied up in interlocking of markets. Middle farmers have better negotiating powers and have income from other small trades. On harvest, they also sell their produce, but only 30–40 per cent is sold to cover the initial cost and debts. They hold on to the rest to be sold later. Likewise, those who produce wheat keep it until the rice season commences, when they sell wheat at a higher price and vice versa. However, in both cases, the traders reap the profit at the cost of the producer (interview of Shiraz bhai from Ahmedabad, October 2011). The traders in Gujarat belong to the agrarian classes such as the capitalist farmer. They are not players coming in from other states, as in the case of the eastern districts of Chhattisgarh.

With big companies such as Reliance and Star Bazaar willing to invest in commercial agriculture, direct sourcing from farmers has started in certain parts of the state. Consequently, a kind of monoculture is arising, as these companies demand particular crops, and farmers supply those crops. Therefore, producing for self-consumption, a chief factor in maintaining food security, is under threat. On the other hand, the entry of such companies could threaten the position of the existing traders, but there are instances of traders finding ways around this. A respondent stated how traders buy 2 kilograms of produce each time (upper limit) from Reliance Fresh, and then sell it in *mandis* for a higher price. This saves their physical effort of procuring from the source and transportation cost, but they nonetheless continue to be important players in the market (interviewee from Ahmedabad, 2011).

Another key actor in the agrarian economy is the cold storage owner. Cold storages are generally located on highways and are used mainly for storing high-value crops such as fruits and exportable vegetables. Their significance lies in the fact that in the absence of government-run warehouses and adequate storage infrastructure, they are the sole providers of storage facilities. Farmers are forced to depend on them. Even the Food Corporation of India has to take godowns on rent from these private owners, increasing the private owners' bargaining power (three interviews: an activist, a farmer, and a bank officer from Ahmedabad, November 2011).

Evidence showed that cold storage owners were lending money to farmers, thereby exercising control on the supply to market. An owner of a chemical plant informed that when he started his factory, he took a loan from a cold storage owner. He explained that this cold storage owner was a big farmer, and exerted significant control over the informal credit economy. Instances of farmers investing their surplus into the credit market and becoming moneylenders were previously noted by Rutten (1986, 2003), and even in a recent Rajasthan study (Levien, 2012), it was seen that cash earned through land transactions by farmers was being lent to farmers, thus contributing to the former's rent income. The picture is quite similar to that of Andhra Pradesh and Tamil Nadu as observed by Swaminathan (2005), Harriss-White (2008), and Ramchandran (2010). Therefore, the merchant class that has roots in the big farmer class has extended its reach beyond agriculture to even industry. Categorising the moneylenders as a distinct class from the big farmer class would be inappropriate, as agrarian surplus is at the root of their diversification into cold storage and moneylending. They have not severed all ties with agriculture and engage in capitalist agriculture, as evidence showed.

Input centricity and privatisation: Serving interests of few

This section puts forth two arguments. First, the privatisation of inputs was meant to benefit the capitalist farmers to augment agricultural growth. Not only were they more capable of adopting these technologies in the aftermath of the Green Revolution, the state also took initiatives to familiarise these classes with new technologies. Second, these policies have helped the capital-rich farmers diversify into petty bourgeois activities such as selling chemical inputs and machinery, in which, to ensure higher sale, they take all kinds of measures.

Gujarat emphasises input centricity even more than Chhattisgarh, given its already mature capitalist agriculture and an existing class of capitalist farmers. Rutten (1986) sheds some light on how big and middle farmers in the 1980s gradually invested their agricultural surplus in agribusiness and then in business outside agriculture, starting a phased transition to becoming capitalists. Since the 1970s, investments have been made outside agriculture into small flour mills, tiny transport companies, tile factories, and private financing companies, which have multiplied many times (Rutten, 1986).

Breman (1989) makes the same observation about south Gujarat, with these farmers diversifying into agro-industries such as sugar mills and using by-products in paper factories. More than two decades later, the same trend can still be observed. The big farmers are investing in agro-business or trading of agricultural products, and accumulating more. A contributory factor is that returns from agriculture have been less than other sectors. However, globalisation and privatisation of inputs have opened new opportunities for those who can invest in retailing of chemical inputs. A mix of petty bourgeoisie and trader class has emerged in the countryside of Gujarat, many of whom are local people. The situation is different from Chhattisgarh where often those in seed–fertiliser–pesticide retailing are Gujaratis, Marwaris, and suchlike coming from other states. However, the situation in Gujarat is similar to findings in Tamil Nadu as discussed in Chapter 3 (Harriss-White, 2004). This is not to suggest that the category of traders is entirely constituted of rural people. Urban traders have also opened shops to make use of the new opportunity. A common interest binds the two, namely the maximising of the sale of inputs from MNCs. They are working as instruments of big industrial capitalists, who are trying to capture the Indian agricultural market through the domestic proprietary class.

Close to the Khudi town centre, for instance, there was a huge market (*mandi*) with many shops selling fertilisers and pesticides. I walked into a seemingly reputed store. The shop owner explained all his products. In the absence of any government subsidy on pesticides, farmers have to depend exclusively on private traders. He added that the farmers were ignorant and did not know what to use for which pest. Hence, the trader could sell more-than-required quantities of pesticides, of different varieties, by scaring them about losing their crop. He added that the farmers often took fertilisers and pesticides on loan, a common practice in this business. But how does the trader ensure that the money comes back to the shop owner? His answer was simple, 'I belong to the nearby village so I know most of these farmers, and so collecting dues is not a problem' (interviewee from Mehsana, November 2011). Hari (another farmer) was also buying fertilisers from a shop situated only 5 kilometres away from the village where the shop owner was from the village. He stated that social ties play an important role in increasing the sale of new chemical products (interviewee from Rajkot, May 2012). The capitalist agenda seeks networks of local big and middle farmer classes to succeed. The rural proprietary classes accumulate through the new opportunity presented by the policy of input centricity.

Respondents mentioned that the capitalist firms, both national and international, prefer giving retail agency to local people (some of whom are farmers) to enhance their sale (interviewee from Mehsana November, 2011). It supports Murugkar's (2006) observations discussed in Chapter 3. In interviews across districts, it was disclosed that the number of input shops have multiplied in the last 15 years. As I approached Ahmedabad and Baroda, I saw many such shops; local people told me that they were owned by traders operating in urban centres. In suburban and remote rural areas, the owners were big farmers who have diversified into input retail.[29] This is particularly important, as the agriculture-input market thrives on credit; therefore, someone who runs a shop has to have two things – local connections and capital. Both are available only to the big and middle farmers. At the other end of the spectrum, this has added to the burden of tiller farmers and landless labourers who are forced to borrow more to survive in the competitive commercial agriculture, thus losing out more under the market-driven regime.

In Surat and Mehsana, I met petty bourgeois shop owners who spoke in the language of the capitalists and not of *kheduts*. They or their family members are farmers, but they supervise their own land which is cultivated mainly by wage labour. They explicitly stated that their objective in starting an inputs business is to maximise the sale of their products, as well as push for more purchase of seeds, fertilisers, and pesticides. They influence tiller farmers to purchase more inputs by using caste and class influence. This escalates the cost of production for ignorant farmers and adds to the profit of traders, who are often the big/capitalist farmers. Similar observations have been made by Glover (2010), NCEUS (2009), and Murugkar (2006).

Adoption of capitalist agriculture stands on the premise of high capital investment (Cleaver, 1972; Byres, 1981). Rutten (1986) found how the class of 'well-to-do farmers' were given preference in technical advice and other facilities from the state. A bureaucrat whose interview has been given in detail in a previous section made it clear that still 'more capable' farmers were extended help from the state. The word 'capable' translates to a certain class with access to infrastructure and investment, the capitalist farmer. Hailing from the big farmer and middle farmer classes, this class has assumed a new character in Gujarat's trajectory of economic development. The logic of pushing growth by providing service to them, as observed previously in Chhattisgarh, manifests here too, although not as candidly. It totally makes sense for the sake of economic growth to reinstate the agrarian proprietary classes as part of the political settlement, especially after 2004.

The state also offers tacit support to the private players. A point triangulated across respondents – as is common across India – is that the Seed Corporation that is entrusted with seed distribution at low price has often failed to deliver quality. Respondents revealed that the low dependability of government seeds eventually led them to give up on them because it landed them in trouble with low yield and/or poor quality of produce. Hence, farmers tend to buy seeds from private stores to ensure quality and yield (interviews of Shiraz bhai from Ahmedabad and Singh from Baroda, November 2011). Dasji, an organic farmer, apprised us that in the last two decades, seed companies must have come to earn many times more as they sell pesticides and fertilisers in addition to seeds. He lamented that although these products are harmful for the soil and cannot sustain high yield over a long period, the sudden rise in yield and hence promise of extra income make it an attractive proposition.

The state initially ensured lower prices for Bt seeds than most other states. The government supported indigenous GM cotton technology and declared its inability to bring informal seed producers, who were breaching WTO agreements, under its control. The state government went a step further to help the local farmers, by imposing a ceiling of ₹750 per packet to ensure that seeds were available at a reasonable price. It resulted in higher Bt cotton seed production in Gujarat and availability of seed at lower prices[30] that aided wider adoption of this high-value crop (Gupta, 2008). However, the state has since moved away from this position, according to interviewees. The state has been advocating procuring private inputs from seed and fertiliser companies for the sake of productivity, coercing farmers to rely on these inputs for Bt cotton (interviewee from Banaskantha, 2012). Input centricity and large-scale technology are the prescriptions from the state.

An indignant university scientist pointed out that corn is facing similar issues. Despite Indian universities developing their own varieties of corn in 2005, the government has initiated projects to subsidise Monsanto corn seeds. To ensure its fast adoption, they are offering free fertilisers with seeds. This has left indigenous varieties unable to compete with foreign seeds, retorted Desai[31] (Kavitha, 2011). These foreign seeds have gone into farmers' hands without being tested in university labs. On some occasions, researchers have expressed doubts about Monsanto's quality, but that has been overlooked. In 2009–10, Monsanto was paid 40 per cent of the corn adoption project money and that too without any tender. Thereafter, the government has been buying seeds from other corporates. Here again, local traders are used to sell the products. Admittedly, traders encourage or even brainwash farmers to buy more fertilisers and pesticides promising higher yield (interview of a farmer from Baroda, November 2011).

While tiller farmers are putting in all efforts to cope with the spiralling rise in the cost of cultivation, the government subsidy for fertilisers is directed towards big fertiliser firms, serving another industrialist lobby constituted of the Indian

Farmers Fertiliser Cooperative (IFFCO), Monsanto, Cargill, DuPont, and other such organisations (Ghosh, 2005; Birner et al., 2011; Mukundan, 2013; discussed in Chapter 3). The subsidised rates pushed the sale of fertilisers higher. Hence, agriculture has gained some state support in the last decade, but is secondary to the industrial sector. The most hegemonic member of the political settlement operating in the state is the industrial capitalist. It was also revealed that high demand and limited supply of fertilisers has resulted in a black market around its sale. This again involves government officials who earn rent in managing the black market. The point was raised by two respondents, but mandates further enquiry (interviewees from Ahmedabad, 2011).

Water: A deal breaker

The issue of water was discussed in an earlier section on policies, including surface irrigation and ground irrigation. The dependence on groundwater is huge, with 80 per cent of irrigation drawn from it (Iyer, 2017). A Green Revolution company has been entrusted with providing micro-irrigation systems to address excess exploitation of groundwater. The mission is part of the second Green Revolution. Within the state, it will work through reputed and authorised micro-irrigation system suppliers, who will install these systems in farms on demand. They will simultaneously provide various agro-services pertaining to irrigation. The aim is to reduce consumption of both water and electricity, while enhancing agricultural productivity. The state has declared this would result in the farmers' prosperity at large[32] (GoG). The government boasts of sprinklers and drip irrigation, but it should be pointed out that these are not resource neutral. Fieldwork showed the farms where I encountered such systems were all more than 10-acre holdings. Consequently, any initiative to privatise the means of irrigation is bound to have serious impacts for the mass of farmers present in the northern, western, and eastern districts (Joshi and Acharya, 2005). The SSP's main and branch canals are serving select regions in south, north, and central Gujarat. Therefore, private irrigation is what most farmers will have to depend on. However, the branch canal work has been slow, because it is facing a major hurdle in acquiring land for creating the network of distributaries, both minor and sub-minor (interviews of a political leader and a farmer from Baroda, November 2011). Out of the 6,188 villages, 34.3 per cent are no-source villages having no definite source of water (Gupta, 2004).

The reality is that against a target of 1.8 million hectares, the SSP is irrigating only 80,000–100,000 hectares, mostly in the Narmada, Bharuch, and Vadodara districts. There are several other canal irrigation systems – Mahi, Ukai-Kakrapar, Karjan, and Damanganga – that distribute water to mostly central and south Gujarat, covering 70 per cent of Gujarat's command areas. These are the areas historically inhabited by capitalist farmers who have diversified into cash crops and trade. All in all, canal irrigation is covering 18 per cent of total irrigation, leaving most farmers to depend on groundwater irrigation.

Building on the example of cotton cultivation, access to land and water plays a determining role in growing cotton. This is a concern that is reflected in the work of Dubash (2002). Access to water in north Gujarat is determined by control over tubewell technology. The history of groundwater extraction has favoured the capitalist farmers (Hardiman, 1998; Yagnik and Sheth, 2005). Prakash (2005) takes Hardiman's argument further to show that the current scenario favours the wealthier section of agrarian society who have access to groundwater. Absence of source of irrigation would mean giving up cotton cultivation. Shah (2005) adds in her appraisal of several cotton-growing villages in Gandhinagar district that only well owners (big farmers) largely from the Patel and Thakore castes grew cotton. Though they do not use the category class, the evidence essentially indicates that those who own capital are the only ones who are able to adopt private irrigation that determines the type of crop a farmer cultivates, cash or food crop, high-value crop or mass crop (Breman, 2007). To quote Hardiman (1998: 1542),

> Such a system survives today because the rural poor continue to lack access to resources, particularly land and water. In the case of water, this gives rise to a situation in which the elites exert their power by controlling and manipulating its supply. It is in their interest for there to be shortages. So long as this nexus prevails, it is hardly possible for more equitable systems of water harvesting and distribution to evolve.

In a recent study, it was found that Dalit farmers were not allowed to put in borewells in the village by Ahirs, who are bigger and higher caste farmers (Iyer, 2017). Across the field area, the author finds caste and class obstructing the access of Dalits and landless labourers to water and land, which determine their success in agriculture (Iyer, 2017). In another study, unequal distribution of land and water in addition to social relations of dependency are found as the cause of rural poverty (Aubron et al., 2015). The deprivation faced by poorer sections has not lessened in the last decade (Aubron et al., 2015).

In such a structural context, in 2012, the state government in Gujarat advocated micro-irrigation. The strategy was adopted to win back farmer support.

Desai in his interview stated how water has been a cause of alienation of farmers from the BJP in the decade following 2000. He conjectured that farmers' votes will decide the fate of the 2012 assembly election. The BJP won the 2012 election but with reduced rural support; he made the crucial observation that the farmers still wield political power. Their strength was displayed in the protests launched just a year ago to lift the ban on wells (interviewee from Ahmedabad, December 2011). Even Modi was compelled to salvage his reputation with the rural vote bank by giving in to demands of the cotton farmer lobby. He lifted the ban on groundwater exploitation across 26 districts (*Times of India*, 2012). This is against his broader stand on irrigation, which advocated and directed state resources towards energy-efficient irrigation methods (such as sprinklers). The 2012 state elections showed the BJP having lost substantial rural support despite Modi's re-election, an issue which needed to be addressed immediately.

The irrigation issue emerged as a key issue after the fieldwork was completed in May 2012. In February 2013, the BJP government steamrollered through the Gujarat Irrigation and Drainage Act passed in March 2013. The Act sought to regulate sinking of borewells on any agricultural land along with use of groundwater available from it. In case of violation, there could be imprisonment up to six months and a fine of ₹10,000. This was met with tremendous opposition in Parliament, including by the Congress. After 2012, this was a turnaround since even the BKS was seen openly resisting the Bill; their core argument was that the farmers have no option other than sinking tubewells given the poor availability of water; rationing the wells will hurt farmers' interest. As many as 17 out of the 26 districts in the state were suffering drought conditions (*The Hindu*, 2013). Regulation of water is required for sustenance of the natural resource. However, the state is tending to make water usage exclusive to those farmers who can procure the required permissions from the government. Access to local administration is for a few (capitalist farmer, or leaders from reserved castes) as observed across fieldwork. Plausibly, this policy will make it harder for tiller farmers to access groundwater because unequal structural relations will pervade the distribution of water.

Access to water has been the key to agricultural success and agrarian dominance in the state; be in investing in tubewells or accessing Narmada canal water, only a few have managed to corner the benefits. Another advantage of owning private irrigation came to light in Khudi village, Mehsana. The big capitalist farmer was reported charging rent from the tiller farmers for using his pump; therefore, technology access is giving him an advantage in generating more surplus and is acting as an additional means of accumulation. The small farmers were reluctant to disclose the rates charged in the presence of the big farmer in the FGD. Similar observations have been made elsewhere in India, particularly in Gujarat (Dubash 2002; Shah, 2007; NCEUS, 2009; Mehta, 2012). It illustrates how the capitalist farmer is extracting rent from small farmers, adding to the accumulation of capitalist farmers and extraction from the rest.

Access to water in commercial input-centric agriculture such as in Gujarat is a deal breaker, as by nature the technology the policy has brought in is a lumpy technology. No water means complete failure, even if all other inputs have been put in. The state has once again come to help those who need it the least. Big and capitalist farmers are cornering big subsidies in the name of technological advancement and also by being able to seek the relevant permission for setting up new pumps. All those who are having to rent private means of irrigation have no share in government subsidy and have to pay hefty rents to the owners of irrigation pumps.

Monopolisation of land resource

Land holds utmost significance as a factor of production in agriculture. This section is devoted to understanding the land acquisition policy in the period under study. The land policy, as it stood in 2012, could be traced back to the 1990s. The government amended the land acquisition policy right after coming to power in 1995. As elsewhere in India during the 1980s, the 'land to the tiller' lobby had a stronghold on government; therefore, it could protect agricultural land from urban classes until the 1980s. But by the end of the 1980s, the state sanctioned large tracts of fertile agricultural land for industrial purposes. Subsequently, the BJP government scrapped the 8-kilometre rule[33] in its very first legislative assembly session by proposing a tenancy bill in 1995. The announcement of this change in policy was followed by a few protests despite significant SC and ST membership of the state legislative assembly, who were supposedly going to be at the losing end. The big farmers welcomed this move, as reflected in the support from *khedut* organisations (Sud, 2012). This gives a sense that the big farmer interest is not exclusively rural.

The government has sought to make land available to big business ever since (Bharwada and Mahajan, 2006). After the debacle at Singur,[34] Tata moved their car-manufacturing project to Gujarat, where it was swiftly allotted land by the state government. This gave the state a favoured destination status for corporate houses and attracted investment from many new private companies. As was reported by different respondents, the process of land transfer has followed a pattern in rural areas – first, the government transfers the grazing land and wasteland to the company without informing the villagers. Once the initial task is accomplished, the farmers are approached for the purchase of their fertile land. 'Since, by this time, some land in the village is already with the private company, and often this land is adjacent to certain farmer's holding, their choice of selling land to the companies and even negotiating prices get drastically reduced' (interview of a farmer from Rajkot, May 2012). A similar instance of illicit transfer of *gochur* (grazing) land by showing it as revenue land was reported in the case of Maruti's new plant in Rajkot (*Times of India*, 2013a). Such cases are reported from other districts as well. For instance, a public interest litigation (PIL) case was pending against the Adani group[35] for encroaching upon 40 acres of grazing land in Kutch district (Balan, 2013). These instances conform to the characterisation of the state as a 'land broker' that works on behalf of the private companies and against people (Levien, 2012).

Who has benefitted from the government's land acquisition policies? Krishnakumar (2007) finds that the industrial capitalist class, both in diamond and other sectors, has gradually acquired land from poor farmers near Surat. Most respondents were of the view that the capitalists, primarily from the Brahmin–Bania castes, constituted the gainers of land acquisition. A few respondents held that the gainers were from 'rich farmers' who were now exerting the most power, and included Patidars among the beneficiaries (interviews of a Left party leader and a scholar from Ahmedabad, December 2011). They accumulated by investing their surplus in agro-processing and industrial sectors. One may conclude that even if they had different castes and origins, their interests have become one and the same. There is a reverse trend of 'concentration' of land, as evident from Table 5.3. Sud (2007) identifies 'nouveau-rich capitalist classes', differentiated from Brahmin–Bania–Khoja mercantile groups, as having assumed the most dominating position over the state apparatus in the neoliberal era.

A common policy between Gujarat and Karnataka is restriction of ownership of agricultural land to agriculturists from the respective state only. Some lands are even classified as non-transferrable to protect rural interests. However, in 2012, the High Court ruled this as discriminatory, allowing agriculturalists from all over India to buy land in the state (*Times of India*, 2012b). This opened the land to urban and out-of-state buyers. Suhel, an activist, reported that the real estate market is thriving on black money.

In practice, to buy land from farmers, big capitalists make use of 'irrevocable power of attorney' from them. This power of attorney allows them to sell land without seeking a consent letter from the farmer. The regulations pertaining to landownership are thwarted in Gujarat. Some urban businessmen also show themselves as farmers, by virtue of owning agricultural land, and, thereby, are eligible to own land anywhere in the state. I witnessed a rich businessman sitting in a café with a rural man – as apparent from his attire – signing a land deed. He also had a technocrat, possibly a lawyer, assisting him and explaining the clauses to the businessman. Later, an activist explained that diamond industry owners are heavily investing in real estate (interviewee from Rajkot, May 2012). Capitalists are found diversifying into real estate as a sector. While these are only individual stories, they do tally with the stories about 'land grab' in the Indian press, from across India, claiming that numerous corrupt and illicit ways of buying land exist.

In line with this is an interview by a renowned scholar[36] who mentioned the existence of a 'Gujarat Land Bank', whose office he has personally visited. They can offer land in any part of Gujarat in keeping with the buyers' demand. While this has helped the capitalists, the state bureaucracy has also been gainers. Whenever a land deed is signed, a significant portion of rent goes to the bureaucracy, while a voucher of 5 per cent of the deed's value is handed to the owner. This was confirmed by three respondents. The amount to be paid for registration of new land has also multiplied manifold from ₹5,000–6,000 to almost ₹100,000 per acre of land over a decade. Hence, the bureaucracy has been accumulating significantly more under the era of privatisation and rapid land transfers from agricultural to non-agricultural purposes, a kind of grand corruption, following Bussell's categorisation of corruption (2012).

Unlike Chhattisgarh, the Gujarat state enjoys more relative autonomy from the capitalist class. Ministers, however, do enjoy personal favours from corporate houses that are in turn compensated by giving them state subsidy and land at a low price (Murat and Praful bhai, interviewed in 2011). Essar bought land at ₹1 per acre, which they later sold at ₹1,500 per acre (interview of Sagarbhai, from Ahmedabad 2011). The figures could not be validated. An Adani plant has been asked to close operations by the Gujarat High Court, which considered their activities as illegal on the grounds of not having environmental clearance (Bahree, 2014). A question can be raised as to how a vigilant bureaucracy did not notice the lapse or was it too keen to guard the interest of the capitalist? Sud (2007) mentions an interview with a revenue officer who informed that the entire department had received a standing instruction that everything should be done to make land available if and when an industry demands. Such service to the capitalists possibly explains why Gujarat has been attracting such high industrial investment although the actual owners of land are paid little heed, both in terms of compensation and alternative employment.

At the village level, evidence showed the petty bourgeoisie working through its kin to facilitate land transfer. The *mukhia* (*panchayat* head) of the particular village was the nephew of the local MLA and has been instrumental in selling land to factories and continues to offer land to external agents (interview of Shashi[37] in October 2011) This is an instance where the local government representative acted as a broker in land transaction, an event suggestive of how decentralisation is furthering the penetration of capital, and relation to the political leaders is critical in setting up such deals. The *mukhia* has accumulated through brokerage activities, thus transforming himself from a middle farmer to a new petty bourgeoisie.

As reported by respondents across districts that land was being bought by NRIs, I met three NRIs who bought land themselves. In Anand district, cases were observed of NRIs settling back in their ancestral villages or towns, after 15–20 years of departure. I met a businessman in Ahmedabad who told me how he has bought land in his traditional village. A professional from London has recently invested in a house in Baroda. This is creating a demand for residential plots and housing, further increasing the land price. It has been a factor for easing the process of land acquisition, thereby transferring land smoothly from farmers to NRI families. Having established that land use has been transferred from agricultural to non-agricultural purposes, the question arises whether this can be equated with a shift of power from agrarian classes to capitalist over the state apparatus? Or has the agrarian class undergone a change in character?

Instances of capitalist farmers speculating in the land market appear in literature as early as the 1980s (Rutten, 1995). Similar observations have been made by Sud (2007). The fieldwork conducted for this study confirmed the presence of an expanding land market and the active participation of big and capitalist farmers in the process of land acquisition, with even capitalist farmers with mid-sized holdings in some instances. A Rajkot farmer expressed disappointment because he could not sell his land as his village came under the red zone,[38] where buying land was prohibited. A middle farmer negotiated prices for land with a private chemical company and continues to assist in their land acquisition, for a cut. Every story of land acquisition had the mention of an intermediary (interviewee from Kheda, October 2011). A kind of unholy alliance seems to have emerged around land deals, with the industrial capitalist as the primary beneficiary, but the rural proprietary class was only second in gaining from the process. Using their connections to urban people, their access to land and access to the larger community of small farmers who might potentially want to sell land, the capitalist farmers have assumed the role of land brokers. Their class character is, thus, changing to that of a new petty bourgeoisie using market opportunities. Instances of the class buying land themselves also came to light.

It is well documented that the capitalist class wants to accumulate land, and this is impossible without a policy shift and a change in material conditions of the owners of land who will be willing to sell their land, thus ensuring a continuous supply of land. Leaving the rural population out of the benefits of its policies had already cost the BJP dearly during the parliamentary election in 2004. Consequently, policies since had to take into consideration the class interest of rural proprietary classes, whose interests are no longer purely agrarian. These aspirations have been managed adequately by the state through the inclusion of these classes in the political settlement, where land deals are accruing profit to capitalist farmers and rent to the bureaucracy, both becoming part of the petty bourgeoisie. Land consolidation at the large-sized holdings indicate that the class has not lost out in the bargain.

Conclusion

Gujarat has manifested itself as a strong state since 2001, marked by Modi assuming power and the party consolidating its support base. This consolidation of Hindu nationalist sentiment received zeal in the aftermath of the Godhra incident in 2002. The state has pushed forward the interests of the industrial capitalist class. This is a marriage of interest, where the mercantile ethos pervades both state and society. Gujarat's state apparatus is rather cohesive, and the state has enjoyed a 'favoured destination' status among investors. The political settlement in Gujarat is comprised of the industrial capitalist class, capitalist farmers (middle and big holdings), and the old and new petty bourgeoisie. Field evidence showed that the state has been paying special attention to smoothing the process of land acquisition and ensuring a steady flow of cheap labour. A new land policy has made acquiring land easier. Labour rights have been thwarted and provisions of seeking justice have been curtailed. All of these work in favour of the capitalist class and point to the hegemonic influence of this class in determining policies (Chatterjee, 2008).

Since 2002, the political leadership that has been taking utmost care to maintain political stability has had a crucial role to play in making Gujarat investment-friendly. The bureaucracy has formed the backbone of the efforts to bring in market forces, facilitating the latter's operations even prior to liberalisation. However, even though the leaders and officials have acquired old petty bourgeois character, the state enjoys some autonomy, as displayed in its support to local companies against the multinational giant Monsanto. Therefore, unlike in Chhattisgarh, the state in Gujarat does not exhibit a 'personal fusion' with the capitalist class.

Since Independence, Gujarat has tread a distinct development path, but well within the paradigm of classical transition of capitalism. Surplus accumulation begins from agriculture and diversifies to trade. Part of this diversification has been owed to adverse natural factors such as dryland, lack of irrigation, and droughts that have compelled the rural proprietary class to move to urban centres and diversify to other sectors. In many cases, diversification to trade extends beyond India to foreign markets to accumulate at a fast pace. Mercantile capitalism thrived on agricultural surplus until the class was ready to move into industrial capitalism. This was the picture that unfolded until the 1970s. In the 1980s, Gujarat began to concentrate on the secondary sector, and by the 1990s, it had achieved commanding heights in manufacturing, not just within the state but across India. What makes Gujarat distinct is that some members of the rural proprietary class were unwilling to delink themselves from agriculture (Rutten, 2003; Sud, 2007; Breman 2007; Damodaran, 2008). The 'Gujaratness' of the story is that a part of the class continues to situate itself in the agrarian economy, and directly dominates the labour class.

Since 2000, the political settlement in Gujarat has witnessed the reinstatement of the rural proprietary class among the dominant classes, and the state has given ample subsidy support to these growers of high-value crops. Unlike in Chhattisgarh, Gujarat's big and middle farmers, better categorised as capitalist farmers, are exclusively cash crop growers, extensively using capitalist methods of agriculture, and target the export market for maximum profits. Indirectly, opportunities fostered by the New Agricultural Policy have included retailing or trading in seeds, fertilisers, pesticides, and machinery, and these reinforce linkages between the sectors. Colluding with the MNCs to maximise the sale of their products, brokerage from land transactions, subsidy on private irrigation, and rent from machinery have contributed to the rising accumulation and influence of this class. The nature of accumulation changes the class character, as utilising market-led opportunities is tending to transform several members of the agrarian class into the new petty bourgeoisie.

On the other hand, the food crop growers are almost always tillers and owners of small holdings with little or no irrigation facility. A separation of interest has arisen among the classes of farmers, hurting the formation of a strong farmer movement. In the late 1980s and 1990s, the farmers' movement under the Khedut Samaj and the BKS welcomed liberalisation. They were supporters of global players entering agrarian production, unlike the KRRS in Karnataka (Brass, 1995). South Gujarat farmers have been forerunners in adopting liberalisation-privatisation and have mostly been affiliated to the Khedut Samaj led by Sharad Joshi and drew their prosperity from sugar cooperatives. The representation of northern and central district farmers has been under the banner of the BKS. The social base for both organisations is that of the Patidars, the well-off peasantry (Brass, 1995). The northern farmers are still a political force, as fieldwork showed. However, Saurashtra has taken a backseat in political representation.

The most critical finding is that the state in Gujarat was found actively pursuing the agenda of capitalist large-scale agriculture in an organised way. There is a tacit recognition that this process will be accompanied by pushing small landholders out of agriculture. The increase in large holdings since 2005 is a clear indication of the direction in which the policies are pushing the sector. Since its objective is clear, it is turning a blind eye to the 'other', the classes who cannot be drivers of capitalist agriculture for lack of access to land, water, and credit resources. They have been left on their own despite being tillers.

Gujarat's strong adherence to the logic of the market has delinked it from the objective of social justice, such as 'land to the tiller'. The state's attitude to tiller farmers and other marginalised groups has been one of alienation and neglect. For instance, there is little effort to provide protection to labour and distributing *patta* to STs under the Forest Rights Act (Bandi, 2012). Instances of caste discrimination and caste affinity in villages, ghettoisation of lower castes who cultivated upper-caste capitalist farmers' land but were excluded from the latter's social life and physical space, and intolerance towards religious minorities (particularly Muslims) were witnessed. Discontent at the grassroots resulted in a shrinking of Modi's support base in Saurashtra, where the opposing Gujarat Parivartan Party (GPP) arose during the 2013 elections. The GPP mobilised its supporters based on an agenda of anti-BJP politics and promised to offer the people a better alternative to the BJP. Beneath the peaceful and developmental image, Gujarat seemed to be a deeply divided society.

The state's stance appears to be that infrastructural support and any other kind of support – monetary or irrigational – has been made readily available to farmers. However, the systematic removal of people from the sector, thereby adding them to the pool of cheap and informal workers, is real. Labour data does not account for footloose labour (Hirway, 2012). In line with scholars such as Indira Hirway and Neha Shah (2011), Rohini Hensman (2014), and Christophe Jaffrelot (2015), this author agrees that it is a deliberate attempt on the part of the state to suppress labour struggles and maintain low wages. Repeated complaints about increasing wages due to the introduction of the MGNREGS (which is as high as minimum wages) and the state's eagerness to tackle the problem by mechanising agriculture reflect shared ideas between the state and capitalist farmers. The scenario matches that of Chhattisgarh in installing technological solutions to manage labour issues affecting tiller farmers negatively. Technological solutions, however, cater to the interest of a few in states who accumulate from different sources but only marginally serve 80 per cent of the farmers who work as labourers.

Distinct from Chhattisgarh, Gujarat is pursuing the agenda of capital but the state has maintained its autonomy, which Poulantzas and Jessop termed as 'relative autonomy'. The bureaucracy maintains an autonomy as a class vis-à-vis the industrial capitalists and is not controlled by the latter. A mercantile ethos pervades the bureaucracy. It is, however, evident from data on corruption that rent collection by the bureaucracy is high. Instances of capitalists directly contesting election were found but Modi maintained a clean image. Nothing suggested that he is personally accumulating from furtherance of capital, which contributes to the state's legitimacy. This is unlike Yeddyurappa in Karnataka and ministers in Chhattisgarh (a case of personal fusion), despite a close connection between the capitalist class and the state.

Notes

1. It is a kind of land relation with the landlord owning the land, and the people, called peasants/tenants, working on it. The peasants are dependent on the landlord.
2. State domestic product is the sum total of goods and services produced within a state.
3. It covers the western districts, Rajkot, Junagadh, Bhavnagar, Porbandar, Jamnagar, Amreli, Surendranagar, Devbhoomi Dwarka, Morbi, Gir Somnath, and some portions of Ahmedabad and Botad.
4. With a view to overcoming the shortcomings experienced on account of the multiplicity of controls and clearances, absence of world-class infrastructure, and an unstable fiscal regime, and with a view to attracting larger foreign investments in India, the SEZs Policy was announced in April 2000 (GoI, Ministry of Commerce).
5. The reach of this organisation can be understood from the fact that the owners acquire license for the diamond merchants to keep pistols with them. According to uncorroborated information from an activist working with diamond labourers,

while the pistols are acquired under the plea of recent robberies, their actual use is in fact in controlling the *karigars* (interviewee from Surat, May 2011).

6. The urban class is constituted of the rural classes who have stakes in multiple sectors.

7. These extra incentives were extended to cultivators of oilseeds under the Technology Mission on Oilseeds, a programme of the state government.

8. This was prior to the introduction of Bt cotton.

9. Person owning more than ₹10 million.

10. Reliance, Essar, and Adani are the three biggest corporates in the state controlling a large chunk of the cement, power, real estate, and oil sectors. They are all Indian companies with headquarters in the state and are big players in the Indian economy.

11. Similar argument can be seen in Rutten (2003: 61), where he finds this across 59 families from Gujarat investing in agro-business and trade.

12. Godhra refers to a communal violence that occurred in central Gujarat in 2002, and evidence finds that it had support from the state officials and was thus a part of the BJP's agenda (Oommen, 2008).

13. It is difficult to assess the validity of these statistics, as 56 MLAs claim to have incurred no expense in fighting elections.

14. Centre for Social Studies working paper. For more details, see Sastry (2014).

15. Calculated as marginal-, small-, and semi-medium farmers as well as agricultural labourers as per 2010–11 data (Planning Commission).

16. By 2006, over 90 per cent of Gujarat's 18,000 villages were covered under the Jyoti Gram Scheme (JGS).

17. Government of Gujarat, Gujarat Urja Vikas Nigam Limited.

18. The movement aimed to stop the building of dams on the Narmada river, which was leading to thousands of villages being submerged in water due to river inundation. It affected people from Gujarat, Madhya Pradesh, and Maharashtra. In 1985, the movement gained momentum under Medha Patkar, who gave the movement a media presence. The movement brought environmentalists, social workers, farmers, *adivasis*, and media personalities together.

19. Bikabhai Gopaldas, Sumanbhai Bababhai, Bipinbhai Maganbhai, Pralatbhai Vikabhai, Girishbhai, Haribhai Mohanbhai (head), and Chandrakant.

20. *Basti* implies small shanties as opposed to big houses owned by upper castes. This is a result of spatial separation among different castes, where families from the lower castes live in a particular neighbourhood away from middle and upper castes.

21. He insisted on payment for organising the meeting which recurred in other instances while conducting fieldwork in Gujarat, an aberration from the other field states.

22. Slum-type housing.

23. Daniel Thorner discusses this category.

24. Projected figures for 2010.

25. Semi-medium is counted in the category of tiller farmers.

26. Raka Ray and Mary Katzenstein, ed, 'Chapter 7', in *Social Movements in India: Poverty, Power and Politics*, 179–202 (Lanham, MD: Rowman and Littlefield).

27. In 2003, the state government had banned exploitation of groundwater in 57 *taluka*s, covering 13 districts.
28. Dark zone refers to those *taluka*s in Gujarat where use of electricity to extract water for irrigation has been restricted by the government due to low water table.
29. Similar evidence has been found in Maharashtra (Aga, 2018).
30. The price fell from ₹1,600 to ₹650 for a 450-gram packet.
31. Head of Navbharat Seeds.
32. Details available at http://www.ggrc.co.in/frmhomepage.aspx.
33. The rule stipulated that landowners–tillers have to reside within 8 kilometres of their landholding to ensure land from the absentee landlords can be transferred to tenants.
34. In May 2006, Tata Motors announced a Nano car plant on 1,000 acres in Singur, West Bengal. The acquisition led to long-standing protests and violence, since the land in question was fertile. After a long legal battle, this culminated in Tata Motors moving their operations out of West Bengal in October 2008. For a complete timeline of the issue, see *The Hindu*, 'Singur Land Acquisition Issue: A Timeline,' 31 August 2016.
35. A major corporate group in the state, allegedly harbouring close relations with the state government.
36. What I found especially fascinating is how she was concerned about Gujarat as a whole. Her concerns for the lowest castes in Gujarat, their culture and tradition, and how these are under assault from present policies, while she was giving the interview, were particularly heartening.
37. This was told by a close confidant of a relative of mine, who was directly involved in acquiring land for a factory.
38. Area demarcated, disallowing land acquisition from the region.

❀

6

Karnataka

State Patronage, Market Opportunism, and Urban–Rural Closing Gap

This chapter aims to analyse Karnataka's political economy in the post-liberalisation phase. It explores the changes in policies, particularly on the agricultural sector, and the way these have affected class formation and consolidation. It examines the relationship between proprietary classes and the state to understand how the state allocates resources, such as land, water, and credit, and infers how the political settlement operates within the state. These questions have been addressed through a thorough literature review and fieldwork conducted in the state between February and July 2012. Although Karnataka has four agricultural universities that publish vast literature, these were of little pertinence to the study. This was primarily due to the technical nature, micro-view, and quantitative approach of these publications. Nonetheless, the information has been included whenever appropriate. Karnataka is a diverse state, and patterns vary between the northern and southern districts; therefore, evidence from fieldwork is juxtaposed with existing literature to present a comprehensive and nuanced picture. The north is less irrigated, has less capitalist agriculture, and has fewer commercial crops in comparison to the south.

In line with the other field-based chapters, this chapter opens with a brief description of the state, and a discussion on the economy, particularly sector growth rates, main sources of investment, and alignment of lobbies. It presents the trajectory of certain agrarian proprietary classes and links it to dominant castes, as the literature is mostly written along the parameter of caste. To make sense of proprietary classes after 1991, the scene prior, during the 1970s and 1980s, has been briefly discussed. This is followed by a brief discussion on three key features of Karnataka – corruption, farmer suicide, and decentralisation. These are relevant for explaining the field findings. Subsequently, political settlement and agrarian class formation and consolidation are reflected upon. Accumulation through diversification by fractions of rich farmers are highlighted along with that of the political leaders and state officials who have transformed into petty bourgeoisie. Field findings suggested that regional variations within the state exist, as demonstrated. Comparative assessment of these findings with Chhattisgarh and Gujarat is attempted. Finally, it is inferred that the nature of the regional state is clientelist, playing a major role side by side the market.

Karnataka's booming economy – the drivers and gainers

The period of 1990–2013 in Karnataka had witnessed rule by various parties – the Congress (until 1994 and again 1999–2004), Janata Dal Secular (1994–99), and the BJP (2007–13). Between 2005 and 2008, there were brief periods of dissolved governments and President's rule. This has resulted in the existence of policies taking multiple directions unlike the other two states, where one political party has dominated the political scene for the entire period under scrutiny. Hence, in the case of Karnataka, initially the economic policies were directed in multiple ways by different political leaders before gaining consistency in the last leg of the period. This section discusses the shift in sectoral distribution in gross state domestic product (GSDP), regional variation, and the classes and castes that have dominated the politics of the state and benefited from government policies and schemes.

Sectoral growth in Karnataka: 2002–12

Karnataka's economic performance has been better than the Indian average over the last decade. In the second half of the 1990s, the average real GSDP growth was about 5.2 per cent in the primary sector, 8.6 per cent in the secondary sector, and 10 per cent in the tertiary sector (GoK, 2003 cited in Assadi, 2010). Table 6.1 shows the above-average performance of the state during 2002–12, which is at par with the all-India average, except for the agricultural sector in 2011–12 that can be attributed to poor rainfall. The state has been successful in attracting 9.1 per cent of the total domestic investment of India and has emerged as the most preferred state for investment. In terms of foreign direct investment (FDI), it has attracted 9 per cent and has been among the top five states. This has translated into a huge economic boom in the state, particularly in the tertiary sector that is predominantly IT driven. The state has been attracting human resources from across the country who are in search of lucrative employment, with its capital Bengaluru as the favourite destination. Compared to Chhattisgarh and Gujarat, Karnataka has maintained closer relations with the World Bank and multinational corporates such as Monsanto and Cargill since the mid-1990s, both in terms of adopting its recommendations and taking favours such as loans[1] and providing land for GM seed trials. In fact, the rise of a major farmer organisation in the state, Karnataka Rajya Raitha Sangh, was in opposition to the inroads being made by foreign organisations into the agricultural sector (Scoones, 2008).

Table 6.1 Sectoral growth rates in Karnataka (in %)

Sector	2002–07	2007–12	2011–12
Agriculture	2.1 (2.4)	5.7 (3.3)	–2.9 (2.5)
Industry	9.5 (9.3)	5.3 (6.7)	3.6 (3.9)
Services	9.2 (9.2)	10.3 (9.9)	10.6 (9.4)
Total GSDP	7.7 (7.8)	8 (7.9)	6.4 (6.9)

Source: Directorate of statistics, multiple years.
Note: Figures in brackets are all-India numbers for the respective years.

Karnataka's agrarian sector contributes about 17 per cent of the GSDP and accounts for the income of 65 per cent of the population. Therefore, income inequality vis-à-vis other sectors is evident, but an analysis of the way agrarian classes have performed and coped with new policies has the potential to explain inequality within the sector. In the early 2000s, the state faced drought conditions that, together with political apathy towards the primary sector, affected the farmers severely (Assadi, 2010) and the sector registered low growth rates. Since then, it has recovered (Table 6.1), though it remains to be seen whether this can be said uniformly across the sector, or to only specific crops and classes. The positive developments in the agricultural sector were mainly because of the adoption of new agrarian policies first by the Congress government in 2006 and then the BJP in 2012. The main tenets of the policies and its key beneficiaries are discussed subsequently in the chapter. It aims to bring out the continuing aspects and new elements of the policy, and how it relates to the political economy of rural Karnataka.

Agro-ecologically, Karnataka can be divided into three regions – coastal, northern, and southern. In the pre-reforms period, each region was characterised by distinctive agrarian features. The coastal part had a high incidence of tenancy (44 per cent of the total land), largely tiny plots of land, and the lowest concentration of landownership resulting in the most equal land distribution. In contrast, the southern region has been marked by the lowest prevalence of tenancy, signifying a greater magnitude of peasant proprietorship. The tenanted area in the northern part ranged from 15 per cent in Dharwad to as little as 2 per cent in Bidar during the pre-reforms period (Figure 6.1). The northern region was marked by a skewed landownership pattern, with Gulbarga, Bijapur, and Bidar displaying a high proportion of holding in the largest size group (over 20 hectares), which is often an indicator of landlordism (Deshpande and Torgal, 2003). These districts have been the most backward in the state in terms of economic and social development. In the post-reform period, southern districts have shown a high rate of commercialisation, with Mandya, Mysore, Dharwad, and Shimoga being the forerunners, registering high agricultural growth, and having performed well in commercial crop production.

Figure 6.1 Karnataka – districts and major towns; districts visited

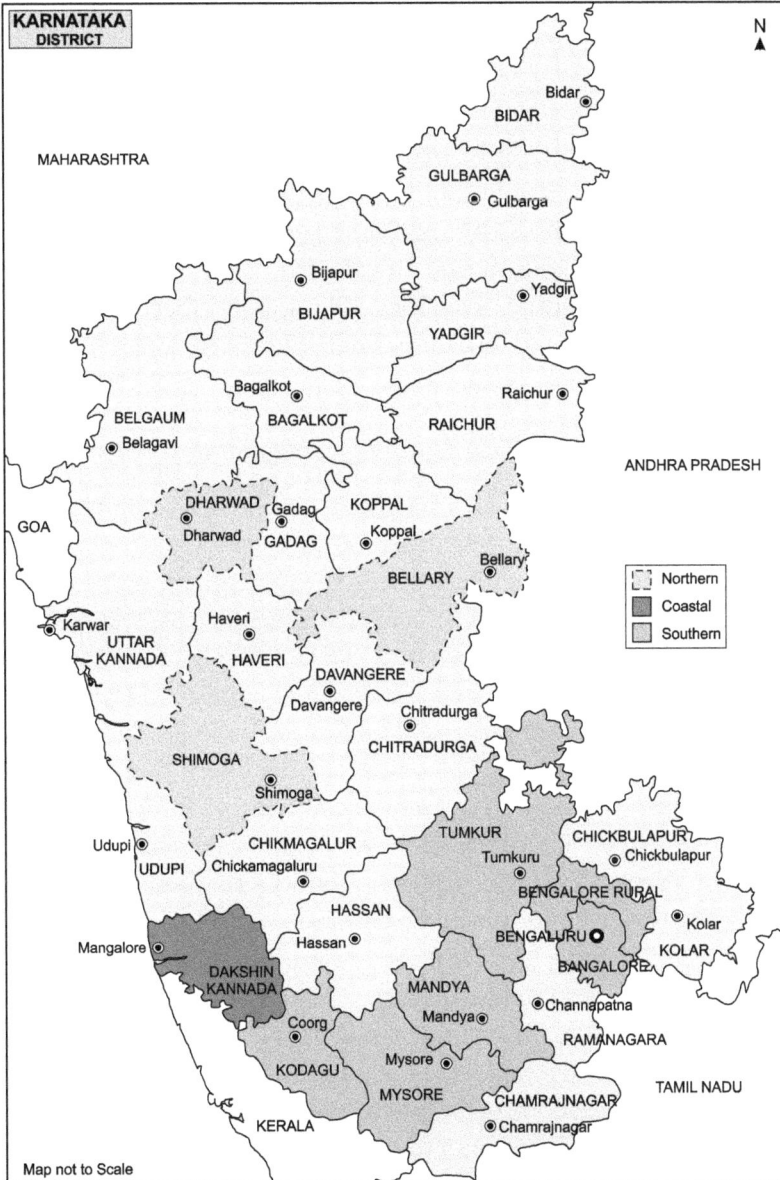

Source: www.mapsofindia.com.

An important factor that separates northern districts from those in the south is the former's lack of irrigation. According to official estimates, about 45 per cent of the agricultural land in these districts requires irrigation, but the current extent of irrigated land is only about 26 per cent (Rao and Gopalappa, 2004). Southern districts have had the advantage of canal irrigation, but since investment in public irrigation has reduced across India from the 1990s, even public tanks (that historically were a crucial source of drinking water and protective irrigation for rural poor people in backward areas) have registered a decline (Rao and Gopalappa, 2004).

Therefore, based on the level of development, the districts in Karnataka can be classified into three categories. The 'most developed' and 'developed' categories cover all districts in south, except Tumkur and Chitradurga, and includes Belgaum and Bellary districts from the north. The remaining northern districts come under the third category, 'highly backward' (Sthanumoorthy and Sivarajadhanavel, 2007). This lopsided intra-state development mirrors the concentration of natural, economic, and political resources in the south.

Karnataka politics: Two dominant castes and state patronage

The political scene of Karnataka has been traditionally dominated by two castes, Lingayats and Vokkaligas. Lingayats are from the dry regions in the north of the state and Vokkaligas are from the wet regions in the south. Both the castes comprise big farmers, white collar professionals, and traders. The only period in the last 60 years when the political stronghold of these two castes dwindled was in the 1970s under the then Chief Minister, Devraj Urs,[2] who tried to implement tenancy reforms. The Karnataka Land Reforms Act was amended in 1979, under which 'agricultural labourers were given an entitlement to seek ownership rights over land inhabited by them'. In his effort to create a support base with the backward classes, Urs introduced reservation for OBCs in public employment. He maintained a fine balance between the two dominant castes by classifying Vokkaligas as a 'backward class', eligible for concessions from the government in educational and government jobs, thus bringing them closer to the regime than the Lingayats.

The land reforms had limited success. Kohli (1987) argues that it was the weakness of the state together with the power of regional propertied classes that interfered with the efficacy of the reforms. Although more than half the reform applications were settled in favour of the applicant, that is, the labourer (Aziz and Krishna, 1997: 20–21), only 6 per cent of surplus land was distributed (Deshpande and Torgal, 2003). Moreover, tenants were forcefully ousted by the landowners before the implementation of the reforms to make sure they did not benefit from them. The actual beneficiaries were landlords, big or small, rather than the landless, and this defeated the stated purpose of land redistribution (Damle, 1989; Nadkarni and Vedini, 1996; Narendar Pani cited in Pani, 1996). Consequently, the economic position of big and middle farmers was strengthened in most cases through consolidation of their holdings, which led them to acquire a strong political voice. It can, thus, be argued that the reform added to the pool of labour as evicted tenants became landless and a stronger big farmer class was created as a whole.[3]

The OBCs, however, gained substantially from the tenancy reform and reservation. Many of them entered various white-collar professions such as the state bureaucracy during the 1970s and the early 1980s. Similar to Chhattisgarh, reservation given to the OBCs for institutional positions has brought the social group into the class of petty bourgeoisie, gaining from close association with the state. What is peculiar about Karnataka are the sub-categories under the OBC category – forward and backward. In Urs' tenure, only the backward groups were included into the OBC category. In 1980, the then Chief Minister, Ramakrishna Hegde, added the forward castes, such as Lingayats, to bring them into the ambit of state patronage (Manor, 1984; *Economic and Political Weekly*, 2005; Assadi, 2006). By 1988, Lingayats and Vokkaligas occupied 51 per cent of the total seats in the *zilla parishad*s, 46 per cent in the state legislative assembly, 54 per cent in the state legislative council, and 54 per cent in both houses of Parliament[4] despite constituting only 26 per cent of the total state population as per the 1988 election data (Radhakrishnan, 1990: 1753; Reddy, 1990). As Justice Reddy (1990) argued, this political dominance is a reflection of the economic dominance of these two groups.

Over the years, the state in Karnataka has proactively created spaces for members from certain caste groups to climb up the class ladder. It consolidated the old petty bourgeois class position within these social groups – OBCs for instance – by making public resources available to its members. The purpose of reservation is to help a group that has been historically disadvantaged, but in reality few members have used the policy to improve their personal material and social position. Thus, arguably only a few from a caste improved their class status. Within the regional power structure, as expected, Brahmins exerted both economic and political power. They were the first to migrate en masse to urban centres, and they now dominate better-paying and prestigious jobs. Population wise, they constitute just 3.5 per cent, but their representation in higher employment is 19.5 per cent and 21.5 per cent in education. With about 41 per cent of all government secretaries coming from their community, the Brahmins virtually are an 'institution' in themselves (Reddy, 1990).

The castes and classes discussed so far thereafter formed two power blocs in state politics in the 1990s. The two political formations came to be denoted as MOVD (Muslims, OBCs, Vokkaligas, and Dalits) and LIBRS (Lingayats and Brahmins). Throughout the 1990s, the *former* maintained their stronghold and paved the path for to two Chief Ministers – H. D. Deve Gowda (1994–96) and S. M. Krishna (1999–2004). Though from different political parties, Janata Dal Secular (JD[S]) and the Congress respectively, their social base was the same. However, the support base of the BJP, the ruling party that assumed power in the state assembly in 2007, was different. They were more deeply entrenched in the Lingayat–Brahmin coalition and came to power by appealing to Hindi (linguistic), Hindu (upper caste), and Hindustan (chauvinistic national) identities. They have successfully built a support base with numerous other groups, especially the OBCs, by offering them a promise of better governance and state patronage in the form of assembly seats (Manor, 2007). The drifting away of the OBCs from the Congress has meant a loss in terms of voters for the party. Since politically they were a support base the party had created, their drift away from the Congress was a failure of long-term strategy for the party. The agrarian policies of 2006 and 2012 are to be assessed in the light of the social structure after reforms, with a bolstered agrarian proprietary class and the OBCs consolidated as part of the petty bourgeoisie.

Farmers' resistance and the rise of commercial crop cultivation

Karnataka, unlike the other two states under scrutiny, has witnessed an autonomous farmers' movement, independent of the political parties. In the 1980s, the farmers' movement took roots with the formation of the KRRS in the district of Shimoga, and it soon spread to other districts. The KRRS conceptualised Indian economic backwardness as 'weak capitalism', where upper caste and capitalists have excluded the masses (peasantry and labourers) by denying them education and a share in property (Assadi, 1994). It also pointed out the urban and industrial bias of the government. Their central argument was that the terms of trade are against agriculture (Assadi, 1994: 218). They demanded higher budgetary allocations and small-scale industrial units to create more employment. In the early 1990s they strongly mobilised against the WTO entering the Indian agricultural sector, especially the input and price markets, as it would further curb farmers' autonomy. However, over the latter part of the 1990s, the movement lost steam.

There have been arguments from Marxian scholars that the KRRS is a rich peasants' movement and is reactionary (Pattenden, 2005: 97). My interviews support the view that the movement and its protests and rallies are a political ploy of the big farmer lobby to display its strength. In an interview on enquiring why the KRRS is particularly strong in Bellary and not in other districts, a leader attributed it to the preponderance of farmers with holdings of over 20 acres, and added, 'When there are big farmers, the KRRS has to be strong.' This was by far the most direct statement showing whom the organisation represents. However, based on the interviews I carried out, I would argue that the KRRS is not reactionary per se; rather it is seeking to appropriate the advantages of neoliberal policies. Inclusion of small farmers serves the purpose of adding numerical strength to the lobby.

The KRRS lost steam in the latter part of the 1990s. Despite being a social movement, it never challenged social hierarchies and caste atrocities. As argued by Banaji (1994), the movement was delinked from pro-labour issues. To that extent, it remained representative of big farmers (Brass, 1994; Nair, 1996; Pattenden, 2011). Ideologically, the movement understood the peasantry as an undifferentiated whole, a perception that rendered caste, class, and other fissures within the peasantry redundant and led to the failure in addressing issues that affected small farmers. It systematically oppressed Dalits and OBCs. Claiming to be a voice for 'all farmers', it practised hostility and oppression towards lower-caste small farmers, including violence against agricultural labour. This affected the legitimacy of the movement and, arguably, proved to be its undoing. The organisation is no longer as relevant in state politics, though it operates as fractions in a few districts as fieldwork showed.

Changes after 1990

A few features have been discussed in this section that at first glance seem to be delinked from agriculture, but eventually have been woven into the field findings to develop a sound understanding of the political economy of the state. With the son-of-the-soil Deve Gowda assuming power in the early 1990s, significant policy changes were introduced. In 1994–95 (the same year when Gujarat undertook its counter reforms), Karnataka implemented a relaxation of land ceilings and allowed sale of agricultural land for non-agricultural purposes. The agricultural sector was, thus, opened to capitalists and professionals. Deve Gowda toed the financial capital line that low ceiling on landownership is an obstacle in market functions and poses a challenge to optimal utilisation of factors of production (Nair, 1996; Jenkins, 1999). Jenkins ascribes the state taking a strong stance to support the regional capitalist classes, who were aspiring to accumulate faster with the arrival of foreign capital.

In the last two decades politics in Karnataka has been marked by three characteristics – corruption, agrarian distress, and the spread of local self-government institutions. A recent study argues that Karnataka has seen the highest proportion of petty corruption among the states in India (Bussell, 2012). A corrupt bureaucracy, exchange of favours among the bureaucracy, police, elected leaders, and industrialists, and vast sums of illicit money from multiple sources (such as mining scams[5]) have characterised state politics (*Headlines Today*, 2011). The press named a former Chief Minister, party leaders, mining magnates holding ministerial positions, and over 600 officials for indulging in corrupt practices that cost the exchequer ₹160.85 billion between 2006 and 2010 (*Headlines Today*, 2011). Analysis of the 2008 election shows the enormous use of money power that played a role in the victory of the BJP in Karnataka. The political class accumulated massively in the past decade, as reflected in the increase of the average wealth of contesting legislators by about 800 per cent (Vasavi, 2008). In the backdrop of the alliance between the industrial capitalist and political classes (state officials and leaders), the third class, the agrarian propertied class, was also keen to reap benefits of the real-estate boom (Nair, 1996).

Liberalisation of the agrarian sector was meant to change the lives of farmers, and it has indeed accomplished that. As economic and social deprivation in parts of the state reached epic proportions, some farmers were driven to as far as committing suicide. The first cases of suicide were reported in 1998 from the underdeveloped districts (Bidar and Gulbarga), but soon spread to the developed, commercial-crop-farming districts. Various reliable sources have uniformly reported higher suicide figures, though the state government denies the number. In 2001, according to such sources, the number of suicides registered was 2,505 (Nagaraj, 2008). After 2000, the number has kept rising. The central government admitted that between 2000–01 and 2005–06, around 8,600 farmers committed suicide in Karnataka – the highest compared to any other state in India (Assadi, 2008). The OBC farmers were particularly affected because they borrowed heavily from informal moneylenders for production of high-value commercial crops. They were attracted towards cotton and shrimp production that were fetching good prices at the time. The unexpected decline in international prices along with unsupervised use of insecticides, which resulted in infestation of the crop, spelled their ruin, and hundreds of farmers ended their lives in desperation (Rao and Suri, 2006; Nagaraj, 2008; NCEUS, 2008). Suicide occurred among small- and medium-sized market-oriented farmers who had incurred high levels of debt trying to adopt capitalist input-centric agricultural production such as deep-tubewell irrigation (Reddy and Mishra, 2009). The argument is that these were fallouts of new agrarian policies and indicate that certain classes bore the burden of the new policies introduced in the mid-1990s. Not all classes were affected by this unfavourably. Does the trend change thereafter?

The third feature of relevance is that Karnataka implemented local self-government institutions even prior to its adoption by the national government. The Panchayati Raj reforms were adopted in the state in the early 1990s.[6] The Janata Party had passed new local government regulations as early as 1983 in the state. M. G. Krishnan (1992) argued that this institutional change arose in response to the democratic consciousness among marginalised sections such as peasants and Dalits. Moreover, various sections of the society were deeply disenchanted and were looking for a (local) alternative to the Congress. Hence, the Janata Party took the initiative in providing a solution. Under the Karnataka Panchayat Raj Act (1983) the *zilla parishad* was given extensive planning, administering, and monitoring powers in matters of local development. An analysis of participation of marginalised caste members in PRIs and access to state resources through reservation policy will be undertaken to comprehend effective inclusion of new members in the circuit of capital. Accumulation here is through connection to the state.

From caste discourses, it can be deduced that the bureaucracy and big farmers/landlords were the primary stakeholders in state politics during the 1980s. Locating the class interest of these caste groups can assist in understanding how agrarian policies are formulated and which classes the benefits accrue to. The political economy picture indicates that indigenous capital in the state is not all-powerful, the way it is in Gujarat. The rapid expansion of the tertiary sector and the dependence on FDI have split the pie between foreign capital investing heavily in the state and domestic capital trying to maximise the opportunities created by new policies.

In this context, the fieldwork focused on three classes: capitalist, the petty bourgeoisie (bureaucracy, professionals, and elected leaders), and big farmers. A large part of the fieldwork concentrated on rural proprietary classes' interests and their inter-linkages with the urban capitalist class. The aim was to answer two main questions: (*a*) What is the role of agricultural policy in relation to agrarian classes after 2000? (*b*) How does the state balance diverse interests within itself and maintain political settlement?

Fieldwork

The total number of interviews conducted were 42, out of which 24 interviewees were farmers, 6 were academics working in related fields, 3 were state officials, 2 were journalists, and 7 were political party members. In the state, there were 2 respondents who were interviewed twice each. There was a need to gather the relevant part of the information provided by them. Over a period of 4 months, 3 FGDs were held, 1 in Mangalore with tribal small farmers, and 2 in Bellary and Shimoga with big capitalist farmers, growing sugarcane and areca nut respectively.

In this section, based on the fieldwork, it is concluded that big farmers and landlords can no longer be characterised solely as rural classes because fresh opportunities created by neoliberal policies have enabled them to diversify to sectors other than agriculture. Their new class position is more of petty bourgeoisie (new and old), which has aligned their interests closer to the urban capitalist class. Many of them regard agriculture as a peripheral activity. However, in some cases they have embarked upon profitable capitalist agriculture as well. At the other end of the rural spectrum, tiller farmers including small, marginal, and semi-medium farmers are facing increasing debt due to privatisation of inputs, and reduced labour use owing to mechanisation, leading to less opportunity for labour. A polarisation has set in between different classes of farmers, which has adversely affected the farmers' movement in the state. Once again, the industrial capitalist emerges as the most dominating class in the political settlement, although the presence of both domestic and foreign capital was noted. Evidence showed that capital has partnered with petty bourgeois elements to penetrate the rural sector. In this instance, the petty bourgeoisie has its roots in the big farmers and landlord class. Here, the agricultural policies of 2006 and 2012 have had a significant role to play. The essence of both policies was promotion of commercial and high-value crops, input centricity, and subsidies to facilitate mechanisation that would tantamount to protecting and promoting the interests of agrarian proprietary classes.

The section opens with a discussion of different classes dominating the state economy and the various political ploys that these classes adopt (such as lobbying for political bargain). Subsequently, a detailed discussion of agrarian classes and policies in the 1990s and changes post-2004 are undertaken to argue that after the defeat of the NDA in the 2004 national elections, regional states have taken utmost care to reinstate big farmers in the political settlement.

Balance of power: State lobbies and their changing dynamics

The following section is concerned with the dominant classes – industrial capital, big farmers, and petty bourgeoisie – and their changing interests. By comparing their functioning in the political realm and ascertaining which lobbies have gained in recent decades, the key economic demands of the capitalist class are assessed. This also informs the nature of 'political settlement' that prevails at the state level.

In the case of Karnataka, political parties are found to be a weaker cementing factor than patron–client relations. Like in the Lingayat stronghold, Shimoga, deep patron–client relations were noted by multiple respondents. A probable reason for this is the underdevelopment in northern districts, which implies that access to state resources is an important source of surplus. Those with cliental relation with Yeddyurappa[7] and Eshwarappa[8] made money in the corruption cases, which explains their economic and political dominance in these districts. A respondent said, 'They have divided the Shimoga district among themselves and are making huge earnings from its natural resources' (interview of a journalist from Bellary, July 2012). Despite them pursuing politics as a vehicle for their individual and clients' economic gain, they have retained political support of their caste on the face. Although hailing from the south, Yeddyurappa has been instrumental in 'bringing in the landlords from northern district into politics', remarked a party leader (interview in Bangalore, April 2012). Some evidence pointed at the benefits of corruption accruing to agrarian proprietary classes in the north, but the issue mandates more investigation.

The northern districts that are gaining prominence in both economic and political spheres have finally posed a challenge to the dominance of southern districts within state politics (interview of a journalist, March 2012). It can be interpreted as the opening of political space to those who were outsiders. At a preliminary glance, the political struggle seems to be among only the castes, but its class character becomes apparent when delving deeper. It is the motive to gain more state resources, as a means of accumulation, that drives the quest to capture state power. The power of the north lobby relative to that of the south lobby can be discerned from the regional shift in politics.

The shift in the power bases of the ruling party can be traced to a change in the position of political lobbies. An eminent technocrat, who has participated in policy processes during the last three decades, provided a clear view of the relationship between state politics and lobbies: 'Politics is an intersection of different interest groups and lobbies. Few interests are unique to one lobby for which they negotiate among themselves, while other interests run across several lobbies and hence are negotiated among them.' This is how the politics of the state works (interviewee from Bangalore, March 2012). The education and the service sector (information technology) lobbies were the dominant lobbies up to the turn of the century. Since 2000, the real estate and mining lobbies have assumed more power and exerted a disproportionate influence over the ruling party (Nanjappa, 2008). Geographically, the real estate lobby has a commanding presence in southern Karnataka, and mining has a tighter hold on the northern districts. The education lobby has been relegated to a third position, and is located primarily in the coastal belt, that is, Dakshin Kannada and Uddupi. Private education institutions and international schools dot both these districts. However, there are instances of a capitalist being influential across lobbies, thereby using multiple opportunities to maximise surplus. For example, Vijay Mallya was an industrialist who held a diversified portfolio; he owned an educational institution, a liquor company, and even a fertiliser company. Real estate has been a sector that has seen a lot of investment from many lobbies.

Several sources, such as Vasavi (2008) and *Pragoti*[9] (Nanjappa, 2008), have analysed how the lobbies assume political power. Quite a few instances of the economically powerful individuals contesting elections were noted across districts, such as Bellary, Shimoga, and Mangalore (Vasavi, 2008). It is widely accepted that in the 2007 state assembly election, the mining lobby concentrated its finances in six districts – Bellary, Chitradurga, Hubli-Dharwad, Haveri, and Tumkur (interview of a senior political leader[10] from Mumbai, August 2012). A journalist argued that the mining lobby spent up to ₹30,000 million in the election. Foreign capital has been key in relation to the regional state.

From fieldwork it can be affirmed that a common interest that binds indigenous and foreign capital is 'acquiring land'. The class is seeking revision of the land acquisition policy to facilitate that objective. Given an upper ceiling on how much agricultural land can be owned and given that the state has declared land as non-transferable to protect agricultural land, the interest of capital has been seemingly at stake. Market ethics has penetrated the agrarian classes. For example, in Bellary district, the respondents (middle and big farmers) were looking for a chance to sell their land to utilise increasing market rates of land. Farmers near Bangalore said they would sell off their land if they got a good price. Industrial capitalists like big farmers, in this instance, seek a political party at the helm of affairs that can materialise their demand for relaxed land laws. Likewise, in the case of Gujarat, a case has already been presented in Chapter 5 in which the industrial capitalists were seeking appropriate political representation to consolidate land. The political leaders are seeking to maximise personal economic gains by perpetuating the interest of the capitalist (Bussell, 2012). Powerful capitalist interests also influence public policy by assuming positions within state institutions, such as taking membership in the Karnataka Vision group, Agricultural Mission, and Karnataka Education Mission that were formed by the government to oversee state development. These commissions had no representation from farmers, Dalits, or religious minorities (Narasappa and Vasavi, 2010). Instead, the decisions have been influenced by the proprietary class assuming positions of power.

The weakening of the farmers' movement in late 1990s translated to a weakening of farmers' lobby, as noted by several respondents[11] (interviews in Bangalore, February–August 2012). However, evidence suggested that a few crop lobbies are still operating in the southern districts. Sugarcane farmers have an independent organisation, the Karnataka Kabbu Belegavara Sangha, to deal with their demands even though their presence is limited to Mysore and Mandya. Here, the number of members and mobilisation become important as a measure of strength of the organisation (interview of a technocrat, 2012). Silk farmers have an organised voice in the same districts. Ramnagar has one of the most effective cocoon markets operating, where the state was found to be actively promoting farmers' interest.

The strength of crop lobbies, such as for sugarcane and areca nut, shows the negotiation power of agrarian capital, but these lobbies are a remote second when pitched against the interests and influence of the capitalists. In 2009, respondents reported that the central government had passed a law that if a state government forces sugarcane mills to pay more than the previous year's rate to farmers for sugarcane, then the excess must be financed by the state government (interview of Dhananjay from Mandya, 2012). Hence, mill owners have been given immunity from farmers' demands. A respondent conjectured that this happened because of Sharad Pawar's (who is a sugar baron) presence in the central government, who voiced the mill owners' interests. As in the case of Chhattisgarh, Karnataka faces a conflict of interest, where the state has to decide as to whom a policy should benefit; in all of this, the interest of the capitalist is the most dominant one. In Bellary, for instance, the local mill owner was from Maharashtra who enjoyed a monopoly on sugarcane processing, therefore curbing farmers' negotiation power; a similar situation was faced in Dakshin Kannada. The upshot of this is that, given the state's nexus with capital, farmers' interest holds a secondary position (interview of an academic from Mangalore, July 2012).

Considering these findings, does it mean that farmers are not a part of the political settlement as concluded in Chhattisgarh and Gujarat? Respondents indicated that the flow of black money and illegal transactions have led to the formation of a petty bourgeoisie within the agrarian structure. This new petty bourgeois class accumulates by grabbing opportunities brought in by the market, as Poulantzas (1973) had predicted. This class comprises mostly farmers, primarily big and a 'few' middle. They have accumulated but not invested enough capital in trade or industry to be categorised as capitalists. They are steadily reducing use of their labour in agriculture but in a few instances middle farmers continue putting their labour in agriculture alongside hired wage labour, whereas the big farmers have thrived exclusively on hired labour and have begun investing in trade, such as coal transport, tractor shops, and contractor business, as evidence showed. The new petty bourgeoisie has links to middle and big farmers and marks the movement of agrarian surplus out of agriculture. A few have managed to go fully into investing capital for profit through a productive activity, thus assuming a rural capitalist character. Khan's (1996, 2000) notion of rent (bribery, corruption, and land deals), which accrues to the elite, can be seen here accruing to the bureaucracy and elected members, which at the district level overlap with middle and big farmers. However, the tendency is to invest in trade and land, and seldom in industry, thus hindering the class' transformation into capitalists. They are keen to reap quick benefits, which trade offers but not in opportunities that have long gestation time, like manufacturing.

They often hold political positions such as *sarpanch*, and have risen to prominence in a short span of 10 to 15 years (interviews of an academic from Bangalore and an activist, 2012). They have preferential access to state resources, an important component of which are the MGNREGS funds, since almost 99 per cent of the MGNREGS resources in the state are disbursed through the *gram panchayat*s. Political positions are used to further economic gains. As reported, the new members of the local self government siphon off funds from cooperative society loans, subsidies on seeds and fertilisers, funds for road construction, and suchlike (interview of a journalist, August 2012, and an activist from Tumkur, 2012). In Tumkur district, the contractors were reported to use machines to complete the MGNREGS work and pocket the money. Simply put, what is witnessed is corruption leading to accumulation. This is in line with the findings of Pattenden's Karnataka village study, where he gives evidence of access to political funds (gatekeeping) feeding into accumulation in the northern districts of Karnataka (2011). This indicates that there are deep cleavages even among the farmers. At the top are the rural proprietary classes, who control and determine access to public resources and gain from private opportunities, and at the bottom, the tiller farmers depend on both agriculture and non-agriculture as sources of employment, lack state support, and face food insecurity.

State at the core of accumulation: Strong patron-client relations

'Karnataka has the highest rate of petty corruption among all states in India (Bussell, 2012). This section substantiates that through case studies and how one kind of class power translates into another and how connections to state resources enable access to economic gains. The cases are assembled from different respondents, including three core informants (all were reliable sources) – an activist from Mandya, a journalist in Bengaluru, and a national political leader. Agrarian roots of many of these individuals have been traced, indicating how surplus accruing from non-agrarian sources protect big farmers from the clutches of agrarian crisis. It also surfaced how common interests emerge and bring proprietary classes closer, particularly around one type of accumulation – 'land acquisition'.

Against this backdrop, the districts of Mandya, Mysore, Bellary, and Shimoga threw up various instances of economic accumulation owing to political influence. Ram Krishna, a public works department (PWD) officer, is a middle farmer and a Congress worker with connections to the state-level bureaucracy during the tenure of S. M. Krishna as chief minister. During this period, he bagged many contracts for public works, and accumulated significantly. After a successful phase of working as a contractor for the PWD, he accumulated enough to own a *kalyan mandappa* (marriage hall), a petrol pump, and over a hundred tractors. A part of the surplus generated from these was invested in consolidating his landholdings. His accumulation drive has been fuelled further through various MGNREGS projects for which he operates as a lead contractor (interview of an activist from Mandya, 2012). A similar case was witnessed on a Bangalore highway where the owner of a convention hall owned a small nursery. He had other businesses in the city and would rarely visit the hall (interview of a nursery worker from Bangalore, 2012).

Govardhan, a rich farmer, similarly acquired assets in Maddur town. His wife won the MLA election. Later, he contested the state election on a Congress ticket and won. Their political opponent was a retired officer of the Karnataka Industrial Development Board. Known to have abused the power and position of his office for private gain, the opponent has also entered politics post-retirement. He initially joined the Congress but later shifted to the BJP. However, he was seen campaigning for the JDS for *taluk panchayat* elections. Change of political alliance here is a way for quicker accumulation, where ideology becomes insignificant. He has aligned with the party that was predicted to assume power to maximise his gain.

Arjun is a two-time MLA. He started off as a middle farmer who joined the KRRS and later shifted to Vokkaliga Sangha. During his political career he has come to own nursing colleges as well as primary and high schools. Once more political connections played an instrumental role in furthering accumulation. In Mandya, S. M. Krishna, the erstwhile Chief Minister, owns the biggest sugar mill along with large holdings of land. His family wields political and economic influence. The accumulation through political position was reported in other cases around Bangalore. Real estate was a common source of accumulation. The owner of a wedding venue (*mandappa*) who is also a political figure was the case in multiple instances.

The prevalence of such activities indicates that dominant proprietary classes actively seek direct political power to fuel, sustain, and protect their accumulation. These are cases of 'personal fusion', as previously noted in the case of Chhattisgarh. Corruption and maintenance of patron–client relation with the state and other illicit practices emerge as a source of accumulation. In terms of class, many of these individuals began as middle/big farmers and went on to invest in other sectors, such as in establishing schools, quarries, contracting, and banks. A part of the surplus is also reinvested in acquiring more land. In some instances where political power preceded large landownership, land has been bought in their name, channelising surplus from other sectors into agriculture.

There are only a few examples of persons who started off from modest backgrounds but whose political connections then brought them economic surplus. The distinction between pure economic power and political power is increasingly blurred, making Poulantzas' perspective on class fitting in the context. Class, for Poulantzas, is a category that operates in both political and economic realms. Existing economic classes (not directly involved in state functioning) tend to capture political power and determine state affairs, and the political leaders indulge in corrupt practices by accepting funds from capitalists and investing it in land, trade, and industry. The separation of capital and state, in this case, seems difficult, leaning towards Mitra's kind of understanding: 'Those who aim at power do so ... to shift the distribution of assets and incomes in society in favour of those groups who support them' (Mitra, 1977).

Agrarian policy in Karnataka: Two phases and its thrust areas

The primary question addressed in this section is – what happened to the agrarian classes under the new policy regime in Karnataka? Policy regime can be divided into two phases: one from 1991 to 2006 and another from 2006 onwards. In the 1990s, WTO intervention, seed imperialism, and preferential price policies ushered a new phase in Karnataka's agrarian sector. The policy objective was marked by a shift from distribution to productivity by harping on input centricity and technology-driven agricultural growth. The state government was very keen to make use of the new opportunities created as a result of liberalisation. Karnataka was an early adopter of technology and private inputs, and cut down public investment in subsidies. As put by Nair (1996), 'Karnataka must prepare to harvest its share of investments in the aquaculture, horticulture, floriculture, and housing industry' (p. 251). The state had a low agricultural growth rate throughout the 1990s until 2000. The agenda was to increase incorporation of cultivators into the market and for that to happen the public sector had to withdraw from crop procurement. Despite the FCI regularly raising the ceiling of agricultural prices, its purchase of cereals fell sharply with the opening of the sector to international trade. This resulted in price uncertainty that influenced farmers to take up cultivation of more market-viable crops (Deshpande and Prachitha, 2006).

Agrarian reforms began to be implemented since the 1990s and resulted in falling sectoral growth and farmer suicides. Though most Indian states adopted the strategy, Reddy and Mishra (2009) blame the Karnataka government particularly for its 1990s policy to 'squeeze investment in agriculture', which resulted in the agrarian crisis that the state faced. This continued into the 2000s. In 2001, the World Bank granted the state an economic restructuring loan. It came with strings attached, underlining most importantly that the government should withdraw from the power sector as a regulator and distributor of power. This led to bifurcation of the electricity board to agricultural and domestic feeders. The outcome was the partial withdrawal of subsidy provided to the farmers in the form of free power. In fact, power tariffs increased drastically. The obvious outcome was more adverse for tiller farmers who would have to pay higher rent to the owners of pumps than a big farmer or a capitalist farmer who could cope with the pressure of paying for electricity.

The defeat of the NDA at the centre in 2004 reminded the political parties that rural proprietary classes were a force to reckon with (Rao and Gopalappa, 2004; Bose, 2006). The change in regime arguably triggered a change in the very essence of policies. The policies undertaken right after that in 2006 and then in 2012 reflect the state paying particular attention to various fractions of rich farmers. The state government distanced itself from the service sector and adopted a rural-friendly language (Vasavi, 2007). It is worth noting that despite the GATT prescriptions of a minimal role of the state in the sector, the state has actually resumed its role in steering the sector's growth soon after 2000 by selecting the crops to be focused on, the items to be subsidised, where formal credit should be targeted, and suchlike. It has introduced e-auction at the APMC in silk cocoon trade to ensure the farmers get good prices. Subsidy on machinery, drip irrigation, and greenhouses have been highly instrumental in mechanisation and shift in cropping pattern. A subsidy of 90 per cent has been offered on drip irrigation by the Chief Minister, which has led to high adoption of drip irrigation in Raichur, Mandya, and so on (Murdeshwar, 2013).

Until 2007, the state had JDS and Congress rule and since 2007 the BJP has been in power except for six months, between November 2007 and May 2008. The government (under Congress and JDS) declared that 'Karnataka agriculture has seen low levels of public investment and not all farmers have been able to access credit, modern technology, irrigation and markets' (Government of Karrnataka, 2003). Despite detailed consultation with agricultural scientists and experts, including Swaminathan,[12] the stated objective of Karnataka's Agriculture Policy of 2006 was not distribution or innovation in indigenous varieties of food grains or other crops that could impact the masses in the sector. The declared agenda was 'doubling agricultural production over the next decade with the help of imported technologies, biotechnology, and corporatisation of agriculture'. Despite its dreadful negative implications for employment generation, corporate agriculture was held as a way forward: agriculture is the most labour-dense sector, yet an investment of ₹30,000 million in coastal Karnataka was found to create employment for only 350 persons (Deshpande and Prachitha, 2006). This could potentially spell disaster for those classes of farmers who have survived by working as agrarian wage labourers. However, the state showed no concern for them; rather, it focused its policy prescriptions to push the agricultural growth to its target of 4.5 per cent per annum, up from 2 per cent in 2002. Post-harvest value addition, better communication between 'lab and land',[13] and better opportunities to enhance a farmer's net income were some of the other aims of the policy. The policy listed hybrid seeds, chemical inputs, and mechanisation as the features of the new agriculture of the state. Like Gujarat, Karnataka is pursuing a second wave of Green Revolution with a change in cropping pattern. A major focus was given to high-value crops with crops such as maize, sunflower, pepper, cotton, groundnut, and horticulture owing to their demand in the export market.

The origin of the farming crisis has often been ascribed to stagnation in public investment (Assayag, 2005). However, the situation has undergone a significant change in the decade after 2000. The agriculture and allied activities outlay approved by the Planning Commission and state government between 2003 and 2008 is ₹4,923.8 million at 2002–03 prices, which is 4 per cent of the total budget and 86.15 per cent higher than the Ninth Plan approved outlay (1997–2002). The Eleventh Plan (2007–12) had an agricultural budget of ₹1,13,200.8 million, which is 8 per cent of the total budget outlay.[14] The government aimed to contribute 8.9 per cent of the Twelfth Plan outlay to agriculture. The budget increase is from ₹19,660 crore to ₹22,310 crore between 2012–13 and 2013–14. Counter to the prescription of a minimalist state, the state has (re)assumed a larger role in the agricultural sector. The favourable disposition towards the sector, however, cannot be equated with gain of all agrarian classes.

Mechanisation of agriculture was touted as the way forward to achieve high growth in the agrarian sector, as was the case in Chhattisgarh and Gujarat as well. However, as seen in the case of those two states, mechanisation comes with the influx of chemical inputs and expensive machinery, newer methods of irrigation, and an automatic laying-off of wage labourers. Input centricity results in burdening small farmers with debt who find it hard to pay for lumpy technology. Against this backdrop, the 2006 agricultural policy makes special provisions for small farmers. It recommends formation of cooperatives to share the high cost of cultivation among tiller farmers, since small-holding cultivation is uneconomic. But ground reality tells a saga of continuing deprivation and farmer suicide among these classes. A reputed technocrat mentioned, 'Like there are principles enshrined in the Indian constitution but never followed, so are we, *bureaucrats* and *government advisors*, enshrined in our official positions, who have no choice but to sign policy documents which will not be implemented.' What the quote meant is that even though tenets of the policy are selectively implemented and scientists who advise policy makers are aware of that, documents are still made official to score political points and capture popular support. 'Forming cooperatives to make small holdings viable' is one such tenet, which promised opportunity to farmers with all size holdings. He pointed at another similar example, the issue of making water available in arid and semi-arid zones; lack of irrigation has been a major cause of farmer distress, which has been mentioned in policy documents but no constructive plan was drawn to address the issue between 2006 and 2012 (interview of a senior policy maker from Bangalore, 2012).

In Karnataka, there was a trend of growing high-value horticulture crops, sericulture, animal husbandry, and moving away from traditional crops (cereals) (Deshpande, 2004; Gowda, 2009). Over 1,82,000 hectares of additional area were brought under horticulture during the Eleventh Plan period (2007–12) under the National Horticulture Mission (Mishra, 2012).[15] In 2007–08, horticulture occupied 2,23,000 hectares, which is only 14.5 per cent of the net cultivated area; however, income from horticulture constitutes over 40 per cent of the total income generated from the entire agricultural sector. High-technology floriculture has emerged as central to the new cropping pattern, with flower export registering a steady rise since 2000. Karnataka accounted for 60 per cent of the total cut-flower exports from the country (Gowda, 2009). Export-driven agriculture has come to define this state's agrarian sector.[16] Another example of the state's export orientation is the emphasis on aquaculture. The Karnataka Reforms Act (1961) was amended to extend facilities to farmers and help them adopt aquaculture, especially shrimp culture, for export purposes (Nair, 1996). Though shrimp export is an area in which India has achieved stunning progress, farmer suicides have been found to occur among those in shrimp culture owing to the requirement of high investment, which when followed by a crash of prices spells disaster for them, as seen in the neighbouring state of Andhra Pradesh (Sridhar, 2006). High capital investment and informal debt surface as the premise on which cultivation of the crop rests.

Another feature of the 2006 agricultural policy is its emphasis on organic farming. Organic produce has a new demand in urban India, and the state government is trying to fund organic farming selectively in some districts such as Coorg. Such measures were unheard of in other districts according to the literature review and interviews. In Coorg there are families trying to become organic farmers to break away from the spiral of increasing cost of production based on chemical inputs. I met two big farmers (both college graduates, a rarity among farmers) owning plantations who spoke about this transition. They explained, 'When you adopt the organic method, the first two years there is poor yield; this loss is difficult to bear for a farmer who has a debt. It is only by the third year that one starts to make profit.' Therefore, in effect, this scheme too can only be used by surplus-producing farmers who can wait until the third year for a higher yield and then benefit from higher returns (interviews of Siddharth and Ravi from Coorg, April 2012).

The liberal land ceiling policy introduced in Karnataka in the early 1990s allowed non-agricultural private/public limited companies to acquire large agricultural lands for purposes of high-technology floriculture. After 2000, floriculture units in Karnataka have increasingly been owned and organised as private limited companies to take advantage of the industrial benefits and subsidies provided by both state and central governments. It seems that among the beneficiaries, several are from outside the state; a large majority of such high-technology floriculture units in and around Bangalore are owned and organised by entrepreneurs from Andhra Pradesh (Gowda, 2009). Evidence showed that relatives of government officials, a part of the old petty bourgeoisie, are investing in nurseries around Bengaluru (interview of Ganesh from Tumkur, 2012).

While capitalist farmers in Gujarat are playing more with open-market prices, minimum support price (MSP) has retained a role in benefiting farmers. Despite the ostensibly 'scientific approach' to the process of arriving at the cost of production, prices of crops were modified as per the recommendation of the political leaders (patrons) to serve the interests of their clients (Deshpande, 2002; Assayag, 2005). Such intervention occurred for a handful of crops, such as paddy and sugarcane, affecting the price parity across crops and minimising the role of input costs in determining the MSP. Through this, the state has been protecting the interests of crop lobbies dominated by big farmers who grow certain commercial crops. This exemplifies a patron–client relation that stands opposed to the World Bank's recommendation of letting the market determine prices. The other gainers are the intermediaries who watch support prices carefully, buy at low prices from the small farmers (who need to sell at the earliest to return their debt due to factor market interlocking), and then pocket the profit by waiting for state procurement (Deshpande and Naika, 2002; Assadi, 2000; interview of a farmer from Mangalore, 2012).

Field evidence showed, as was the case in the 1990s, that intervention of stakeholders at state level has a significant role in price setting for select commercial crops, such as sugarcane and cotton. However, in October 2009, the central government had tried to protect interests of sugar mill owners by trying to minimise the role of state governments in deciding the MSP. A new order was brought in place of the Sugarcane (Control) Order (1966) where the concept of a statutory minimum price (SMP) was replaced by the fair and remunerative price (FRP) of sugarcane. Herein again, the difference between big and tiller farmers emerge; in line with what was reported in the literature, despite the 'intervention price' that guarantees a buying price, tiller farmers are coerced to sell to local traders and merchants at a price lower than the MSP. There are several hidden costs involved that force farmers to sell to the traders – the cost of transporting cotton to the Cotton Corporation of India office, long waiting time (extending up to several days) at the office, and the compulsion to pay loan interest on time. Farmers could not afford to wait to encash the cheques issued by corporations (Assadi, 2000) and they still cannot. Therefore, new institutions and enhanced prices have limited impact for those at the bottom of the agrarian structures (interviews of an activist from Mysore, June 2012, and a technocrat from Bangalore, 2012). In the event of the government writing off farmer loans in drought-prone districts as after the 2009 and 2012 drought conditions, the distribution was biased. The allocated funds covered those who took loans from institutional sources that covered fractions of the rural proprietary class (Narasappa and Vasavi, 2010; interviewee from Dharwad, 2012).

All this leads to the argument that an incentive structure is created for a class of big farmers and capitalist farmers under the garb of deliberately directing the flow of resources towards export-oriented crops. Concerns about food security or the livelihood of tiller farmers who are mainly food crop producers (because of their politically and economically marginal position) have been systematically sidelined by the state. The big and capitalist farmers have become a part of the political settlement and their interests are being safeguarded through agricultural policies and informal practices in other sectors, as further elicited in the following sections.

Who gains from the policies? Different classes of farmers in Karnataka

Having had a successful Green Revolution in the past, Karnataka has embarked on planning a new technological revolution in agriculture since 2006, as the last section highlighted. This section discusses the changes in social structures that were brought about by new policies and interventions by global forces in the state. *The Hindu* (2006) reported that capitalist agriculture has destroyed traditional farming and abolished structures of interdependence. Field findings indicate that there are three fractions within the agrarian proprietary class operating in the state who come from diverse class backgrounds and are reaping the benefits of globalisation. The hardships faced by tiller farmers in sustaining agriculture are highlighted in this section, along with evidence of their diversification and their coping mechanisms in the changing scenario.

Big farmers

Big farmers hold social and economic significance in the countryside. From among the respondents, most owned holdings of 15 acres or more. Table 6.2 shows a fall in the number of large holdings, but it arguably is an estimate of traditional big farmers alone, and income depends on what is farmed and how it is farmed as much as on the size of a farm. The class also has added several new avenues of income, so agriculture may not be central to their accumulation. In Mandya, an activist gave a vivid description of commission agents[17] and *mandi* owners (often big farmers) as important economic players who rose to prominence since the late 1990s. Their significance has steadily grown with privatisation and the state receding from extension service, subsidised inputs, and procurement (Nagaraj, 2008). A common phenomenon is that big farmers have set up pesticide and fertiliser shops, a very lucrative business in this era of privatisation, given that new cropping patterns depend primarily on chemical inputs. Big farmers and commission agents also operate as moneylenders. In hilly tourist districts, converting old period houses into guest houses or home-stay houses[18] has emerged as a common form of income diversification.

Table 6.2 Landholding pattern in Karnataka

	2005–06		2010–11		Variation (in %)	
	Number of landholdings (in thousand ha)	*Total area (in thousand ha)*	*Number of landholdings (in thousand ha)*	*Total area (in thousand ha)*	*Number of landholdings*	*Total area (in thousand ha)*
Marginal	3,656	1,651	3,849	1,851	5.28	12.08
Small	2,013	2,876	2,138	3,020	6.21	5.01
Semi-medium	1,278	3,468	1,267	3,393	-0.89	-2.17
Medium	554	3,205	511	2,904	-7.83	-9.41
Large	79	1,184	68	994	-14.94	-16.06
Total	7,832	12,161	7,581	12,385	3.32	-1.80

Source: Agristat, 2010–11.

Big farmers are primarily into cultivation of cash crops. In Tumkur coconut, pulses, and flowers are grown. In Mandya there is a trend towards sericulture and sugarcane. In these regions such a cropping pattern is aided by the availability of good canal irrigation. In comparison, big farmers in Bangalore (rural) district have adopted horticulture and floriculture, given the constraints of falling landholding size, access to a big market, and the availability of technology. Siddhesh,[19] from a Lingayat-dominated village, painted a vivid picture of changes in the last decade. His grandfathers are two brothers, each with three sons. The two grandfathers individually owned 12 and 16 acres of land. Two of his uncles are still in agriculture and their land is completely tilled by lower-caste labourers from an adjoining village. The other four uncles have diversified into other professions: government clerk, input merchant, fodder shop owner, and milk-van supplier. One of them also owns a shop selling *shikakai*[20] and *ragi*; this uncle has built a big house. Siddhesh cites the example of another farmer from his village who started a petrol pump and subsequently built a house costing ₹10 million. According to him, 'Those who have money, can diversify.' Dairying has a strong presence in the village and Siddhesh's grandfather was the chief supplier of Jersey cows. Farmers from as far as Dharwad used to come to the village to purchase cows from him.

It can be deduced that the surplus from a big holding helped in the first diversification when his grandfather took up the cattle trade. The next generation has gained from the surplus and taken to input shops and milk supply business, while one brother has become a government officer. Another farmer from Tumkur has opened a battery shop in Mandya. His land is cultivated on sharecropping while he looks after his shop. Another farmer owns three big machinery shops in the rural districts of Tumkur, Chanapatna, and Bangalore. They sell harvesting, wood-cutting tractors, and weeding machines. Another big farmer from Hassan has started a Mahindra tractor shop in Mandya. Such diversification to non-agrarian avenues by the big farmer has been observed by other scholars (Ramachandran et al., 2010; Harriss White, 2004, 2008; Lerche, 2014).

Mandya has capitalist agriculture taking roots; evidence of contract farming was found in the Tumkur village. The latter is far more dependent on external links than Mandya is. The demand for cucumber for export has shot up in Siddhesh's *taluka*. An MNC provides the start-up funds to farmers. They also provide other inputs such as pesticides, and they buy the produce after harvest. It presents a case of interlocking where the company is controlling the factor market and sale of produce, leaving little autonomy to the farmers. He pointed out that 15 years ago inter-cropping was practised to maintain soil fertility; the same land was used to grow green gram, then *ragi*, and smaller plots were kept for chillies, onion, and other such crops. It helped farmers retain both their autonomy and food security. However, with the spread and domination of market imperatives, monocropping has taken over. Families are increasingly growing only areca nut and coconut.[21] The majority of them sell their produce to a government agency located 12 kilometres from the village. Two cases of absentee farmer were also reported in Tumkur where farmers had taken up business in other districts, such as owning a battery shop.

An educated respondent further remarked that the two factors that determine the success of a farmer are education and water. Being a university-educated person himself, he counted the boons. Pump irrigation has been in vogue for the last 25 years, and 6 years ago the village also initiated canal irrigation. Abundance of water has made commercial cropping viable. The farmers have been approached by big companies to partake in contract farming for exportable crops (interviewee from Bangalore, 2012). With this case, we saw the various avenues of diversification available to middle and big farmers in Tumkur, but the autonomy of farmers has become a casualty in the face of contract farming. Traditional crops and mechanisms are being replaced by new methods and crops (interview of a scholar from Bangalore, 2012; Deshpande and Indira, 2010). In the long term, this can potentially affect their food security as well.

Landlords

A form of absentee landlordism was noted in Chikmanglur, Coorg, Shimoga, and Thirthalli *taluka*. The farms were under managers[22] who would run the estates, and the owners would come to visit once every six months or a year. These were primarily large plantation estates. For example, the holding size of landlords in Chikmanglur and Coorg was 50 acres or more. Such large landholdings have been possible because plantation crops were exempt from land ceiling laws and escaped land reforms. Many landlords moved to urban jobs in industry or the service sector from Shimoga and Hassan districts and continued to extract rent from agriculture by giving their land on lease (interviewees from Shimoga and Coorg, 2012). Their interviews indicated that they are distanced from the real issues of agriculture such as irrigation and the rising cost of cultivation. They operate as a rentier class for whom agriculture holds little direct economic relevance. The rent they get is not invested into productive capitalist agriculture but in other sectors. It distinguishes the fraction of landlords from capitalist farmers; the latter have consistently invested profit from agriculture to use better technology to increase profitability.

A respondent from Shimoga was an erstwhile landlord. Before land reforms, his family was that of a *zamindar* household owning 250 acres of land. During the 1970s reforms, they lost 150 acres of land owing to the land ceiling and the remaining land was distributed among four brothers. Henceforth, his landholding size has been 25 acres (areca, coconut, and pepper) and another 5 acres is devoted to paddy. Under the present circumstances, he should be categorised as a big farmer having adopted commercial crops and employed 40 wage labourers. He does not live off rent and invests surplus in better chemical inputs for the sake of higher profits. In paddy, the system is of sharecropping with 60:40 share where the landless cultivator gets 40 per cent of the produce. The other three brothers are urban professionals, placed in high government positions, transforming into old petty bourgeoisie. Their farms are run by managers and they earn rent from their land, signifying that they are landlords. The respondent sounded disappointed that his son, unlike all his cousins, decided not to study or settle in the city. He mentioned that all his nephews and nieces have become professionals – doctors, IT engineers, and some of them even went abroad. This was a matter of great pride. He emphasised how opportunities in Shimoga were limited and there was not much one could achieve. In his words, 'A farmer does not aspire his son to be a farmer.' The emerging picture is different from Gujarat, where the capitalist farmers exhibited pride in rural life and agriculture and never felt like they were left behind in the race.

Many instances of landlords and big farmers' sons pursuing higher education and joining the IT sector or senior level bureaucracy jobs were observed in Coorg, Shimoga, Mangalore, Dharwad, and even Hassan. Across districts such as Tumkur or Dakshin Kannada, where levels of urbanisation is high, big and middle farmers are seeking urban life and education for children, thus detaching themselves from agriculture as a vocation. Evidence of both selling off land and retaining holding were observed, however. Tumkur has recently established itself as the new Silicon Valley and has seen similar levels of urban migration as the predominantly plantation districts such as Coorg. This phenomenon is seen across districts. The organisation and articulation of farmer interests, as in the case of these absentee landlords, gets diluted as the next generation has steadily moved into non-agrarian arenas such as engineering, self-employment, and medicine. They have little stakes in agriculture. An emerging trend is of employing managers at plantations to look after the cultivation, while landlords live in cities (Mumbai and Bangalore). A petty bourgeoisie with technical expertise comes to the fore, reducing the gap between the rural and the urban. It is weakening the old ties in agrarian society, as Breman (2007) had observed in Gujarat.

A finding unique to Karnataka is that the landlord class exerts a powerful influence in the state's vision, as several members of this class have assumed government positions. They have become part of the old petty bourgeoisie, adhering to the definition given by Khan (1996, 2000). In Chhattisgarh, the presence of the class is far more scattered and, thus, the influence is less cohesive. In Gujarat, the agrarian class has not directly penetrated the bureaucracy the same way. The notion of large-scale mechanised farming is seen as the way forward, as Murthy voiced it (interviewee from Shimoga, 2012). The same perspective of mechanised large-scale farming as the way forward was voiced by bureaucrats and agricultural scientists in their interviews (interviewees from Bangalore, 2012). Even if landlords and big farmers do not have organisational strength to influence policy decisions, their individual presence within the bureaucracy and agricultural universities lends support to state policies where the two have arrived at a common interest. It creates a vocal support base for the government's new policies and, to that extent, they form a part of the political settlement.

Capitalist farmers or gentleman farmers

Agrarian relations are undergoing manifold changes. Global forces are transforming existing class relations, bringing new classes and new practices into the sector. Contract farming, employing huge machinery for irrigation, weeding, and harvesting, and thus replacing labour use are some such practices. The new players include capitalist farmers and gentleman farmers. As evident from Tables 5.2 and 6.2, the proportion of large holdings has decreased in Karnataka, indicating that agriculture has not proved to be as profitable an enterprise in Karnataka as it did in Gujarat. A high rate of diversion of agricultural land for non-agricultural purposes can also be inferred from this.

Capitalist farmers are mostly located in the southern districts, belong to upper and middle castes, or have an inherited land status. Their class characteristics are derived from surplus accumulation through application of technological innovations, which has been (re)invested in agricultural and other sectors. They are quick adopters of new crops, such as flowers, maize, cotton, and vegetables. Gentleman farmers are those who invest surplus generated from other sectors into agriculture. The size of their landholdings varies and typically starts from 5 acres. They have made good use of the opening of borders since liberalisation by investing in cultivation of high-value crops. They indulge in speculation and sell their produce when prices are high, thereby maximising their profits.

In Tumkur and rural Bangalore, floriculture has become a favoured choice for capitalist farmers who see high returns from the crop. A local farmer-cum-academic who has been working on agrarian relations over the past two decades reported that traders of agricultural crops or local commission agents have also opened nurseries, such as those along the Mysore highway and outskirts of Bangalore (interview of Raman from Bangalore and an activist from Mandya, 2012). Some of these nurseries are built on land bought by non-agriculturalists in lucrative locations. The legal provision which allows non-agriculturalists to buy agricultural land has created a network of local people operating as land brokers or intermediaries who buy land from farmers and sell it to political leaders and capitalists at higher rates, thus making huge profits. The close relationship of these traders with political leaders, professionals, and district officials helps them get critical information on agricultural support prices and procurement early which in turn helps them in speculation and profit maximisation. It is the profit from speculating in crop sale that is being reinvested in floriculture and horticulture, by way of buying agricultural land between 5 and 50 acres (interviews of a farmer from Bangalore, 2012, and a journalist from Bangalore, August 2012). The land size is difficult to ascertain, but the phenomenon of bringing in surplus from other sectors and investing in a profitable sub-sector of agriculture was mentioned by several respondents. High-technology floriculture is highly capital intensive and employs technology such as the greenhouse that costs ₹400,000–500,000 per acre which only a few can adopt.

Karuturi Global is an enterprise that started off in Karnataka, and in 2014 it supplied flowers the world over. They own firms in Ethiopia, Kenya, and India, among others. Farms closer to Bangalore benefit from their proximity to highways. The high-value variety of flowers, such as roses, carnations, orchids, anthuriums, and birds of paradise, cater to Bangalore, Mumbai, and export markets. The technology, market, and capital set it apart from small farmers who produce gerbera and gladioli, which are sold within the state (Gowda, 2009).[23] Such nurseries dot Ramoulli, close to Bangalore. The owners have shifted from roses to decorative plants of a wide variety. One nursery had 5,000 varieties of plants. Labourers toiled as the owners sat in air-conditioned houses. The bigger nurseries and farms have an intermediary class of managers who are educated, fluent in English, and manage the farms and sale of products. Fruits and horticulture are also being grown side by side. They have a strong presence in urban markets, both retail and wholesale. They supply to designers for interior decoration and those who sell in Bangalore. Some of the nurseries on the road are owned by members of the same family.

In Mandya, these new farmers were termed 'corporate lords' by a respondent to denote their access to land and technology in contrast to that of traditional big farmers who continue growing silk, sugarcane, and areca nut. The owners of the nurseries come from Tamil Nadu and Andhra Pradesh also. The government has specific websites for the educated gentleman farmers. They are aided through subsidies and availability of inputs and irrigation by the government. Machinery is imported from Holland, Israel, France, and the USA for the petty bourgeoisie In recent years, many corporate houses such as ESSAR group, TATA group, Reliance (Jamnagar Farms), ITC, and Bharti have invested in the flower sector (Singh, 2006). An instance of contract farming of fruits in the northern districts, engaging primarily the big farmers, came to light. As per the theoretical classification, the industrial capitalists and gentleman farmers have entered the agricultural sector by bringing in surplus from other sectors and taking control, thereby being the drivers of agricultural growth. They are the beneficiaries of market opportunities. Big farmers are gaining more through the state than the market. The distinction was not as severe in Gujarat where capitalist farmers have bought land and employed tiller farmers on contracts to cater to supermarkets such as Star Bazaar and Reliance Fresh.

To summarise, the presence of landlords is concentrated in the northern and plantation districts of Karnataka, like in the northern districts of Chhattisgarh. Some of them just maintain a relation of rent extraction with agriculture and others have invested in upgrading technology, thus transforming to capitalist farmer class position. The trend of capitalist farmers diversifying to other sectors is similar to Gujarat, but with one difference. In Gujarat, the diversification is more due to market forces, whereas in Karnataka, patronage of state is essential for any diversification and accumulation. The gentleman farmers are most visible in Karnataka, unlike Chhattisgarh and Gujarat. It suggests a presence of new petty bourgeoisie class that is mature.

Escalating input costs due to privatisation have pushed up the overall cultivation costs for traditional crops. This, in addition to the fact that returns from rice, paddy, and millets are quite low, makes small-scale farming difficult. The cost of production is said to be more than the minimum support prices for paddy (interview of a farmer from Mysore, June 2012). This could not be independently validated, but is common in the literature, reflecting the sheer apathy of the state towards farmers growing food crops (NCEUS, 2008). Small farmers were found experimenting with sericulture and flowers on a part of their holdings where reliable water sources were available. The investment required for these crops is high and, thus, they borrow money from local *mandi* owners or big farmers and, in turn, have to sell the produce to them at below-market rates (interview of a technocrat from Bangalore, 2012). Hence, the benefits of competitive global prices do not reach them.

Tiller farmers are facing livelihood threat from external factors, such as industrialisation and rapid urbanisation. Agriculture has low returns, whereas land prices have been rising. Selling land can bring immediate money for them. As a respondent spoke of his experience, 'In Tumkur, I have observed small farmers giving up their land owing to the liability of cultivation and low-crop prices, in addition to the traders who charge them high interest. Even I want to sell off my land' (interview of Siddhesh from Bangalore, August 2012). What ought to be noted is that under the same policy, big farmers and landlords have come to command more avenues to diversify and own newer means of production, thereby adding to their accumulation. The entire agrarian sector is no longer facing a crisis, but the policy has perpetuated the crisis faced by tiller farmers which affects even middle farmers to an unforeseen magnitude. The brunt of privatisation is borne by the lower classes, while the proprietary classes are receiving state support to cope with market-led opportunity of capitalist high-value agriculture.

Agrarian distress

Intensifying agrarian distress and growing farmer suicides

Among the states affected by farmer suicides, Karnataka has been on top of the hit list. Despite a strong farmer movement, the issue did not make it to the top priority of the movement on the ground. Who such a farmer movement represents is a question worth pursuing. The suicides have been ascribed to poor irrigation, lack of livelihood options, and neoliberal policies (Nagaraj, 2008). It began in 1997, and by the early 2000s, the phenomenon had spread to the relatively advanced agricultural regions, particularly in the districts of Mandya, Hassan, Shimoga, Davanagere, Koppal, and even Chickmagalur. Literature has shown that this is related to fast adoption of cash crops that require high investment (Reddy and Mishra, 2009). An exception is coastal Karnataka, where people's dependence on non-agrarian activities and wider linkages to other sectors (except for a few pockets of areca nut), migrating to metropolitan cities such as Mumbai and even the Middle East, have acted as a buffer against debt (interviews of an academic and a local businessman from Mangalore, July 2012).[24]

After 2000, the number of farmer suicides kept rising. Despite moderate to high agricultural growth in the decade (Table 6.1), high rates of suicide persisted that points to a differentiated nature of agrarian society. For the period 2000–01 to 2005–06, the central government data on farmer suicides for the state is around 8,600, which is the highest compared to any other state. This was also a period of acute agrarian crisis. In 2003 the state experienced severe drought in over 13 districts. In 2003–04 alone, 708 farmers committed suicide, with Hassan reporting the highest number. The year 2004–05 saw a fall in number of suicides with improvement in rainfall. But even with a declining overall trend, Hassan continued to report the highest number (37) of suicides followed by Belgaum (33) (Assadi, 2011). These are also districts where cultivation of high investment commercial crops, such as maize, cotton, and tobacco, was extensive, which likely drove small farmers to desperation (Mishra and Reddy, 2009). A senior leader of a Left party fixed the figure of those who have died in the state since the mid-1990s at 36,000 (interview in Bangalore, April 2012). High suicide rates in these districts signify the close interconnections between market-oriented agriculture and suicides (interview in Bangalore, April 2012; Suri and Rao, 2006). The lure of higher yield brought in by new seed and chemical inputs holds a promise to break away from poverty, which the class of tiller farmers seek; however, for these farmers, these advantages are actually made redundant by the existing structural inequalities. The only difference could possibly be made by the state, but persistence of their suffering testifies to the lack of proactive state effort to create any safety valve for these classes.

The scenario that emerges is that five prime players, mentioned in various interviews as different stakeholders – contractor, moneylender, agricultural input-shop owner, commission agents, and *mandi* owners – often overlap with big farmers and capitalist farmers and, in a few instances, with middle farmers. Not only are they more capable of adopting high-value crops but they also have tapped new sources of generating surplus through privatisation of inputs and irrigation. Evidently, they are emerging as gainers in neoliberal policies.

To conclude, the way agrarian policies were crafted by the state in Karnataka between 2006 and 2012 has polarised the agrarian society – the agrarian proprietary class has gained from market forces, ensured by the state, while also going through differentiation with the class.

Rich farmers survive amid agrarian distress: State in action

In Karnataka, survival of a farmer is evidently dependent on two factors – making use of market opportunities and maintaining political clout. Agrarian crisis has had severe impact on the state but given the differentiated impact of agrarian policies, some classes have accumulated during the same period. Successful economic diversification and direct or indirect access to political power are commonly observed among big farmers as well as a few middle farmers. For example, in Dharwad, an erstwhile landlord[25] owned the biggest private dairy in 2012. He is also an elected leader, having contested elections independently and once on a BJP ticket. Interestingly, it was only after the economic reforms in the early 1990s that the dairy was started. Another big farmer shared information on land deals and upcoming property projects, as he works as a contractor. He too has political connections. Another example is of a senior government officer who revealed his antipathy towards the Congress because he suffered loss of landholdings under the land reforms. A big farmer's brother was a senior bureaucrat and another had a brother in the national party. Then there are those who wield power owing to KRRS's leadership. These landlords and big farmers enjoy a lot of power locally; small and middle farmers look up to them for guidance for negotiating crop prices, accessing cooperatives, and suchlike for subsidies[26]; a kind of patron–client relation resurfaces as outlined in previous sections.

Several farmers were carrying green stoles, as a symbol of the KRRS. Interviews revealed that these farmers have managed to accumulate through whichever channel they could use, mostly trade and business ventures. The green stole has come to hold a symbolic significance of 'being a farmer', since the movement had taken a backseat in the face of self-aggrandisement. The respondents stated that the leaders have aligned themselves with the Congress and the BJP, despite being KRRS members, to earn state favours and get their followers some privileges. Respondents pointed out that the KRRS was broken from within. Each district has its own brand of the KRRS.

Another farmer-cum-leader's power can be gleaned from how others viewed him. He lives in Bangalore city and owns a house there where his sons are receiving education. Back in his village he owns big landholdings. He invited me to a high-end hotel which serves political guests. The crowd was affluent, and while waiting for him, I observed many young well-dressed men walking in, most of them with political connections, as the waiter narrated. When my respondent arrived, he did so in a big white car with a green light glaring on top, quite like the bureaucrats – *red batti*[27] cars. Other district leaders from Bellary and Daongidhi pointed out that the BJP government treats him as an insider. Another district leader informed that when there is any problem, *saab* (boss) would sort it out with the political party in Bangalore. He even gets them appointments with the MLA concerned. The confidence among these district heads about their leader indicated that his political connection played a key role in securing big farmer interests. A hierarchical structure like that of any party operated here.

Farmers' Forum, an outfit of the KRRS, operates as a bargaining tool for big farmers who negotiate with the state at the district level. In his words,

> Small agitations take place every week and the Deputy Commissioner agrees to send our petitions to the upper level. This is all that comes out of protests. On approaching the MLA, he promises to raise issues, but that is all. In 2012, the MLA was from the Congress with the BJP heading the state assembly, which has made matters harder for him to negotiate. (Interview of a big farmer from Shimoga, August 2012).

The testimony reflected his comfort and contact with the political leaders at the district level. He also pointed out that the MLA was the owner of a paper mill and had little interest in agriculture. Likewise a famous leader owns the biggest sugar factory in Mandya with large holdings. The cases point to an overlap between the state and capitalists where 'personal fusion' surfaces, as previously observed in Chhattisgarh. In addition, the respondent listed the numerous positions he has held at the district level, including the head of the local government for decades, director of a local government college, and social respect for being an erstwhile landlord within the *taluk*.[28] The entrenched relation between the agrarian proprietary class and the state has not been undone by the entry of global forces.

In another district, the respondent Iqbal made it amply clear that the KRRS extends support to those farmers who come under their banner. In his words, 'when our leader comes to the district, it shows "who we are"; if farmers want protection and advantages, they have to join the KRRS.' Like any other party, the powerful are offering patronage to the weaker sections of farmers.

Show of political power is key to attracting members. Another show of his social status was when he mentioned building a *darga* (shrine), which would cost ₹1.5 million, in his village. It was to signify his newly achieved affluence by the coal transporting business and, at the same time, appeal to people of his faith (interview in Bellary, August 2012). The KRRS seems to be operating like any other political party, using religious symbols to attract members.

The above instances make a case for how relations between rich farmer fractions and the state continue unabated, and the proprietary class enjoys access to political resources. Distress thus affects the tiller farmers disproportionately more.

The BJP links itself with the masses

Democracy entails elections and gaining popular mandate, and political parties aim to win legitimacy from the rural population that form the majority of the voters. This section examines how political parties operate in Karnataka and the way they engage with the rural population to gain their votes.

Petty bourgeoisie: Old and new and their political influence

Poulantzas' (1973) notion of petty bourgeoisie is divided into two fractions – old and new. The old petty bourgeoisie accumulates through state resources, while the new petty bourgeoisie accumulates through market forces and by serving the interests of the capitalist class.[29]

The new petty bourgeoisie serve the interests of the capitalists by acting as intermediaries in land deals, as moneylenders, or as input-shop owners. In towns respondents stated that the commission agents and *mandi* owners maintain close ties and even act as linchpins of the ruling political party at the state level (interviews of a farmer, Bangalore, 2012, and a reporter, Bangalore, 2012). They have accumulated significantly since privatisation picked up pace in the new millennium. Opening pesticide–fertiliser shops and tractor and other machine dealerships have been a prime source of surplus. Big farmers act as moneylenders, who have benefitted all the more from commercial crop cultivation. The rent accruing from hiring out tractors is also common. A Bangalore-based rural reporter stated that ₹ 400 per hour is charged for hiring a tractor. Interlocking of factors, credit, and product markets is very high in agriculture, as triangulated across interviews. This leaves tiller farmers vulnerable and dependent on moneylenders, big farmers, and commission agents, and vulnerable to layered exploitation.

Another avenue of accumulation brought in by urbanisation is land contracting. It is indeed a part of the globalisation–privatisation vision of development. In Dharwad, the son of a big farmer has become a contractor, since the city is undergoing rapid urbanisation owing to its proximity to an airport in its twin city, Hubli. The location of the city on the national highway connecting Bengaluru and Mumbai has contributed to the land value appreciating fast. The contractor introduced me to an MLA, whom he referred to as a friend. This MLA happened to be from a big-farmer background. Through him, I got introduced to a senior government officer who is an erstwhile *jagirdar*'s[30] son. The powerful in the district are part of a close network. As already discussed, big farmers have diversified into different urban professions, politics, contracting, transport business, and agro-trade. Additionally, these classes enjoy political clout to the extent of personal fusion. It can be deduced that the antagonism between three dominant classes, as Bardhan had seen, has weakened – big farmers who tend to be petty bourgeoisie are aligning with the industrial capitalist class, thereby bridging the latter's antagonism with big farmers. Their changing class character into petty bourgeoisie, old[31] or new, has meant a simultaneous shift in focus to urbanisation and capital accumulation from multiple sources introduced by the market. This is because these classes, though as distant second to industrial capitalists, have managed to be counted among the beneficiaries of globalisation. They have also secured state support and are enjoying the benefits of agricultural subsidies, formal credit, and higher MSPs. Another avenue to draw surplus is land transaction, where they are often the contact point for the industrial capitalist class. All persons straddle multiple geographical spaces at any given point in time, align themselves with political parties, and wield political influence.

The story in Bellary unfolded in an FDG that confirmed the pattern seen so far. A farmer owns 40 acres of land and employs 80 labourers. His land is irrigated by Tungabhadra river canals, and he grows paddy and sugarcane. He is also a political leader, who in front of four other farmers present in the FGD declared having made ₹5 million from mining and working as a coal transporter, and was elated with the new opportunities that coal mining had presented in the district. He listed problems such as water being affected with high chloride content, the resulting increase in incidents of asthma, cancer, and kidney problems, borewells having to be dug deeper for accessing water since the water table was falling, and high siltation; however, the significant achievements of the state were the quick and high income he and his fellow farmers made.

In the FGD, it was found that another farmer had started a transport business for moving coal from one place to another. He added, 'Some farmers in Hospet have also started iron ore businesses in past one decade' (interview of Sukhia from Hospet, 2012).

As a result of such developments, the perception of land has changed. Land is no longer associated with agriculture alone. In view of the classes being ready to grab new profitable opportunities, an alliance binding the agrarian and non-agrarian classes makes consolidating an opposition to capital almost impossible. The respondents were aware that land prices have shot up with mining and spread of the Hospet city. A few of them mentioned they were waiting for their agricultural land to come within city limits and then they could get good prices by selling it. Such an interest is distancing these big farmers from other farmers and linking them to the powerful coal mafias, the capitalists.

Iqbal's class position was displayed in the way he negotiated with the family of his son's bride-to-be. He told the bride's family that arrangements for the wedding had to be in Bellary city; if it were to be in the village, then the *barati* (groom's family and friends) would not attend it. The pride of accumulation earned from mining and the stamp of being a political leader made him doubly dominant. Added to this, his brother had joined the Congress party. It can be inferred that a prominent big farmer's family is useful for political parties to reach a wider vote bank of small farmers. The social class holds significance to the extent that political lines actually cease to matter. Manoj, on the other hand, is a farmer's son-turned-contractor and part of the real-estate sector. He is involved in land transactions.[32] He was privy to a lot of information about land prices and shared it with other big farmers in his village in Dharwad, especially where prices were expected to rise. He, too, maintained political relations and acted as a broker. Both these individuals commanded respect among the village population, which is a probable explanation of why political parties would be keen to safeguard their interests. One of them is a Muslim while the other one belongs to an upper caste Hindu family; therefore, caste cannot be seen as playing a determining role, at least not in these cases.

The evidence conformed to an observation made by Pattenden (2005) that even though politicians are expected to regulate the way merchants and traders operate, in reality 'they would not because of the two groups' mutual support' (Pattenden, 2005: 292). In fact, the state has not given up its pivotal position as the patron. The state officials and leaders have also gained in the process, thus narrowing the interest difference between the adjudicator and the beneficiary. Political leaders are now petty bourgeoisie. Similar conclusions were drawn in Chhattisgarh.

Ideological weapons of the BJP

In India, political parties have used ideology as a plank to attract a huge number of supporters, so much so that even if the promise of market fails, ideology triumphs in keeping the masses with the party. Across the country, sub-organisations of political parties have been instrumental in mobilising masses from different fractions of the society. For instance, Yuvaka Mandal and Mahila Samaj[33] are spread across Dakshin Kannada district popularising the agenda of the RSS. 'These outfits are regarded as good employers by the younger generation in the district, who join it for secure employment,' a respondent opined. Despite the district being open to economic transactions with other states and countries, given the location of a port, it had limited employment opportunity. Two interviewees also reported that secular newspapers have been swept out of the district and have been replaced by the ideological monopoly of the right wing.

The OBCs who had gained political and economic power in the 1980s have shifted their loyalties from the Congress to the BJP. The present generation identifies either with the ABVP, Bajrang Dal, or the Hindu Yuva Sena,[34] and there is no room for any other discourse (interviews of an activist and an academic from Mangalore, July 2012). As responses were assessed, it seemed likely that employment security was making many youngsters align with the organisations. The rise of the petty bourgeoisie in the district, with a fall in dependence on agrarian income, is also a cause of shift to the BJP that seems to hold the greatest promise for their rapid economic gain. The civil society has experienced saffronisation with organisations such as the Karnataka Rakshana Vedike (KRV) and the Art of Living sect capturing people's imagination (Vasavi, 2007). KRV has been representing the interest of Kannada language and Kannadiga identity in the larger national politics, and Art of Living teaches how to lead a moral life, but is essentially a Hindu sect.

The close association between the state and right-wing organisations can also be inferred from the way the government has been silent on cases filed against the Bajrang Dal for its violent activities in 2008.[35] The newspaper *Karavali Ale* was targeted by Bajrang Dal and other right-wing groups for reporting their attacks on churches. Several cases filed against the members of the Bajrang Dal, Vishwa Hindu Parishad, BJP, and Sri Ram Sena with regard to their illegal activities around the Baba Budangiri shrine in Chikmagalur were withdrawn in the last week of December 2008 (Narasappa and Vasavi, 2010). Effectively, the BJP has successfully polarised the urban voters with a significant part in its favour.

Cropping pattern in Karnataka: Elite crops versus mass crops

A notable difference has emerged within agrarian classes between growers of two kinds of crops – those that are grown by big farmers and capitalist farmers are termed as 'elite crops', and those grown by tiller farmers[36] are 'mass crops'. Commonly, the first category includes commercial crops, such as oilseeds, cotton, maize, and silk and, in the new millennium, vegetables, fruits, and flowers; the second category includes food grains, millets, and pulses. The classification is significant as it is linked to which crops gain state support and which crops drive the export. The state is attentive to elite crops such as flowers and vegetables, as they are drivers of high growth in the sector. Nadkarni and Vedini (1996) showed how more than 70 per cent of land owned by small and marginal farmers was used for growing cereals and pulses, as well as food grains. Noting these classifications among farmers becomes crucial in identifying the real beneficiaries of agrarian policies that focus overtly on commercial crop cultivation.

The literature review also testified that the state exhibited preferential treatment towards cultivators of some crops against others, such as silk, areca nut, and sugarcane. For instance, it made serious efforts to rescue coffee and tobacco cultivators during the 1990s at the time of crisis rather than dry-land farmers of the northern districts (Assadi, 1995). This was apparent in the establishment of a Coffee Board to buy their produce, exemption of their land from ceiling legislation, and concerted efforts to seek concession from the central government to overcome the crisis in the 1990s. Recently, the e-auction facility for silk cocoon has also worked to secure the interests of another commercial crop. The coffee growers made it apparent that they were well organised and had old ties with political parties and even the central government; however, these ties with the state have dwindled after 2000. It was ascribed to the lobbying power of the plantation owners and horticulture taking precedence[37] (interviews of a Ravi from Coorg, May 2012, and a technocrat from Bangalore, 2012). They claimed their connection to other big cities, such as Bengaluru and Mumbai, and even foreign countries affords them a special visibility that leads to easy access to state resources.

Coffee has been a favoured crop, but was facing competition from gentleman farmers. The coffee farmers expressed concern that price fluctuations were making it harder for them in the present era. The respondents mentioned the entrance of corporates into plantations (interviews of Ravi and Siddharth from Coorg, April 2012). Plantation crops have seen infiltration of gentleman farmers (both professionals and big corporate) and are directly affected by liberalisation. The conventional capitalist farmers are finding it hard to sustain coffee production. Land in Coorg is also most attractive for tourism, and coffee farmers are facing threat from those who eye their land for both agrarian and non-agrarian purposes.

A senior technocrat expressed his concerns that elite crop bias is affecting tiller farmers, whose holdings are being rendered uneconomical, especially since the mid-2000s. In such a situation, taking policy measures such as mechanisation and promoting HYV seeds that cater to large farms will hurt the tiller farmers' interests more (interviewee from Bangalore, 2012). A similar point has been raised that the new policies are benefitting a limited section of agrarian society (Deshpande and Prachitha, 2006). Table 6.3 presents a comprehensive state-level understanding of cropping patterns and provides details of acreage for the important crops in the state.

Elite crops grown for commercial purpose, such as fruits, maize, and vegetables, have had an increase in acreage, whereas mass crops, which include paddy, soybean, ragi, and wheat, have stagnated or have fallen. Cotton cultivation has been encouraged by the state for the sake of agricultural growth. In 2007, the state government drafted a new textile policy, and cotton gained prominence. Anand, the Joint Director at the state's department of handlooms and textiles, gave an interview stating that cotton's rising growth rate is a cause for pinning hope on the sector (Nandy, 2008). The linking of cultivation with agro-processing holds promise, but only for that class of farmers who will be able to sell to factories directly. Therefore, tiller farmers are likely to miss such an opportunity.

Table 6.3 Cropping pattern in Karnataka: 2001–2011

Crop	2001–02			2010–11		
	Area under production (in million ha)	*Production (in million tonnes)*	*Yield (in kg/ ha)*	*Area under production (in million ha)*	*Production (in million tonnes)*	*Yield (in kg/ ha)*
Gram	0.48	0.28	587	0.96	0.63	656
Tur	0.48	1.47	306	0.89	0.53	596
Groundnut	0.85	0.58	685	0.85	0.74	871
Vegetables	0.36	0.42	7.9	0.47	0.91	16.5
Sugarcane	0.41	33	81,122	0.42	39.66	94,429
Oilseeds	1.91	1.02	587	1.62	1.27	784

Contd.

Paddy	1.48	38	2281	1.54	42	2719
Wheat	2.60	1.99	763	2.55	2.79	1094
Flowers				0.027	6,063.9 (cut and loose	-
Soybean	48.4	40.2	831	0.17	0.15	882
Ragi	0.95	1.539	1614	0.79	1.588	2015
Onion				0.19	2.59	13,607
Potato				40	0.40	10,010
Tobacco				0.13	0.13	1,072
Sunflower	0.58	0.262	449	0.41	0.25	610
Cotton	0.61	0.61	171	0.55	1.20	371
Maize	0.58	1.5	250	1.3	4.4	345
Coconut				0.42	1.50	3573
Cashew nut				0.12	.06	491
Fruits	0.26	4.03	15.7	0.38	6.27	-

Source: India Horticulture Database 2001 and 2011, Agriculture Statistics, Directorate of Economics and Statistics.

Sugarcane, the crop which receives the biggest share of irrigation, is in common parlance regarded as an elite crop, confined as it is to areas with abundant irrigation and grown by better-off farmers. The area under sugarcane has seen a steep increase over the past three decades from around 100,000 hectares to nearly 400,000 hectares. Sugarcane growers have been receiving assured administered prices, a privilege that growers of cereals and millets do not receive. Even groundnut and cotton have not managed to garner such protection and that probably explains their non-stabilising acreage. However, sugarcane also remains immune from price fluctuations, given strong linkages to agro-business. Sugarcane growers form a strong crop lobby in the districts of Mysore, Mandya, and Hassan. As a big farmer informed, sugarcane growers are well connected with political leaders; this is exemplified by the fact that they approach the District Collector directly to raise prices of sugarcane produce (interviews of a farmer from Shimoga and another from Bellary, 2012).[38] Maize has also been directed to agro-processing units in bulk rather than sold for consumption. The state has been consistent in supporting maize producers because of its high export demand. That explains how the area under maize in the state has registered an increase from 64,000 hectares in 1970–71 to nearly 1.3 million hectares in 2010–11, a 20-fold increase (Table 5.3).

Another organised crop lobby is that of areca nut, which is classified as an elite crop. In Mangalore, an academic[39] explained that areca nut farmers came together with the aspiration of fighting for higher prices, but they were also looking to open a chocolate factory. This ambition was realised with the opening of CAMPCO[40] (the Central Arecanut and Cocoa Marketing and Processing Co-operative Limited) that continues to run well. The organisation that mobilised these farmers is the BKS, affiliated to the RSS. Due to its already organised status, areca nut has also enjoyed the support of eminent political leaders who cut across ideological lines to protect their interests (Kammardi, 2012).[41] Areca nut growers are also concentrated in Malnad, where they are affiliated closely with the KRRS. Political leaders from both the Congress and the JDU have often highlighted areca nut farmers' issues and joined rallies; this is because of the strength of the crop lobby, so in these districts ignoring them could be fatal for political reasons. The collective bargaining power of the lobby has decreased as sugar mill owners now get more concessions and have gained an upper hand,[42] but the state has tried to keep the big farmers happy by securing their economic interests and maintaining patron–client relations with them. These findings were triangulated.

Unlike the elite crops illustrated so far, all other crops are mass crops, such as cereals, coconut, pulses, and groundnut, which have been left out of the state's blessings. The producers of mass crops face severe interference of traders and depressed prices, resulting in fall in acreage. Despite being grown in the same districts – Dakshin Kannada and Tumkur – coconut, a mass crop, has not had similar importance (and negotiation power for its growers) as areca nut. Karnataka alone produced 46.9 per cent of areca nut grown in the country in 2010–11 (Indian Horticulture Database, 2011). An interviewee argues that this can be ascribed to all classes of farmers growing coconut, while areca nut is attributed to big and middle farmers alone who have invested in forming cooperatives, similar to cotton (interviews of an academic and a farmer, both from Mangalore, July 2012). The same is the condition of millets, turmeric, and pulses that go unmentioned in politicians' speeches and farmers' protests. What the tiller farmers grow holds little significance, but their land and labour are crucial, which need to be made available for exploitation by the proprietary classes in the current era.

The privileged status of certain crops and their protection by the state exists in the literature. The fact that the state is increasingly focusing on investing heavily in particular high-value crops whose cultivation costs can be borne comfortably by big farmers and capitalist farmers suggests a bias that will alienate and ruin those who cannot afford such capital investment. The southern districts are among the beneficiaries, but not Tumkur; however, growers of elite crops in the northern districts were doing well too. The BJP requires their support and has kept them within the ambit of state patronage. While this feeds into economic growth, it holds political significance too. These rural proprietary classes affect the poorer farmers' voting decisions and command their allegiance. Thus, keeping the former aligned with the BJP serves the party's interests. The state is 'building on the best', a phenomenon Cleaver (1972) had identified during the Green Revolution.

Input centricity polarises agrarian classes

This section outlines the state government's approach to agricultural credit, seeds, fertilisers, and pesticides that have been privatised since the mid-1990s. The chemical inputs have created a spiral of rising costs of cultivation that the capital-poor farmers find unbearable.

Agricultural credit

Reversal in providing credit by nationalised banks to farmers and a drastic fall in the number of branches serving rural areas since the 1990s have been noted by several scholars. This has created room for private lenders. The All India Debt and Investment Survey (2002) confirms that credit to the rural sector has been increasingly coming from private sources since the 1990s. Since then, the percentage of institutional credit fell from 78 per cent in 1991 to 67 per cent in 2002, and informal sources increased by 50 per cent over the decade. Within formal lending institutions, the general reasons for preference towards big farmers are appropriate collateral, correct paper work, and secure returns. The rest of the story is similar to the other states. Several interviews showed uniformly that farmers who availed loans from the cooperative societies had landholdings above 10 acres. Within big farmers, 'the nationalised banks preferred giving loans to big farmer growing sugarcane' (interview of an activist from Mandya, May 2012). The sugarcane growers often supply to factories in bulk, so the factories act as a safety net to pay back the bank; therefore, loan recovery is easier (interview of farmers from Mysore and Bellary, July 2012). While banks are protecting their assets, the state was found protecting the interests of its ally. As droughts had affected over 100,000 farmers in 2012, farmers have been incurring debts with little prospect of repayment. The response of the BJP was to waive farmers' loan amounts, for which Yeddyurappa[43] demanded ₹10,000 million from Jagadish Shettar, the new Chief Minister (*The Hindu*, 2012). However, the loan waiver would potentially cover only borrowers from formal sources.

In line with the above, a big farmer informed us that when they approach the cooperative societies for loans, the amount given is ascertained by the size of holding. 'I can take loans up to ₹100,000 for my land size,' he said. The institution charges interest rate at 1 per cent, which is the privilege of a few who can repay on a regular basis because of cash crops and diversified incomes. Most tiller farmers fail to repay the loans, and then they stand disqualified to take any further loans from the cooperative society, and are forced to approach informal sources (interviewee from Shimoga, August 2012; Assadi, 2010). In Bellary, a farmer stated, 'Government gives loans but you need connections to get loans' (interview in 2012). So *panch, sarpanch*, and *zilla panchayat* members are often the first to get loans. According to *The Hindu* (2011), 'Followers of the president of the society and those of the leaders of the dominant political party in that village corner the loans, and poor farmers are left in the lurch.' State patronage is essential even for credit access, which the state chooses to limit to the class of big farmers and capitalist farmers.

A new angle to the problem surfaced when a respondent stated that in cases where the big farmers and landlords live in cities, and have nothing to do with the production process, it is hard to get loans from formal sources. The tenants who are responsible for acquiring the credit for inputs and hiring machinery do not have *pattas*[44] in their names and hence are not eligible to get loans from any formal institution (interview of a farmer from Shimoga, 2012). A similar observation was made in Coorg that faces instances of absentee landlordism.

The corporate sector pervades the seed, machinery, and fertiliser sectors under different brand names. Contract farming and direct purchase of agricultural land have also begun in the state (interview of an agriculturalist from Dharwad, March 2012). In Coorg, two plantation owners informed that Tata has bought more than 1,000 acres of land and are cultivating coffee on their own plantation. The plantation owners complained that they could not afford the machinery that Tata employed, which put them at a disadvantage. Tumkur has seen the emergence of contract farming for vegetables such as cucumber and potato. It is creating monocropping, thereby curbing farmers' autonomy. Such unequal competition is making formal credit further inaccessible to tiller farmers, vis-à-vis giant corporations, the capitalists. Those who till the soil are falling out of the race for their lack of access to capital.

Moneylenders, operating in the informal credit market, can be classified into two kinds – those from the rural setting, that is, big or capitalist farmers, and those from the urban, comprising traders, *mandi*-owners, and commission agents (interviews of a technocrat from Bangalore, 2012, and a farmer from Bangalore, June 2012). According to Assadi (1998), unlike earlier decades, moneylenders in the present scenario of globalisation are not interested in appropriating land when farmers fail to pay the rent. He conjectures that the reasons for this is uncertainty in the agrarian economy and requirement of investing time and physical labour in agriculture, which the latter is not keen on. This signifies landlord-class behaviour, where the actor operates with a 'pure extraction' agenda (Assadi, 1998). What emerged from interviews is that interlocking prevails in factor, credit, and output markets. Moneylenders can be commission agents or traders who fall into two categories – *pakka* (they are traders and also buy the final produce) and *kachha* (they facilitate transactions and operate as middlemen in selling; they are not final buyers of produce). The *kachha* commission agents lend to farmers and pre-fixes the price of crops. In the Yaswanthpur market, one such commission agent monopolises the entire fish sale. He conducts a transaction of 2000 kilograms of fish a day, all in cash.

Lack of access to agricultural credit for tiller farmers is evident from the increasing rates of farmers' suicides, as discussed in detail in Chapter 5. The following sections highlight this relation between privatisation of chemical inputs and farmers' distress more closely.

Harbinger of GM seed

In previous chapters it has been acknowledged that Karnataka was a forerunner in inviting foreign MNCs into the seed sector. The state policy documents since the 1990s show its inclination to adopt GM seeds, a feature that remains unaltered in the 2006 document. While in Gujarat there was state support to indigenous Bt seeds at one point, Karnataka chose to toe the line of the World Bank that private chemical inputs would break the low agricultural growth and lead to fast growth in the sector. The Chhattisgarh government is keen to invite foreign seed companies, but penetration has been slow as has been the adoption of commercial crops. The Karnataka government has withdrawn support in seeds, particularly for commercial and high-value crops, which has left the farmers vulnerable and coerced them to depend on the market to procure both inputs and sell the crops (interview of an agriculturalist from Dharwad, March 2012).

The same emphasis on agro-business and industry resurfaces in the 2012 policy documents. A public assertion of this position was witnessed previously when the state hosted the Asian-Pacific Seed Association meet in Bengaluru in September 2000, where the state government officially granted concessions to international agricultural companies. At the time of this conference Karnataka was producing 50 per cent of the seeds in India (Assayag, 2005). Several respondents indicated that universities were keen to push for private technologies. For instance, in Dharwad a middle farmer informed us that they were being pushed to adopt Bt cotton due to the absence of any alternative seed. He named some indigenous varieties, such as DH I and II, along with Varalaxmi and Jayalaxmi, which were developed under Dr B. H. Katarki more than a decade ago. Since then, innovation has seldom occurred. Even if there are innovations, they remain in the lab and never reach the farmers (interviews of a farmer and a university professional from Dharwad, March 2012).

The private companies have taken over the market and penetrated distant villages. Indigenous companies are present, but the market is dominated by foreign players. For instance, Cargill Seed Company has received support from the Karnataka government in the opening of the India Maize Development Association. Monsanto has been supported by the state government since the economic reforms. This indicates a high rate of penetration of foreign capital in the sector. As articulated by a senior state official, privatisation of seed in the state is 'almost complete' (interviewee from Dharwad, August 2012), unlike Chhattisgarh where farmers are sticking to using their own seeds from one year to another. Market dependence is huge, with the state retreating from the sector. In 2009, the Seed Corporation organised a Seed Convention to make Karnataka a global destination for seed production and also to promote the seed industry in Karnataka with over 5,000 seed-producing farmers.

A growing nexus between the state, public universities, and private companies was noted. Employment opportunities in private agro-companies for public university graduates works as a big incentive. Once they get recruited, they toe the private company line. The state has been reluctant to spend on agricultural research, which has created a vacuum in terms of domestic solutions to agricultural problems. The sector has been left to depend on private companies for any employment and innovation. As a result, new graduates are inclined to join private companies where research falls prey to private interest. 'We supply them with their workers', was stated (interview of an academic from Dharwad, August 2012). The professional class becomes a petty bourgeoisie allying with industrial capitalists, as is observed here. Innovation remains limited to a few commercial crops and seldom focuses on dry-land crops and cereals. Technology thus invented is geared towards the cultivation of commercial crops and can only be afforded by farmers who own capital. Resource-neutral technology is a far cry under these circumstances.

Fertiliser and pesticide

Unlike seeds, the state still controls a part of fertiliser and pesticide supply, but private retail shops dot the roads connecting towns and villages. They have penetrated the remote rural markets. DuPont, like other MNCs, has been using a big network of salesmen originally from villages to sell their products. Capitalism draws a wedge among the rural classes, where those who run these retail stores become the exploiters of other farmers. Mangalore reported a different trend, where urban businessmen are opening retail shops to sell the agricultural inputs.

Studies on the cost of cultivation conducted by an agricultural university show a rising cost of production across crops, which can be attributed to privatisation of inputs. The cost of cultivation per acre of areca nut has increased from ₹260,000 to ₹365,000 in Karnataka. The cost includes seedling, fertiliser, pesticide, labour, land rent, and depreciation of permanent items such as fencing, machinery and processing yards (Kammardi, 2012). The cost of cultivation of cotton has risen due to hybrid seeds and chemical pesticides and fertilisers. High-technology floriculture incurs a cost of ₹300,000–₹400,000 per acre. Cultivation of sugarcane per acre costs ₹83,000 (2010–11). The National Sample Survey Organisation (2005) reports that the rising cost of chemical inputs are causing farmers to incur higher debt, which is at the root of the agrarian crisis. What adds to the plight of the farmers is spurious seeds and pesticides leading to poor yields that further cuts down profit (interviews of a farmer from Bangalore, 2012, and another from Mangalore, July 2012; Rao and Gopalappa, 2004; NCEUS, 2008). Such an approach to transform agriculture into a capital-intensive sector may achieve growth, but will exclude many more farmers and build on the proprietary classes.

Input shops, owned by traders or big farmers, lend informal credit to farmers at high interest rates (interviews of farmers from Mandya and from Bangalore, June 2012). This 'chemical input trader' combines usury with advice that farmers seek regarding chemical inputs (Assayag and Fuller, 2005). It ties the farmers from multiple directions to a class of exploiters. A farmer had to sell his kidney so he could save his family by paying back debts of ₹50,000 or above (interview of a small farmer from Mysore, June 2012; Shiva Kumar, 2013).

Fertiliser is a product that benefits two of the state's allies; it is a direct gain for the industrial capitalists due to the subsidy allotted to fertilisers. The fertiliser lobby is organised and has an active representation through influential figures such as Vijay Mallya (Chairman, Mangalore Chemicals and Fertilisers Ltd.) negotiating on their behalf. They add a mark-up over the cost of production, and it is against this total that they ask for subsidy. It has been impossible to contend with their power and allot the subsidy directly to farmers, despite repeated proposals from farmer organisations. Political settlement demands attention be given to big farmers and capitalist farmers (interview of a technocrat from Bangalore, 2012; Birner et al., 2011). Subsidised fertilisers by cooperative societies are cornered by these fractions, as triangulated in interviews. The state directs the subsidy to its two close allies within the agrarian sector. The policy has inflicted an increased burden of high cost onto tiller farmers owing to its overt focus on chemical inputs and lumpy technology.

Water: A privilege not a right

Irrigation is a crucial factor in Karnataka since more than 70 per cent of the state is arid and semi-arid, and has faced three droughts between 2000 and 2013. It is one input without which new technologies cannot work, given their lumpy nature. Irrigation covers 26 per cent of the cultivated area in Karnataka, below the all-India average of 46 per cent. Until the 1980s, canal irrigation was rising, but this has stagnated at 39 per cent since 1994. Tank irrigation has reduced drastically, while well irrigation (tube and bore) doubled in the 1990s, which is now covering 37 per cent of the irrigated area (Deshpande and Prachitha, 2006). All along, public investment has been directed to irrigated regions as part of the state budget (Deshpande and Indira, 2010). This has resulted in huge regional difference among the districts in terms of gross irrigated area (GIA). South Karnataka has pockets of canal irrigation, such as Mysore and Mandya, while most of the northern districts are dependent upon pump sets and private irrigation techniques. The district-wise percentage of GIA to gross cropped area data up to 2001–02 shows that 7 out of 27 districts, including Bellary, Davangere, Shimoga, Belgaum, Dakshin Kannada, Mandya, and Bagalkote, have above 40 per cent coverage, while 12 districts have below 20 per cent coverage (Deshpande and Indira, 2010).[45] The situation is worsened by reduced government investment in irrigation infrastructure.

Implementation of public irrigation is subject to political bargaining rather than being a technical decision. The following case shows big farmers' influence on the state apparatus. In Dharwad, the big farmers informed how they sabotaged the introduction of canal irrigation into their village. To avert land ceiling on their irrigated landholdings and retain their large holdings, they stalled the process by using their network with the local bureaucracy[46] (FGD in Dharwad,

March 2012). They were, of course, the farmers who owned pumps or could pay for borewells and had adopted commercial crops; these farmers are charging rent from others for using their pumps, an income that they certainly do not want to lose. As a result, numerous tiller farmers are stuck in a water-deficit situation and have to stick to traditional crops. The case illustrates the connection between the state and big farmers, who come from, as in this case, an upper caste.

Concentration of resources on elite crops is a direct indication of state protection for interests of big farmers and capitalist farmers. The latter is also capable of bearing the cost of private irrigation machinery. An indication of their rise and consolidation can be deduced from the doubling of acreage under wells since the 1990s. Subsidising pumps and charging for electricity have benefitted those classes who can bear the remaining cost of both. The lumpy nature of the technology (Lerche, 1999; Deshpande et al., 2004) prevents the benefits of high yield from reaching those who cannot seek water, despite incurring the cost of other inputs.

The politics of land acquisition: Big gainers and petty gainers

A foray into land acquisition – the process, the policy, the gainers, and losers – will lead to developing a political economy understanding of land, which is a crucial input for production. Under Chief Minister Devraj Urs (1972–80), Karnataka saw the implementation of land ceiling and land redistribution measures that negatively affected landlords. Since then, land-related policies have played a determining factor in the state politics – in terms of alignment with and against political parties. Those who lost land harbour a resentment against the Congress for implementing the land reforms (interview of a landlord from Dharwad, March, 2012). From the early 1990s the state has undertaken a reversal of the land reform policy like many other states in India.

The state has been proactive in altering the land acquisition law to facilitate conversion of agricultural land to land that can be used for non-agricultural purposes. The amendment was brought in 1995. Jenkins (1999) links it to the presence of a regional capitalist class whose support was sought by the political party, which explains the policy revision. At the same time, the class was hoping for faster accumulation with the arrival of foreign capital and reduced dependence on national capitalists. Since then, Karnataka has experienced unabated land acquisitions, legal and illegal. Nair (1996) spells out the principal amendments in the Karnataka Land Reforms (Amendment) Act. The Act restores the leasing of land in the districts of Uttara Kannada and Dakshina

Kannada for aquaculture at lease rents. It revises the ceiling on landholding for specified purposes, such as industrial development, educational institutions, places of worship, housing projects, floriculture, and horticulture. The most alarming part was that all restrictions were exempted if the state government deemed that the land was to be used 'in public interest and for reasons to be recorded in writing'; such a law can be bent by politicians and officials at their will (Nair 1996, Jenkins, 1999).

The Land Reforms Amendment Act (1995) made exceptions for land alienation under Section 109, meaning that certain kinds of land were excluded from the purview of prescribed land ceilings. For industrial development the Land Reforms Amendment Act has fixed the upper limit at 20 units of agricultural land (120 acres of dry land or 20 acres of irrigated land with two crops). The present amendment has enhanced the ceiling to 216 acres of dry land. These amendments have assisted the free flow of capital into acquisition of agricultural land. The industrial capitalist has succeeded in accessing land in the most remote corners of the state (Jenkins, 1999). The agrarian rich have also diversified into real estate as a business opportunity (Nair, 1996). The migration of the rural rich to cities is leading to rising demand for land and the associated rise in bribery, fraud, and middlemen charges.

As evident from policy statements, the state is geared towards converting agriculture to a high-value, large-scale, mechanised sector. In an interview with Murthy (interview of a farmer, Shimoga, 2012), he informed that 'in 2004–06, when areca nut prices crashed, many farmers committed suicide; others had to sell their land to pay off the debts, but the state did nothing to secure us good prices'. Dayanand, another big farmer quite experienced in his trade, remarked:

> For those who lost land, it was their livelihood and for those who bought land, it was just their recreation. Those who only earn from agriculture cannot dream of going to the city for medical treatment or children's schooling. The price fluctuation makes it a high-risk sector, and thus cultivating farmers prefer to sell land and become wage labourers, so that they can at least earn a regular salary. For those who live in Bangalore, and work in the IT sector, ₹1.5 million per acre is not difficult to pay, so they are buying land in our region as an investment. (Interview in Shimoga, 2012)

In Dakshin Kannada, another investment avenue has surfaced. Those individuals who went to Mumbai and the Gulf in the 1980s are keen to invest their surplus in real estate. They are also buying land in their native places, often their villages, but are not interested in agriculture (interview of a professor from Mangalore, July 2012). The respondent himself has bought land in his village, one generation after moving out. The land is being used to start shops, guest houses, and suchlike, and the ongoing land market rate offered is very lucrative for farmers who have an annual income of ₹20,000 or more (interview of a farmer, Mangalore July 2012; Assyag and Fuller, 2005). In Bengaluru, 20 IT professionals, as well as a few from middle and big farmer background, have invested as shareholders to develop a huge apartment complex in the northern part of the city. They have retained ownership of one floor each and the rest is being sold. The class seen benefitting here is the new petty bourgeoisie arising from the well-paid professional class and the agrarian rich. The big farmer families in this case came from the adjacent state of Andhra Pradesh (interview of Surya, 2012). Market-led opportunities arc bringing professional and big farmer classes closer on the basis of their new interest.

Similar cases were reported from Coorg, where urbanisation and tourism have led to land buying by white-collar professionals and industrial capitalists. Though the local population has organised themselves to stop infiltration by 'outsiders', they stated that many people from the Reddy[47] community have been buying land there. Coorg is one district where resistance to outsiders was prominent, which can probably be explained by locals' higher education, better income from capitalist agriculture, and pride in owning their plantations. Informally, official terms such as 'notification' and 'de-notification' are used to procure huge tracts of land by big farmers, petty bourgeoisie, and the industrial class (interview of a farmer from Bangalore, May 2012). As an activist narrated, 'The middleman comes and tells a group of farmers in the village that the government is about to notify the land of their village for acquisition', which means that the government will take over the land for public purpose at low prices. This works as a threat, and farmers sell land before the notification is implemented to make as much money as possible. Farmers owning less than 5 acres often sell their land in the event of any personal emergency. Fluctuating crop prices since the mid-1990s have increased their vulnerability. Land is often bought by intermediaries who start some small business or a nursery and, in some cases, also sell the land to urban professionals or big industries later. A similar pattern was observed in Shimoga.

A recent trend observable across the state is monopolisation of land by capitalists and petty bourgeoisie, which is a reversal of land reforms. The state officials themselves are among the beneficiaries, owing to bribe involved in such land deals. The state has taken a wider political position of being capital friendly, and thus is making all arrangements to make land available to the capitalists. The real estate lobby has steadily gained prominence in the last decade.

There have been regular reports of irregularities in land transfer to private builders (Balasubramanian, 2012[48]; *Hindustan Times*, 2012). V. Balasubramanian opines that the Bangalore Development Authority held around 1,000 acres of open space in 2012, which according to records is 3,000 acres. Hence, 2,000 acres have been encroached upon by private companies. He ascribes the land grab to a nexus between public officials and private companies, which has been shielded from the public eye by politicians. Previously in 2007, the A. T. Ramaswamy Joint Legislature Committee on land encroachments showed that out of a total of 1,50,000 acres of government land in Bengaluru Urban district, 24,000 acres was under encroachment; it was valued at ₹400 billion. The Yeddyurappa cabinet in 2009 had to form a task force to recover land. Direct accumulation by political leaders is an added factor as to why the government has extended support to manoeuvre policy to smoothen the process of acquisition. Political leaders in this new era are either petty bourgeoisie or capitalists.

A young boy in Dharwad informed that after completing a Masters in Computer Application, he has taken up a job of data entry manager in a factory (white-collar job) to be able to send money home. This is the only way he can pay back the *mahajan* and save their land. They own 15 acres of land but the income is still insufficient for the family. If this is the state of a farmer who owns 15 acres, we can well imagine those farmers with less than 5 acres. The uncertain and insufficient income from agriculture, debt crisis, poor surface irrigation, and rising costs of inputs are making self-cultivation difficult for tiller farmers. In this situation, Assadi's (1995) prediction that new policy will facilitate transfer of land from agriculturist to non-agriculturist, paving the way to corporate landlordism, holds true.

Across districts, the functioning of petty gainers in real estate has been validated. The big gainers are capitalists (domestic and foreign), but each such acquisition requires the support of the petty bourgeoisie who have, from a rural context, good relations with farmers who are lured to generate surplus. Unfortunately, agriculture in Karnataka is not an honourable profession or sector, which is not the case in Gujarat or western Chhattisgarh. Therefore, a widely prevailing idea is to use land to get out of agriculture or generate as much money from the sector as possible in an exploitative way. The big and middle farmers, therefore, are the petty gainers. Simultaneously, urban professionals were also found to be accumulating in the process. This is creating a rift within the agrarian society since capital has partnered with the rural proprietary classes, who apparently are big farmers (very rarely landlords) but in the neoliberal era have assumed a petty bourgeois position with a close alliance with the capitalists. The political settlement has the petty bourgeoisie (old and new), big farmers, capitalist farmers, and industrial capitalist as its members with the capitaists as the most powerful. Thus, Bardhan's (1984) idea of opposing interests of classes between big farmer and industrial capital loses relevance with an overlap of interests between them.

The role of Panchayati Raj Institutions

This section presents two major arguments – first, propertied classes infiltrate state institutions to perpetuate their class interest and, second, access to positions in political institutions has led to economic gain and accumulation and brought about a change in class character among small farmers. A two-way process has unfolded, which is bringing in a few more members in the circuit of capital and state patronage.

Decentralisation: Another way to foster a political elite

In an evaluation conducted after two decades of their formation, a study found *panchayat*s to be merely organs of the central and state governments whose chief function is implementation of policies conceived by the government's higher echelons (Rajasekhar et al., 2012). They are not evoking demands from below to challenge structural inequality, nor to influence institutional decisions (Kudva, 2003). Reddy (1990) in the Backward Class Commission report found an overarching presence of Lingayats and Vokaliggas in political institutions, pointing to the dominance of the big farmer and landlord class. Most often, big landowners had maintained their dominance on *zilla parishad*s (Ray and Kumpatla, 1987). A chief stronghold is the position of the president of the *zilla parishad* and 63 per cent of the past presidents belonged to the socially dominant class of big farmers. This is an indicator that entrenched social inequalities exerted influence on new institutions until the 1990s. However, it can be argued that the class exerting control over PRI has seen a transformation in the last two decades, bringing members from middle farmers and some from small farmers within the political class (Pattenden, 2011). That said, the erstwhile big farmers remain part of the class.

Manor (2007) finds that PRIs are more effective channels between the villages and the upper echelons of the government than the political parties creating a pool of beneficiaries. Those who have been elected in PRIs due to reservations get access to state resources (Palaniswamy and Krishnan, 2012). The most effective way of accumulating through state resources is from corruption.

Increase in the number of political posts has increased the number of claimants to the commission pie (Vijayalakshmi, 2008). Approximately 55 to 65 per cent of the development funds are used for pay-offs and commissions (Vijayalakshmi, 2008). The fieldwork revealed a similar stronghold of new entrants on the local self-government institutions, who are not from an upper or dominant caste, but their access to political institutions has enhanced their economic status. The institution has penetrated rural life, garnering support for the regional state by distributing patronage.

Be it Mangalore or Shimoga, respondents replied that the capitalists (contractors) and political parties use money and muscle power to intervene and influence *panchayat* elections. Though these elections are supposed to be non-political and formally not fought under party banners, parties exert tremendous control on the candidates and ensure their victory (interview of a political cadre from Mangalore, July 2012). Murthy, a big farmer in Shimoga, confirmed that *panchayat* elections are political and parties put money and push their candidates indirectly. After winning elections, people work as per the diktat of the political party that is aligned to the capitalist class. With limited education the poor farmer cannot decide on official matters independently. Thus, they submit to the will of the capitalist who sponsored their election through a party (interview in Shimoga, August 2012). The nexus between capital and the state once again becomes conspicuous. The elected representatives with their new-found access to capital have altered their class position to old petty bourgeoisie. These farmers are simultaneously perpetuating the interest of capital by easing the process of land acquisition and fostering self-accumulation.

A political activist alluded to how reservation in *panchayat* elections has created a new trend over the past decade. Newly elected members often have poor education, so they put their signature on documents as per the secretary's instructions in fear of being framed, and in lieu they get their share of the corruption money (interviews of an activist-farmer from Mandya, May 2012, and an academic from Bangalore, August 2012). There are projects that only exist on paper and the entire project fund gets distributed among the stakeholders. He stated, 'At present, funds have increased, and so have bribes gathered by this class.' Like in the case of the MGNREGS, despite a roll call at the beginning of each day, once the officer leaves, so do the labourers. There is a serious lack of accountability and, as a result, developmental work suffers (interview in Shimoga, 2012). In each project, state funds are shared among all ranks from the *sarpanch* to the MLA (interviews of a scholar from Bangalore, a journalist from Bangalore, and an activist from Mandya, 2012). A recent report (Rajasekhar et al., 2012) concludes that elite capture has taken place in the scheme. However, not all of these elites are from upper castes or landlord families. These elites come from varied caste and class backgrounds and accumulate through political connections. Consequently, state patronage and corruption have created a new class of beneficiaries in rural India, altering earlier agrarian class structures. They fall under fractions of the old petty bourgeoisie accumulating from rent.

In the past two decades, a few members from middle farmers and small farmers have assumed old petty bourgeois character. The state has accomplished the task of creating 'an elite', not entirely overlapping with the upper caste, through manoeuvring of reservation that acts as another scheme for distribution of state patronage. It makes the hold of the state stronger and makes structural inequalities deeper by bringing a few more people within the fold of capital. These farmers no longer regard agriculture as central to their sustenance, as the state provides them with new sources of accumulation. This new class position sets them apart from their caste members, as they seek surplus in the form of rent and want to make use of the market to grow the surplus, thus aligning themselves closer to capital. This matches Jessop's (1983) characterisation of an advanced capitalist state pursuing decentralisation to access the smallest areas of surplus production.

Conclusion

At first glance, the state's argument for a 'paradigm shift' in agrarian policy would seem like treating all agrarian classes alike, but a closer look at it tells a differentiated story. The benefits of such policy measures have been accrued unequally due to the structural inequality. Under the garb of phrases such as 'cooperatives' and 'a serious note of the marginal and small farmers who have lost out in the sector chasing growth' (Policy Document, 2006), the government chose to focus its energy on input centricity, high-value crops, and mechanisation of agriculture. These policies have promoted the interest of the big farmers and capitalist farmers, who are important allies for the state.

The state in Karnataka is in the thick of class formation and consolidation despite the political instability during the last couple of decades. A high incidence of corruption and instances of accumulation through political positions or relations led to the characterisation of the state as a 'clientelist' state. It is a weak state as compared to Gujarat. Karnataka has seen prolific penetration of market forces in all sectors since the mid-1990s, but that has not resulted in a retreat of the state. The state is very much present in these transactions, and hence capital and the state operate in a close nexus, whereby state officials and political leaders are the direct beneficiaries.

The political settlement in the state is constituted of the industrial capitalist, big farmers and capitalist farmers, and the new and old petty bourgeoisie. The new petty bourgeoisie has a significant presence in the state, more pronounced than the other two states. Drawn from the professional classes, the new petty bourgeoisie fraction has been making use of opportunities brought in by globalisation and privatisation. The IT sector has contributed to the economic boom. New input companies such as Cargill and DuPont have also created a demand for university-educated professionals. They are ardent advocates of privatisation. The old petty bourgeoisie is thriving on state resources, which is a significant source of accumulation. Among the three states, this trend is most conspicuous in Karnataka. A part of these two fractions of the petty bourgeoisie are drawn from big farmers and landlords, but there are elements from other farmers who have also joined the class due to OBC reservation. The petty bourgeoisie (including state officials) has been benefitting from land transactions, mining, and new projects in the form of rent accumulation.

During the last few decades, the state has skillfully formed and consolidated new classes through its policies; the 'new petty bourgeoisie', who have gained in the process of privatisation of agricultural inputs, credit, and land transaction, is the closest ally to capital. They invest in real estate to generate more surplus, as cases in Bangalore and Shimoga showed. An expansion of the old petty bourgeoisie has been undertaken by allocating funds to schemes such as the MGNREGS and taking the reservation to local government forward. Consolidation of members from backward OBCs into the petty bourgeoisie has meant their disassociation from their respective caste groups and alliance with capital, which adds to the argument that class is a defining identity in recent decades. They play a crucial role in politically connecting the countryside to state capital. This is probably why petty bourgeois elements have been observed contesting district and sub-district level elections.

Capitalist agriculture is more predominant in the southern districts and in Bellary in the north. Irrigation and state support are intensely focused on these The capitalist farmers in these districts are using market opportunities to their advantage. The state has concentrated on these classes, for instance, by forming the Agricultural and Processed Food Products Export Development Authority to facilitate the sale of their products abroad or subsidising technology such as greenhouse technology. The gap between the big/capitalist and tiller farmers has widened along with differentiation within the agrarian capital. The conclusion is similar to Gujarat but with a difference. Unlike Gujarat, the state officials in Karnataka were found to play a direct role in ascertaining crop prices and procurement.

The space occupied by the KRRS has indeed shrunk, but that does not mean that the countryside has gone out of the ambit of state patronage. Issues such as MSP, irrigation, rural credit, and subsidised inputs have not lost significance. Through lobbying and personal contact with political leaders and district-level bureaucrats, big and middle farmers, especially those with political connections, continue to corner the institutional credit and subsidies, on machines, and influence MSPs of a few crops. A minimum of 1 hectare of land is required to avail many of the subsidies, which excludes marginal farmers automatically. Accessing these benefits often hinge on upper-caste connections which overlap with big farmers predominantly in the northern districts and capitalist farmers in south. The BKS in the other two states has chosen to represent capitalist farmers, leaving the rest to fight their own battles.

In the 2004 general elections the NDA's loss taught both the national parties about the need to gain back the confidence of different fractions of the agrarian proprietary class. The argument made is that this has been the precise intention with which the 2006 and 2012 agricultural policies were formulated and implemented. While developments such as mining corruption and rapid growth in information technology have been in the limelight, the state took a bold step by declaring the 'Karnataka Agri-Business Development Policy' in 2010, bringing opportunities to that class of farmers who produce for export and metropolitan markets. The aim was to bolster the primary sector by export-driven growth, where investments would be channelled for building agro-business linkages. With the turn of globalisation, these proprietary classes are looking for mechanisation and technology to make agriculture profitable. The policies highlighting technology and private inputs without any agrarian structural changes, in liaison with the relaxation of land ceiling, are likely to ensure accumulation in agriculture directly, but only in the hands of those who can hold the capital. Playing with the market also requires hoarding capacity. Therefore, the policy is in no way resource neutral.

The indirect benefit accruing to big farmers or landlords is in the form of diversification into other sectors. The landlords' lingering connection to agriculture is rent; their class position has broadly altered to petty bourgeoisie as they have become part of the state bureaucracy or the professional class. A few instances of landlords transforming into capitalist farmers by investing surplus in agriculture have been noted. Big farmers continue to be significant in state politics given their access to and control over a huge pool of voters and their continued dominant caste status. However, this is not observed uniformly across the state since the southern districts have seen a greater impact of modernisation and old social hierarchies have weakened (Pattenden, 2011). The agrarian policies have also resulted in the proliferation of trading in chemical inputs and machinery, moneylending, commission agencies, and owning *mandis*. In many cases these activities were found to be taken up by the big and middle farmers. Therefore, these avenues of diversification have indirectly helped in the accumulation of the rural proprietary class.

The state has entered the capitalist mode of agriculture but only in parts, unlike Gujarat where the phenomenon is much more widespread. This need for continuous technical innovation has built bridges between universities, private companies such as Monsanto, Cargill, and DuPont, the white-collar professionals (petty bourgeoisie), and the bureaucracy. The state has increasingly created space for private companies to enter the input market and their presence has increased with floriculture and horticulture taking off, since private players are supplying the machinery. The efficacy of technology is directly connected to large-scale, irrigated landholdings. Hence, both foreign capital and capitalist farmers stand to gain from such a policy decision, thereby narrowing the interest between the agrarian and non-agrarian proprietary classes, namely big farmers, petty bourgeoisie, and industrial capital. It is these reasons that have propelled the entry of gentleman farmers into the profitable floriculture and horticulture sectors, acquiring agricultural land and investing surplus from other sectors. As long as they drive the agricultural growth upwards, the state is happy to support them, and even allow tax evasions.

The tiller farmers, with no capital and little access to irrigation, are left at the brink of survival, where leaving agriculture and selling off their land would most likely make their lives easier. Literature substantiated by field evidence points to the deprivation that the tiller farmers have been facing, as reflected in the continuity of farmer suicides. Consequently, conditions are ripe to give up self-cultivation. In the process, a continuous supply of land is being created, which serves the interest of capital, the petty bourgeoisie, and even the state, each of whom have accumulated through land transactions. These rural intermediaries located in the rural context either organise the transaction or buy land that they then sell to the petty bourgeoisie or the capitalists.

Polarisation among classes has set the agrarian society between those who own capital and those who depend on labour. A few individuals from lower castes have gained access to capital due to the PRIs and caste-based reservation, indicating the intricate ways in which capital and the state function by building allies in the pockets that they want to invade. Through economic and political routes, fractions have accumulated, which shows class differentiation within the agrarian capitalist class.

This is secured by oppressing the tiller farmers. In some instances members of two classes would belong to the same caste. Seizing the poor farmers' resources to perpetuate capitalists' agenda explains the inequality that characterises rural India. Jessop's theorisation comes alive in the case where pauperisation takes place as capital penetrates the remote rural areas.

To differentiate the role of different classes, the industrial class is the driver of the policy, while big and capitalist farmers are the gainers of policies. The former provides the funds in contesting politics, dictates the terms, and even assume political positions in some districts. The change in the new millennium is that alongside the interest of the capitalist, the agrarian proprietary class has found their way back into the political settlement. The former wants land and the latter has access to land. The farmers regard land as valuable, not as a factor of production in agriculture, but for its sale value. This is a change that neoliberalism has brought about. This makes Karnataka stand apart from Gujarat. Here, most respondents did not regard agriculture as an honourable profession and hence were looking for a way out. Jodhka (2008) has previously made a similar observation about agriculture. In Gujarat, most respondents took pride in agriculture and saw promise in it. Chhattisgarh had a mixed reaction. This possibly explains why the number of large holdings have not risen in Karnataka and capitalist agriculture has not consolidated, unlike in Gujarat. If politics is about maintaining a fine balance between the different classes, then the state in Karnataka has accomplished the task by guarding the 'agrarian proprietary class' interest after 2004 by taking them back under the wing of state patronage and ensuring that benefits of market opportunities accrue to them. The clientelist state is active. It has been creating a class of petty bourgeoisie which cements the distance between big and capitalist farmer, as it existed prior to the 1990s.

Notes

1. It has been earlier discussed in Chapter 3.
2. The Chief Minister of the fifth state assembly.
3. A few cases of genuine loss for the landlord surfaced during fieldwork. It was more an exception.
4. These data are from the 1988 elections.
5. For further details, refer to Bussell (2012). The scams came to light thanks largely due to an efficient *lokayukta*, the corruption ombudsman organisation at the state level.
6. The strong tradition of decentralisation has its roots in the Mysore state.
7. Yedyurappa came to power as the Chief Minister in 2007 based on his Lingayat support base (Padmavathi and Shastri, 2009). He eventually had to resign owing

to corruption charges for one of India's biggest mining scams under his chief ministership. However, Yedyurappa indirectly continues to influence state policies. Some respondents said that to keep the Lingayat constituency happy, the BJP has been paying heed to him.

8. A senior BJP leader who was a cabinet member in 2007 holding the power portfolio. He was elected as the BJP state president in 2010.

9. It is a publication of a Left organisation in India.

10. A senior leader of a regional party, he is known to me through a reliable source and shared the information on grounds of anonymity.

11. A senior technocrat was a key informant. I met him on several occasions between February and August 2012.

12. A leading authority on agriculture who has highlighted the plight of small farmers and has documented the rising cost of cultivation in the post-liberalisation era.

13. Bridging the gap between latest research and farmers, so that the latter can make use of technologies.

14. For more details, refer to http://planning.kar.nic.in/sites/planning.kar.nic.in/files/State%20Budget.pdf and http://planningcommission.nic.in/plans/stateplan/index.php?state=b_outbody.htm (accessed on July 2014).

15. For more details, refer to http://smartinvestor.business-standard.com/market/Compnews-143771-Compnewsdet-National_Horticulture_Mission_cheers_Karnataka_farmers.htm#.WmoemainE54 (accessed on July 2018).

16. Like in the service sector, IT is the dominant sub-sector that has been winning state support. The state's alliance with foreign capital is prominent in both these instances where capturing foreign market is the dominant intent.

17. They are people who work for commercial purpose between vendors and buyers.

18. Old period houses are open to guests. The food is provided by the owner of the house and is often the cuisine of the region. It is meant to give an authentic cultural experience of the region.

19. He was a key informant since he is a fellow student at a university where I was residing and was recommended by friends as a reliable source.

20. A herbal seed used to wash hair in India.

21. In 2010–11, the state was the third largest producer of coconut in India, contributing 13.8 per cent, after Tamil Nadu and Andhra Pradesh (GoK, 2012a, 2011).

22. The managers who run the farms, often a local person or a labourer, are salaried employees and do not have the same stake in agriculture as an owner. Hence, the kind of attention they pay is minimal.

23. The small farmers have diversified to cultivation of flowers which might add to their income but they are not part of the technological revolution. This differentiation within the sector was agreed upon across interviews in Mandya, Tumkur, and Bangalore.

24. This observation was of an insider who has grown up in the district and been part of its transitions in the past two decades.

25. He is a landlord since his ownership of land is historical.
26. When I met the MLA, in his dairy there were more than 20 farmers who had assembled to seek his advice on various problems related to agriculture and land.
27. Red light on cars is a privilege for VIPs in India, which he copies by putting a similar green light. Green symbolises the colour of the KRRS movement.
28. The day we reached there, it was the day of Nagpanchami. It is an important festival for farmers as they ask for forgiveness from the snake god for having killed snakes in their fields. His son informed that he has been performing the ritual for many years for their village, despite being a Kshatriya. This indicates that in social order the family is regarded very highly.
29. Mushtaq Khan talks about the role of the petty bourgeoisie acting on behalf of the capitalist.
30. *Jagirdari* is a feudal system of landownership practised in British India in the Deccan regions. The person owning the land was called the *jagirdar* who was responsible for paying revenue to the British government.
31. Intelligentsia is regarded as old petty bourgeoisie in Poulantzas' classification.
32. He offered to give me a tour of some prime properties that were available, where he could act an intermediary to get me the best prices.
33. Yuvak Mandal is the youth wing of the RSS, and Mahila Samaj is the women's wing of RSS.
34. This is a Hindutva outfit.
35. I made several attempts to interview an RSS leader to delve deeper into the issue but it could not materialise, since he could not make time.
36. Tiller farmers include farmers with semi-medium, small and marginal holdings without other sources of income, such as a *panchayat* position.
37. Plantation land in Kerala was given the same exemption.
38. These respondents spoke in an FGD, where presence of other respondents prevented providing wrong information.
39. He comes from a family that has been closely associated with the formation of the cooperative.
40. The CAMPCO has now become a multi-state cooperative under relevant Indian laws. The organisation is mainly into procurement, marketing, selling, and processing of areca nut and cocoa.
41. For more details, see T. N. P. Kammardi, 2012, 'Areca Nut Economy at the Cross Roads', Department of Agricultural Economics, Government of India.
42. This is linked to the special treatment given to them by Sharad Pawar, the UPA agricultural minister, who hails from the sugar lobby.
43. He was exerting control on the government even after resignation. He was putting pressure on the government and the new Chief Minister to cater to big and capitalist farmers' interests.
44. Land deeds to confirm ownership.

262262

262262262

262262262

262262

45. For more details, refer to Deshpande and Indira (2010).
46. Permissible landholding of unirrigated land classified as type D is 54 acres, which for irrigated land, type A with two crops, vary between 10 and 18 acres. So, if irrigation was implemented, they feared losing land.
47. Reddy is a landed caste from Andhra Pradesh, which has diversified to other sectors.
48. V. Balasubramanian was appointed the chairman of Karnataka's Task Force for Recovery and Protection of Public Lands on land grabbing in the state. He wrote a report on land grab which was not available in public domain during my fieldwork.

7

State in Action, Political Settlement, and the Agrarian Flux

The task taken upon in the book was to demonstrate why, even in the globalisation era, the need to investigate the nature of the state and state–class relation remains pivotal, and to examine the extent to which the state is autonomous from proprietary classes, if at all. The point was to reflect on the agrarian transformation by asking questions about economic structures and their interplay with the state. The interplay is of two types: the differentiated effects of class on state apparatus and, therefore, on policy formulation, and the effects of policies on the agrarian classes. The aim was to document an empirically informed understanding of agrarian classes, and a differentiation within the agrarian capitalist class in particular to reflect on the growing inequality. The method followed was empirical observations based on which conceptual categories were drawn. The methodology is particularly important given that a critique of Marxist political economy has been that it has tended to generalize, particularly about the Global South, without paying enough attention to the empirical reality and cultural context (Skocpol, 2010; Poulantzas, 1973). To understand the role of the state, I scrutinized state agrarian policies between 2004 and 2013 and three other policies that relate to rural life and their effect on classes. The class structure cannot be understood without the employment reservation policy and PRI policy which cater to specific castes but, as demonstrated, foster accumulation. Hence a discussion on these policies was also included. In the Introduction, I asked: is the inequality new or structural? The answer is it is both.

The period is chosen to understand if the state made concerted efforts to bring the agrarian capitalist class into a political settlement through specific policies in reaction to the loss of the BJP in the 2004 general elections. The study thus adopted a triangular frame bringing together political–economic–social processes to understand the relations between class and state. This book raised four key questions which are answered in the subsequent sections. The book found four fractions of the agrarian proprietary class to be relevant – big farmer, landlords, gentleman farmers,[1] and capitalist farmers – and their sources of accumulation and political bargaining. It showed differentiation within the class with only two fractions accumulating from agriculture directly. The other fractions have gained from secondary relations of exploitation made possible by agrarian policies, land policy, and other policies. A cross-sectoral flow of capital was observed from agrarian to non-agrarian and, more interestingly, from non-agrarian to agrarian. The state was found to play an important role in policy making and the agrarian structures shaped the state policies and vice versa. Such accumulation by the agrarian proprietary class explains the inequality that has intensified in India, thereby indicating why globalisation is not a grand equaliser. The research drew on fieldwork in three Indian states – Chhattisgarh, Gujarat, and Karnataka – bringing out the richness of a comparative study.

Agriculture is varied across states (Lerche, 2014); therefore, to capture the heterogeneity, the unit of analysis in the study was chosen to be regional state. A three-state comparison has been drawn here, and the states were chosen on the basis of one overarching similarity and a crucial difference. The states have largely been under the BJP's rule since 2000 and have had fewer years under the Congress. While there has been an ideological continuity between their state governments and politics, their economies differ substantially. While Chhattisgarh is primarily dependent on agriculture, the economies of Gujarat and Karnataka are driven by manufacturing and services sectors, respectively.

Theoretically, the book builds on the work of Poulantzas (1973), Jessop (1983), Bardhan (1998), Mitra (1977), and Khan (2010) on one hand and that of Kohli (1987) and Sinha (2005) on the other. The goal is to understand the state–class relation and rests on the premise that class is a key factor attended to in policy making. Such policies differentially affect class and their fractions. The case study is India after 2004. Chapter 2 provided theoretical insights from these five key thinkers. Given this understanding of class, what is the influence of class interest on state functioning in India? A class that cannot exert political power is neither a class for itself nor a class at all as Poulantzas defined.

The dynamics between state and class are critical to understand the impact of global forces in the specific context of the Indian state. Capitalism is a global force shaping life almost everywhere, but with a wide variation. Jessop (1983) wrote about state power and the nature of the state, postulating a personal fusion is possible between capitalists and the state, with decentralisation and 'immiseration' of the proletariat. These are features of capitalism. In this strain, Khan (2004, 2005) argues that power is balanced among the dominant groups in each country on an 'operational settlement' that underlines political stability and economic growth. Following these ideas, a 'functional coalition' was identified in each state and the interrelations among its components, that is, the proprietary classes, were analysed. This helped to answer the critical question about 'the nature of the state'.

Fieldwork was undertaken in 24 districts across the three states during 2011–12 to meet stakeholders such as farmers, political leaders, journalists, academics, and social activists. These districts were selected based on substantive presence of farmer lobby or big farmers who are influential in state politics and form the core of this study. Most of the respondents were big farmers, and a few were landlords.

The fieldwork in addition to literature review brought to light some important themes. First, under the current policy regime, self-cultivation has been made increasingly unsustainable for small farmers who are facing dispossession (Sainath, 2004) with skewed land distribution and high cost of cultivation as discussed in the Introduction (Chapter 1). This is a contribution of the literature on agrarian crisis (Nagaraj, 2008; Mishra and Reddy, 2009; Banerjee, 2011; Patnaik, 2002). A rising burden of informal credit is reported on farmers since the mid-1990s, and it has adversely affected self-cultivation (NCEUS, 2005, 2008). There is no denying the agrarian crisis. However, this picture does not account for all farmers; in fact, agrarian India is divided within itself with policies benefitting a few and not the others. A class of farmers have accumulated wealth during this period. In line with the findings of Harriss-White (2004, 2008), the fieldwork also showed that this class of farmers is thriving on the sale of chemical inputs, moneylending, land transactions, and procurement. In Chhattisgarh, many of the non-agricultural sources of income revolve around mining projects. In Gujarat and Karnataka, these relate to industrial projects and real estate with mining in some parts, such as in Bellary. The findings agree with scholars like Jodhka (2014) and Lerche (2014) and the NCEUS which reported about 50 per cent of big farmers' and capitalist farmers' income coming from non-agricultural sources (NCEUS, 2003). Hence I argue the agrarian may not be understood exclusively in terms of the rural. Third, evidence suggests the state affecting a weakening of a united farmers' movement across states, with a rupture of interest between classes who seek opportunities to accumulate and the rest who get dispossessed. Farmer movement had been reduced to a mouthpiece of big farmers, as previously argued by Banaji (1994), Brass (1994), and Pattenden (2005), until the 2020 farmer protests when tiller farmers gained a voice.

The four subsections in this chapter are divided to answer the four questions raised in the Introduction. The first elucidates the features of the agrarian policies of Chhattisgarh, Gujarat, and Karnataka and argues how these protect and promote the interests of big farmers and capitalist farmers alongside the new fraction of gentleman farmers who invest surplus from non-agrarian sectors in profitable elite crops such as floriculture and horticulture. The second section deals with the agrarian proprietary class fractions, their consolidation, alteration, and formation during the last two decades. The third section looks at three powerful classes – capitalist, petty bourgeoisie, and rich farmers (its different fractions), political leaders being a part of either capitalists or the petty bourgeoisie – and analyses their inter-dynamics.

Agrarian policy and land policy: The benefactor and beneficiaries

This section answers the first question raised in the Introduction – have agrarian policies since globalisation been continuous and homogeneous across regional states? If not, is the state an important factor causing variation? In all the states, meeting and interviewing leaders of farmer organisations and their associates was prioritised to understand the demands they champion, who are at the forefront of pushing their demands vis-à-vis the state, and how these demands have influenced new policies since the early 2000s. Scholars have pointed out that the defeat of the NDA in the 2004 general elections indicated the strength of the power of the rich rural classes to influence electoral outcomes (Bose, 2006; Vasavi, 2008). The agricultural policies that each state formulated occurred around the 2004 general election results. The agrarian crisis in the late 1990s resulted from blindly taking to the prescriptions of the GATT agreement as well as cutting agricultural budget and subsidies. However, the states soon realised that continuance of such deprivation of all rural classes had the potential to defeat their own political aspirations. Since the late 1990s, the agrarian sector has been in crisis (Patnaik, 2002; Sainath, 2004). Yet the BJP chose to focus on urban India in the India Shining campaign, leading to its defeat in the general elections. Could that remain the strategy if the BJP wanted to make a comeback to power? This book aimed to examine if in the aftermath of 2004, the new policy regime would attempt to alter agrarian policies, and bring the rural proprietary classes back among the beneficiaries of state policies? If so, what would such policies do for the rich farmers? The primary conclusion of this book, in light of the empirical evidence, is that in the neoliberal period global forces do wield power but the state remains important, and so does the class structure, which is not evened out. Rather, global forces work upon existing structures through the state apparatus. The state, therefore, had to guard the interests of the proprietary classes within the broader framework of following prescriptions of international organisations. To that extent, class dynamics hold significance in understanding matters of both state and policy.

Agrarian policy's differential outcome: What purpose does it serve?

Fieldwork-based evidence showed that the proprietary classes continue to have linkage to the state, but predominantly through personal connections rather than organisations or lobbies. These relations of big farmers with political parties and leaders, their association with district-level bureaucracy, and their assumption of positions of power in local government point to them being considered in policy making by those in the state apparatus. The class is well represented within the bureaucracy, with many family members in the bureaucracy and among local leaders. This has also been observed previously by Manor (2007), Harriss-White (2008), Jeffrey and Lerche (2000), and Pattenden (2005), among others.

The more organised farmer voice is dominated by the agrarian proprietary class. The presence of the Bharatiya Kisan Sangh (BKS) was noted in agriculturally developed districts of Chhattisgarh and Gujarat, while the Karnataka Rajya Raitha Sangha's (KRRS) presence was more significant in those districts of Karnataka that were dominated by commercial crops. These districts were, without fail, more irrigated, employed more mechanised methods of farming, and engaged with commercial crops. The members of these farmers' organisations were primarily commercial-cropping farmers. While this reflected the ability of big farmers to better organise themselves, it also indicated that the capacity to mobilise and negotiate was absent among food crop growing tiller farmers. The KRRS acted as the negotiating platform for capitalist farmers and big farmers, while the BKS operated only in districts that had the presence of capitalist farmers, such as mainland Gujarat. The incidence of such connection was the highest in Karnataka, where almost every big farmer and landlord seemed to harness political ties, then followed by Gujarat and Chhattisgarh.

However, evidence pertaining to the role of these organisations in policy formulation was tentative. No direct evidence could be collected regarding big farmers forming part of policy-making forums. Anecdotal evidence regarding a politician or bureaucrat taking a position in policy formulation forums in favour of big farmers was noted. With that said, during interviews, the bureaucrats commonly did not take a supportive stance towards capitalist farmers, but rather spoke about 'agricultural growth'. The growth bias meant the political leaders shared an overlapping perspective with the agrarian capitalist class about the future of agrarian sector and shared the concern of growing cost of labour, labour that includes the small and marginal farmers. Following Mitra's (1977, 2004) argument, it can be inferred as a sign of the proprietary class using the state to maximise its profit motive, which manifests in shaping policies to guard their interests. Both big farmers and capitalist farmers were most agitated by the high cost of labour that had increased particularly due to the NREGA since 2005 (Khera, 2011). To save on labour costs and extend their profits, these fractions of the rural proprietary class turned to mechanisation. From the interviews, it appeared that they were willing to invest in advanced machinery such as tractor, weeding, and sprinkler irrigation to cut the cost of labour. The concern for reducing labour costs was prioritised by the bureaucracy and political leaders as the issue circumscribing all possibilities of agriculture, and prescribed mechanisation as the solution for this. It was established that, in the decade following 2000, subsidy has been channelised towards mechanisation and high-value crops within agriculture, which was a result of the new policies adopted during this time to address the demands of capitalist farmers.

The focus areas of the New Agricultural Policy across the states were fourfold: chemical input centricity, high-value crops, private irrigation, and subsidised mechanisation. There are many other aspects in the long policy documents, but they are not pursued in earnest by the states, such as the stipulation for cooperatives to tackle the issue of non-economical small holdings or attention to small farmers' access to inputs. The crops that are the claimants of the largest share of state resources are horticulture and floriculture. Subsidies on machinery and subsidies through cooperative societies providing cheaper seeds and fertilisers are largely cornered by big farmers and capitalist farmers (and a few landlords in the case of Karnataka).

The Chhattisgarh 2010 Vision document declares that the 30 per cent of farmers constituting big and middle farmers will be the drivers of growth in the sector. It is shocking for a state to shift its focus from the tillers! In Gujarat, the impersonal push given to the 'capable farmers' (as a bureaucrat called it) in the form of subsidy for irrigation machinery and 25 per cent subsidy on greenhouses was also intended to benefit the same fractions. Karnataka has the landlords and big farmers under state patronage in the form of subsidies, with special provisions for farmers growing elite crops. Tiller farmers may also grow cash crops, but they cannot bear the cost of machinery, even if they get a 50 per cent subsidy. For high-yielding seeds and pumps, they must enter the vicious cycle of informal credit. They hardly enjoy the benefits of subsidies, inputs from cooperatives, and credit from formal institutions since they neither have political connections nor is their produce contributing significantly to state agricultural growth. So, a state keen to achieve high growth has sided with the class that can drive such growth, directing public resources to those who can make private investments, thereby leaving the rest with little support.

As per the backward linkages to policy, in broad terms, it can be concluded that the agrarian proprietary class is able to promote its class interest into the state apparatus. They are well represented within the bureaucracy and are supporting government policies of large-scale farming and mechanisation from within the apparatus. Big farmers have voiced their demands for higher prices, cheaper inputs, subsidies on machinery, and non-taxation of agricultural income, which have all been made available to them by the state. The need for high agricultural growth and decreasing land availability, along with the display of power of the rural proprietary class in the 2004 election, have reinstated the agrarian proprietary classes in the political settlement of all three states, albeit as a second to the capitalists. While their interests are accommodated in agricultural policy formulation, NREGA, PRI, and land acquisition policy aided accumulation. Other policies ostensibly catering to caste groups such as reservation in employment have also been found to bolster avenues of accumulation by the same class. State patronage and corruption have added new members from marginalised caste groups into a class of beneficiaries in rural India, thus altering earlier agrarian class structures.

This part answers the second question – what has been the disaggregated impact of policies, both agrarian and others, on proprietary classes and their fractions? Does it lead to the formation of a new class or/and consolidation of existing class structure? The answer is that the impact of policies is quite disaggregated and shows differentiation within the class. Drawing on Byres' (1981) argument, fieldwork confirmed that such technologies are not resource neutral; the book affirms that those farmers who have land, capital, and political connection are the ones who can adopt such new agricultural technology. The states' focus on high-value crops and a shift in cropping pattern have aided capitalist farmers to reproduce themselves in both Chhattisgarh and Gujarat. In Karnataka, in addition to capitalist farmers, big and a few middle farmers have also cornered state favours due to extensive patronage networks. Chhattisgarh's big farmers, mainly those from the plains, were found maintaining a cordial relationship with political leaders. Broadly, tribal districts lagged behind in receiving state patronage, with a few exceptions. In cornering state favours, the OBCs have fared better than other social groups across the three states.

The big farmers who have continued with food crops and not adopted new technology were found making little profit from agriculture. A case in point is that of the paddy-producing big farmers of Bilaspur and Dhamtari districts of Chhattisgarh. As a safety net, these farmers relied on occupational diversification into professional employment such as white-collar jobs or the bureaucracy. In this context, the fraction of big farmers is distinct from that of capitalist farmers; rather, the former more aptly should be classified as the petty bourgeoisie. In the case of Karnataka, the state secured high prices for big farmers' produce such as sugarcane and areca nut, where evidence showed a patron–client relation operating between the fraction and bureaucrats at the district level. Even here, there were instances of landlord and big farmer families taking up professional jobs or retailing in agricultural inputs and machinery, thus becoming petty bourgeoisie. The point to note is that all fractions still accumulating capital within agriculture are essentially doing so through secondary relations of exploitation within the sphere of exchange like input credit, money credit, and output commissions. Only two fractions, the capitalist farmer and the gentleman farmer, are accumulating through the primary relation of exploitation of labour within the sphere of production, as seen in Gujarat in particular, with a few instances in western Chhattisgarh and southern Karnataka. In Gujarat, agriculture has proved to be a profitable enterprise under state policy since Narendra Modi assumed power in the state. Rising profitability explains the increase in the number of large landholdings in the state. This is unlike the situation in Chhattisgarh and Karnataka, suggesting that those who are profiting from agriculture are consolidating their landholdings (Table 5.3). Those who cannot afford these capital-intensive technologies are finding it hard to sustain agriculture but not equally across the states. In Karnataka, patron–client protection acts as a buffer against market forces for the proprietary class. In Chhattisgarh, the state is not as careful about protecting their interest as the demand for land extraction looms large. However, minimum support price and procurement of paddy have been regarded by most as the state looking after farmers.

Further, the benefits of input and credit privatisation have accrued to rural, propertied classes by providing them an indirect avenue of diversification.

They now operate as 'private players' such as input-shop owners, moneylenders, and commission agents more than ever in India (Janaiah, 2002; Murugkar, Ramaswamy, and Shelar, 2006; Raghavan, 2008). Privatisation of inputs has meant a larger degree of marketisation of the production process. Owing to the lumpy nature of technology (Cleaver, 1972; Deshpande, 2004), the only way technology can succeed is if farmers deploy all the necessary inputs, including water. The absence of any ingredient would result in failed crops. Evidently this has led to more opportunities for accumulation by big farmers and capitalist farmers, as previously observed by Barbara Harriss-White (2004, 2008) in her fieldwork in West Bengal and Tamil Nadu, and Ramachandran, Rawal, and Swaminathan (2010) in Andhra Pradesh. In the three states under scrutiny, the landlord fraction has diversified into professional and bureaucracy jobs. For the landlord class, rent collection is their only connection with agriculture, hence they should aptly be characterised as petty bourgeoisie. The other fraction of rich farmers is more into trade and moneylending, all being instances of extracting surplus from the tiller farmers. Hence the new agricultural policies have had differentiated impact on these agrarian classes. This conclusion is in agreement with Jeffery et al. (2008), Ramachandran et al. (2010), Breman (2007), Nair (1996), and Rutten (1995) in their works on Uttar Pradesh, Andhra Pradesh, Gujarat, and Karnataka.

Across the three states, the essence of the new agrarian policy has been to create new and multiple avenues of income for the agrarian proprietary class and, simultaneously, acting as a tool of oppression for the capital-poor tiller farmers. The latter are being exploited twice – by a distant capital (Monsanto, Cargill, and DuPont, among others) and by these agrarian capitalists themselves who are carrying forward the agenda of capital within the Indian agrarian society. Evidence showed these elements are extracting by pushing for higher sale of expensive inputs by 'threat and lure' tactics, as previously observed by Murugkar et al. (2006) and Shiva and Crompton (1998). The tiller farmers are particularly vulnerable because the state, by gradually withdrawing from agricultural extension services, has left them solely dependent on the private sellers for information on the use of new chemical inputs (Deshpande and Prachitha, 2006). To increase sales, the petty bourgeoisie makes false promises, for example, winning over farmers with the promise of crop protection with the use of extra insecticide or insisting that using more fertilisers will lead to better yield. Consequently, private players extract higher profits, and tiller farmers[2] bear higher costs. Interlocking of credit and factor markets was reported and triangulated across states, as previously observed by Harriss-White (2004, 2008), Swaminathan (2005), and Ramchandran, Rawal and

Swaminathan (2010). Informal credit is making adoption of new technology harder for the mass of farmers who are struggling to self-cultivate. The differential effect of the agricultural policy across classes has been identified by Ramachandran (2011), which finds more evidence in the study.

A defining aspect of agricultural policy is subsidies on private irrigation and on machinery. It was affirmed that the big farmers continue to corner the available subsidy on machinery that cater to large-scale cultivation. Subsidies on drip and sprinkler have been a positive, but this is so for the same fractions of the class who can afford the remaining amount required for the private irrigation. Aptly utilising the subsidy, big farmers and a few middle farmers are taking up capitalist agriculture. They are simultaneously moving to high-value crops such as floriculture and horticulture. The same fractions are accumulating through seed-fertiliser-pesticide shops, tractor dealerships, as well as rent on pumps and tractors, all secondary relations of exploitation.

Jessop (1983) predicted that 'immiseration' of a proletariat will occur as capital matures and tightens its grip on the state. The rising misery of the proletariat will be accompanied by the loss of control of resources, as data on land holdings show. Field findings show that objective conditions such as informal credit, interlocking, and rising cost of inputs have increased extraction from tiller farmers which in part is accruing to the agrarian proprietary classes who trade in inputs, machinery, provide informal credit, buy their crops, etc. The resulting situation has deeply marginalised tiller farmers. Both Chhattisgarh and Karnataka have reported a high incidence of farmer suicides – an indication of the severity of the crisis. Gujarat has seen concentration of land in large holding category. Since 2004, in Punjab, a similar observation has been made about the severity of deprivation faced by small farmers (Singh and Bhogal, 2014) and elsewhere (Chandra and Taghioff, 2016). In the light of the evidence presented that classes within agriculture are reaping benefits at the cost of other classes within the sector, the agrarian crisis in India has affected numerous farmers but not all. In fact, the extraction of surplus is carried out among certain agrarian classes corroborating the larger picture of growing inequality in India. This reaffirms that despite the severity of the agrarian crisis, state policy has managed to create opportunities and provide support in a way that structural inequality is deepened and the majority of farmers have been facing dispossession (Chandra and Taghioff, 2016). A key finding is that fractions such as big farmers gain more from the state whereas the capitalist farmers and gentleman farmers make bigger gains from the market. A crucial fallout is the rupture in 'farmer interest'. In the 2024 elections that will be a crucial factor in forming alliances – whether a class is looking for state support to accumulate or is open to market-led opportunities is linked to the nature of the state operating regionally. The state in Karnataka, for instance, is characterised as clientelist; hence here the farmers would be inclined to support a political party that offers more patron–client exchange. This is not true for Gujarat, which is less dependent on the state. New sources of accumulation for one class excluding the others have reduced the possibility of farmers supporting any one political party as a voting bloc. The other crucial factor to consider in the 2024 elections is regional variation. The political irrelevance of the agrarian tiller class (small and semi-medium farmers) was quite undemocratic but farmer movements since 2018 have been actively working to mobilise them and the success of their mobilisation was witnessed in the 2020–21 farmer protests in India, dominated by the north but joined by farmers from other parts of India. In Poulantzas' categorisation, tiller farmers did not qualify as a class during 2004–14 but the 2024 elections may show tiller farmers are more capable of mobilising and acting politically, as Pattenden and Bansal predicts (2021), thus challenging such a categorisation. The agrarian proprietary class has reinstated itself as a class in the political settlement since 2004.

This can be inferred from the fact that the state apparatus is consistently pushing for a policy framework that is harming and disempowering the tiller farmers with little organised, political representation from these classes. Even those policies which are explicitly aimed for empowering marginalised castes and tribes like reservation in employment and PRIs tend to open up rent-seeking opportunities, thus fostering accumulation by a few who join a privileged class. I observed a number of middle farmers in local state institutions who accumulate from accessing state resources, and very few instances of tiller farmers, who are from SC and ST groups, gaining. Therefore, they would be unlikely to mobilise for caste empowerment; rather, the policy facilitates members of marginalised castes and tribes gain mobility (Rajasekhar et al. 2011).

The policy contributes another significant aspect to meet the demands of the dominant classes. Under the current policy regime with no other major change in circumstances, a number of tiller farmers would likely find it hard to sustain in agriculture, as pointed out by Chandra and Taghioff (2016); thus more land would likely become available for sale to meet the demand of capital. Despite diverse fractions within, all capitalists uniformly seek land. Agricultural policy is contributing towards creating a continuous supply of land crucial to satisfy the capitalist class.

Land policy and the emergence of the petty bourgeoisie

Land is integral to farmers, but it has become a necessity to the capitalists with the real estate boom in India. The issue of 'land acquisition', its illicit transactions, and partisan motive have been prominent in Indian debates since 2000. In 1995, both Gujarat and Karnataka amended their respective land acquisition policies to allow agricultural land to be used for non-agricultural purposes in the name of development. Conversion of agricultural land to non-agricultural and relaxing the ceiling on holding have aided strategic accumulation of land by the capitalists, an observation made by Sud (2007), Nair (1996), and Gowda (2009). The process has been underlined by displacement and dispossession of tiller farmers, stirring concern from activists, academics, journalists, and development professionals (Fernandes, 2014). The fieldwork findings are in agreement with the existing scholarly views that industrial capital has benefitted from such a policy shift. It, however, poses an ancillary question – is capital alone in cornering all profits?

Evidence confirmed that big farmers and, in a few instances, middle farmers are acting as intermediaries and accruing profit across the three states. Beyond the realm of formal transactions, land is transferred from a farmer to a capitalist or a political leader informally every day. The techniques used for this were found to be irreversible power of attorney, showing the transaction as a gift or using scare factors such as notification by the government, thereby forcing farmers to sell land to the available buyers and cheating the sellers, among others. These informal techniques require involvement of people from villages who know the owners of land, often small and marginal farmers, and have the confidence to carry out the transaction smoothly. However, following Poulantzas' arguments, those carrying out such transactions are operating outside the agrarian production and hence the appropriate classification would be new petty bourgeoisie rather than as middle or big farmers in these cases, given the preponderance of non-agricultural sources in their accumulation. This class is accumulating and reproducing itself by utilising opportunities created through the market such as land sale, agricultural input shops, and commission agencies, and has aligned itself to the interest of capitalists. The phenomenon has been observed by Levien (2011, 2012) in Rajasthan and by Rutten (1995) in Gujarat, although they have not been characterised as petty bourgeoisie.

Globalisation, through the careful act of state policies, has brought more actors within the circuit of capital. The evidence runs counter to the prescribed shrinking of the state in the era and the book argues this would have been impossible without an active role played by the state. For instance, one such group that has been newly inducted into the circuit is that of the elected leaders of *panchayat*s. Reservation policy has brought members from lower castes, often middle and small farmers, within the fold of beneficiaries at the district level. In this instance the state is adding a few members to the class structure. The new avenues of accumulation and fear of being penalised for not supporting the agenda of the state are the two factors that result in them giving their consent to a development project, thus smoothening the process of acquiring common property resources, for instance. This was observed with land acquisition of public land, grazing land, or forest land that requires a consent form PRI elected members. This was observed in Chhattisgarh and Gujarat. Karnataka presents the strongest case of rent-seeking opportunities at the level of local self-government. By benefitting from state resources, public funds accrue to these few elected members, hence affecting their class position. They no longer subscribe to caste empowerment or strive for it. This possibly explains the rise in the pool of landless labourers, as observed in Punjab (Singh and Bhogal, 2014), whose resources are being concentrated in the hands of the capitalist class or concentration of landholdings in Gujarat among big farmers. This process would not be as smooth without the support of the elected members of PRIs and other farmers with political connections. These new beneficiaries can be characterised as petty bourgeoisie accumulating from land transactions and state resources through corruption and taking large shares of public schemes such as the PDS and the MGNREGS. In the cases of Chhattisgarh and Gujarat, reservation has similarly absorbed members of OBC groups into the bureaucracy, given them access to state resources and included them in the operative political settlement. Expansion of the old petty bourgeois class was predominant in Karnataka. The new state in Chhattisgarh has recruited members from middle and big farmer classes (mainly OBCs, a few SCs) into the state bureaucracy, so an expansion of the old petty bourgeoisie has taken place here as well. Dependence on state resources for self-perpetuation is comparatively lower in Gujarat. Instead of caste empowerment, we have noted bolstering of the existing class structure through these policies.

New class within India: State creation and destruction

The methodology was to empirically locate fractions within the agrarian proprietary class in each state on field and then conceptually identify them.

This was key to developing an embedded understanding of the agrarian proprietary class and its fractions. Given varying contexts, the location and operations of the fractions displayed a wide variety across the states. The fraction of big farmers predominantly came from middle castes. They generated surplus from sources other than agriculture. The nature of classes has and still is undergoing transformation, especially since the 1990s. A new kind of class dynamic and consolidation was observed, breaking the binaries of rural and urban, agrarian and non-agrarian.

Capitalist farmers are present across all three states, but in Chhattisgarh they are regionally concentrated in western districts such as Durg and Bemetara, whereas the eastern districts have big farmers who continue to grow paddy and have been slow in adopting mechanised methods of cultivation. New seeds and technology have made some inroads, but it is far behind the other states. In Gujarat, big and medium farmers have assumed either capitalist farmer or merchant capital class identity. This was triggered by the success of the Green Revolution and widespread adoption of groundnut production and then Bt cotton. As data shows, since 2005, the percentage and number of large holdings have seen a rise in the state, pointing to the profitability of agriculture. In Chhattisgarh and Karnataka, the accumulation by capitalist farmers, both within and outside agriculture, has been augmented by their connection to political parties and the state. In Karnataka, sugarcane and areca nut are some of the commercial crops grown by the capitalist farmers while the last decade has also seen the wide adoption of technology-intensive floriculture and horticulture, targeting the export market. Therefore, the shift in cropping pattern has propelled agriculture towards the production of high-value crops. Thus, the agrarian sector has been receiving capital from other sectors and even other states. The high growth figure is due to the boost the sector has received from contributions of the gentleman farmers. Non-agrarian surplus is feeding the agricultural sector.

Big farmers, landlords, and some middle farmers who have access to political power no longer consider land and agriculture as central to their income, owing to avenues of diversification (Harriss-White, 2004, 2008; Lerche 2014). While Harriss-White's evidence was drawn from Tamil Nadu and West Bengal, similar findings emerged across the three states under scrutiny, albeit not uniformly. Even capitalist farmers were found to be keen to sell their land and make money in districts where mining, construction of airports, or industrial projects that require large tracts of land have taken place. But where high-value crops have taken roots with the availability of irrigation and farmers were earning well from the export market, there they were happy to remain in agriculture. Gujarat capitalist farmers exhibited a pride in agriculture that was mostly missing in Karnataka. Chhattisgarh fell in the middle with a mixed representation.

A confirmed conclusion is that big and capitalist farmers have diversified into various non-agrarian sectors in the globalisation era, thereby generating handsome surplus. The promise of agrarian policies to make the sector perform better has been achieved by reinstating the agrarian proprietary class and non-agrarian classes who have invested in high value crops and by supporting them to access market opportunities. As argued in the previous section, it is appropriate to classify them in Karnataka and Chhattisgarh as new petty bourgeoisie who have gathered capital but not invested in trade or industry. Gujarat is an exception where the surplus has been invested in trade; hence, a big finding is that rural does not overlap with agrarian as categories in India after 2000.

The policy of input-centricity and propagation of chemical inputs like hybrid seeds, pesticides, and fertilisers have curbed farmers' autonomy, coercing them to source inputs from the market – a phenomenon termed as 'accumulation by dispossession' by Kloppenburg (2010). More importantly, it necessitated the development of a channel between capital (private company) and tiller farmers, allowing the shopkeeper selling these products to gain from the process. He is a retailer while the company (capitalist) selling the products is a distant wholesaler. While the market has penetrated villages through these shops, many private companies were found employing agents from adjacent villages to go door-to-door to convince farmers to buy these products, resulting in higher consumption of chemical inputs. Demonstration effect is instrumental in commercial-crop farmers opting for expensive chemical inputs. Extension services, originally made available by the state, have seen a retreat since the mid-1990s, and this has made farmers more dependent on private companies as knowledge providers, rupturing farmer interest into exploited and exploiter.

Eminent scholars such as Partha Chatterjee (1997), Harold Gould (1995), and Atul Kohli (2004) argued that the ruling party in early decades after Independence did not build a new structure of power in the localities; rather, the method of gaining dominance was by adopting the existing dominant groups within the fold of their parties and government. The same does not currently explain the states under the BJP that are found to actively create its own allies. Evidence showed the state (particularly under the BJP, since all three states under study are predominantly ruled by one party) drafted policies to carefully recruit a few beneficiaries from the deprived classes and backward castes through primarily two channels, informal land transactions and reservation in the formal institution of PRI and bureaucracy. Consequently, this has fostered accumulation in the hands of a few middle farmers and small farmers whose class position has changed to petty bourgeoisie; owing to the new class position, they have shifted their allegiance to capitalists. They are situated in rural India but are perpetuating interests of the industrial capital by organising land transactions with small farmers on the former's behalf. They are instrumental in dispossessing other tiller farmers from their caste group. Their elected status as PRI representatives has allowed them access to state resources, accumulating through rent, adding a new source of wealth generation. Their election campaigns receive handsome donations from local contractors and political parties, as evidence showed. Hence, their rise to the petty bourgeois class serves the interest of capital by helping it to penetrate the rural market. The theoretical characterisation of Jessop (1983) that decentralisation will aid the process of capital's infiltration into the furthest corners of an economy has come alive in the present scenario which does not necessarily deepen democracy.

State over society or society over state?

This section answers the third question raised in the Introduction – what do we know about the nature of the state and its autonomy from proprietary classes? Chapters 4, 5, and 6 presented the distinctiveness of Chhattisgarh, Gujarat, and Karnataka, respectively, and highlighted several important regularities among them – similar objective and tenets in agricultural policy, capitalist farmers benefitting from such policies, interlocking of credit and factor markets, big farmers' diversification to secondary sources of accumulation, identifying beneficiaries in land transactions, and reservation policy fostering accumulation by members of marginalised caste and tribal groups who are tiller farmers. The discussion on these issues was initiated in Chapter 3 with a literature review and the following chapters built on those arguments with the empirical findings adding depth and breadth on several issues. Capitalists are uniformly found to be part of the political settlement and they drive policies by being the closest ally of the state (Chatterjee, 2008). But on the question of the nature of the state, Chhattisgarh is best characterised as a case of personal fusion with capitalists themselves assuming power as elected members. After 2000, fractions of the rural proprietary class became part of the political settlement, and are in a comfortable position to receive patronage and subsidies rather than being the decision-makers. They are happy to be benefitting even though they are relegated to the position of a secondary partner.

In Chhattisgarh the landlords are thriving through diversification into non-agrarian income sources and making their political claims by entering bureaucratic positions. Big farmers pursuing food crops are not the prime beneficiaries of agricultural policy but gain from reservation for OBCs in several instances. Therefore, the capitalist farmers are concentrated in the western districts. In Gujarat, the last decade has seen policies pushing high-value crops and mechanisation that has benefitted capitalist farmers. There are overlaps between the big capitalist farmers and merchant capital. Since the economy is in transition, these characters cannot be put in either of these categories exclusively. In furthering the interests of capital, the state is simultaneously paying attention to the other ally but way less than the big corporates belonging to the industrial capitalists like Reliance, Essar, and Adani. The state has been successful in instilling a sense of pride in capitalist agriculture, which is in line with the mercantile ethic that pervades Gujarat. In Karnataka the state is attending to patronage distribution and is not as focused as Gujarat towards productive investment. The pride in agriculture is dwindling. The capitalist farmers are among the beneficiaries of subsidies for high-value crops and so are the gentleman farmers. Coming from other sectors, gentleman farmers are attracted by high profit and high subsidies. The landlord class has maintained its control through bureaucratic positions and accesses rent through state power but aptly should be characterised as petty bourgeoisie. Corruption is widespread in the state. The rampant land acquisition has provided another source of accumulation for big and some middle farmers.

The relation with state officials at the district level has surfaced as a critical factor in enhancing access to surplus for the proprietary classes. Literature has shown that local state officials and merchants collude with each other to protect and enhance their interests (Harriss-White, 2004). Evidently, rich farmers have been co-opted at the local state level institutions in Uttar Pradesh (Jeffrey and Lerche, 2000). The beneficiaries are political brokers and economically powerful, richer farmers who exert control on state resources. Field interviews across states indicated that PRIs provide additional source of accumulation. Two key purposes are served by the PRI – distributing state patronage, thus, finding allies for capital among agrarian population who support the formal procedures of land acquisitions and allow social mobility among a few members of marginalised caste groups. A position in PRI means access to state resources, which alters the position of members from caste groups such as an OBC middle farmer to the old petty bourgeois class. Accessing the pool of land is a purpose served best in Gujarat where *panchayat* gives a no-objection certificate to land acquisition of common-property land. State resources continue to support the old petty bourgeoisie's sustenance and nurture it. Funds under the MGNREGS have contributed significantly in their perpetuation, particularly in Karnataka. Field evidence shows that not all beneficiaries are upper caste; instead, they hail from other middle and lower castes in all three states, an aspect that has also been pointed out by some scholars already (Pattenden, 2005; Rajasekhar et al., 2011). Thus, it is affirmed that the state has, by a careful manoeuvring, succeeded in including members from OBC, SC, and ST into the circuit of capital. Hence, paying attention to both caste and class emerges as important to understanding and analysing Indian politics.

As far as political lobbying is concerned, a change in the dominant lobbies was observed in Gujarat from diamond, textile, and oil to real estate and chemical/gas; it emerged that Gujarat has also experienced a shift from small to big corporates dominating the economic scene. In Karnataka, the shift in dominance was from education and IT to mining and real estate. Chhattisgarh, since its formation, has been dominated by mining, cement, and real estate. Despite these shifts in influential lobbies, what remains undisputed is the dominance of capital, as Chatterjee (2008) pointed out, and the all-pervasiveness of the interest of these classes in 'land'. So, for a state that has the capitalist class as the most dominant member in the political settlement, it is imperative to ensure the access and supply of land. How does the state ensure that? Case studies show agrarian policies are playing a significant role in coercing those who solely contribute labour, like tiller farmers, out of self-cultivation.

A close nexus between capitalists and the state (bureaucracy and political leaders) was noted across states, with several instances of the two classes interchanging their positions. If this is considered to be the most dominant aspect of the relationship between the state and the agrarian classes, all three states provided some variation. Despite commonality, each state presented a different kind of relationship. Chhattisgarh is best characterised as a case of 'personal fusion' as Jessop (1983) and Miliband (1969) had argued. This is owing to the absence of both land reforms and Green Revolution in the state, such that big farmers are not in a position to pose any formidable challenge to other classes. Surplus from agriculture is not feeding industrialisation.

Gujarat is a case of relative autonomy, which Poulantzas wrote about, where the state is perceived as having a separate entity from capital, thanks to the language of market adopted by state officials and leaders. Within the state though, evidence of grand corruption was recently detected (Bussell, 2012); it shows rent collection is widespread by the bureaucracy and leaders. However, undeniably, Gujarat is the strongest state among the three. It can be ascribed to the mature nature of Gujarat's economy where the capitalists prefer growing through market opportunities rather than thriving on state resources, precisely the sentiment the BJP has thrived upon. The state in this case plays a supportive function of providing the infrastructure like policy, roads, and power for such rapid economic growth to be possible (Sood, 2012). Karnataka has a clientelist state, a feature Mushtaq Khan (2005) characterises South Asia with, where state patronage is almost imperative for economic accumulation. Admittedly, instances of patron–client relation and personal fusion at the district level were observed across the states but nowhere near the level of Karnataka. The state has been most welcoming to foreign capital in all sectors.

In their recent work, Harriss, Corbridge, and Jeffrey (2012) acknowledged the shift of the Indian state towards the business class or 'elite'. Chatterjee (2008) finds the capitalist class as hegemonic. They mention that 'greater costs of participating in India's competitive politics led a growing number of politicians to finance their campaigns illegally' (ibid: 15–16). Capitalists funding elections as party donations or contesting elections were noted across interviews. *Karnataka Election Watch* (ADR, 2008, 2013) finds elections were increasingly contested by the millionaires who could spend 'big'. The money is spent not just on elaborate campaigns and air travels but also to dole out things like cash and blankets to voters (ADR, 2008).

Kohli (2009) characterizes the Indian state as pro-business and not pro-market after 2000, a shift from his state-above-society position in his earlier works (1990, 2004). The two main positions that emerged in the literature review are of 'state over society' and 'state partnering social actors'. Fieldwork findings indicate that class has become so integral to the state through connections with political parties, taking party membership, funding elections, and capitalists' direct assumption of political power that the boundary between the state and society has become more permeable than ever. Judged on the evidence relating to agrarian policies and land policies, the state does not reign over social forces in India. In this field at least, the present scenario is one where those wielding socio-economic power exerts tremendous control on the state apparatus at different levels.

This answers the fourth question raised in the Introduction – whether policies of liberalisation and privatisation have expanded farmers' playing field to urban areas or has it been further limited to the rural area. Fieldwork led to the conclusion that the classic rural–urban divide, which scholars such as Atul Kohli (2012) have upheld, would not amount to an accurate portrayal of contemporary Indian politics and society. Rather, portrayal by scholars like Dipankar Gupta (2015) and Jens Lerche (2014) depict the reality. Gupta sheds some light on the closing gap between the categories of rural and urban, coining the term 'rurban'. Beneficiaries of neoliberal globalisation policies are present as much in the rural context as in the urban. In fact, the passage between the state at the district level and the regional state (state capitals) is controlled by the proprietary classes who have access to both, and who, in the garb of private players, have accumulated and managed to reclaim their political relevance since 2000. Their playing field has been extended to urban India. This finds support in Khan's (2005) notion of the petty bourgeoisie that is constituted of college and university graduates and middle and big peasants. They act as agents for political parties, as political entrepreneurs, who lead both organised and informal politics. Analysis of evidence suggests the fact that this class is constituted of members from middle and big farmers, input shop owners who may also be traders or big farmers, white collar professionals, and the bureaucracy. Another factor that has closed the gap between rural and urban is the interest of gentleman farmers in high-value crops, bringing in capital from other sectors into agriculture. It may contribute to the growth but not driven by tiller farmers.

Concluding remarks

The relevance of state–class as a frame has been demonstrated where evidence pointed at class as an important consideration in how the state formulates policies and how classes influence policy making. Class definitionally is as much determined by political and ideological relations as economic relations (Poulantzas, 1973). To realise their economic aspirations, proprietary classes have come to occupy political positions and they directly/indirectly influence different institutions of state, which makes it peculiar to the context. Hence globalisation has not evened out pre-existing structures, nor erased the role of the state, which reasserts the relevance of this study of particular states, state–class relation, and the nature of the state.

The other critical inference pertains to agrarian structures. It is a widely held view that peasants are losing out entirely under the neoliberal policies. The peasant–globalisation dichotomy (McMichael, 1997, 2008; Patnaik, 2006) is the most preponderant, such that differentiation within rural classes do not matter and all peasants are set to lose with the expansion of corporates' hold on agriculture. The book agrees about the severity of the agrarian crisis, but points at the few fractions of the agrarian class who have accumulated in the era between 2004 and 2014. To that extent, the inequality within agrarian India has grown, making the crisis worse for those who lose access to means of production and state support.

This has put 'farmer', as a category, in a state of flux with the advent of new avenues of diversification and means of accumulation. Certain classes of farmers are on a path to getting transformed into petty bourgeoisie and others into capitalists depending on their location and beginning point. Professionals and corporates are taking to farming and joining the category of gentlemen farmers. Both market and the state are providing the new means of accumulation. A kind of polarisation of agrarian classes has set in – those acquiring more capital in the neoliberal era have more sources of surplus from agricultural and non-agricultural sources, particularly in the post-2004 policy regime, and those on the labour side losing their landholdings due to the high cost of cultivation, informalisation of credit, lack of water, and high demand for land, making class differences an important consideration to comprehend agrarian India. The mention of such polarisation can be found in Lerche's writing (2013). This process is aided by the state that has provided extra sources to the capital-owning classes by creating opportunities of diversification. The policy thrust on elite crops for the sake of generating agricultural growth has led to competition between the two classes and thereby alienation of the tiller farmer from land. State does not lose its significance; instead, it makes a comeback in a distinct role. The state has reinstated big farmers and capitalist farmers into the political settlement. The other class, the petty bourgeoisie, in the settlement, however, is created by both the state and the market, which allows them access to thrive on non-agricultural income like private input trade, sale of machinery, rent on machinery and irrigation, and state resources.

I argue that Bardhan's three dominant proprietary classes do not exist as exclusive classes in new India but in fact have a set of overlapping interests and are no longer antagonistic to one another. Privatisation of inputs and demand for land have brought these three classes closer in interest.

Extending the playing field of the industrial capitalist and the professional class to high-value agriculture and of big/capitalist farmers into private inputs and land transactions have drawn them closer. The circuit of capital has widened, creating more opportunities for the proprietary classes, and the gap between the rural and the urban have narrowed in the process, with the classes straddling multiple productive sectors. Mitra (1977) remains relevant as his idea that political power is a tool to shift assets in favour of classes comes alive. A class of petty bourgeoisie has been crafted out of state policy, as evident across states. Predictions by Poulantzas (1998) and Jessop (1983) fit into India after liberalisation. Class takes on a political route to secure economic gains. Penetration of capital in distant corners of rural India has been aided by decentralisation as a policy. Picking allies and including them in the petty bourgeoisie has been observed across states.

Finally, capitalism does not work from a distance without touching structures. It mitigates old structures, negotiates with existing classes, and creates new classes and fractions to extract surplus. Evidence from all three states showed class differentiation within the agrarian capitalist class. The process requires the state to help at every step, as the case on India confirms. The state is using old structures and carefully creating new ones to smoothen the process of capitalist penetration in the furthest corners of the country.

Post-liberalisation India has seen two fractions emerge within the petty bourgeoisie, the new and the old. The former has been consolidated by rapid urbanisation, a real estate boom, global investments, and the IT boom. The latter is aided by retailing in agricultural inputs and machinery, land acquisition, mining, etc. Corruption has contributed to the sustenance of the old petty bourgeoisie and kept the rent coming in. The consolidation of these fractions has very much touched the agrarian classes since the processes of consolidation cut across rural and urban India. While undoubtedly the agrarian crisis persists, the agrarian proprietary classes have escaped its clutches aided by the state, especially after 2004, leaving the mass of tiller farmers to face monoculture, loss of food sovereignty, heightened food insecurity, dispossession, and dwindling employment opportunities due to quick mechanisation of agriculture (Chandra and Taghioff, 2016).

Politically, this polarisation poses a challenge to mobilise the farmer interest for the 2024 elections; additionally, given the differentiation within the agrarian proprietary class into several fractions with interests cutting across urban and rural India, they would likely find it hard to align themselves with rural India alone if they think it erodes new opportunities in the non-agrarian sector.

Under these circumstances, the burden of mobilising and representing the farmer interest will fall on those who have been hurt by the agrarian crisis the most and attacked by the 2020 farm laws the most (Pattenden and Bansal, 2021). The factor of how a fraction accumulates is linked to the nature of the state which will also play a pivotal role in their political position. Members of a clientelist state will vote differently from those operating under a state categorised by relative autonomy in response to the three farm laws. Dependence on the state to accumulate will mean a greater tendency to support the state, which can continue with clientelism, rather than a shift to market forces. The two dominant scholarly positions are both shown to be inadequate through the findings.

The scholarly position that globalisaton has reduced the need to look into state–society relations since a kind of homogeneity of policies has been imposed by the global institutions is found to be not entirely correct; in fact we noted discontinuous policies before and after 2004 and variation across the regional states which suggest the state still retains power. One notable conclusion about the state as seen after the loss of the NDA in 2004 is that the state not only adopts existing structures but also alters them by bringing in new members into classes, even by caste-based policies. Hence certain classes gain more than others. Thus the second scholarly position that the agrarian crisis has uniformly unfolded in India is also found to be inadequate. The state uses specific policies to spread its reach to marginalised social groups and recruit members from these castes into a better class position, simultaneously accessing resources from the remotest corners. Such a process of spread of capitalism being associated with decentralisation in rural areas was predicted by Bob Jessop (1983).

The victory of the BJP in these regional states and then in the 2014 national election bore testimony to how the promise of rapid development had to be extended to the rural voters. To this extent, paying attention to regional politics would be crucial to predicting the outcome of the 2024 elections. If we recall the anti-globalisation protests, the farmers headed by the KRRS in Karnataka had a very different stance from those under the BKS in Gujarat. The state has created robust changes in the structure and amidst these structures, the state stands firmly. Agrarian policy and the other three policies meant for caste groups have been at the core of this transformation. Consequently, the three proprietary classes are no longer antagonistic but in alliance, even have shared interest, for the common purpose of accumulation. The three classes in the political settlement have accumulated unduly through policies and often from multiple sources, thereby excluding the others more effectively, setting India on a most unequal path of development. Those who have gained or stand to gain from such a path are unlikely to band together against the state which has fed them. Mobilising for a farmer movement is one thing; however, it is quite different from a general election where class and caste matter much more than the identity of a farmer.

Notes

1. In our later work, we have referred to them as nouveau riche rural capitalist (Das Gupta and Mehrotra, 2021), especially since this class has a prominent presence of women; hence the earlier term misrepresents the reality.
2. Middle farmers can also fall in the category depending on their political connection.

Bibliography

Aga, Aniket. 2018. 'Merchants of knowledge: Petty retail and differentiation without consolidation among farmers in Maharashtra, India.' *Journal of Agrarian Change* 18: 658–676.

Agricultural Policy of Karnataka. 2006. Bangalore: Government of Karnataka.

Agriculture Census 2010-2011: All India Report on Number and Area of Operational Holdings. 2014. Government of India. Accessed July 2018. Available at http://agcensus.nic.in/document/agcensus2010/agcen2010rep.htm.

Alagh, Yoginder K. 1988. 'Pesticides in Indian Agriculture.' *Economic and Political Weekly* 23(38): 1959–1961, 1963–1964.

———. 2004. *State of the Indian Farmer: A Millennium Study* . New Delhi: Academic Foundation.

Amin, Samir. 2011. 'India, a Great Power?' *Monthly Review* 56(9). Accessed July 2019. Available at https://monthlyreview.org/2005/02/01/india-a-great-power/.

Anand, I., A. Banerjee, and A. Dasgupta. 2021. 'How to Define a Farmer.' *Indian Express*. Accessed January 2022. Available at https://indianexpress.com/article/opinion/columns opinion /farmers-protest-india-farm-laws-7607697/.

Anupama, Saxena and Praveen Rai. 2009. 'Chhattisgarh: An Emphatic Win for the BJP.' *Economic and Political Weekly* 44(39): 125–127.

Arjjumend, Hasrat. 2001. 'Drilling of Rice Bowl and Conservation of Seeds: Response of Peasant Society to Globalisation of Agriculture in Chhattisgarh.' *Leisa India* 2(2): 18–19.

Assadi, Muzaffar. 1995. 'Karnataka's New Agricultural Policy: Making Way for Corporate Landlordism.' *Economic and Political Weekly* 30(52): 3340–3342.

———. 1997. *Peasant Movement in Karnataka* 1980–1994. Delhi: Shipra.

———. 2000. 'Seed Tribunal: Interrogating Farmers' Suicides.' *Economic and Political Weekly* 35(43-44): 3808–3810.

———. 2006. 'Karnataka: The Muted Anti-Reservation Agitation.' *Economic and Political Weekly* 41(29): 3146–3150.

———. 2008. 'Farmers' Suicide in India: Agrarian Crisis, Path of Development and Politics in Karnataka.' *La Via Campesina*, 13 November. Accessed July 2019. Available at http://viacampesina.net/downloads/PDF/Farmers_suicide_in_india%283%29.pdf.

———. 2010. 'Path of Development and Farmers' Suicide.' In *Agrarian Crisis and Farmer Suicide*, edited by Ram S. Deshpande and Saroja Arora, 94–117. London, New Delhi: Sage Publications.

Assadi, Muzaffar and S. Rajendran. 2000. 'Changing Shape of Caste Conflict.' *Economic and Political Weekly* 35(19): 1610–1612.

Assayag, Jackie. 2005. 'Seeds of Wrath: Agriculture, Biotechnology and Globalization.' In *Globalizing India: Perspectives from Below,* edited by Jackie Assayag and Chris Fuller, 65–88. London: Anthem Press.

Association for Democratic Reforms (ADR). 2008. 'Criminal and Financial Background of MLAs and Candidates 2008 Assembly Elections.' *Karnataka Election Watch.* Accessed 12 March 2015. Available at www.adrindia.org.

———. 2012. *Gujarat Election Watch 2012: Analysis of Criminal, Financial and Other Details including Election Expenditure of MLAs and Contesting Candidates from Gujarat.* New Delhi.

———. 2013. *Karnataka Assembly Elections 2013: Analysis of Financial, Criminal Background and Other Details of Newly Elected MLAs in the Chhattisgarh Assembly Elections.* New Delhi.

Aubron, Claire, Hugo Lehoux, and Corentin Lucas. 2015. 'Poverty and Inequality in Rural India: Reflections Based on Two Agrarian System Analyses in the State of Gujarat.' *EchoGeo.* Accessed June 2015. Available at https://echogeo.revues.org/14300?lang=en.

Awasthi, Dinesh N. 2000. 'Recent Changes in Gujarat Industry: Issues and Evidence.' *Economic and Political Weekly* 35(35–36): 3183–3187, 3189–3192.

Aziz, Abdul and Sudhir Krishna. 1997. *Land Reforms in India: Karnataka: Promises Kept and Missed.* New Delhi: Sage Publications.

Bagchi, Amiya. 2005. 'Rural Credit and Systemic Risk.' In *Financial Liberalisation and Rural Credit in India,* edited by V.K. Ramchandran and Madhura Swaminathan, 39–50. New Delhi: Tulika Books.

Bahree, Megha. 2014. 'Doing Big Business in Modi's Gujarat.' *Forbes India,* 12 March. Accessed July 2019. Available at http://www.forbes.com/sites/meghabahree/2014/03/12/doing-big-business-in-modis-gujarat/3/.

Bailey, Alison. 2017. 'Tracking Privilege-preserving Epistemic Pushback in Feminist and Critical Race Philosophy Classes.' *Hypatia* 32(4): 876–892.

Baka, Jennifer. 2013. 'The Political Construction of Wasteland: Governmentality, Land Acquisition and Social Inequality in South India.' *Development and Change* 44(2): 409–428.

Balan, Premal. 2013. 'Gujarat HC Notice to Adani Power over Chinese Colony.' *Business Standard.* Accessed 20 June 2013. Available at http://www.business-standard.com/article/current-affairs/gujarat-hc-notice-to-adani-power-over-chinese-colony-113062000677_1.html.

Balasubramanian, V. 2012. 'Land Grabbing in Karnataka: Need for Protection of Commons with Innovations.' Centre for Innovations in Public Systems. Accessed July 2019. Available at http://www.cips.org.in/public-sector-systems-government-innovations/documents/land_grabbing_in_karnataka.pdf.

Banaji, Jairus. 1994. 'The Farmers' Movements: A Critique of Conservative Rural Coalitions.' *Journal of Peasant Studies* 21(3–4): 228–245.

Banerjee, Arindam. 2011 'The Impact of Neo-liberal Policy on Indian Peasantry.' South South Forum on Sustainability, Lingnan University, Tuen Mun, Hong Kong, 12–14 December.

Bardhan, Pranab. 1984. *The Political Economy of Development in India.* New Delhi: Oxford University Press.

———. 1998. *The Political Economy of Development in India.* Expanded edition. New Delhi: Oxford University Press.

————. 2002. 'Decentralization of Governance and Development.' *Journal of Economic Perspectives* 16(4): 185–206.

Barrow, Clyde W. 2000. 'The Marx Problem in Marxian State Theory.' *Science and Society* 64(1): 87–118.

Basant, Rakesh. 1994. 'Economic Diversification in Rural Areas: Review of Processes with Special Reference to Gujarat.' *Economic and Political Weekly* 29(39): A107–A116.

Basu, Priya. 2005. 'A Financial System for India's Poor.' *Economic and Political Weekly* 40(37): 4008–4012.

Bernstein, Henry. 2010. *Class Dynamics of Agrarian Change.* Halifax, NS, and Sterling, VA: Fernwood Publishing and Kumarian Press.

Berthet, Samuel and Girish Kumar, eds. 2011. *New States for a New India: Federalism and Decentralization in the States of Jharkhand and Chhattisgarh.* New Delhi: Manohar Publishers.

Bharwada, Charul and Vinay Mahajan. 2006. 'Quiet Transfer of Commons.' *Economic and Political Weekly* 41(4): 313–315.

Bhatia, Bela and Jean Drèze. 2006. 'Employment Guarantee in Jharkhand: Ground Realities.' *Economic and Political Weekly* 41(29): 3198–3202.

Bhatia, Kiran and B.G. Banerjee. 1988. *Tribal Demography of the Gonds.* New Delhi: Gyan Publishing House.

Bhatt, Himansshu. 2013. 'South Gujarat Units to Hike Sugarcane Procurement Price.' *Times of India*, 11 September. Accessed 22 January 2014. Available at http://timesofindia.indiatimes.com/city/surat/South-Gujarat-units-to-hike-sugarcane-procurement-price/articleshow/22475367.cms.

Bhaumik, Sankar K. 2008. *Reforming Indian Agriculture: Towards Employment Generation and Poverty Reduction: Essays in Honour of G.K. Chadha.* New Delhi: Sage Publications.

Birner, Regina, Surupa Gupta, and Neeru Sharma. 2011. *The Political Economy of Agricultural Policy Reform in India: Fertilizers and Electricity for Irrigation.* Washington DC: International Food Policy Research Institute. DOI: 10.2499/9780896291720.

Bose, Nilav and Sanjeev Mehra. 2012. 'Beyond the Rosy Picture.' *Business Today.* 15 April. Accessed 16 August 2014. Available at http://businesstoday.intoday.in/story/karuturi-global-challenges-ram-karuturiagriculture/1/23499.html.

Bose, Prasenjit. 2006. 'Liberalisation with a Human Face: An Oxymoron.' *Economic and Political Weekly* 41(23): 2297–2301.

Brass, Paul. 1994. 'The Politics of India since Independence.' In *The New Cambridge History of India*, Volume IV: I, edited by Paul R. Brass, 403. Second edition. Cambridge: Cambridge University Press.

Breman, Jan. 1985. 'Between Accumulation and Immiseration: The Partiality of Fieldwork in Rural India.' *Journal of Peasant Studies* 13(1): 5–36.

————. 1989. 'Agrarian Change and Class Conflict in Gujarat, India.' *Population and Development Review, Supplement – Rural Development and Population: Institutions and Policy* 15: 301–323.

———. 1993. *Beyond Patronage and Exploitation: Changing Agrarian Relations in South Gujarat*. Delhi: Oxford University Press.

———. 2007. *The Poverty Regime in Village India* . New Delhi: Oxford University Press.

Bunsha, Dionne. 2007. 'Farmers Are Dying in Gujarat Too.' *Frontline* 24(11).

Business Standard. 2003. 'JPC Not to Probe Judeo Case: PM.' 12 December. Accessed 3 December 2011. Available at http://www.business-standard.com/article/economy-policy/jpc-not-to-probe-judeo-case-pm-103121201053_1.html.

———. 2014. 'Chhattisgarh Hikes Subsidy for Drip Irrigation.' 24 August. Accessed July 2019. Available at http://www.business-standard.com/article/economy-policy/chhattisgarh-hikes-subsidy-for-drip-irrigation-114082400798_1.html.

Bussell, Jennifer. 2012. *Corruption and Reform in India: Public Services in the Digital Age*. New York: Cambridge University Press.

Byres, Terence J. 1981. 'The New Technology, Class Formation and Class Action in the Indian Countryside.' *Journal of Peasant Studies* 8(4): 405–454.

———, ed. 1997. *State, Development Planning and Liberalisation in India*. Delhi: Oxford University Press.

———. 1998. 'State, Class and Development Planning in India.' In *The State, Development Planning and Liberalisation in India*, edited by Terence J. Byres, 36–81. New Delhi: Oxford University Press.

Chadda, Maya. 2012. 'India in 2011: The State Encounters the People.' *Asian Survey* 52(1): 114–129.

Chakrabarti, Saumya and Anirban Kundu. 2009. 'Rural Non-Farm Economy: A Note on the Impact of Crop-Diversification and Land-Conversion in India.' *Economic and Political Weekly* 44(12): 69–75.

Chancel, L.., T. Piketty, E. Saez, G. Zucman, et al. 2022. *World Inequality Report, 2022*. Paris: World Inequality Lad. Accessed on 25 May 2023. Available at https://wir2022.wid.world/.

Chandra, Uday and Daniel Taghioff. 2016. *Staking Claims: The Politics of Social Movements in Contemporary Rural India*. New Delhi: Oxford University Press.

Chang, Ha-Joon. 2002. *Kicking Away the Ladder: Development Strategy in Historical Perspective*. London: Anthem Press.

Chatterjee, Partha. 1997. *State and Politics in India*. New Delhi: Oxford University Press.

———. 1998. *State and Politics in India*. New Delhi: Oxford University Press.

———. 2008. 'Democracy and Economic Transformation in India.' *Economic and Political Weekly* 43(16): 53–62.

Chattopadhyay, S. S. 2004. 'Saffronising the Tribal Heartland.' *Frontline* 21(6). Accessed 12 March 2014. Available at http://www.hindu.com/fline/fl2106/stories/20040326004601900.htm.

Chaudhury, Pradipta. 2004. 'The Creamy Layer.' *Economic and Political Weekly* 39(20): 1989–1991.

Chavan, Pallavi. 2007. 'Access to Bank Credit: Implications for Dalit Rural Households.' *Economic and Political Weekly* 42(31): 3219–3224.

———. 2011. 'Microfinance under Neoliberalism.' *Review of Agrarian Studies* 1(2). Accessed July–December 2011. Available at http://ras.org.in/microfinance_under_neoliberalism.

Chavan, Pallavi and R. Ramakumar. 2007. 'Revival of Agricultural Credit in the 2000s: An Explanation.' *Economic and Political Weekly* 42(52): 29.

Clay, Edward J. and Bernard B. Schaffer, eds. 1984. *Room for Manoeuvre: An Exploration of Public Policy in Agriculture and Rural Development.* London: Heinnemann Educational Books.

Cleaver, Harry M., Jr. 1972. 'The Contradictions of the Green Revolution.' *The American Economic Review* 62 (1/2): 177–186.

Cole, Shawn. 2009. 'Fixing Market Failures or Fixing Elections? Agricultural Credit in India.' *American Economic Journal: Applied Economics* 1(1): 219–250.

Corbridge, Stuart, John Harriss, and Craig Jeffrey. 2013. *India Today: Economy, Politics and Society.* Cambridge: Polity Press.

CPI(M). 2000. Available at http://cpim.org/content/party-programme.

Daily Bhaskar. 2012. 'Realtors Throw in Towel, Begin Distress Sale.' 3 April. Accessed 19 April 2013. Available at http://daily.bhaskar.com/article/GUJ-AHD-realtors-throw-in-towel-begin-distress-sale-3053129.html.

Daily News and Analysis (DNA). 2013. 'Why Big Business Strongly Favours Narendra Modi.' 18 April. Accessed 12 August 2013. Available at http://www.dnaindia.com/analysis/1823847/ column-why-big-business-strongly-favours-narendra-modi.

Damle, Chandrashekhara Bhat. 1989. 'Impact of Tenancy Legislation and Changing Agrarian Relations: A Case of Dakshina Kannada District, Karnataka.' *Social Scientist* 17(11–12): 83–97.

Damodaran, Harish. 2008. *India's New Capitalists: Caste, Business, and Industry in a Modern Nation.* Basingstoke: Palgrave Macmillan.

Damodaran, H. and S. Agarwal. 2021. 'Revealing India's Actual Farmer Population.' *Indian Express.* Accessed February 2022. Available at https://indianexpress.com/article/opinion/columns/revealing-indias-actual-farmer- population-7550159/.

Dand, Sejal A. and Sujoy Chakravarty. 2006. 'Food Insecurity in Gujarat: A Study of Two Rural Populations.' Accessed 3 June 2006. *Economic and Political Weekly* 41(22): 2248–2258.

Das Gupta, Sejuti. 2013. 'New Seed Policy as a Source of Oppression or Liberation? A Political Economy Perspective from Chhattisgarh Agriculture Post-1990.' *IFFCO Bulletin* 1: 36–48.

———. 2013. 'With Flowers and Capsicum in the Driver's Seat, Food Sovereignty is Impossible: A Comparison of the Politics of Agricultural Policy in Two Indian States, Gujarat and Chhattisgarh.' *Food Sovereignty: A Critical Dialogue.*

Das Gupta, Sejuti and Ishita Mehrotra. 2021. 'Who Is a farmer in India?' *Sikh Research Journal.* Accessed September 2022. Available at https://www.aqs.org.uk/who-is-a-farmer-in-india/.

Das Gupta, Sejuti, Ishita Mehrotra, and Aparajita Bakshi. 2022. 'Who Are Farmers in India After All? A Conceptual Exercise and a Policy Question.' *Sikh Research Journal* 7(1).

Das, S. K. 2005. 'Reforms and the Indian Administrative Service.' In *The Politics of Economic Reforms in India*, edited by Jos Mooij, 171–198. New Delhi: Sage Publications.

D'Costa, Anthony P. and Achin Chakraborty, eds. 2017. *The Land Question in India: State, Dispossession, and Capitalist Transition.* New Delhi: Oxford University Press.

Deshpande, Ram S. 2002. 'Suicide by Farmers in Karnataka: Agrarian Distress and Possible Alleviatory Steps.' *Economic and Political Weekly* 37(26): 2601–2610.

———. 2004. 'In the Name of the Farmer: Central and Karnataka State Budget, 2004–05.' *Economic and Political Weekly* 39(31): 3433–3434.

Deshpande, Ram S. and J. Prachitha. 2006. *Agricultural Policy in India: Towards a Policy Matrix in a Federal System.* Bangalore: Institute of Social and Economic Change.

Deshpande, Ram S. and M. Indira. 2010. 'Rainfed Agriculture in Karnataka.' In *Rainfed Agriculture in India: Perspectives and Challenges,* edited by Surjit Singh and M.S. Rathore. Jaipur: Rawat Publications.

Deshpande, Ram S. and Saroj Arora. 2011. *Agrarian Crisis and Farmer Suicides.* New Delhi: Sage Publications.

Deshpande, Ram S. and T. Raveendra Naika. 2002. *Impact of Minimum Support Prices on Agricultural Economy: A Study in Karnataka.* Bangalore: Institute of Social and Economic Change.

Deshpande, Ram S., M. J. Bhende, P. Thippaiah, and M. Vivekananda. 2004. *Crops and Cultivation, State of Indian Farmer: A Millennium Study.* New Delhi: Academic Foundation.

Dev, S. Mahendra. 2012. 'Small Farmers in India: Challenges and Opportunities.' Working Paper 2012–2014. Mumbai: Indira Gandhi Institute of Development Research. Accessed June 2012. Available at http://www.igidr.ac.in/pdf/publication/WP-2012-014.pdf

Development Channel. 2012. 'Karnataka Becomes Most Preferred Destination for Domestic investment.' Accessed 05 June 2012. Available at http://www.developmentchannel.org/development/economy/1519-karnataka-becomes-most-preferred-destination-for-domestic-investment.

Dholakia, Ravindra H. 2000. 'Liberalisation in Gujarat: Review of Recent Experience.' *Economic and Political Weekly* 35(35–36): 3121–3124.

Dholakia, Archana R. 2002. 'Non-Tax Revenue and Subsidies in Gujarat.' In *Dynamics of Development in Gujarat,* edited by Indira Hirway, Surendra P. Kashyap, and Amita Shah. New Delhi: Concept Publishing.

Di John, Jonathan and James Putzel. 2009. 'Political Settlements.' Governance and Social Development Resource Centre. Issues Paper. Accessed June 2009. Available at https://core.ac.uk/download/pdf/103642.pdf

Dixit, Anita K. 2008. 'Economic Growth and the Agricultural Sector in Gujarat.' PhD dissertation, Jawaharlal Nehru University, New Delhi.

———. 2009. 'Agriculture in a High Growth State: The Case of Gujarat (1960 to 2006).' *Economic and Political Weekly* 44(50): 64–71.

———. 2012. 'Agrarian Poverty, Nutrition and Economic Class – A Study of Gujarat, India.' *Journal of Agrarian Change* 13(2): 263–281.

Dubash, Navroz K. 2002. *Tubewell Capitalism: Groundwater Development and Agrarian Change in Gujarat.* New Delhi: Oxford University Press.

————. 2007. 'The Electricity-Groundwater Conundrum: Case for a Political Solution to a Political Problem.' *Economic and Political Weekly* 42(52): 45–55.

Economic and Political Weekly. 1988. 'Launching a Second Green Revolution.' 23(12): 560.

————. 1996. 'Congress versus Swatantra in Gujarat: District-by-District Analysis of Prospects.' 1(10): 398–403.

Engelshoven, Miranda. 1999. 'Diamonds and Patels: A Report on the Diamond Industry of Surat.' *Contributions to Indian Sociology* 33(1–2): 353–377.

Engineer, Asghar A. 2003. 'Assembly Elections: Good Tactics Pays.' *Economic and Political Weekly* 38(50): 5232–5235.

Fafchamps, Marcel. 1992. 'Cash Crop Production, Food Price Volatility, and Rural Market Integration in the Third World.' *American Journal of Agricultural Economics* 74(1): 90–99.

Fernandes, Walter. 1998. 'Development Induced Displacement in Eastern India.' In *Antiquity to Modernity in Tribal India: Volume I: Continuity and Change among Indian Tribals*, edited by Shyama C. Dube, 217–300. New Delhi: InterIndia Publications.

————. 2008. 'Sixty Years of Development-Induced Displacement in India.' In *India – Social Development Report Development and Displacement*, edited by Hari Mohan Mathur. New Delhi: Oxford University Press.

————. 2011. 'Land as Livelihood vs Land as Commodity.' *Infochange Agenda.* Accessed 30 March 2014. Available at http://www.indiawaterportal.org/articles/battles-over-land-land-commodity-and-land-livelihoods-special-issue-infochange.

————. 2014. 'Land as livelihood vs Land as Commodity.' Infochange Agenda, Accessed 30 March 2014. http://www.infochangeindia.org/agenda/battles-over-land/land-as-livelihood-vs-land-as-commodity.html.

Frankel, Francine R. 2005. *India's Political Economy, 1947–2004: The Gradual Revolution* New Delhi: Oxford University Press.

Fuller, Christopher and Jackie Assayag, eds. 2005. *Globalizing India: Perspectives From Below. Anthem South Asian Studies.* London: Anthem Press.

Geertz, A. Clifford. 1973. *The Interpretation of Cultures: Selected Essays.* New York: Basic Books.

Gerring, John. 2004. 'What Is a Case Study and What Is It Good For.' *The American Political Science Review* 98(2): 341–352.

Ghosh, Jayati. 2005a. 'The Political Economy of Farmers' Suicides in India.' *Macroscan.* Accessed 10 August 2012. Available at http://www.macroscan.com/fet/dec05/pdf/freedom_hunger.pdf.

————. 2005b. 'Trade Liberalization in Agriculture. An Examination of Impact and Policy Strategies with Special Reference to India.' *Human Development Reports.* Accessed July 2019. Available at http://hdr.undp.org/en/content/trade-liberalization-agriculture.

Gill, Anita. 2004. 'Interlinked Agrarian Credit Markets: Case Study of Punjab.' *Economic and Political Weekly* 39(33): 3741–3751.

Glover, Dominic. 2010. 'Is BT Cotton a Pro-Poor Technology? A Review and Critique of the Empirical Record.' *Journal of Agrarian Change* 10(4): 482–509.

————. 2012. 'Biotechnology and Agricultural Development.' Review of *Biotechnology and Agricultural Development: Transgenic Cotton, Rural Institutions and Resource-Poor Farmers*, edited by Robert Tripp. *Journal of Agrarian Change* 12(4): 616–619.

Golait, Ramesh. 2007. 'Current Issues in Agriculture Credit in India: An Assessment.' *Reserve Bank of India Occasional Papers* 28(1): 78–100.

Government of Chhattisgarh (GoC). 2012. 'Irrigation Potential'. Available at http://www.cgwrd.in/organisation/activities/irrigation-potential.html.

Government of Gujarat (GoG). 2011. *Summit 2011*. Government of Gujarat. Accessed July 2019. Available at http://www.vibrantgujarat.com/food-agro.htm.

Government of India (GoI). 2012. *Indian Seed Sector*. Government of India. Accessed 22 December 2012. Available at http://seednet.gov.in/material/IndianSeedSector.htm.

Government of Karnataka (GoK). 2003. *The Millennium Biotech Policy*. Bangalore: Government of Karnataka.

———. 2012a. *Annual Report 2012–2013*. Bangalore: Government of Karnataka.

———. 2012b. *Twelfth Five Year Plan*. Bangalore: Government of Karnataka.

Gould, Harold A. 1995. *Grass Roots Politics in India: Century of Political Evolution in Faizabad District*. New Delhi: Oxford and IBH.

Gowda, M.V. Srinivasa. 2009. 'High Tech Floriculture in Karnataka.' Department of Economic Analysis and Research, National Bank for Agriculture and Rural Development. Occasional Paper 49.

Grossman, Nick and Dylan Carlson. 2011. 'Agriculture Policy in India: The Role of Input Subsidies.' United States International Trade Commission Executive Briefings on Trade. Accessed July 2019. Available at https://www.usitc.gov/publications/332/EBOT_IndiaAgSubsidies.pdf

Gudavarthy, Ajay. 2019. *India After Modi*. New Delhi: Bloomsbury.

Guha, Ramachandra. 2010. 'Unacknowledged Victims.' *Outlook*. Accessed 08 October 2013. Available at http://www.outlookindia.com/article/Unacknowledged-Victims/265069

Guillen, Mauro F. 2001. 'Is Globalization Civilizing, Destructive or Feeble? A Critique of Five Key Debates in the Social Science Literature.' *Annual Review of Sociology* 27(1): 235–260.

Guion, Lisa A., David C. Diehl, and Debra McDonald. 2011. 'Triangulation: Establishing the Validity of Qualitative Studies.' Institute of Food and Agricultural Sciences. Florida: University of Florida. Accessed July 2019. Available at https://sites.duke.edu/niou/files/2014/07/W13-Guion-2002-Triangulation-Establishing-the-Validity-of-Qualitative-Research.pdf.

Gujarat Agrovision 2010: Action Plan. 2010. Department of Agriculture Cooperation and Farmers Welfare: Government of Gujarat. Accessed 30 July 2012.

Gulati, Ashok. 1988. 'Effective Incentives and Subsidies for Groundnut Cultivators in India.' *Economic and Political Weekly* 23 (52–53): A157–A162.

Gulati, Ashok and Anil Sharma. 1995. 'Subsidy Syndrome in Indian Agriculture.' *Economic and Political Weekly* 30(39): A93–A102.

Gupta, Akhil. 1989. 'The Political Economy of Post-Independence India – A Review Article: The Political Economy of Development in India by Pranab Bardhan.' *The Journal of Asian Studies* 48(4): 787–797.

———. 1998. *Postcolonial Developments: Agriculture in the Making of Modern India*. Durham: Duke University Press.

———. 2008. 'Modified Yarn.' *Outlook Business*. Accessed 15 September 2010. Accessed July 2019. Available at http//business.outlookindia.com/newolb/article.aspx?ioi597.

Gupta, Dipankar. 2005. 'Whither the Indian Village? Culture and Agriculture in "Rural" India.' *Review of Development and Change* 10(1): 1–20.

———. 2015. 'Tracking Changes in a Traditional Setting: The Importance of Being Rurban.' *Economic and Political Weekly* 50(24): 37–43.

Hardiman, David. 1998. 'Well Irrigation in Gujarat: Systems of Use, Hierarchies of Control.' *Economic and Political Weekly* 33(25): 1533–1544.

Harriss, John. 1999. 'Comparing Political Regimes Across Indian States: A Preliminary Essay.' *Economic and Political Weekly* 34(48): 3367–3377.

Harriss, John, Stuart Corbridge, and Craig Jeffrey. 2012. *India Today: Economy, Politics and Society*. Cambridge: Polity Press.

Harriss-White, Barbara. 1996. *A Political Economy of Agricultural Markets in South India: Masters of the Countryside*. London: Sage Publication.

———. 2002. 'Development, Policy and Agriculture in India in the 1990s.' Queen Elizabeth House. Working paper no. 78. Accessed July 2019. Available at http://www3.qeh.ox.ac.uk/RePEc/qeh/qehwps/qehwps78.pdf.

———. 2003. *India Working: Essays on Society and Economy*. Delhi: Cambridge University Press.

———. 2008. *Rural Commercial Capital: Agricultural Markets in West Bengal*. New Delhi: Oxford University Press.

Harriss-White, Barbara and S. Janakarajan. 2004. *Rural India Facing the 21st Century: Essays on Long Term Village Change and Recent Development Policy*. London: Anthem Press.

Harvey, David. 2009. 'The "New" Imperialism: Accumulation by Dispossession.' *Socialist Register* 40: 63–87.

Headlines Today. 2011. 'Mining Scam: Karnataka Lokayukta Santosh Hedge Submits Report, Indicts Yeddyurappa and Reddy Brothers.' 27 July. Accessed 4 March 2014. Available at http://indiatoday.intoday.in/story/karnataka-lokayukta-report-on-mining-scam-submitted/1/146274.html.

Hensman, Rohini. 2014. 'The Gujarat Model of Development: What Would It Do to the Indian Economy?' *Economic and Political Weekly* 49(11). Accessed 15 March 2014. Available at http://www.epw.in/journal/2014/11/reports-states-web-exclusives/gujarat-model-development.html.

Herring, Ronald J. 1999. 'Embedded Particularism: India's Failed Developmental State.' In *The Developmental State*, edited by Meredith Woo-Cummings, 306–307. New York: Cornell University Press.

———. 2005. 'Miracle Seeds, Suicide Seeds and the Poor: GMOs, NGOs, Farmers and the State.' In *Social Movements in India: Poverty, Power, and Politics*, edited by Mary Fainsod Katzenstein and Raka Ray, 203–232. Lanham, MD: Rowman and Littlefield.

———. 2008. 'Opposition to Transgenic Technologies: Ideology, Interests, and Collective Action Frames.' *Nature Reviews Genetics* 9: 458–463.

Hirway, Indira. 2000. 'Dynamics of Development in Gujarat: Some Issues.' *Economic and Political Weekly* 35 (35/36): 3106–3120.

———. 2012. 'Gujarat "Growth Story": A Distorted Model Which Promotes Crony Capitalism.' *Counterview*. Accessed 1 October 2012. Available at http://counterview.

org/2012/10/01/gujarat-growth-story-a-distorted-model-which-promotes-crony-capitalism/.

Hirway, Indira and Neha Shah. 2011a. 'Labour and Employment in Gujarat.' *Economic and Political Weekly* 46(44–45): 62–64.

———. 2011b. 'Labour and Employment Under Globalisation: The Case of Gujarat.' *Economic and Political Weekly* 46 (22): 57–65.

Hirway, Indira, Surendra P. Kashyap, and Amit Shah, eds. 2002. *Dynamics of Development in Gujarat.* Ahmedabad: Concept Publishing.

IBN Live. 2007. 'Polls Are New Business for Gujarat Industrialists.' 24 November. Accessed 1 March 2012. Available at http://ibnlive.in.com/news/polls-are-new-business-for-gujarat-industrialists/52935-3-2.html.

Iyer, Pushpa. 2017. 'The Politics of Muddled Waters in Gujarat: A Religious Nationalist Development Model's Treatment of Water.' In *The Politics of Fresh Water: Access, Conflict and Identity (Earthscan Studies in Water Resource Management)*, edited by Catherine M. Ashcraft and Tamar Mayer. New York: Routledge.

Jakobsen, Jostein. 2019. 'Neoliberalising the Food Regime "Amongst Its Others": The Right to Food and the State in India.' *The Journal of Peasant Studies* 46(6): 1219–1239.

Jaffrelot, Christophe. 1996. 'Interpreting Madhya Pradesh Voting Patterns.' *Economic and Political Weekly* 31(49): 3207–3208.

Jalal, Ayesha. 1995. *Democracy and Authoritarianism in South Asia.* Cambridge: Cambridge University Press.

Jan, Muhammad A. and Barbara Harriss-White. 2012. 'The Three Roles of Agricultural Markets: A Review of Ideas about Agricultural Commodity Markets in India.' *Economic and Political Weekly* 47(52): 39–52.

Janaiah, Aldas. 2002. 'Hybrid Rice for Indian Farmers: Myths and Realities.' *Economic and Political Weekly* 37(42): 4319–4328.

Jayal, Niraja G. 1999. *Democracy and the State: Welfare, Secularism and Development in Contemporary India.* Delhi: Oxford University Press.

Jeffrey, Craig. 2001. 'A Fist Is Stronger than Five Fingers: Caste and Dominance in Rural North India.' *Transactions of the Institute of British Geographers* 26(2): 1–30.

———. 2002. 'Caste, Class, and Clientelism: A Political Economy of Everyday Corruption in Rural North India.' *Economic Geography* 78(1): 21–41.

Jeffrey Craig and Jens Lerche. 2000. 'Stating the Difference: State, Discourse and Class Reproduction in Uttar Pradesh, India.' *Development and Change* 31(4): 857–878.

———. 2001. 'Dimensions of Dominance: Class and State in Uttar Pradesh.' In *The Everyday State and Society in Modern India,* edited by Christopher J. Fuller and Veronique Benei, 91–114. London: Hurst.

Jeffrey, Craig, Patricia Jeffery, and Roger Jeffery. 2008. *Degrees Without Freedom? Education, Masculinities, and Unemployment in North India.* Stanford: Stanford University Press.

Jenkins, Rob. 2000. *Democratic Politics and Economic Reforms in India.* Cambridge: Cambridge University Press.

Jessop, Bob. 1983. *The Capitalist State.* Oxford: Martin Roberston and Company.

Jha, Dhirendra K. 2009. 'Jatland in Chhattisgarh.' *Open*. Accessed 26 September 2009. Available at http://www.openthemagazine.com/article/india/jatland-in-chhattisgarh.

Jodhka, Surinder S. 1995. *Debt, Dependence and Agrarian Change*. Jaipur: Rawat Publishers.

———. 2008. 'The Decline of Agriculture.' In *Reforming Indian Agriculture*, edited by Sankar K. Bhaumik. New Delhi: Sage Publications.

———. 2014. 'What's Happening to the Village Revisiting Rural Life and Agrarian Change in Haryana.' CAS Working Paper Series. Centre for the Study of Social Systems. Jawaharlal Nehru University, New Delhi.

Joshi, Vidyut and Akash Acharya. 2010. 'Addressing Agricultural Power Subsidy: A Case of North Gujarat.' *Centre for Social Sciences*. Working Paper No. 2.

Jung, Najeeb. 2011. 'The Sound of Silence.' *Times of India*, 1 February. Accessed 06 February 2012. Available at http://articles.timesofindia.indiatimes.com/2011-02-01/edit-page/28379182_1_forests-adivasis-chhattisgarh.

Kaiser, Ejaz. 2011. 'Bhaskar Group's Coal Mining Plans Face Public Ire.' *Hindustan Times*, 10 March 2011. Available at http://www.hindustantimes.com/india/bhaskar-group-s-coal-mining-plans-face-public-ire/story-MdF8MuNnMVvYzTIPYcgM0I.html.

Kalecki, Michal. 1972. *Essays on the Economic Growth of the Socialist and the Mixed Economy*. London: Cambridge University Press.

Kammar, Aravind. 2010. 'Economics of Land Use and Cropping Pattern in Northern Transitional Zone of Karnataka.' M.Sc. dissertation, Department of Agricultural Economics, Dharwad University of Agricultural Sciences.

Kashyap, Surendra P. 2006. *Agriculture and Irrigation Development in Gujarat: Strategies and Issues* (Mimeograph). Ahmedabad: Gujarat Institute of Development Research.

Kavitha. 2011. 'Navbharat Seeds.' Accessed 18 March 2012. Available at http://www.agricultureinformation.com/mag/2011/02/navbharat-seeds/.

Kennedy P. 1993. *Preparing for the Twenty-First Century*. New York: Random House.

Khan, Asgar. 2011. '90,000 Litres of Banned Insecticide Seized.' *Daily Bhaskar*. Accessed July 2019. Available at http://daily.bhaskar.com/news/MP-RAI-90000-litres-of-banned-insecticide-seized-2179813.html?D3-RAI.

Khan, Mushtaq H. 1996. 'The Efficiency Implications of Corruption.' *Journal of International Development* 8(5): 683–696.

———. 2000. 'Rent-Seeking as Process.' In *Rents, Rent-Seeking and Economic Development: Theory and Evidence in Asia*, edited by Mushtaq H. Khan and Jomo K. Sundaram, 70–144. Cambridge: Cambridge University Press .

———. 2004. 'State Failure in Developing Countries and Institutional Reform Strategies.' In *Toward Pro-Poor Policies. Aid, Institutions, and Globalization. Annual World Bank Conference on Development Economics, Europe (2003),* edited by Bertil Tungodden, Nicholas Stern, and Ivar Kolstad, 165–195. New York: Oxford University Press and World Bank.

———. 2005. 'Markets, States and Democracy: Patron–client Networks and the Case for Democracy in Developing Countries.' *Democratization* 12(5): 704–724.

———. 2010. 'Political Settlements and the Governance of Growth-Enhancing Institutions.' Unpublished paper in Research Paper Series on 'Growth-Enhancing Governance.'

Khera, Reetika. 2011. 'Labour Freedom Won, Battle on Against Wage Delays'. *The Economic Times*, 22 July.

Kloppenburg, Jack. 2010. 'Impeding Dispossession, Enabling Repossession: Biological Open Source and the Recovery of Seed Sovereignty.' *Journal of Agrarian Change* 10(3): 367–388.

Kobrin S.J. 1997. 'The Architecture of Globalization: State Sovereignty in a Networked Global Economy.' In *Governments, Globalization, and International Business*, edited by J.H. Dunning, 146–171. New York: Oxford University Press.

Kochanek, Stanley A. 1974. *Business and Politics in India*. Berkeley: University of California Press.

———. 1995. 'The Transformation of Interest Politics in India.' *Pacific Affairs* 68(4): 529–550.

———. 1996. 'Liberalisation and Business Lobbying in India.' *The Journal of Commonwealth and Comparative Politics* 34(3): 155–173.

Kohli, Atul. 1987. *The State and Poverty in India: The Politics of Reform*. New York: Cambridge University Press.

———. 1990. *Democracy and Discontent: India's Growing Crisis of Governability*. Cambridge: Cambridge University Press.

———. 2001. *The Success of Indian Democracy*. Cambridge: Cambridge University Press.

———. 2004. *State-Directed Development Political Power and Industrialization in the Global Periphery*. Cambridge: Cambridge University Press.

———. 2006. 'Politics of Economic Growth in India, 1980–2005.' *Economic and Political Weekly* 41(14): 1361–1370.

———. 2009. *Democracy and Development in India: From Socialism to Pro-Business*. New Delhi: Oxford University Press.

———. 2012. *Poverty Amid Plenty in the New India*. New York: Cambridge University Press.

Krishnan, M.G. 1992. *Panchayat Raj in India*. New Delhi: Mittal Publications.

Krishnakumar. 2007. 'Advantage Modi in South Gujarat.' Rediff. Accessed 17 April 2013. Available at http://www.rediff.com/news/2007/dec/10gujpoll6.htm

Kudva, Neema. 2003. 'Engineering Elections: The Experiences of Women in Panchayati Raj in Karnataka, India.' *International Journal of Politics, Culture and Society* 16(3): 445–463.

Kulkarni, Manu N. 2004. 'Biotechnology: Policing or Regulating?' *Economic and Political Weekly* 39(46–47): 5063–5064.

Kulkarni, Vishwanath. 2012. 'Surging Cultivation Costs Behind Hike in Support Price.' *Business Line*. Accessed 13 April 2014. Available at http://www.thehindubusinessline.com/economy/agri-business/surging-cultivation-costs-behind-hike-in-support-price/article3547422.ece.

Kumar, Hitesh. 2011. 'Research Paper on Tobacco Plantation, Institute of Rural Management, Anand'. Unpublished paper.

Kumar, M. Dinesh, Lokesh Singhal, and Pabitra Rath. 2004. 'Value of Groundwater: Case Studies in Banaskantha.' *Economic and Political Weekly* 39(31): 3498–3503.

Kumar, Sanjay. 2002. 'Creation of New States: Rationale and Implications.' *Economic and Political Weekly* 37(36): 3705–3709.

Kumar, Satendra. 2022. 'New Farm Bills and Farmers' Resistance to Neoliberalism.' *Sociological Bulletin* 71(4): 483–494.

Lerche, Jens. 1999. 'Politics of the Poor: Agricultural Labourers and Political Transformations in Uttar Pradesh.' *Journal of Peasant Studies* 26(2–3): 182–241.

———. 2013. 'The Agrarian Question in Neoliberal India: Agrarian Transition Bypassed?' *Journal of Agrarian Change* 13(3): 382–404.

———. 2014. 'Regional Patterns of Agrarian Accumulation in India.' In *Indian Capitalism and Development*, edited by Judith Heyer and Barbara Harriss-White, 46–65. London: Routledge.

Lerche, Jens, Alpa Shah, and Barbara Harriss-White. 2013. 'Introduction: Agrarian Questions and Left Politics in India.' *Journal of Agrarian Change* 13(3): 337–350.

Levien, Michael. 2011. 'Special Economic Zones and Accumulation by Dispossession in India.' *Journal of Agrarian Change* 11(4): 454–483.

———. 2012. 'The Land Question: Special Economic Zones and the Political Economy of Dispossession in India.' *Journal of Peasant Studies* 39(3–4): 933–969.

Lieten, Georges K. 1996. 'Panchayats in Western Uttar Pradesh – Namesake Members.' *Economic and Political Weekly* 31(39): 2700–2705.

Lieten, Georges K. and Ravi Srivastava. 1999. *Unequal Partners: Power Relations, Devolution and Development in Uttar Pradesh*. New Delhi: Sage Publications.

Lindberg, S. 1995. 'Farmers' Movements and Cultural Nationalism in India: An Ambiguous Relationship.' *Theory and Society* 24(6): 837–868.

Mahadevia, Darshini. 2005. 'From Stealth to Aggression: Economic Reforms and Communal Politics in Gujarat.' In *The Politics of Economic Reforms in India*, edited by Jos E. Mooij, 291–321. New Delhi: Sage Publications.

Mahurkar, Uday. 2011. 'Babus Modified.' *India Today*, 21 October. Accessed 19 August 2013. Available at http://indiatoday.intoday.in/story/gujarat-chief-minister-narendra-modi-trains-bureaucrats/1/157048.html.

Manor, James. 1984. 'Blurring the Lines between Parties and Social Bases: Gundu Rao and Emergence of a Janata Government in Karnataka.' *Economic and Political Weekly* 19(37): 1623–1632.

———. 2004. 'Towel over Armpit: Small-Time Political Fixers in India's States.' In *India and the Politics of Developing Countries: Essays in Memory of Myron Weiner*, edited by Ashutosh Varshney, 61–83. New Delhi: Sage Publications.

———. 2007. 'Change in Karnataka over the Last Generation: Villages and the Wider Context.' *Economic and Political Weekly* 42(8): 653–660.

McCartney, Matthew. 2010. *Political Economy, Growth and Liberalisation in India, 1991–2008*. London: Routledge.

McMichael, Philip. 1997. 'Rethinking Globalization: The Agrarian Question Revisited.' *Review of International Political Economy* 4(4): 630–662.

———. 2008. 'Peasants Make Their Own History, But Not Just as They Please.' *Journal of Agrarian Change* 8(2–3): 205–228.

Mehrotra, Ishita. 2012. 'Political Economy of Rural Female Labour: A Study of Labour Relations in East Uttar Pradesh, India.' PhD dissertation, SOAS, University of London.

Mehta, Niti. 2012. 'Performance of Crop Sector in Gujarat during High Growth Period: Some Explorations.' *Agricultural Economics Research Review* 25(2): 195–204.

Mehta, Shray and Shreya Sinha. 2022. 'The Rise and Fall of Agrarian Populism in Post-colonial India: Farmers' Movements and Electoral Politics at Crossroads.' *Indian Sociological Society* 71(4): 601–618.

Menon, Meena. 2002. 'From Rice Bowls to Fruit Farms.' Accessed 22 July 2011. Available at http://indiatogether.org/agriculture/articles/richaria1.htm.

Miliband, Ralph. 1969. *The State in Capitalist Society*. London: Weidenfeld and Nicolson.

Minot, Nicholas and Devesh Roy. 2006. 'Impact of High-Value Agriculture and Modern Marketing Channels on Poverty: A Conceptual Frame Work.' Draft report MTID. Washington, DC: IFPRI.

Mitra, Ashok. 1977. *Terms of Trade and Class Relations*. London: Frank Cass and Company Ltd.

———. 2004. *Terms of Trade and Class Relations: An Essay in Political Economy*. Reprint. New Jersey: Routledge.

Morriss, Sebastian and Ajay Pandey. 2007. 'Towards Reform of Land Acquisition Framework in India.' *Economic and Political Weekly* 42(22): 2083–2090.

Morse, Stephen, Richard Bennett, and Yousouf Ismael. 2007. 'Inequality and GM Crops: A Case-Study of Bt Cotton in India.' *The Journal of Agrobiotechnology Management and Economics* 10(1): 44–50.

Mukundan, R. 2013. 'Fertiliser Subsidy: Fix It Right.' *The Business Line*. Accessed 19 July 2013. Available at http://www.thehindubusinessline.com/opinion/fertiliser-subsidy-fix-it-right/article4932160.ece.

Murdeshwar, V. 2013. '90 Percent Subsidy for Drip Irrigation: CM.' *Indian Express*, 23 September. Accessed 23 August 2014. Available at http://newindianexpress.com/states/karnataka/90-percent-subsidy-for-drip-irrigation-CM/2013/09/23/article1798818.ece.

Murugkar, Milind, Bharat Ramaswami, and Mahesh Shelar. 2006. 'Liberalization, Biotechnology and the Private Seed Sector: The Case of India's Cotton Seed Market.' Indian Statistical Institute, New Delhi. Discussion paper 06-05. Accessed January 2006. Accessed July 2019. Available at http://www.isid.ac.in/~pu/dispapers/dp06-05.pdf.

Nadkarni, Mangesh Venkatesh, and Vedini K. Harishchandra. 1996. 'Accelerating Commercialisation of Agriculture: Dynamic Agriculture and Stagnating Peasants?' *Economic and Political Weekly* 31(26): A63–A73.

Nagaraj, K. 2008. *Farmers' Suicides in India: Magnitudes, Trends and Spatial Patterns*. Chennai: Madras Institute of Development Studies.

Nair, Janaki. 1996. 'Predatory Capitalism and Legalised Landgrab: Karnataka Land Reforms.' *Economic and Political Weekly* 31(5): 251–252.

Nandy, Madhurima. 2008. 'Karnataka Drafts New Textile Policy to Attract Investment.' *Live Mint,* 4 June. Accessed 3 March 2013. Available at http://www.livemint. com/2008/06/04224346/Karnataka-drafts-new-textile-p.html.

Nanjappa, V. 2008. 'The Lobbies That Matter in Karnataka.' *Pragoti.* Accessed 6 April 2012. Available at www.pragoti.in/node/1339.

Narayanamoorthy, A. and S. S. Kalamkar. 2006. 'Is Bt Cotton Cultivation Economically Viable for Indian Farmers?' *Economic and Political Weekly* 41(26): 2716–2724.

Narayanan, S. 2020. *'The Three Farm Bills.'* The India Forum. Accessed May 2022. Available at https://www.theindiaforum.in/article/three-farm-bills.

National Sample Survey Organisation. 2005. *Indebtedness of Farmer Households.* Situation Assessment Survey, 59th Round, Report no. 498. Ministry of Statistics and Programme Implementation, Government of India.

National Commission for Enterprises in the Unorganised Sector (NCEUS). 2007. *Report on Conditions of Work and Promotion of Livelihood in Unorganised Sector.* National Commission for Enterprises in the Unorganised Sector, Ministry of Small Scale Industry, Government of India, New Delhi.

———. 2008. *A Special Programme for Marginal and Small Farmers.* New Delhi: Government of India. Accessed July 2019. Available at http:// nceuis.nic.in/Special_Programme_for_ Marginal_and_Small_Farmers.pdf.

Nielsen, Kenneth and Alf Nilsen. 2016. *Social Movements and the State in India: Deepening Democracy?* New York City: Springer Link.

Oommen, Tharailath Koshy. 2008. *Reconciliation in Post-Godhra Gujarat: The Role of Civil Society.* New Delhi: Pearson Longman.

Pai, Sudha. 1993. *Uttar Pradesh: Agrarian Change and Electoral Politics.* New Delhi: Shipra Publications.

Pal, Suresh. 2008. 'Agricultural R&D Policy and Institutional Reforms: Learning from the Experiences of India and China.' *Economic and Political Weekly* 43(26–27): 145, 147–155.

Palaniswamy, Nethra and Nandini Krishnan. 2012. 'Local Politics, Political Institutions, and Public Resource Allocation.' *Economic Development and Cultural Change* 60(3): 449–473.

Pandit, Virendra. 2010. 'Gujarat Racing Ahead in Floriculture, Horticulture.' Accessed 09 May 2013. Available at http://www.thehindubusinessline.in/2010/05/27/ stories/2010052752752100.htm.

Panini, M. 1999. 'Trends in Cultural Globalisation: From Agriculture to Agribusiness in Karnataka.' *Economic and Political Weekly* 34(31): 2168–2173.

Parashar, Neeraj. 2010. 'Impact of Coal Bed Methane Mining in Korba and Raigarh District of Chhattisgarh.' Paper presented at International Conference on Land-Water Resources, Biodiversity and Climate Change at the Bhopal School of Social Sciences, Bhopal. Accessed 27 October 2012. Available at http://www.slideshare.net/ neerajparashar/impact-of-coal-bed-methane-cbm-in-korba-and-raigarh

Paroda, Rajendra Singh. 2012. *Keynote Address.* National Seed Corporations, Golden Jubilee Year Celebrations.

Patnaik, Prabhat. 2001. 'Alternative Paradigms of Economic Decentralisation.' *Social Scientist* 29(9/10): 48–59.

Patnaik, Utsa. 1987. *Peasant Class Differentiation: A Study in Method with Reference to Haryana.* Delhi: Oxford University Press.

———. 2002. 'Deflation and Deja-Vu.' In *Agrarian Studies: Essays on Agrarian Relations in Less Developed Countries,* edited by Madhura Swaminathan and V. K. Ramchandran. Delhi: Tulika.

———. 2003. 'Global Capitalism, Deflation and Agrarian Crisis in Developing Countries.' *Journal of Agrarian Change* 3(1–2): 33–66.

———. 2006. 'The Agrarian Crisis and Importance of Peasant Resistance.' *People's Democracy* 30(5).

Pattenden, Jonathan. 2005. 'Horizontality and the Political Economy of Social Movement: The Anti-Capitalist Globalisation Movement, the Karnataka State Farmers Association and Dynamics of Social Transformation in Rural South India.' PhD thesis. SOAS, University of London.

———. 2011. 'Gatekeeping as Accumulation and Domination: Decentralization and Class Relations in Rural South India.' *Journal of Agrarian Change* 11(2): 164–194.

Pattenden, Jonathan and Gaurav Bansal. 2021. 'A New Class Alliance in the Indian Countryside? From New Farmers' Movements to the 2020 Protest Wave.' *Economic and Political Weekly* 56(26–27): 22–29.

Planning Commission. 'State-wise Growth Rate (Annual Average in %) of Agriculture and Allied Sector in India: 1996–97 to 2013–14.' Government of India. Available at http:// planningcommission.nic.in/data/datatable/data_2312/DatabookDec2014%20 60.pdf.

Poulantzas, Nicos. 1973. *Political Power and Social Classes.* London: NLB and Sheed and Ward.

PRIA, 2010. 'Citizenship DRC: Synthesis and Communication Study Report.' Unpublished report. Development Resource Centre, Participatory Research in India.

Prakash, Anjal. 2005. 'The Dark Zone: Groundwater Irrigation Politics and Social Power in North Gujarat.' PhD thesis, Wageningen University.

Pray, Carl E. and Bharat Ramaswami. 1999. 'Liberalization's Impact on the Indian Seed Industry: Competition, Research, and Impact on Farmers.' *International Food and Agribusiness Management Review* 2(3–4): 407–420.

———. 2001. 'The Impact of Economic Reforms on R&D by the Indian Seed Industry.' *Food Policy* 26(6): 587–598.

Purohit, Makarand. 2013. 'Power Hub Becomes Pollution Hub.' *India Water Portal.* Accessed 16 October 2013. Available at http://www.indiawaterportal.org/articles/ power-hub-becomes-pollution-hub.

Radhakrishnan, P. 1990. 'Karnataka Backward Classes.' *Economic and Political Weekly* 25(32): 1749–1754.

Raghavan, M. 2008. 'Changing Pattern of Input Use and Cost of Cultivation.' *Economic and Political Weekly* 43(26-27): 123–129.

Rajasekhar, D., M. Devendra Babu and R. Manjula. 2011. *Elite and Programme Capture in Grama Panchayats of Karnataka, Centre for Decentralisation and Development, Institute for Social and Economic Change.* Bangalore: National Council of Applied Economic Research.

Raju, Saraswati and Sucharita Sen. 2006. 'Globalisation and Expanding Markets for Cut-Flowers: Who Benefits?' *Economic and Political Weekly* 41(26): 2725–2731.

Rakshit, Santanu. 2011. 'Capital Intensification, Productivity and Exchange – A Class-Based Analysis of Agriculture in West Bengal in the Current Millennium.' *Journal of Agrarian Change* 11(4): 505–535.

Ramachandran, V.K. 2011. 'The State of Agrarian Relations in India Today.' *The Marxist* 27 (1–2): 51–89. Accessed 2 April 2013. Available at https://protect-eu.mimecast. com/s/eDa8CPjEjUKyyzPIzQlWV?domain=cpim.org"http://www.cpim.org/ marxist/201101-agrarian-relations-vkr.pdf.

Ramachandran, V.K. and Madhura Swaminathan. 2001. 'Does Informal Credit Provide Security? Rural Banking Policy in India.' *International Labour Organisation.* Accessed July 2019. Available at https://pdfs.semanticscholar.org/17c3/ bb07b9b713c3f3d7648870163b1b807a572c.pdf.

———, eds. 2005. *Financial Liberalisation and Rural Credit in India.* New Delhi: Tulika Books.

Ramachandran, V.K., Vikas Rawal, and Madhura Swaminathan, eds. 2010. *Socio-Economic Surveys of Three Villages in Andhra Pradesh: A Study of Agrarian Relations.* New Delhi: Tulika Books.

Ramakumar, R. 2014. 'Economic Reforms and Agricultural Policy in India.' Paper presented at Foundation of Agrarian Change Tenth Anniversary Conference, draft paper, Kochi. 9–12 January. Accessed July 2019. Available at http://www.networkideas. org/ideasact/jan09/PDF/Ramakumar.pdf.

———. 2017. 'Jats, Khaps and Riots: Communal Politics and the Bharatiya Kisan Union in Northern India.' *Journal of Agrarian Change* 17(1): 22–42.

———. 2022. *Distress in the Fields.* New Delhi: Tulika Books.

Rao, Narasimha P. and K.C. Suri. 2006. 'Dimensions of Agrarian Distress in Andhra Pradesh.' *Economic and Political Weekly* 41(16): 1546–1552.

Rao, V.M. and D.V. Gopalappa. 2004. 'Agricultural Growth and Farmer Distress: Tentative Perspectives from Karnataka.' *Economic and Political Weekly* 39(52): 5591, 5593–5598.

Ray, Amal and Jayalakshmi Kumpatla. 1987. 'Zilla Parishad Presidents in Karnataka: Their Social Background and Implications for Development.' *Economic and Political Weekly* 22(42–43): 1825–1827, 1829–1830.

Ray, Manas. 2022. *Crisis of Liberal Deliberation: Facets of Indian Democracy.* Primus Books.

Reddy, D. Narasimha and Srijit Mishra. 2009. *Agrarian Crisis in India.* New Delhi: Oxford University Press.

Reddy, A. Bheemeshwar and Madhura Swaminathan, 2014. 'Intergenerational Occupational Mobility in Rural India: Evidence from Ten Villages.' *Journal, Review of Agrarian Studies* 4(1): 95–134.

Reddy, G. Ram. 1990. 'The Politics of Accommodation: Caste, Class and Dominance in Andhra Pradesh.' In *Dominance and State Power in Modern India*, Volume II, edited by Francine Frankel and M. S. A. Rao, 265–321. Delhi: Oxford University Press.

Reddy, O. Chinnappa. 1990. *The Justice-journey of the Karnataka Backward Classes, Volume 1.* Bangalore: Third Karnataka Backward Classes Commission, Government of Karnataka.

Roche, Chris. 1999. *Impact Assessment for Development Agencies: Learning to Value Change.* Oxford: Oxfam Publication.

Rodrik, D. 1997. *Has Globalization Gone Too Far?* Washington, DC: Institute of International Economics.

Roy, Arundhati. 2009. 'Business as Usual: Vedanta Mine Plans Threaten India's Poorest.' Accessed July 2019. Available at https://www.theguardian.com/environment/cif-green/2009/jul/27/arundhati-roy-orissa-mine.

Rudolph, Lloyd I. and Susanne H. Rudolph. 1987. *In Pursuit of Lakshmi: The Political Economy of the Indian State.* Hyderabad: Orient Longman.

———. 1980. 'The Centrist Future of Indian Politics.' *Asian Survey* 20(6): 575–594.

Rutten, Mario. 1986. 'Social Profile of Agricultural Entrepreneurs: Economic Behaviour and Life-Style of Middle-Large Farmers in Central Gujarat.' *Economic and Political Weekly* 21(13): A15–A23.

———. 1995. *Farms and Factories: Social Profile of Large Farmers and Rural Industrialists in West India.* Delhi: Oxford University Press.

———. 2003. *Rural Capitalists in Asia: A Comparative Analysis on India, Indonesia, and Malaysia.* New York: Routledge.

Rutten, Mario and Pravin J. Patel. 2002. 'Twice Migrants and Linkages with Central Gujarat: Patidars in East Africa and Britain.' In *Development and Deprivation in Gujarat,* edited by Ghanshyam Shah, Mario Rutten and Hein Streefkerk, 314–328. Delhi: Sage Publications.

Sainath, Palagummi. 2004. 'When Farmers Die.' *India Together.* Accessed 01 June 2004. Available at http://indiatogether.org/farmdie-op-ed.

Sau, Ranjit. 2007. 'Second Industrialisation in India: Land and the State.' *Economic and Political Weekly* 42(7): 571–577.

Scoones, Ian. 2008. 'Mobilizing Against GM Crops in India, South Africa and Brazil.' *Journal of Agrarian Change* 8(2 and 3): 315–344.

Sen, Abhijit and Manjeet S. Bhatia. 2004. *State of the Indian Farmer: Cost of Cultivation and Farm Income.* New Delhi: Academic Foundation, Department of Agriculture and Cooperation, Ministry of Agriculture, Government of India.

Sethi, Aman. 2012. 'Environmental Activist Shot and Wounded in Chhattisgarh.' *The Hindu.* Accessed July 2019. Available at http://www.thehindu.com/news/national/environmental-activist-shot-and-wounded-in-chhattisgarh/article3613848.ece.

Shah, A., et al. 2007. 'Income and Employment Pattern in Rural Area of Chhattisgarh: A Micro View.' *Agricultural Economics Research Review* 20(2): 395–406.

Shah, Alpa. 2010. *In the Shadows of the State: Indigenous Politics, Environmentalism, and Insurgence in Jharkhand, India.* New Delhi: Oxford University Press.

Shah, Esha. 2005. 'Local and Global Elites Join Hands: Development and Diffusion of Genetically Modified Bt Cotton Technology in Gujarat.' *Economic and Political Weekly* 40(43): 4629–4639.

Shah, Ghanshyam. 2002. *Caste and Democratic Politics in India.* Delhi: Permanent Black.

Shah, Tushar. 2006. *Groundwater and Human Development: Challenges and Opportunities in Livelihoods and Environment.* Vallabh Vidyanagar: International Water Management

Institute, Gujarat. Accessed July 2019. Available at http://publications.iwmi.org/pdf/H035884.pdf.

———. 2007. 'Crop Per Drop of Diesel? Energy Squeeze on India's Smallholder Irrigation.' *Economic and Political Weekly* 42(39): 4002–4009.

Shah, Tushar and Shilpa Verma. 2008. 'Co-Management of Electricity and Groundwater: An Assessment of Gujarat's Jyotirgram Scheme.' *Economic and Political Weekly* 43(7): 59–66.

Shah, Tushar, et al. 2009. 'Secret of Gujarat's Agrarian Miracle after 2000.' *Economic and Political Weekly* 44(52): 45–55.

Sharma, Sachin. 2013. 'Baria Royals Attend Sadbhavana Fasts.' *Times of India*, 21 February 2012. Accessed 06 March 2013. Available at http://articles.timesofindia.indiatimes.com/2012-02-21/vadodara/31082396_1_devgadh-baria-bjp-state-general-secretary-nationalist-congress-party.

Sharma, Supriya. 2010. 'Korba Scam: Go-ahead without Checks'. *Times of India*, 9 September. Available at https://timesofindia.indiatimes.com/india/korba-scam-go-ahead-without-checks/articleshow/6521877.cms.

———. 2011. 'Ash Dam Damaged, NTPC's Production from Plant Hit.' *The Economic Times*, 27 September 2011. Accessed 14 September 2013. Available at http://articles.economictimes.indiatimes.com/2011-09-27/news/30208400_1_ash-disposal-ntpc-s-korba-500mw.

———. 2012. 'Secret of Jindal's Success: Get Coal Cheap, Sell Power at High Prices.' *The Economic Times*. Accessed 9 September 2012. Available at https://economictimes.indiatimes.com/industry/indl-goods/svs/metals-mining/secret-of-jindals-success-get-coal-cheap-sell-power-at-high-prices/articleshow/16320221.cms.

Shastri, Sandeep and B.S. Padmavathi. 2009. 'Karnataka: The Lotus Blooms…Nearly.' *Economic and Political Weekly* 63(6): 42–45.

Shetty, P. K. 2004. 'Socio-Ecological Implications of Pesticide Use in India.' *Economic and Political Weekly* 39(49): 5261–5267.

Shiva Kumar, M.T. 2013. 'Exploitation Persists, Say Holalu Residents.' *The Hindu*, 4 January 2013. Accessed 24 May 2015. Available at http://www.thehindu.com/todays-paper/tp-national/tp-karnataka/exploitation-persists-say-holalu-residents/article4271321.ece

Shiva, Vandana. 2007. *Cargill and the Corporate Hijack of India's Food and Agriculture*. New Delhi: Navdanya.

Shiva, Vandana, Afsar H. Jafri, Ashok Emani, and Manish Pande. 2000. *Seeds of Suicide: The Ecological and Human Costs of Globalization of Agriculture*. Delhi: Research Foundation for Science, Technology and Ecology.

Shiva, Vandana and Tom Crompton. 1998. 'Monopoly and Monoculture: Trends in Indian Seed Industry.' *Economic and Political Weekly* 33(39): A137–A141, A144–A151.

Shylendra, H.S. and Uma Rani. 2000. *Sustainable Rural Livelihood in the Context of Growing Occupational Diversification and Rural–Urban Linkages*. Delhi: Sage Publications.

Sinha, Shreya. 2020. 'The Agrarian Crisis in Punjab and the Making of the Anti-farm Law Protests.' *The India Forum.* Accessed March 2023. Available at https://www.theindia forum.in/article/agrarian-crisis-punjab-and-making-anti-farm-law-protests.

Singh, Surjit and Vidya Sagar. 2004. *Agricultural Credit in India, State of the Indian Farmer: A Millennium Study, Volume 7.* New Delhi: Academic Foundation.

Singh, Sukhpal. 2006. 'Corporate Farming in India: Is It Must for Agricultural Development?' Working Paper no. 2006-11-06. Ahmedabad: Indian Institute of Management.

———. 2020. 'Farm Acts: Farmers' Freedom at Stake.' *Frontline.* Accessed 23 October 2022. Available at https://frontline.thehindu.com/cover-story/farmers- freedom-at-stake/article32758989.ece.

Singh, Sukhpal and Shruti Bhogal. 2014. 'Thriving or Deteriorating? Punjab's Small Peasantry.' *Economic and Political Weekly* 49(26–27): 95–100.

Singh, Surjit and M.S. Rathore, eds. 2010. *Rainfed Agriculture in India: Perspectives and Challenges.* New Delhi: Manohar Publications.

Sinha, Aseema. 2005. *The Regional Roots of Developmental Politics in India: A Divided Leviathan.* Bloomington: Indiana University Press.

Sinha, Shreya. 2017. 'Agrarian Accumulation in Liberalised India: A Study of Capitalist Farmers in Punjab.' PhD thesis, School of Oriental and African Studies.

Siva, Meera. 2013. 'Pitfalls in Buying Farmland.' *Business Line.* Accessed 9 March 2012. Available at https://premium.thehindubusinessline.com/portfolio/Pitfalls-in-buying-farmland/article20939218.ece.

Sood, Atul. 2012. *Poverty Amidst Prosperity: Essays on the Trajectory of Development in Gujarat.* New Delhi: Aakar Books.

Sridhar, V. 2006. 'Why Do Farmers Commit Suicide? The Case of Andhra Pradesh.' *Economic and Political Weekly* 41(16): 1559–1565.

Srivastava, Devyani. 2008. 'Mining War in Chhattisgarh. Naxalite Violence.' Article no. 2577. Institute of Peace and Conflict Studies. Accessed 18 July 2011. Available at http://www.ipcs.org/article/naxalite-violence/mining-war-in-chhattisgarh-2577.html.

Srivastava, Ravi. 1999. 'Rural Labour in Uttar Pradesh: Emerging Features of Subsistence, Contradiction and Resistance.' *Journal of Peasant Studies* 26(2–3): 263–315.

———. 2012. 'Changing Employment Conditions of the Indian Workforce and Implications for Decent Work.' *Global Labour Journal* 3(1): 63–90.

Sthanumoorthy, R. and P. Sivarajadhanavel, eds. 2007. *Karnataka Economy: Performance, Challenges and Opportunities.* Hyderabad: The Institute of Chartered Financial Analysts of India University Press.

Stone, Glenn D. 2011. 'Field versus Farm in Warangal: Bt Cotton, Higher Yields, and Larger Questions.' *World Development* 39(3): 387–398.

Subbarao, K. 1985. 'State Policies and Regional Disparity in Indian Agriculture.' *Development and Change* 16 (51): 523–546.

Subramani, M.R. 2013. 'Onion Cartel.' *Frontline.* Accessed 23 May 2014. Available at http://www.frontline.in/other/data-card/onion-cartel/article5228816.ece.

Subramaniam, Vincent. 2011. 'The Government Found His Report Too Hot to Print.' *Citizen Matters*. Accessed July 2019. Available at http://bangalore.citizenmatters.in/articles/3270-task-force-report-on-land-grabbing.

Sud, Nikita. 2007. 'From Land to the Tiller to Land Liberalisation: The Political Economy of Gujarat's Shifting Land Policy.' *Modern Asian Studies* 41(3): 603–637.

———. 2009. 'Nano and Good Governance in Gujarat.' *Economic and Political Weekly* 43(50): 13–14.

Suthar, Sudhir Kumar. 2022. *Dilapidation of the Rural: Development, Politics, and Farmer Suicides in India*. Singapore: Palgrave Macmillan US.

Swaminathan, M. and V.K. Ramachandran 2005. *Agrarian Studies 2: Financial Liberalisation and Rural Credit*. New Delhi: Tulika Press.

Swaminathan, Madhura. 2012. 'Who Has Access to Formal Credit in Rural India? Evidence from Four Villages.' *Review of Agrarian Studies* 2(1). Accessed 12 October 2013. Available at http://ras.org.in/who_has_access_to_formal_credit_in_rural_india_evidence_from_four_villages.

Swaminathan, Monkombu Sambasivan. 2007. *Agriculture Cannot Wait: New Horizons in Indian Agriculture*. New Delhi : Academic Foundation.

Swaminathan, S. and Anklesaria Aiyar. 2009. 'Agriculture: Secret of Modi's Success.' *The Economic Times*. Accessed 4 March 2011. Available at http://swaminomics.org/agriculture-secret-of-modis-success.

Taylor, Marcus. 2012. 'The Antinomies of "Financial Inclusion": Debt, Distress and the Workings of Indian Microfinance.' *Journal of Agrarian Change* 12(4): 601–610.

Thaker, Hrima and Vijay Paul Sharma. 2010. 'Fertiliser Subsidy in India: Who Are the Beneficiaries?' *Economic and Political Weekly* 45(12): 68–76.

The Economic Times. 2007. 'Farmers Take Up Floriculture in South Gujarat.' 7 December. Accessed 10 July 2013. Available at http://economictimes.indiatimes. com/news/economy/agriculture/farmers-take-up-floriculture-in-south-gujarat/articleshow/2602867.cms.

———. 2012a. 'Essar Oil to Pay Sales Tax to Gujarat Government in 8 Installments: Supreme Court.' 13 September. Accessed 22 August 2013. Available at http:// articles. economictimes.indiatimes.com/2012-09-13/news/33816982_1_prestigious-unit-scheme-essar-oil-gujarat-high-court ET 2007.

———. 2012b. 'India's Seed Industry to Grow by 53% by 2015: Assocham.' 9 December. Accessed July 2019. Available at http://economictimes.indiatimes.com/news/economy/agriculture/indias-seed-industry-to-grow-by-53-by-2015-assocham/articleshow/17542847.cms.

The Hindu. 2004. 'CEC Warns against Model Code Violation in Chhattisgarh.' 4 November. Accessed 12 March 2014. Available at http://www.hindu.com/2003/11/05/stories/2003110507500100.htm.

———. 2006. 'Green Revolution Destroyed Traditional Farming: Vedike.' 24 June. Accessed 18 August 2011. Available at http://www.hindu.com/2006/06/24/stories/2006062405780300.htm.

———. 2011. 'Agricultural Production Witnesses Healthy Growth.' 2 April. Accessed July 2019. Available at http://www.thehindu.com/todays-paper/tp-national/agricultural production-witnesses-healthy-growth/article1593458.ece.

———. 2013. 'Modi Govt Denies CAG Charges on Land Allotment to Corporate Houses.' 4 April. Accessed 19 August 2013. Available at http://www.thehindubusinessline.com/ news/states/modi-govt-denies-cag-charges-on-land-allotment-to-corporate-houses/ article4580853.ece.

———. 2016. 'Singur Land Acquisition Issue: A Timeline.' 31 August. Accessed July 2019. Available at http://www. thehindu.com/news/national/other-states/Singurland-acquisition-issue-A-timeline/ article14599981.ece.

The Indian Express. 2009. 'Vadodara Horticulturists See Export Potential in Dutch Rose.' 1 June. Accessed 17 July 2011. Accessed July 2019. Available at http://indianexpress. com/article/cities/ ahmedabad/vadodara-horticulturists-see-export-potential-in-dutch-rose/.

The Navhind Times. 2012. 'Narendra Modi Attempts Conquering Keshubhai's Bastion Surat.' 12 December. Accessed 30 December 2013. Available at http:// www.navhindtimes. in/india-news/narendra-modi-attempts-conquering-keshubhai-s-bastion-surat.

Times of India. 2011. 'Chhattisgarh Government Scraps Elephant Reserve Plan for Coal Mining.' 16 January. Accessed July 2019. Available at https://timesofindia.indiatimes. com/india/Chhattisgarh-govt-scraps-elephant-reserve-plan-for-coal-mining/ articleshow/7294639.cms.

———. 2012a. 'Ground Water to Flow Free in Fields.' 29 February. Accessed 02 May 2013. Available at http://articles.timesofindia.indiatimes.com/2012-02-29/ahmedabad/ 31110481_1_dark-zones-groundwater-talukas.

———. 2012b. 'Gujarat's Agricultural Land Is Up for Grabs!' 23 June. Accessed 23 June 2013. Available at http://timesofindia.indiatimes.com/city/ahmedabad/Gujarats-agricultural-land-is-up-for-grabs/articleshow/14350980.cms.

———. 2013a. '5,000 Gujarat Farmers Protest against Maruti Plant.' 17 August. Accessed July 2019. Available at http://timesofindia.indiatimes.com/india/5000-Gujarat-farmers-protest-against-Maruti-plant/articleshow/21873062.cms.

———. 2013b. '75 % MLAs in Chhattisgarh Are Crorepatis.' 16 December. Accessed July 2019. Available at http://timesofindia.indiatimes.com/city/raipur/75-MLAs-in-Chhattisgarh-are-crorepatis/articleshow/27456340.cms.

———. 2013c. 'Land Acquisition Bill passed by Parliament.' 5 September. Available at https://timesofindia.indiatimes.com/india/land-acquisition-bill-passed-by-parliament/ articleshow/22344968.cms

Thimmaiah, G. and Abdul Aziz. 1983. 'The Political Economy of Land Reforms in Karnataka, a South Indian State.' *Asian Survey* 23(7): 810–829.

Thorner, Daniel. 1956. *The Agrarian Prospect in India.* Delhi: University Press.

Tillin, Louise. 2013. *Remapping India: New States and Their Political Origins.* London: Oxford University Press.

United Nations Development Programme (UNDP). 2005. *Human Development Report 2005: International Cooperation at a Crossroads.* New York: United Nations Development Programme.

———. 2011. *Chhattisgarh Economic and Human Development Indicators*. New Delhi. Accessed 16 February 2012. Available at http://www.in.undp.org/content/dam/india/docs/chhattisgarh_factsheet.pdf.

United Nations World Food Programme (UNWFP). 2013. *Food Security Atlas of Rural Chhattisgarh*. New Delhi: Institute for Human Development and UN World Food Programme. Accessed 29 June 2013. Available at http://www.ihdindia.org/Atlas%20of%20Rural%20India.html.

Vaid, Divya. 2012. 'The Caste–Class Association in India: An Empirical Analysis.' *Asian Survey* 52(2): 395–422.

Vakulabharanma, Vamsi. 2010. 'Does Class Matter? Class Structure and Worsening Inequality in India.' *Economic and Political Weekly* 45(29): 67–76.

Vanaik, Anish and Siddhartha. 2008. 'Bank Payments: End of Corruption in NREGA?' *Economic and Political Weekly* 43(17): 33, 35–39.

Varma, R.C. 1995. *Indian Tribes through the Ages*. New Delhi: Ministry of Information and Broadcasting.

Varshney, Ashutosh. 2012. 'The Business–Politics Nexus.' *The Indian Express*. Accessed 18 November 2013. Available at http://www.indianexpress.com/news/the-businesspolitics-nexus/971862/.

———. 1995. *Democracy, Development and the Countryside: Urban-Rural Struggles in India*. Cambridge: Cambridge University Press.

Vasavi, A.R. 2008. 'Caste, Capital and Captaincy in the Karnataka Elections.' *Economic and Political Weekly* 43 (24): 10–11.

Verma, P. 2013. *The Indian Seed Industry: Country Report, National Seed Association of India*. Accessed 18 May 2013. Available at http://www.apsaseed.org/images/lovelypics/Documents/Technical%20Session08/India_%20Country%20Report.pdf.

Vijayshankar, P.S. 2005. 'Four Decades of Agricultural Development in MP: An Agro-Ecological Sub-Region Approach.' *Economic and Political Weekly* 40(48): 5014–5024.

Vijayalakshmi, V. 2008. *Corruption and Local Governance: Evidence From Karnataka*. Institute of Social and Economic Change.

Vyas, Vijay Shankar. 1994. 'Agricultural Policies for the Nineties: Issues and Approaches.' *Economic and Political Weekly* 29(26): A54–A63.

Weiner, Myron. 2001. 'The Struggle for Equality.' In *The Success of India's Democracy*, edited by Atul Kohli, 193–225. Cambridge: Cambridge University Press.

World Bank. 2016. 'Chhattisgarh: Poverty, Growth and Inequality.' 20 May. Accessed July 2019. Available at http://documents.worldbank.org/curated/en/166551468194958356/pdf/105848-BRI-P157572-PUBLIC-Chhattisgarh-Proverty.pdf.

———. 2018. 'Rural Population (% of total population-India).' Available at https://data.worldbank.org/indicator/SP.RUR.TOTL.ZS?locations=IN.

Wood, John R. 1987. 'Reservation in Doubt: The Backlash Against Affirmative Action in Gujarat, India.' *Pacific Affairs* 60(3): 408–430.

Yadav, Kiran. 2012. 'Finding Fortune in the Field.' *Business India*. Accessed 14 May 2013. Available at http://www.championagro.com/pdf/890-corporate-reports-champion-agro-1.pdf.

Yadav, Yogendra and Suhas Palshikar. 2003. 'From Hegemony to Convergence: Party System and Electoral Politics in the Indian States, 1952–2002.' *Journal of Indian School of Political Economy* 15: 5–44.

Yagnik, Achyut and Suchitra Sheth. 2005. *The Shaping of Modern Gujarat, Plurality, Hindutva and Beyond*. New Delhi: Penguin Books.

Yadav, Yogendra. 1999. 'Electoral Politics in the Time of Change: India's Third Electoral System, 1989–1999.' *Economic and Political Weekly* 34(34–35): 2393–2399.

Index

Milton Keynes UK
Ingram Content Group UK Ltd.
UKHW040734141124
451073UK00006BA/122

9 781009 481335